THE SHAVUOT
ANTHOLOGY

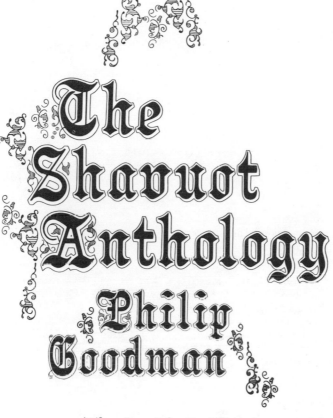

The Shavuot Anthology

Philip Goodman

The Jewish Publication Society of America

PHILADELPHIA

The editor herewith expresses his sincere appreciation to the following publishers and authors who have kindly granted permission to use the material indicated from their published works.

Acum Ltd., Tel Aviv, Israel: "Not a Chirp Was Heard" from *My Holidays: Holiday Stories for Children* by Levin Kipnis, trans. by Israel M. Goodelman. N. Tversky, Tel Aviv, 1961.

American Academy for Jewish Research, New York: "Strength Comes through Belief" from *Epistle to Yemen* by Moses Maimonides. Edited by Abraham S. Halkin, trans. by Boaz Cohen. American Academy for Jewish Research, New York, 1952.

The American Sephardi, New York: *"Dialogo dos Montes,"* trans. by Philip Polack, from *The American Sephardi,* vol. 1, nos. 1–2 (Autumn 1970). Copyright by Yeshiva University.

The American Zionist, New York: "At the Western Wall" from "A Harvest of Spring Holidays in Israel" by Yaacov Luria from *The American Zionist* 63, no. 9 (June 1973). Reprinted by permission of the publisher and the author.

A. S. Barnes & Company, Inc., Cranbury, N. J.: "The Torah Is Accepted Again in Buchenwald" from *The Yellow Star* by S. B. Unsdorfer, Thomas Yoseloff, New York, 1961.

Behrman House, Inc., New York: "The Myriad Angels' Songs" from *The Traditional Prayer Book for Sabbaths and Festivals,* trans. by David de Sola Pool, 1960; "Shavuot" from *Tales of the Jewish Holidays as Told by the Light of the Moon* by Charlotte Bronstein, 1956; "Who Will Be My Surety?" by Seymour Rossel from *Lessons from Our Living Past,* ed. by Jules Harlow, 1972; "The Feast of Weeks" from *Poems for Young Israel* by Philip M. Raskin, 1925; "*Barukh Elohenu,* "*Yisrael ve-Oraita,*" "*Torat Emet*" from *The New Jewish Song Book* by Harry Coopersmith, 1965; "*Kumu ve-Naaleh,*" "At Mount Sinai" from *The Gateway to Jewish Song* by Judith Kaplan Eisenstein, 1939. Reprinted by permission of Behrman House, Inc., 1261 Broadway, N.Y., N.Y. 10001.

Bloch Publishing Co., New York: "The Supreme Influence of the Decalogue" from *The Authorised Daily Prayer Book: Hebrew Text, English Translation with Commentary and Notes* by Joseph H. Hertz, 1948; "Spring and the Feast of Weeks" by Mendele Mocher Sefarim from *Echoes of the Jewish Soul: Gleanings from Modern Literature,* ed. and trans. by Joseph Cooper Levine, 1931; selections from *Rejoice in Thy Festival: A Treasury of Wisdom, Wit and Humor for the Sabbath and Jewish Holidays* by Philip Goodman, 1956; "Shavuot in Modern Israel" from *The Story of Modern Israel for Young People* by Dorothy F. Zeligs, 1961; "Lifting of the Torah" and "For Shavuot" from *Around the Year in Rhymes for the Jewish Child* by Jessie E. Sampter, 1920; "Heroes of the Law" from *A Jewish Child's Garden of Verses* by Abraham Burstein, 1940. Reprinted by permission of Bloch Publishing Co.

B'nai B'rith Hillel Foundations, Washington, D.C.: "The Source of Jewish Power" from *What Is This Jewish Heritage?* by Ludwig Lewisohn, 1954.

Board of Jewish Education, New York: "At Sinai" by Deborah Pessin from *Lag Be'Omer and Shavuot: Jewish Life and Customs: Unit Seven,* ed. by Ben M. Edidin, 1942; "King Agrippa and the Firstfruits" by Samuel Shihor from *The New World Over Story Book,* ed. by Ezekiel Schloss and Morris Epstein, 1968; "Mountains of *Blintzes*" by Sydney Taylor from *World Over,* vol. 19, no. 15 (May 16, 1958).

Brandeis University, Waltham, Mass.: "Shavuot in the Soviet Union" from *The Jewish Religion in the Soviet Union,* by Joshua Rothenberg, Philip W. Lown Graduate Center for Contemporary Jewish Studies and Ktav Publishing House, 1971.

Branden Press, Inc., Boston: "Song of Adorning" by Abraham Shlonsky and "A Shavuot Offering in Exile" by Abraham Nathan Perlberg from *Gems of Hebrew Verse: Poems for Young People,* trans. by Harry H. Fein, Bruce Humphries, Boston, 1940.

Ruth F. Brin, Minneapolis: "The Ten Commandments" from *Interpretations for the Weekly Torah Reading,* Lerner Publications Co., Minneapolis, 1965.

Arthur A. Cohen, New York: excerpts from "Why I Choose to Be a Jew" by Arthur A. Cohen, *Harper's Magazine* 218, no. 1,307 (April 1959). Copyright © 1959 by *Harper's Magazine* Reprinted by permission of the author.

East and West Library, London, England: "The Belief in Divine Providence" from *Kuzari: The Book of Proof and Argument* by Judah Halevi, ed. by Isaak Heinemann, 1947.

Farrar, Straus & Giroux, Inc., New York: "Sinai" from *The Seeker and Other Poems* by Nelly Sachs. Copyright © 1970 by Farrar, Straus & Giroux, Inc.; "The Idea of Revelation" from *God in Search of Man: A Philosophy of Judaism* by Abraham Joshua Heschel. Copyright © 1955 by Abraham Joshua Heschel. Reprinted with the permission of Farrar, Straus & Giroux, Inc.

Follet Publishing Co., Chicago: "Play for Shavuot" from *All-of-a-Kind Family Uptown* by Sydney Taylor, Wilcox and Follet, Chicago, 1958.

Samuel E. Goldfarb, Mercer Island, Wash.: *"Der Oibershter Iz Der Mechutten," "Kabbalat ha-Torah"* from *The Jewish Songster,* Parts I and II, by Israel Goldfarb and Samuel E. Goldfarb, Brooklyn, N.Y.

Mrs. Hirsch L. Gordon, New York: "Karo and Alkabetz Hold a *Tikkun Shavuot* in Salonika" by Solomon Levi Alkabetz, trans. by Hirsch L. Gordon, from *The Maggid of Caro* by Hirsch L. Gordon, Pardes Publishing House, 1949.

Uri Zvi Greenberg, Ramat Gan, Israel: "Thoughts on the Feast of Weeks" by Uri Zvi Greenberg, trans. by Herbert Parzen, from *Mahanaim* 57 (1961).

Harvard University Press and The Loeb Classical Library, Cambridge, Mass.: "Moses Delivers the Decalogue," "Pentecost in Wartime" from *Josephus,* vols. 2 (1927) and 4 (1930), trans. by H. St. J. Thackeray and vol. 7 (1943), trans. by Ralph Marcus. Copyright © The President and Fellows of Harvard College, 1927, 1930, 1943; "Why the Torah Was Given in the Desert," "Why the Laws Are Addressed to Every Individual" from *Philo*, vol. 7 (1937), trans. by F. H. Colson.

Hebrew Publishing Co., New York: "The Counting of the *Omer*" from *A Book of Jewish Concepts* by Philip Birnbaum, 1964; "Shavuot on a Farm in Connecticut" from *The Days of Our Years: Personal and General Reminiscence (1859–1929)* by Israel Kasovich, 1929; "Epilogue to the Book of Ruth" from *And It Came to Pass: Legends and Stories about King David and King Solomon* by Hayyim Nahman Bialik, 1938. Copyright by Hebrew Publishing Co. and used with permission.

Hebrew Union College Annual, Cincinnati: excerpts from "Hazkarath Neshamoth" by Solomon B. Freehof from *Hebrew Union College Annual*, vol. 36 (1965).

The Jewish Chronicle, London, England: "The Torah's Marriage in Gibraltar" by Cecil Roth from *The Jewish Chronicle*, no. 3,397 (May 18, 1934); *"Tikkun Lel Shavuot"* by David Frischman, trans. by J. Israelstam, *The Jewish Chronicle Supplement*, no. 101 (May 31, 1929); "Heaven and Earth" from *A Guide to Shavuoth* by Chaim Pearl, Jewish Chronicle Publications, London, 1959.

Jewish National Fund of America, New York: "The Festival in Haifa" and *"Bikkurim* in Kibbutz Matzuba" by Gershon Ahituv; "The Radish and the Cucumber" by Anda Amir, "My Garden's Firstfruits" by Aharon Zeev, "The Midnight Wish" by Myrim from *Shavuot Sheaves*, ed. by Yehuda Haezrahi, Jewish National Fund Youth Department, Jerusalem, 1965.

Jewish Publication Society of America, Philadelphia: selections from *The Torah: The Five Books of Moses: A New Translation . . . according to the Masoretic Text;* selections from *The Five Megilloth and Jonah: A New Translation;* selections from *Mekilta de-Rabbi Ishmael*, trans. and ed. by Jacob Z. Lauterbach; selections from *Ma'aseh Book*, trans. by Moses Gaster; selections from *Sefer ha-Ikkarim (Book of Principles)* by Joseph Albo, ed. and trans. by Isaac Husik; "Out of the Midst of the Fire" from *Selected Essays* by Ahad Ha-Am; "The Date of Shavuot" from *The Pharisees: The Sociological Background of Their Faith* by Louis Finkelstein; "The Bringing of the Firstfruits During the Second Commonwealth" from *The Rise and Fall of the Judaean State: A Political, Social and Religious History of the Second Commonwealth* by Solomon Zeitlin; "The Voice of Simeon Bar Yohai" from *Legends of Palestine* by Zev Vilnay; "Among the Jews of Algeria" from *Travels in North Africa* by Nahum Slouschz; "Pentecost in Svislovitz" from *Forward from Exile: The Autobiography of Shmarya Levin*, trans. by Maurice Samuel; "The First Confirmation in New York" from *The Rise of the Jewish Community of New York, 1654–1860* by Hyman B. Grinstein; "Where Is That Mountain?" by Charles Reznikoff from *The Menorah Treasury: Harvest of Half a Century*, ed. by Leo W. Schwarz; "We Will Do and We Will Obey" from *Kiddush Ha-Shem: An Epic of 1648* by Sholom Asch, trans. by Rufus Learsi; "The Address to the Sixty" from *For the Sake of Heaven* by Martin Buber, trans. by Ludwig Lewisohn.

Keter Publishing House, New York: "Shavuot among the Samaritans" by Binyamin Tsedaka from *Encyclopaedia Judaica*, Keter Publishing House, Jerusalem, 1971, vol. 14.

Ktav Publishing House, New York: "A New Commandment" from *My Holiday Story Book* by Morris Epstein. Reprinted by permission of the publisher.

Labor Zionist Alliance, New York: "Letters from a Desert in North Africa" from *Letters from the Desert* by Moshe Mosenson, Sharon Books, 1945.

Joseph Leftwich, London, England: "The Vision of Moses" by I. M. Lask from *The Golden Peacock: An Anthology of Yiddish Poetry,* ed. by Joseph Leftwich, Sci-Art Publishers, Cambridge, Mass., 1939.

Merkos L'Inyanei Chinuch, Inc., Oak Park, Mich.: "We Repair Faded Letters" from *A Thought for the Week,* adapted from the works of Rabbi Menachem M. Schneerson, vol. 3, no. 2 (October 17, 1969).

William Morrow & Company, Inc., New York: "Loud Rang the Voice" from *Festivals of the Jewish Year: A Modern Interpretation and Guide* by Theodor H. Gaster, William Sloane Associates, New York. Copyright, 1952, 1953, by Theodor H. Gaster.

Jeremy U. Newman, Far Rockaway, N. Y.: "The Pledge of Israel" and "But God Chose Sinai" from *Trumpet in Adversity and Other Poems* by Louis I. Newman, Renascence Press, New York, 1948.

October House Inc., New York: "Dead Men Don't Praise God" by Jacob Glatstein from *The Selected Poems of Jacob Glatstein.* Translated from the Yiddish and with an Introduction by Ruth Whitman. Copyright © 1972 by Ruth Whitman. Reprinted by permission of October House Inc.

Dr. Raphael Patai, Forest Hills, N.Y.: "Shavuot as Celebrated by the Jews of Kurdistan," trans. by Herbert Parzen, from *Yehude Kurdistan: Mehker Etnologi* by Erich Brauer, ed. by Raphael Patai, Palestine Institute of Folklore and Ethnology, Jerusalem, 1947.

Rabbi Chaim Pearl, Riverdale, N.Y.: "Heaven and Earth" from *A Guide to Shavuoth* by Chaim Pearl, Jewish Chronicle Publications, London, 1959.

Petahim, Jerusalem, Israel: "*Tikkun Lel Shavuot* at Yifat" by Meir Eyali from *Petahim,* no. 4 (1968).

Rabbi David Polish, Evanston, Ill.: "The Covenant at Mount Sinai" from *The Higher Freedom: A New Turning Point in Jewish History* by David Polish, Quadrangle Books, 1965.

The Rabbinical Assembly and United Synagogue of America, New York: "Before the Words of God Are Read," trans. by Joseph Marcus, from *Sabbath and Festival Prayer Book: With a New Translation, Supplementary Readings and Notes.* Copyright 1946. Reprinted by permission of The Rabbinical Assembly and United Synagogue of America.

Mrs. Cecil Roth, New York: "The Torah's Marriage in Gibraltar" by Cecil Roth from *The Jewish Chronicle,* no. 3,397 (May 18, 1934).

Schocken Books Inc., New York: "Shavuot among Brothers and Friends," reprinted by permission of Schocken Books Inc. from *A Guest for the Night* by S. Y. Agnon. Copyright © 1968 by Schocken Books Inc.; "*Yismehu Adirim,*" reprinted by permission of Schocken Books Inc. from *A Treasury of Jewish Folksong* by Ruth Rubin. Copyright © 1950 by Schocken Books Inc.; excerpts from midrashim, reprinted by permission of Schocken Books Inc. from *Hammer on the Rock: A Short Midrash Reader* edited by Nahum N. Glatzer. Copyright © 1948, 1962 by Schocken Books Inc.

Benjamin Schreiber, New York: "Shavuot in Vamia, Hungary" from *Zechor Yemos Olam (Remember the Early Days)* by Benjamin Schreiber, 1969.

The Soncino Press Limited, London, England: selections from *The Babylonian Talmud,* trans. under the editorship of Isidore Epstein, 1935–1950; selections from *Midrash Rabbah,* trans. under the editorship of H. Freedman and Maurice Simon, 1939–1951; "The Decalogue Established the World," "The Bride and The Bridegroom," "One Day Only for the Feast of Weeks" from the *Zohar,* trans. by Harry Sperling, Maurice Simon, and Paul P. Levertoff, 1931–1934;

"The Oral Tradition" from *Judaism Eternal: Selected Essays* by Samson Raphael Hirsch, trans. by I. Grunfeld, 1956. Reprinted by permission of The Soncino Press. All rights reserved by The Soncino Press Limited.

Dr. A. Alan Steinbach, Hollywood, Florida: "Revelation Eternal" from *Spiritual Cameos: Reflections and Meditations on the Holy Days and Festivals,* Gertz Bros., New York.

Union of American Hebrew Congregations, New York: "The Jewish Child's Initiation into School" from *The Lifetime of a Jew throughout the Ages of Jewish History* by Hayyim Schauss; "Shavuot in Eastern Europe" from *The Jewish Festivals: From Their Beginnings to Our Own Day* by Hayyim Schauss, trans. by Samuel Jaffe; "The Ten Commandments" from *The First Rainbow: A Book of Rhymes from Bible Times* by Ilo Orleans. Reprinted by permission of the publisher.

Union of Sephardic Congregations, New York: "Introduction to *Azharot"* from *Prayers for the Festivals according to the Custom of the Spanish and Portuguese Jews,* ed. and trans. by David de Sola Pool, 1947.

United Synagogue Commission on Jewish Education, New York: *"Alu, Alu" "Dundai," "Tanu Rabanan"* from *The Songs We Sing* by Harry Coopersmith, 1950; *"Torah Tzivah Lanu," "Naaleh le-Har Tziyon"* from *More of the Songs We Sing* by Harry Coopersmith, 1971; *"Yismah Mosheh"* from *Songs of Childhood* by Judith Eisenstein and Frieda Prensky, 1955. Reprinted by permission of the United Synagogue Commission on Jewish Education.

Women's League for Conservative Judaism, New York: "How K'tonton Wished a Wish on Shavuot Night" from *The Adventures of K'tonton: A Little Jewish Tom Thumb* by Sadie Rose Weilerstein, 1935; "The First Shavuot" from *The Singing Way: Poems for Jewish Children* by Sadie Rose Weilerstein, 1946.

World Zionist Organization, Youth and Hechalutz Department, Jerusalem, Israel: "The Uniqueness of the Ten Commandments" from *The Modern Jew Faces Eternal Problems* by Aron Barth, 1965.

Yale University Press, New Haven: excerpts from *The Midrash on Psalms,* trans. by William G. Braude, 1959; excerpts from *Pesikta Rabbati: Discourses for Feasts, Fasts and Special Sabbaths,* trans. by William G. Braude, 1968.

Credits for the illustrations are included in the list of illustrations that follows the contents.

* *

מוקדש
לנכדתי הצברה
תהלה
בת אברהם חיים ושרה מינדל

PREFACE

The prime significance of Shavuot today lies in its commemoration as the anniversary of the theophany on Mount Sinai when Moses received the Ten Commandments. This spectacular and unparalleled event was the culmination of the exodus from Egypt. The saga of Israel's sojourn in the desert after their emancipation from Egyptian bondage is climaxed at Mount Sinai with spiritual freedom embodied in the Torah. Thus, following Passover, the Season of Our Freedom, comes Shavuot, the Season of the Giving of Our Law. The Decalogue is introduced with a reminder of the liberation from Egyptian slavery: "I the LORD am your God who brought you out of the land of Egypt, the house of bondage" (Exodus 20.2).

The revelation of the Torah—both the Written and the Oral Law—which according to talmudic tradition occurred simultaneously, was in essence the birthday of the Jewish religion. The Torah, the spiritual legacy covenanted between God and Israel on Shavuot, is the life-giving elixir that has sustained the Jewish people and has given vital meaning to their lives in all generations. It has been Israel's glorious contribution to the world, and its Ten Commandments have been engraved on the hearts of mankind as the cardinal moral basis of modern civilization.

The distinctive characteristic of Shavuot, as originally observed prior to the destruction of the Second Temple and the subsequent exile from the Land of Israel, was its agricultural aspect, marked by the bringing of the firstfruits to Jerusalem. The joyous and colorful rite of the firstfruits offering in the early days of Jewish history admonished the people that "the earth is the LORD's and the fulness thereof" (Psalms 24.1), and that they were His custodians, obligated to share the soil's fertile yield with the poor man and the stranger. This ancient ceremony has been symbolically revived in modern Israel, where processions and pageantry mark Shavuot.

This second of the three pilgrimage festivals is also named the Feast of the Harvest. Through the daily counting of the *omer* for seven weeks it is linked with Passover, when an *omer* of the barley harvest was brought as an offering to the Temple in Jerusalem. Indeed, Shavuot is called Atzeret, the conclusion of Passover, even as Shemini Atzeret is the final day of Sukkot. There is, however, a sharp contrast between Shavuot and the other festivals. There are no symbolic commandments to be performed on Shavuot, like the eating of unleavened bread on Passover and the dwelling in booths and the use of the Four Species on Sukkot. Moreover, in the Diaspora, Passover is celebrated for eight days, Sukkot for nine, and Shavuot for only two days. Though the Season of the Giving of Our Law does not include the engrossing ritual of the other festive days and is of shorter duration, it occupies a paramount position in Jewish life as the festival of nature and revelation.

The traditional observance of Shavuot symbolizes both its agricultural and historical connotation. It occurs at a period of the year when the earth is blanketed with fragrant greenery, adorned with blooming flowers, and verdant with the rich yield of fields and orchards, attesting to God's recurring and bountiful benedictions to man. At the same time it is a reminder of the universal principles promulgated in the Torah—faith in God, the brotherhood of man, and the ideals of justice, compassion, truth, and peace—that the children of Israel undertook to fulfill.

The Shavuot Anthology aims to convey the spirit of the festival in its variegated aspects. It also presents the diverse ways in which the Feast of Weeks has been observed in all generations. Like the preceding volumes in the Sabbath and Jewish Holiday Series of The Jewish Publication Society of America—Abraham E. Milgram's *Sabbath: The Day of Delight,* Emily Solis-Cohen, Jr.'s

Hanukkah: The Feast of Lights, and this writer's *The Rosh Hashanah Anthology, The Yom Kippur Anthology, The Sukkot and Simhat Torah Anthology, The Purim Anthology,* and *The Passover Anthology*—this book contains selections from the major sources of Jewish literature in which references to Shavuot are to be found and from the writings of modern authors. It is the first comprehensive compilation in English on the Festival of Weeks intended for laymen and professionals, for adults and children.

It is my pleasure to express deep appreciation to the many colleagues and friends who have extended to me their generous cooperation. Original contributions to this book were made at my request, as follows: "Recipes for Shavuot" by Mrs. Hanna Goodman, author of *Jewish Cooking around the World: Gourmet and Holiday Recipes;* "Shavuot in Art" by Dr. Joseph Gutmann, professor of art history at Wayne State University and author of erudite studies on Jewish art; "Music for Shavuot" by Cantor Paul Kavon, director of the Department of Music, United Synagogue of America; and the sonnet "The Ever-living Moses" by Dr. A. Alan Steinbach, author of the poetry collections *Bitter-Sweet* and *When Dreamers Build.* Several articles were newly translated from the Hebrew by Solomon Feffer, chairman of the Department of Hebraic Studies, Rutgers University, Newark, N. J., and Dr. Herbert Parzen, author of *Architects of Conservative Judaism* and other scholarly works. The unsigned articles and translations for which no source is given in the notes are my work.

I wish to thank Dr. I. Edward Kiev, librarian of the Hebrew Union College–Jewish Institute of Religion Library in New York, and Mrs. Sylvia Landress, director of the Zionist Archives and Library, and their staffs for making available to me the rich resources of their holdings. I used advantageously the personal library and files of my son-in-law, Rabbi Irving Rubin of Congregation Kesher Israel, West Chester, Pennsylvania. Dr. Samuel D. Freeman, consultant in adult programing, National Jewish Welfare Board, and Dr. Jacob Kabakoff, professor of Hebrew, Lehman College of the City University of New York, offered helpful suggestions.

I am greatly indebted to David C. Gross, former executive vice-president of The Jewish Publication Society of America, for his kind encouragement and ready aid. Mrs. Kay Powell, the Society's associate editor, reviewed the manuscript with meticulous care. Credit for the beautiful design of the book is due to Mrs. Adrianne Onderdonk Dudden.

Dr. Sidney B. Hoenig, the noted historian and dean of the Bernard Revel Graduate School of Yeshiva University, carefully examined a preliminary draft of the typescript and offered much constructive criticism. I am sincerely indebted to him for the benefit of his profound knowledge of Jewish law and lore. Dr. A. Alan Steinbach, distinguished rabbi, author, and editor of both *Jewish Book Annual* and *Jewish Bookland,* likewise critically reviewed the manuscript and made numerous erudite and helpful suggestions. He is also responsible for improving the literary style. For his liberal and wholehearted assistance, which was a great boon, I am most grateful.

I also wish to thank the Memorial Foundation for Jewish Culture, New York, for assisting me by the grant of a fellowship.

My partner in life, Hanna, shared in the preparation of this anthology as she has so willingly done with my previous books. If not for her patience, encouragement, and devotion, I would not have been able to pursue my literary interests.

Philip Goodman

New York City
September 6, 1974

CONTENTS

ILLUSTRATIONS

THE SHAVUOT
ANTHOLOGY

SHAVUOT IN THE BIBLE

The Bible denotes Shavuot as the Feast of the Harvest (Exodus 23.16), the Feast of Weeks (ibid. 34.22), and the Day of the Firstfruits (Numbers 28.26). These names characterize this festival of the wheat harvest, which, according to tradition, was observed seven weeks after the second day of Passover by bringing the firstfruits of the land as an offering to the Temple in Jerusalem. It is one of the three agricultural or pilgrimage feasts prescribed in the Torah.

After the destruction of the Second Temple, Shavuot was identified with the theophany at Mount Sinai, as the anniversary of the giving of the Torah to the Israelites. While there is no reference in the Bible to Shavuot as the "Season of the Giving of Our Law," this appellation is found in the liturgy. Hence, on the first day of the festival the biblical account of the Sinaitic revelation covenanting Israel with God is read from the Torah (Exodus 19–20) during the synagogue services. The Ten Commandments —the spiritual, moral, and ethical blueprint that undergirds the civilized world and constitutes the cornerstones of the major religions—are read as the congregation rises. The version of the Decalogue as given in Exodus is cited below; the Ten Commandments are repeated in Deuteronomy 5.6–18 with some word variations.

The idyllic Book of Ruth, one of the five biblical scrolls, is also read on Shavuot. Various reasons are advanced to explain this practice. Since the Scroll of Ruth vividly limns charming pastoral scenes of the harvest season in ancient Judea, it is considered appropriate for reading on the Feast of the Harvest. Furthermore, Shavuot marks the Israelites' acceptance of God's Law, even as the heathen Moabite Ruth embraced the religion of the Jewish people. It is also maintained that the Book of Ruth was written to trace the ancestry of King David, a direct descendant of the heroine Ruth. It concludes with an account of his lineage, and since David was born and died on Shavuot, according to tradition, the Scroll of Ruth is read in his honor.[1]

*

*The Feast of the Harvest

Three times a year you shall hold a festival for Me: You shall observe the Feast of Unleavened Bread—eating unleavened bread for seven days as I have commanded you—at the set time in the month of Abib, for in it you went forth from Egypt; and none shall appear before Me empty-handed; and the Feast of the Harvest, of the firstfruits of your work, of what you sow in the field; and the Feast of Ingathering at the end of the year, when you gather in the results of your work from the field. Three times a year all your males shall appear before the Sovereign, the Lord. . . .

The choice firstfruits of your soil you shall bring to the house of the LORD your God.

Exodus 23.14–17, 19[2]

The LORD spoke to Moses, saying: Speak to the Israelite people and say to them:

When you enter the land which I am giving to you and you reap its harvest, you shall bring the first sheaf of your harvest to the priest. He shall wave the sheaf before the LORD for acceptance in your behalf; the priest shall wave it on the day after the sabbath. On the day that you wave the sheaf, you shall offer as a burnt offering to the LORD a lamb of the first year without blemish. The meal offering with it shall be two-tenths of a measure of choice flour with oil mixed in, an offering by fire of pleasing odor to the LORD; and the libation with it shall be of wine, a quarter of a *hin.* Until that very day, until you have brought the offering of your God, you shall eat no bread or parched grain or fresh ears [of the new crop]; it is a law for all time throughout the ages in all your settlements.

And from the day on which you bring the sheaf of wave offering—the day after the sabbath—you must count [off] seven weeks. They must be complete: you must count until the day after the seventh week—fifty days; then you shall bring an offering of new grain to the LORD. You shall bring from your settlements two loaves of bread as a wave offering; each shall be made of two-tenths of a measure of choice flour, baked after leavening, as firstfruits to the LORD. With the bread you shall present, as burnt offerings to the LORD, seven yearling lambs without blemish, one bull of the herd, and two rams, with their meal offerings and libations, an offering by fire of pleasing odor to the LORD. You shall also offer one he-goat as a sin offering and two yearling lambs as a sacrifice of well-being. The priest shall wave these—the two lambs—together with the bread of firstfruits as a wave offering before the LORD; they shall be holy to the LORD, for the priest. On that same day you shall hold a celebration; it shall be a sacred occasion for you; you shall not work at your occupations. This is a law for all time in all your settlements, throughout the ages.

And when you reap the harvest of your land, you shall not reap all the way to the edges of your field, or gather the gleanings of your harvest; you shall leave them for the poor and the stranger: I the LORD am your God.

Leviticus 23.9–22

On the day of the firstfruits, your Feast of Weeks, when you bring an offering of new grain to the LORD, you shall observe a sacred occasion: you shall not work at your occupations.

Numbers 28.26

You shall count off seven weeks; start to count the seven weeks when the sickle is first put to the standing grain. Then you shall observe the Feast of Weeks for the LORD your God, offering your freewill contribution according as the LORD your God has blessed you. You shall rejoice before the LORD your God with your son and daughter, your male and female slave, the Levite in your communities, and the stranger, the fatherless, and the widow in your midst, at the place where the LORD your God will choose to establish His name. Bear in mind that you were slaves in Egypt, and take care to obey these laws.

Deuteronomy 16.9–12

When you enter the land that the LORD your God is giving you as a heritage, and you occupy it and settle in it, you shall take some of every firstfruit of the soil, which you harvest from the land that the LORD your God is giving you, put it in a basket and go to the place where the LORD your God will choose to establish His name. You shall go to the priest in charge at that time and say to him, "I acknowledge this day before the LORD your God that I have entered the land which the LORD swore to our fathers to give us."

The priest shall take the basket from your hand and set it down in front of the altar of the LORD your God.

You shall then recite as follows before the LORD your God: "My father was a fugitive Aramean. He went down to Egypt with meager numbers and sojourned there; but there he became a great and very populous nation. The Egyptians dealt harshly with us and oppressed us: they imposed heavy labor upon us. We cried to the LORD, the God of our fathers, and the LORD heard our plea and saw our plight, our misery, and our oppression. The LORD freed us from Egypt by a mighty hand, by an outstretched arm and awesome power, and by signs and portents. He brought us to this place and gave us this land, a land flowing with milk and honey. Wherefore I now bring the firstfruits of the soil which You, O LORD, have given me."

You shall leave it [the basket] before the LORD your God and bow low before the LORD your God. And you shall enjoy, together with the Levite and the stranger in your midst, all the bounty that the LORD your God has bestowed upon you and your household.

Deuteronomy 26.1–11

*

*The Giving of Our Torah

On the third new moon after the Israelites had gone forth from the land of Egypt, on that very day, they entered the wilderness of Sinai. Having journeyed from Rephidim, they entered the wilderness of Sinai and encamped in the wilderness. Israel encamped there in front of the mountain, and Moses went up to God. The LORD called to him from the mountain, saying, "Thus shall you say to the house of Jacob and declare to the children of Israel: 'You have seen what I did to the Egyptians, how I bore you on eagles' wings and brought you to Me. Now then, if you will obey Me faithfully and keep My covenant, you shall be My treasured possession among all the peoples. Indeed, all the earth is Mine, but you shall be to Me a kingdom of priests and a holy nation.' These are the words that you shall speak to the children of Israel."

Moses came and summoned the elders of the people and put before them all the words that the LORD had commanded him. All the people answered as one, saying, "All that the LORD has spoken we will do!" And Moses brought back the people's words to the LORD. And the LORD said to Moses, "I will come to you in a thick cloud, in order that the people may hear when I speak with you and so trust you ever after." Then Moses reported the people's words to the LORD, and the LORD said to Moses, "Go to the people and warn them to stay pure today and tomorrow. Let them wash their clothes. Let them be ready for the third day; for on the third day the LORD will come down, in the sight of all the people, on Mount Sinai. You shall set bounds for the people round about, saying, 'Beware of going up the mountain or touching the border of it. Whoever touches the mountain shall be put to death: no hand shall touch him, but he shall be either stoned or shot; beast or man, he shall not live.' When the ram's horn sounds a long blast, they may go up on the mountain."

Moses came down from the mountain to the people and warned the people to stay pure, and they washed their clothes. And he said to the people, "Be ready for the third day: do not go near a woman."

On the third day, as morning dawned, there was thunder, and lightning, and a dense cloud upon the mountain, and a very loud blast of the horn; and all the people who were in the camp trembled. Moses led the people out of the camp toward God, and they took their places at the foot of the mountain.

Now Mount Sinai was all in smoke, for the LORD had come down upon it in fire; the smoke rose like the smoke of a kiln, and the whole mountain trembled violently. The blare of the horn grew louder and louder. As Moses spoke, God answered him in thunder. The LORD came down upon Mount Sinai, on the top of the mountain, and the LORD called Moses to the top of the mountain and Moses went up. The LORD said to Moses, "Go down, warn the people not to break through to the LORD to gaze, lest many of them perish. The priests also, who come near the LORD, must purify themselves, lest the LORD break out against them." But Moses said to the LORD, "The people cannot come up to Mount Sinai, for You warned us saying, 'Set bounds about the mountain and sanctify it.' " So the LORD said to him, "Go down, and come back together with Aaron; but let not the priests or the people break through to come up to the LORD, lest He break out against them." And Moses went down to the people and spoke to them.

God spoke all these words, saying,

I the LORD am your God who brought you out of the land of Egypt, the house of bondage: You shall have no other gods beside Me.

You shall not make for yourself a sculptured image, or any likeness of what is in the heavens above, or on the earth below, or in the waters under the earth. You shall not bow down to them or serve them. For I the LORD your God am an impassioned God, visiting the guilt of the fathers upon the children, upon the third and upon the fourth generations of those who reject Me, but showing kindness to the thousandth generation of those who love Me and keep My commandments.

You shall not swear falsely by the name of the LORD your God; for the LORD will not clear one who swears falsely by His name.

Remember the sabbath day and keep it holy. Six days you shall labor and do all your work, but the seventh day is a sabbath of

1. Moses giving the Torah to Israel. *Mahzor Lipsiae.*
South Germany. Circa 1320. See Chapter 8.

the LORD your God: you shall not do any work—you, your son or daughter, your male or female slave, or your cattle, or the stranger who is within your settlements. For in six days the LORD made heaven and earth and sea, and all that is in them, and He rested on the seventh day; therefore the LORD blessed the sabbath day and hallowed it.

Honor your father and your mother, that you may long endure on the land which the LORD your God is giving you.

You shall not murder.

You shall not commit adultery.

You shall not steal.

You shall not bear false witness against your neighbor.

You shall not covet your neighbor's house: you shall not covet your neighbor's wife, or his male or female slave, or his ox or his ass, or anything that is your neighbor's.

All the people witnessed the thunder and lightning, the blare of the horn and the mountain smoking; and when the people saw it, they fell back and stood at a distance. "You speak to us," they said to Moses, "and we will obey; but let not God speak to us, lest we die." Moses answered the people, "Be not afraid; for God has come only in order to test you, and in order that the fear of Him may be ever with you, so that you do not go astray."

Exodus 19.1—20.17

The LORD spoke those words—those and no more—to your whole congregation at the mountain, with a mighty voice out of the fire and the dense clouds. He inscribed them on two tablets of stone, which He gave to me. When you heard the voice out of the darkness, while the mountain was ablaze with fire, you came up to me, all your tribal heads and elders, and said, "The LORD our God has just shown us His majestic Presence and we have heard His voice out of the fire; we have seen this day that man may live though God has spoken to him. Let us not die, then, for this fearsome fire will consume us; if we hear the voice of the LORD our God any longer, we shall die. For what mortal ever heard the voice of the living God speak out of the fire, as we did, and lived? You go closer and hear all that the LORD our God says, and then you tell us everything that the LORD our God tells you, and we will willingly do it."

The LORD heard the plea that you made to me, and the LORD said to me, "I have heard the plea that this people made to you; they did well to speak thus. May they always be of such mind, to revere Me and follow all My commandments, that it may go well with them and with their children forever! Go, say to them, 'Return to your tents.' But you remain here with Me, and I will give you the whole Instruction—the laws and the rules—which you shall impart to them, for them to observe in the land that I am giving them to possess."

Be careful, then, to do as the LORD your God has commanded you. Do not turn aside to the right or to the left: follow only the path that the LORD your God has enjoined upon you, so that you may thrive and that it may go well with you, and that you may long endure in the land you are to occupy.

Deuteronomy 5.19–30

I had ascended the mountain to receive the tablets of stone, the Tablets of the Covenant that the LORD had made with you, and I stayed on the mountain forty days and forty nights, eating no bread and drinking no water. And the LORD gave me the two tablets of stone inscribed by the finger of God, with the exact words that the LORD had addressed to you out of the fire on the day of the Assembly.

At the end of those forty days and forty nights, the LORD gave me the two tablets of stone, the Tablets of the Covenant. And the LORD said to me, "Hurry, go down from here at once, for the people whom you brought out of Egypt have acted wickedly; they have been quick to stray from the path that I enjoined upon them; they have made themselves a molten image." The LORD further said to me, "I see that this is a stiffnecked people. Let Me alone and I will destroy them and blot out their name from under heaven, and I will make you a nation far more numerous than they."

I started down the mountain, a mountain ablaze with fire, the two Tablets of the Covenant in my two hands. I saw how you had sinned against the LORD your God: you had made yourselves a molten calf; you had been quick to stray from the path that the LORD had enjoined upon you. Thereupon I gripped the two tablets and flung them away with both my hands, smashing them before your eyes. I threw myself down before the LORD—eating no bread and drinking no water forty days and forty nights, as before—because of the great wrong you had committed, doing what displeased the LORD and vexing Him. For I was in dread of the LORD's fierce anger against you, which moved Him to wipe you out. And that time, too, the LORD gave heed to me. . . .

Thereupon the LORD said to me, "Carve out two tablets of stone like the first, and come up to Me on the mountain; and make an ark of wood. I will inscribe on the tablets the commandments that were on the first tablets which you smashed, and you shall deposit them in the ark."

I made an ark of acacia wood and carved out two tablets of stone like the first; I took the two tablets with me and went up the mountain. The LORD inscribed on the tablets the same text as on the first, the Ten Commandments that He addressed to you on the mountain out of the fire on the day of the Assembly; and the LORD gave them to me. Then I left and went down from the mountain, and I deposited the tablets in the ark that I had made, where they still are, as the LORD had commanded me. . . .

I had stayed on the mountain, as I did the first time, forty days and forty nights; and the LORD heeded me once again: the LORD agreed not to destroy you.

Deuteronomy 9.9–19, 10.1–5, 10

*

*The Scroll of Ruth

In the days when the chieftains ruled, there was a famine in the land; and a man of Bethlehem in Judah, with his wife and two sons, went to reside in the country of Moab. The man's name was Elimelech, his wife's name was Naomi, and his two sons were named Mahlon and Chilion—Ephrathites of Bethlehem in Judah. They came to the country of Moab and remained there.

Elimelech, Naomi's husband, died; and she was left with her two sons. They married Moabite women, one named Orpah and the other Ruth, and they lived there about ten years. Then those two—Mahlon and Chilion—also died; so the woman was left without her two sons and without her husband.

She started out with her daughters-in-law to return from the country of Moab; for in the country of Moab she had heard that the LORD had taken note of His people and given them food. Accompanied by her two daughters-in-law, she left the place where she had been living; and they set out on the road back to the land of Judah.

But Naomi said to her two daughters-in-law, "Turn back, each of you to her mother's house. May the LORD deal kindly with you, as you have dealt with the dead and with me! May the LORD grant that each of you find security in the house of a husband!" And she kissed them farewell. They broke into weeping and said to her, "No, we will return with you to your people."

But Naomi replied, "Turn back, my daughters! Why should you go with me? Have I any more sons in my body, who might be husbands for you? Turn back, my daughters, for I am too old to be married. Even if I thought there was hope for me, even if I were married tonight and I also bore sons, should you wait for them to grow up? Should you on their account debar yourselves from marriage? Oh no, my daughters! My lot is far more bitter than yours, for the hand of the LORD has struck out against me."

They broke into weeping again, and Orpah kissed her mother-in-law farewell. But Ruth clung to her. So she said, "See, your sister-in-law has returned to her people and her gods. Go follow your sister-in-law." But Ruth replied, "Do not urge me to leave you, to turn back and not follow you. For wherever you go, I will go; wherever you lodge, I will lodge; your people shall be my people, and your God my God. Where you die, I will die, and there I will be buried. Thus and more may the LORD do to me if anything but death parts me from you."

When [Naomi] saw how determined she was to go with her, she ceased to argue with her; and the two went on until they reached Bethlehem.

When they arrived in Bethlehem, the whole city buzzed with excitement over them. The women said, "Can this be Naomi?" "Do not call me Naomi ["Pleasantness"]," she replied. "Call me Mara ["Bitterness"], for Shaddai has made my lot very bitter. I went away full, and the LORD has brought me back empty. How can you call me Naomi, when the LORD has dealt harshly with me, when Shaddai has brought misfortune upon me!"

Thus Naomi returned from the country of Moab; she returned

with her daughter-in-law, Ruth the Moabite. They arrived in Bethlehem at the beginning of the barley harvest.

Now Naomi had a kinsman on her husband's side, a man of substance, of the family of Elimelech, whose name was Boaz.

Ruth the Moabite said to Naomi, "I would like to go to the fields and glean among the ears of grain, behind someone who may show me kindness." "Yes, daughter, go," she replied; and off she went. She came and gleaned in a field, behind the reapers; and as luck would have it, it was the piece of land belonging to Boaz, who was of Elimelech's family.

Presently Boaz arrived from Bethlehem. He greeted the reapers, "The LORD be with you!" And they responded, "The LORD bless you!" Boaz said to the servant who was in charge of the reapers, "Whose girl is that?" The servant in charge of the reapers replied, "She is a Moabite girl who came back with Naomi from the country of Moab. She said, 'Please let me glean and gather among the sheaves behind the reapers.' She has been on her feet ever since she came this morning. She has rested but little in the hut."

Boaz said to Ruth, "Listen to me, daughter. Don't go to glean in another field. Don't go elsewhere, but stay here close to my girls. Keep your eyes on the field they are reaping, and follow them. I have ordered the men not to molest you. And when you are thirsty, go to the jars and drink some of [the water] that the men have drawn."

She prostrated herself with her face to the ground, and said to him, "Why are you so kind as to single me out, when I am a foreigner?"

Boaz said in reply, "I have been told of all that you did for your mother-in-law after the death of your husband, how you left your father and mother and the land of your birth and came to a people you had not known before. May the LORD reward your deeds. May you have a full recompense from the LORD, the God of Israel, under whose wings you have sought refuge!"

She answered, "You are most kind my lord, to comfort me and to speak gently to your maidservant—though I am not so much as one of your maidservants."

At mealtime, Boaz said to her, "Come over here and partake of the meal, and dip your morsel in the vinegar." So she sat down beside the reapers. He handed her roasted grain, and she ate her fill and had some left over.

When she got up again to glean, Boaz gave orders to his workers, "You are not only to let her glean among the sheaves, without interference, but you must also pull some [stalks] out of the heaps and leave them for her to glean, and not scold her."

She gleaned in the field until evening. Then she beat out what she had gleaned—it was about an *ephah* of barley—and carried it back with her to the town. When her mother-in-law saw what she had gleaned, and when she also took out and gave her what she had left over after eating her fill, her mother-in-law asked her, "Where did you glean today? Where did you work? Blessed be he who took such generous notice of you!" So she told her mother-in-law whom she had worked with, saying, "The name of the man with whom I worked today is Boaz."

Naomi said to her daughter-in-law, "Blessed be he of the LORD, who has not failed in His kindness to the living or to the dead! For," Naomi explained to her daughter-in-law, "the man is related to us; he is one of our redeeming kinsmen." Ruth the Moabite said, "He even told me, 'Stay close by my workers until all my harvest is finished.' " And Naomi answered her daughter-

2. Ruth amid the reapers. *Mahzor.* Illuminated manuscript on vellum. South Germany. Circa 1320. See Chapter 8.

in-law Ruth, "It is best, daughter, that you go out with his girls, and not be annoyed in some other field." So she stayed close to the maidservants of Boaz, and gleaned until the barley harvest and the wheat harvest were finished. Then she stayed at home with her mother-in-law.

Naomi, her mother-in-law, said to her, "Daughter, I must seek a home for you, where you may be happy. Now there is our kinsman Boaz, whose girls you were close to. He will be winnowing barley on the threshing floor tonight. So bathe, anoint yourself, dress up, and go down to the threshing floor. But do not disclose yourself to the man until he has finished eating and drinking. When he lies down, note the place where he lies down, and go over and uncover his feet and lie down. He will tell you what you are to do." She replied, "I will do everything you tell me."

She went down to the threshing floor and did just as her mother-in-law had instructed her. Boaz ate and drank, and in a cheerful mood went to lie down beside the grainpile. Then she went over stealthily and uncovered his feet and lay down. In the middle of the night, the man gave a start and pulled back—there was a woman lying at his feet!

"Who are you?" he asked. And she replied, "I am your handmaid Ruth. Spread your robe over your handmaid, for you are a redeeming kinsman."

He exclaimed, "Be blessed of the LORD, daughter! Your latest deed of loyalty is greater than the first, in that you have not turned to younger men, whether poor or rich. And now, daughter, have no fear. I will do in your behalf whatever you ask, for all the elders of my town know what a fine woman you are. But while it is true I am a redeeming kinsman, there is another redeemer closer than I. Stay for the night. Then in the morning, if he will act as a redeemer, good! let him redeem. But if he does not want to act as redeemer for you, I will do so myself, as the LORD lives! Lie down until morning."

So she lay at his feet until dawn. She rose before one person could distinguish another, for he thought, "Let it not be known that the woman came to the threshing floor." And he said, "Hold out the shawl you are wearing." She held it while he measured out six measures of barley, and he put it on her back.

When she got back to the town, she came to her mother-in-law, who asked, "How is it with you, daughter?" She told her all that the man had done for her; and she added, "He gave me these six measures of barley, saying to me, 'Do not go back to your mother-in-law empty-handed.' " And Naomi said, "Stay here, daughter, till you learn how the matter turns out. For the man will not rest, but will settle the matter today." . . .

So Boaz married Ruth; she became his wife, and he cohabited with her. The LORD let her conceive, and she bore a son. And the women said to Naomi, "Blessed be the LORD, who has not withheld a redeemer from you today! May his name be perpetuated in Israel! He will renew your life and sustain your old age; for he is born of your daughter-in-law, who loves you and is better to you than seven sons."

Naomi took the child and held it to her bosom. She became its foster mother, and the women neighbors gave him a name, saying, "A son is born to Naomi!" They named him Obed; he was the father of Jesse, father of David.

Ruth 1.1—3.18, 4.13–17[3]

SHAVUOT IN POSTBIBLICAL WRITINGS

Among the classical postbiblical books are the Apocrypha and the Pseudepigrapha and the writings of Flavius Josephus. During the period from circa 330 B.C.E. to 200 C.E., Diaspora Jewry created major literary works in the Greek language. Among these Hellenistic Jewish writings is the Septuagint made in Alexandria, a Greek translation of the Hebrew Pentateuch which later incorporated the books of the Apocrypha that had been excluded from the biblical canon. Excerpts from the apocryphal Tobit and II Maccabees are given below.

The *Book of Jubilees,* a parallel to Genesis and parts of Exodus, is found in the Pseudepigrapha written in the same period as the Apocrypha. An elaborate account of Moses receiving the tablets of the Law as well as the legend of the observance of Shavuot by Noah and the biblical patriarchs are quoted from *Jubilees.*

Another Greek author was Philo of Alexandria (c. 20 B.C.E.–c. 50 C.E.), an observant Jew who was noted for his contributions to religious philosophy and for his role as an astute interpreter of Plato's philosophy. Accepting the Bible literally and historically, he added his own allegorical interpretations. In his *Decalogue,* he expounds why the giving of the Torah took place in the desert and not in an urban locale. The same work cites his rationale as to why the laws are addressed to the individual rather than to the people as a whole.

Flavius Josephus (c. 38 C.E.–c. 100 C.E.), gifted with a creative and imaginative mind, paraphrased the Bible, adding original embellishments. His *The Jewish Antiquities* and *The Jewish War* are considered major sources for the history of the Second Temple period. Culled from Josephus' writings are his interpretation of Moses delivering the Ten Commandments and two instances of Shavuot observance in wartime.

*

*Moses Receives the Tablets of the Law

And it came to pass in the first year of the exodus of the children of Israel out of Egypt, in the third month, on the sixteenth day of the month, that God spake to Moses, saying, "Come up to Me on the mount, and I will give thee two tables of stone of the Law and of the commandment, which I have written, that thou mayest teach them." And Moses went up into the mount of God, and the glory of the Lord abode on Mount Sinai, and a cloud over-shadowed it six days. And He called to Moses on the seventh day out of the midst of the cloud, and the appearance of the glory of the Lord was like a flaming fire on the top of the mount. And Moses was on the mount forty days and forty nights, and God taught him the earlier and the later history of the division of all the days of the Law and of the testimony. And He said, "Incline thine heart to every word which I shall speak to thee on this mount, and write them in a book in order that their generations may see how I have not forsaken them for all the evil which they have wrought in transgressing the covenant which I establish between Me and thee for their generations this day on Mount Sinai. And thus it will come to pass when all these things come upon them, that they will recognize that I am more righteous than they in all their judgments and in all their actions, and they will recognize that I have been truly with them." . . .

And Moses fell on his face and prayed and said, "O Lord my God, do not forsake Thy people and Thy inheritance, so that they should wander in the error of their hearts, and do not deliver them into the hands of their enemies, the gentiles, lest they should rule over them and cause them to sin against Thee.

Let Thy mercy, O Lord, be lifted up upon Thy people and create in them an upright spirit, and let not the spirit of Beliar rule over them to accuse them before Thee, and to ensnare them from all the paths of righteousness, so that they may perish from before Thy face. But they are Thy people and Thy inheritance, which Thou has delivered with Thy great power from the hands of the Egyptians: create in them a clean heart and a holy spirit, and let them not be ensnared in their sins from henceforth until eternity." And the Lord said unto Moses, "I know their contrariness and their thoughts and their stiffneckedness, and they will not be obedient till they confess their own sin and the sin of their fathers. And after this they will turn to Me in all uprightness and with all [their] heart and with all [their] soul, and I will circumcise the foreskin of their heart and the foreskin of the heart of their seed, and I will create in them a holy spirit, and I will cleanse them so that they shall not turn away from Me from that day unto eternity. And their souls will cleave to Me and to all My commandments, and they will fulfill My commandments, and I will be their Father and they shall be My children."

Book of Jubilees 1.1–6, 19–24[1]

* Moses Delivers the Decalogue

FLAVIUS JOSEPHUS

Moses now, having convoked the assembly, told them that he himself was departing to Mount Sinai, intending to commune with God and, after receiving from Him some oracle, to return to them; for their part, he bade them transfer their camp close to the mount, in honor preferring the neighborhood of God. Having spoken thus, he went up to Sinai, which was the highest of the mountains in those regions, having proportions so massive and cliffs so precipitous as put it not only beyond men's power to scale but even to contemplate without tiring the eye; still more did the rumor of God's sojourning thereon render it awful and unapproachable. However the Hebrews, in compliance with the behests of Moses, shifted their camp and occupied the foot of the mountain, exulting in the thought that Moses would return from God's presence with that promise of blessings which he had led them to expect. In festal fashion they awaited their leader, practicing purity in general and abstaining in particular from union with their wives for three days, as he had enjoined upon them, while beseeching God to be gracious in His converse with Moses and to grant him a gift which would promote their happiness. Withal they partook of more sumptuous fare and arrayed themselves, along with their wives and children, in splendid attire.

So for two days they continued in festivity. But on the third, before the sun arose, a cloud settled down over the whole camp of the Hebrews, who had seen not the like before, enveloping the spot whereon they had pitched their tents; and, while all the rest of heaven remained serene, blustering winds, bringing tempestuous rain, came sweeping down, lightning terrified the beholders, and thunderbolts hurled from aloft signified the advent of God propitious to the desires of Moses. Of these happenings each of my readers may think as he will; for my part, I am constrained to relate them as they are recorded in the sacred books. As for the Hebrews, the sights that they saw and the din that struck their ears sorely disquieted them, for they were unaccustomed thereto and the rumor current concerning this mountain, that there was the very resort of God, deeply dismayed their minds. They kept to their tents, dispirited, imagining that Moses had perished beneath the wrath of God and expecting a like fate for themselves.

Such was their mood when suddenly Moses appeared, radiant and high-hearted. The mere sight of him rid them of their terrors and prompted brighter hopes for the future; the air too became serene and purged of its recent disturbances on the arrival of Moses. Thereupon he summoned the people to assemble to hear what God had said to him, and, when all were collected, he stood on an eminence whence all might hear him and "Hebrews," said he, "God, as of yore, has received me graciously and, having dictated for you rules for a blissful life and an ordered government, is coming Himself into the camp. In His name, then, and in the name of all that through Him has already been wrought for us, scorn not the words now to be spoken, through looking only on me, the speaker, or by reason that it is a human tongue that addresses you. . . . He it is who favors you with these commandments, using me for interpreter. Let them be had by you in veneration; battle for them more jealously than for children and wives. For blissful will be your life, do ye but follow these: ye will enjoy a fruitful earth, a sea unvexed by tempest, a breed of children born in nature's way, and ye will be redoubtable to your foes. For I have been admitted to a sight of God, I have listened to an immortal voice: such care hath He for our race and for its perpetuation."

That said, he made the people advance with their wives and children, to hear God speak to them of their duties, to the end that the excellence of the spoken words might not be impaired by human tongue in being feebly transmitted to their knowledge. And all heard a voice which came from on high to the ears of all, in such wise that not one of those ten words escaped them which Moses has left inscribed on the two tablets. These words it is not permitted us to state explicitly, to the letter, but we will indicate their purport.

The first word teaches us that God is one and that He only must be worshiped. The second commands us to make no image of any living creature for adoration, the third not to swear by God on any frivolous matter, the fourth to keep every seventh day by resting from all work, the fifth to honor our parents, the sixth to refrain from murder, the seventh not to commit adultery, the eighth not to steal, the ninth not to bear false witness, the tenth to covet nothing that belongs to another.

The people, having thus heard from the very mouth of God that of which Moses had told them, rejoicing in these commandments dispersed from the assembly.

Jewish Antiquities 3.5.1–6[2]

*

* *Why the Torah Was Given in the Desert*
PHILO OF ALEXANDRIA

To the question why he [Moses] promulgated his laws in the depths of the desert instead of in cities we may answer in the first place that most cities are full of countless evils, both acts of impiety toward God and wrongdoing between man and man. For everything is debased, the genuine overpowered by the spurious, the true by the specious, which is intrinsically false, but creates impressions whose plausibility serves but to delude. So too in cities there arises that most insidious of foes, Pride [or vanity], admired and worshiped by some who add dignity to vain ideas by means of gold crowns and purple robes and a great establishment of servants and cars, on which these so-called blissful and happy people ride aloft, drawn sometimes by mules and horses, sometimes by men, who bear the heavy burden on their shoulders, yet suffer in soul rather than in body under the weight of extravagant arrogance. . . .

He [Moses] had also a second object in mind. He who is about to receive the holy laws must first cleanse his soul and purge away the deep-set stains which it has contracted through contact with the motley, promiscuous horde of men in cities. And to this he cannot attain except by dwelling apart, nor that at once, but only long afterwards, and not till the marks which his old transgressions have imprinted on him have gradually grown faint, melted away and disappeared. . . . Naturally therefore he first led them away from the highly mischievous associations of cities into the desert, to clear the sins out of their souls, and then began to set the nourishment before their minds—and what should this nourishment be but laws and words of God?

He had a third reason as follows: just as men when setting out on a long voyage do not begin to provide sails and rudders and tillers when they have embarked and left the harbor, but equip themselves with enough of the gear needed for the voyage while they are still staying on shore, so Moses did not think it good that they should just take their portions and settle in cities and then go in quest of laws to regulate their civic life, but rather should first provide themselves with the rules for that life and gain practice in all that would surely enable the communities to steer their course in safety, and then settle down to follow from the first the principles of justice lying ready for their use, in harmony and fellowship of spirit and rendering to every man his due.

Some, too, give a fourth reason which is not out of keeping with the truth but agrees very closely with it. As it was necessary to establish a belief in their minds that the laws were not the inventions of a man but quite clearly the oracles of God, he led the nation a great distance away from cities into the depths of a desert, barren not only of cultivated fruits but also of water fit for drinking, in order that, if after lacking the necessaries of life and expecting to perish from hunger and thirst, they suddenly found abundance of sustenance self-produced—when heaven rained the food called manna and the shower of quails from the air to add relish to their food—when the bitter water grew sweet and fit for drinking and springs gushed out of the rock—they should no longer wonder whether the laws were actually the pronouncements of God, since they had been given the clearest evidence of the truth in the supplies which they had so unexpectedly received in their destitution. For He who gave abundance of the means of life also bestowed the wherewithal of a good life; for mere life they needed food and drink which they found without making provision; for the good life they needed laws and ordinances which would bring improvement to their souls.

These are the reasons suggested to answer the question under discussion: they are but probable surmises; the true reasons are known to God alone.

Decalogue 1–5[3]

*

Why the Laws Are Addressed to Every Individual

PHILO OF ALEXANDRIA

The ten words or oracles, in reality laws or statutes, were delivered by the Father of all when the nation, men and women alike, were assembled together. Did He do so by His own utterance in the form of a voice? Surely not: may no such thought ever enter our minds, for God is not as a man needing mouth and tongue and windpipe. I should suppose that God wrought on this occasion a miracle of a truly holy kind by bidding an invisible sound to be created in the air more marvelous than all instruments and fitted with perfect harmonies, not soulless, nor yet composed of body and soul like a living creature, but a rational soul full of clearness and distinctness, which giving shape and tension to the air and changing it to flaming fire, sounded forth like the breath through a trumpet an articulate voice so loud that it appeared to be equally audible to the farthest as well as the nearest. . . .

So much for the divine voice. But we may properly ask why, when all these many thousands were collected in one spot, He thought good in proclaiming His ten oracles to address each not as to several persons but as to one, Thou shalt not commit adultery, Thou shalt not kill, Thou shalt not steal, and so too with the rest. One answer which must be given is that He wishes to teach the readers of the sacred Scriptures a most excellent lesson, namely, that each single person, when he is law-abiding and obedient to God, is equal in worth to a whole nation, even the most populous, or rather to all nations, and if we may go still farther, even to the whole world. . . .

A second reason is that a speaker who harangues a multitude in general does not necessarily talk to any one person, whereas if he addresses his commands or prohibitions as though to each individual separately, the practical instructions given in the course of his speech are at once held to apply to the whole body in common also. If the exhortations are received as a personal message, the hearer is more ready to obey, but if collectively with others, he is deaf to them, since he takes the multitude as a cover for disobedience.

A third reason is that He wills that no king or despot swollen with arrogance and contempt should despise an insignificant private person but should study in the school of the divine laws and abate his supercilious airs, and through the reasonableness or rather the assured truth of their arguments unlearn his self-conceit. For if the Uncreated, the Incorruptible, the Eternal, who needs nothing and is the Maker of all, the Benefactor and King of kings and God of gods could not brook to despise even the humblest, but deigned to banquet him on holy oracles and statutes, as though he should be the sole guest, as though for him alone the feast was prepared to give good cheer to a soul instructed in the holy secrets and accepted for admission to the greatest mysteries, what right have I, the mortal, to bear myself proud-necked, puffed-up and loud-voiced toward my fellows, who, though their fortunes be unequal, have equal rights of kinship because they can claim to be children of the one common mother of mankind, nature? . . . For as I am a man, I shall not deem it right to adopt the lofty grandeur of the pompous stage, but make nature my home and not overstep her limits. I will inure my mind to have the feelings of a human being, not only because the lot both of the prosperous and the unfortunate may change to the reverse we know not when, but also because it is right that even if good fortune remains securely established, a man should not forget what he is. Such was the reason, as it seems to me, why He willed to word the series of His oracles in the singular form, and delivers them as though to one alone.

Decalogue 9–10[4]

*

*The Patriarchs Celebrate Shavuot

He gave to Noah and his sons a sign that there should not again be a flood on the earth. He set His bow in the cloud for a sign of the eternal covenant that there should not again be a flood on the earth to destroy it all the days of the earth. For this reason it is ordained and written on the heavenly tablets that they should celebrate the Feast of Weeks [Oaths] in this month once a year to renew the covenant every year. And this whole festival was celebrated in heaven from the day of creation till the days of Noah—twenty-six jubilees and five weeks of years: and Noah and his sons observed it for seven jubilees and one week of years, till the day of Noah's death, and from the day of Noah's death his sons did away with it until the days of Abraham. . . . But Abraham observed it, and Isaac and Jacob and his children observed it up to thy days, and in thy days the children of Israel forgot it until ye celebrated it anew on this mountain. And do thou command the children of Israel to observe this festival in all their generations for a commandment unto them: one day in the year in this month they shall celebrate the festival. For it is the Feast of Weeks and the Feast of Firstfruits: this feast is twofold and of a double nature: according to what is written and engraven concerning it, celebrate it. . . .

And it came to pass in the first week in the forty-fourth jubilee, in the second year, that is, the year in which Abraham died, that Isaac and Ishmael came from the Well of the Oath to celebrate the Feast of Weeks—that is, the feast of the firstfruits of the harvest—to Abraham, their father, and Abraham rejoiced because his two sons had come. . . . And he ate and drank, and blessed the Most High God,

> Who hath created heaven and earth,
> Who hath made all the fat things of the earth,
> And given them to the children of men
> That they might eat and drink and bless their Creator.
> *Book of Jubilees* 6.15–21, 22.1, 6[5]

*

*Tobit's Feast Turned into Mourning

At our feast of the Pentecost, which is the holy Feast of the Weeks, there was a good dinner prepared me; and I laid me down to dine. And the table was set for me, and abundant victuals were set for me, and I said unto Tobias my son, Go, my boy, and what poor man soever thou shalt find of our brethren of the Ninevite captives, who is mindful of God with his whole heart, bring him and he shall eat together with me; and lo, I tarry for thee, my boy, until thou come. And Tobias went to seek some poor man of our brethren and returned and said, Father. And I said to him, Here am I, my child. And he answered and said, Father, behold, one of our nation hath been murdered and cast out in the marketplace, and he hath but now been strangled. And I sprang up and left my dinner before I had tasted it, and took him up from the street and put him in one of the chambers until the sun was set, to bury him. Therefore I returned and washed myself, and ate food with mourning, and remembered the word of the prophet which Amos spake against Bethel, saying,

> Your feasts shall be turned into mourning,
> And all your ways into lamentation.
> *Tobit* 2.1–6[6]

*

Pentecost in Wartime

FLAVIUS JOSEPHUS

When Antiochus undertook an expedition against the Parthians, Hyrcanus set out with him. On this we have the testimony of Nicolas of Damascus, who writes as follows: "After defeating Indates, the Parthian general, and setting up a trophy at the Lycus river, Antiochus remained there two days at the request of the Jew Hyrcanus because of a festival of his nation on which it was not customary for the Jews to march out." Nor does he speak falsely in saying this; for the festival of Pentecost had come round, following the Sabbath, and we are not permitted to march either on the Sabbath or on a festival.

Jewish Antiquities 13.8.4[7]

It was the arrival of Sabinus which gave the Jews an occasion for insurrection. For this officer endeavored to force the guardians of the citadels to hand them over to him and instituted an exacting search for the royal treasures, relying for this task not only on the soldiers left by Varus, but on a crowd of his own slaves, all of whom he armed and employed as instruments of his avarice. So, on the arrival of Pentecost—thus the Jews call a feast which occurs seven weeks after [Passover], and takes its name from the number of intervening days—it was not the customary ritual so much as indignation which drew the people in crowds to the capital. A countless multitude flocked in from Galilee, from Idumaea, from Jericho, and from Peraea beyond the Jordan, but it was the native population of Judea itself which, both in numbers and ardor, was preeminent. Distributing themselves into three divisions, they formed three camps, one on the north of the Temple, another on the south, adjoining the hippodrome, and the third near the palace, on the west. Thus investing the Romans on all sides, they held them under siege.

The Jewish War 2.3.1[8]

*

*The Maccabean Warriors Observe the Feast of Weeks

Setting out from thence they [Judah the Maccabee and his army] marched in haste against Scythopolis, which is six hundred furlongs from Jerusalem, but since the local Jews testified to the goodwill shown them by the Scythopolitans and to their humane conduct during periods of misfortune, they simply thanked them and enjoined them to continue well-disposed to their race in future. Then they marched up to Jerusalem, as the Feast of Weeks was close at hand.

After the feast called Pentecost they hurried against Gorgias, the governor of Jamnia.

II Maccabees 12.29–32[9]

SHAVUOT IN TALMUD
AND MIDRASH

The divine revelation on Mount Sinai, commemorated on the Festival of Pentecost, gave rise to numerous ethical instructions, parables, and legendary tales embodied in the Talmud and midrash. The legends serve to dramatize this historic occasion, when the children of Israel accepted the divine Law. The aggadic portion of the Talmud and the expository literature of the midrashim are intended to delineate religious principles and moral insights, infuse love of God, and inspire devotion and loyalty to the Torah. The selections in this chapter illustrate these purposes.

The Talmud is an inexhaustible mine from which the Jewish people have extracted spiritual and educational ores that have served as their guide and inspiration for a millennium and a half. This monumental work has been a vital source that nourished the Jews in their long, tortuous sojourn in the Diaspora. Indeed, it became the indispensable link in the "Chain of Tradition" that began with Moses at Mount Sinai. About the year 200 C.E., Rabbi Judah ha-Nasi, a revered and prestigious scholar, compiled the laws taught by the *tannaim* (teachers) into the Mishnah. It was arranged systematically according to subject matter into six sections or orders. The Gemara, which was finally redacted in the fifth century, is the product of the *amoraim* (interpreters) who expounded and amplified the teachings of the Mishnah. The

Mishnah and the Gemara combined constitute the Talmud. In this chapter the passages from the Mishnah are cited by chapter and paragraph (i.e., 1.2), while those from the Gemara are indicated by page number (i.e., 12a).

There are two versions of the Talmud: the Jerusalem (Yerushalmi) Talmud, which is the product of the study of the Mishnah by scholars within Palestine, and the Babylonian (Bavli) Talmud, by far the more popular of the two. Unless passages in this book are identified as coming from the Yerushalmi Talmud, they are from the Babylonian Talmud.

While there are talmudic tractates, either in name or in theme, that deal with the other festivals and High Holidays, there is no tractate titled Shavuot. There is one tractate named *Bikkurim* ("Firstfruits") in the Order of *Zeraim* ("Seeds") that devotes three of its four chapters to procedures for the offering of the firstfruits on Shavuot.

Replete with legends, homilies, parables, and allegories, the midrash is the elaboration of the Bible, abounding in edifying and penetrating interpretations. Among the earliest midrashim dating from the tannaitic period are *Mekhilta de-Rabbi Ishmael* ("Rule of Rabbi Ishmael"), a commentary on a portion of Exodus, and *Sifra* ("Books"), an exposition on Numbers and Deuteronomy. Also considered one of the oldest of the midrashim is *Pesikta de-Rav Kahana* ("Section of Rabbi Kahana"), a collection of homilies ascribed to Rabbi Kahana.

Pesikta Rabbati ("Large Section"), which includes homilies and discourses drawn from early sources for the festivals, fast days, and special Sabbaths, was probably redacted in Palestine in the seventh century. *Pirke de-Rabbi Eliezer* ("Chapters of Rabbi Eliezer") is attributed to Eliezer, son of Hyrcanus, of the first and second centuries C.E., but it was most likely edited in the ninth century. The ethical-religious books, *Seder Eliyahu Rabbah* ("Large Order of Elijah") and *Seder Eliyahu Zuta* ("Small Order of Elijah"), were composed in the tenth century and feature parables and moral exhortations. In the next century Rabbi Toviah ben Eliezer edited *Pesikta Zutarta* ("Small Section"), also named *Lekah Tov* ("Good Teaching"), which is a commentary on the Pentateuch and the Five Scrolls. Dealing with the same biblical books is the *Midrash Rabbah* ("Great Midrash"), a basic source of homiletic interpretations redacted in the twelfth century which is the product of many hands over a long period of time. Homilies based on verses in the Book of Psalms are found in *Midrash Tehillim* ("Midrash on Psalms"), compiled from the third to the thirteenth century.

*

The Mountain Chosen for the Revelation

Moses was keeping the sheep of Jethro for forty years. . . . And he led the flock until he came to Horeb, as it is said, *Now Moses . . . drove the flock into the wilderness, and came to Horeb, the mountain of God* (Exodus 3.1). There the Holy One, blessed be He, was revealed unto Moses from the midst of the thornbush. Moses saw the bush burning with fire, and the fire did not consume the bush, and the bush did not extinguish the flames of fire. Now the bush does not grow in the earth unless it has water beneath it. Moses saw and was wondering very much in his heart, and he said, "What kind of glory is there in its midst? I will turn aside and see this great sight, why the thornbush is not burnt." The Holy One, blessed be He, said to him, "Moses! Stand where thou art standing, for there in the future will I give the Torah to Israel, as it is said, *And He said, "Do not come closer. Remove your sandals from your feet, for the place on which you stand is holy ground"* (ibid. 5). . . .

From the day when the heavens and the earth were created, the name of the mountain was Horeb. When the Holy One, blessed be He, was revealed unto Moses out of the thornbush, because of the word for the thornbush *(seneh)* it was called Sinai *(Sinai),* and that is Horeb. And whence do we know that Israel accepted the Torah at Mount Horeb? Because it is said, *The day you stood before the* LORD *your God at Horeb* (Deuteronomy 4.10).

Pirke de-Rabbi Eliezer 40, 41[1]

When the Holy One, blessed be He, sought to give the Torah to the children of Israel, Mount Carmel came from Aspamea and Mount Tabor came from Beth-elim. Later revelation refers to their coming in the verse *As I live, saith the King, whose name is the* LORD *of hosts, surely like Tabor among the mountains, and like Carmel by the sea, so shall he come* (Jeremiah 46.18). The one said, "I am called Mount Tabor. It is fitting that the Presence should rest upon me, for I am the highest of all the mountains, and not even the water of the deluge overwhelmed me." And the other said, "I am called Mount Carmel. It is fitting that the Divine Presence should rest upon me, for I put myself in the middle of the Red Sea, and it was by my help that the children of Israel got across." The Holy One, blessed be He, replied, "By the blemish of arrogance in you, you have already made yourselves unworthy of My presence. Each of you is unworthy of My presence." . . .

All the mountains then began to thunder protests and to make a commotion, as is said *The mountains quaked in* [*contesting for*] *the presence of the* LORD (Judges 5.5). Thereupon the Holy One, blessed be He, asked, *"Why look ye askance* (Psalms 68.17) [that is, why do you wish to contend with Sinai?] Ye are all *peak-backed mountains* [ibid.]!" Here "peak-backed" has the sense of "blemished," as in the verse *No one at all who has a blemish shall be qualified . . . no man . . . who is peak-backed* (Leviticus 21.18–20).

God said, "My wish is to dwell only on Sinai because Sinai is the lowliest of all of you," for, as Scripture says, *I dwell in the high and holy place, with him also that is of a contrite and lowly spirit* (Isaiah 57.15).

Whence did Sinai come? R. Jose taught: Out of Mount Moriah, out of the place where our father Isaac had been bound as a sacrifice, Sinai plucked itself as a priest's portion is plucked out of the bread. For the Holy One, blessed be He, said: "Since their father Isaac was bound upon this place, it is fitting that his children receive the Torah upon it."

Midrash on Psalms 68.9[2]

Man should always learn from the mind of his Creator; for behold, the Holy One, blessed be He, ignored all the mountains and heights and caused His Divine Presence to abide upon Mount Sinai, and ignored all the beautiful trees and caused His Divine Presence to abide in a bush [similarly, man should associate with the humble].

Sotah 5a[3]

The Holy One, blessed be He, considered all generations and He found no generation fitted to receive the Torah other than the generation of the wilderness; the Holy One, blessed be He, considered all mountains and found no mountain on which the Torah should be given other than Sinai.

Leviticus Rabbah 13.2[4]

Now Moses . . . came to Horeb, the mountain of God (Exodus 3.1). The mountain had five names: the mountain of God, the mountain of Bashan, the mountain of peaks, the mountain of Horeb, and the mountain of Sinai. The mountain of God—because there Israel accepted the godhead of the Holy One, blessed be He. The mountain of Bashan—because everything that man eats with his teeth *(be-shen)* is given for the sake of the Torah which was given on the mount. . . . The mountain of peaks *(gavnunim)*— pure as cheese *(gevinah)* and pure from every blemish. The mountain of Horeb—because from it the Sanhedrin derived power to slay with the sword *(herev)*. R. Samuel b. Nahman says, The idol worshipers received their sentence from there, as it is said, *those nations shall be utterly wasted—harov yeheravu* (Isaiah 60.12), from Horeb they shall be destroyed *(yeheravu)*. Sinai— because hatred *(sinah)* descended to idolaters thence [as they hated Israel for accepting the Torah].

Exodus Rabbah 2.4

One of the Rabbis asked R. Kahana, Hast thou heard what the mountain of Sinai [connotes]? The mountain whereon miracles *(nissim)* were performed for Israel, he replied. Then should it be called Mount Nisai? But [it means] the mountain whereon a happy augury *(siman)* took place for Israel. Then it should be called Mount Simanai. . . . R. Jose son of R. Hanina said, It has five names: The Wilderness of Zin, [meaning] that Israel were given commandments there; the Wilderness of Kadesh, where the Israelites were sanctified *(kadosh)*, the Wilderness of Kedemot, because a priority *(kedumah)* was conferred there; the Wilderness of Paran, because Israel was fruitful *(paru)* and multiplied there; and the Wilderness of Sinai, because hostility toward idolaters descended thereon. While what was its [real] name? Its name was Horeb. Now they disagree with R. Abbahu who said, Its name was Mount Sinai, and why was it called Mount Horeb? Because desolation *(hurvah)* to idolaters descended thereon.

Shabbat 89a–b

I would bring you to the house of my mother (Song of Songs 8.2):
this is Sinai. R. Berekiah said, Why is Sinai called "house of my
mother"? Because there Israel became like a newborn child.

Song of Songs Rabbah 8.2

✱

✱ *When the Torah Was Given*

Why was the Torah given during Sivan and not in Nisan or
during any one of the other months? What parable applies as an
answer to this question? That of a king who was arranging the
festivities for his daughter's wedding. And a man, one of the
royal dignitaries, said, "It would be seemly for the princess, after
she is seated in the palanquin, to have her ride on an elephant
and so raise her among all the nobles of the kingdom." Another
answered and said, "An elephant stands high, but is without
splendor. A horse, however, is beautiful—it has splendor as well
as beauty. And since the princess is lovely, it would be more
seemly to have her mount a horse and thus show her loveliness
among all the notables of the kingdom." Then a man spoke up
and said, "An elephant stands high, and a horse is comely; but
neither has a mouth to speak with, hands to clap together, or feet
to dance with. Hence it is fitting for me to extol the princess, for
I have a mouth to speak with, hands to clap together, and feet
to dance with; and so I would have her mount on my shoulders
to display her loveliness." Even so the Holy One, blessed be He,
did not give the Torah in Nisan nor in Iyar, because the sign of
Nisan in the Zodiac is a lamb, and the sign of Iyar is an ox, and
it is not fitting for them to extol and praise the Torah. Hence the
Holy One, blessed be He, gave the Torah in Sivan, because the
sign of Sivan is twins, and the twins are human, and being human
have mouths to speak with, and hands to clap together, and feet
to dance with.

Pesikta Rabbati 20.1[5]

Blessed be the Merciful One who gave a threefold Torah
[Pentateuch, Prophets, and Hagiographa] to a threefold people
[Israel, consisting of Priests, Levites, and Israelites] through a

3. Moses receiving the tablets of the Law. *Mahzor.*
   Illuminated manuscript on vellum. South Germany. Circa 1320. See Chapter 8.

thirdborn [Moses, born after Miriam and Aaron] on the third
day [of their abstinence from their wives] in the third month.

Shabbat 88a

By rights Israel should have been given the Torah immediately on their departure from Egypt; but the Holy One, blessed
be He, said, "The bloom of My children has not yet returned.
From slaving with clay and bricks have they just emerged, and
they are unable to receive the Torah at once." To what is the
matter like? To a king whose son arose from his sickbed, and
people said to him, "Let your son go to his school." He replied,
"The bloom of my son has not yet returned and you say that he
should go to his school! Let my son recuperate for two or three
months with food and drink and get well; after that he will go
to his school." Similarly spake the Holy One, blessed be He,
"The bloom of My children has not yet returned. From slaving
with clay and bricks have they just been released, can I then give
them the Torah! Let my children recuperate for two or three
months with the manna, the well of water and the quails; after
that I will give them the Torah." When was it given? *On the third
new moon after the Israelites had gone forth from the land of Egypt*
(Exodus 19.1).

Ecclesiastes Rabbah 3.11

When Israel came out of Egypt the vast majority of them were
afflicted with some blemish. Why? Because they had been working in clay and bricks and climbing to the tops of buildings.
Those who were engaged on building became maimed through
climbing to the top of the layers of stone; either a stone fell and
cut off the worker's hand, or a beam or some clay got into his
eyes and he was blinded. When they came to the wilderness of
Sinai, God said, "Is it consonant with the dignity of the Torah
that I should give it to a generation of cripples? If, on the other
hand, I wait until others take their place, I shall be delaying the
revelation." What, then, did God do? He bade the angels come
down to Israel and heal them.

Numbers Rabbah 7.1

Why were the Ten Commandments not said at the beginning
of the Torah? The Rabbis give a parable. To what may this be

compared? To the following: A king who entered a province said to the people, "May I be your king?" But the people said to him, "Have you done anything good for us that you should rule over us?" What did he do then? He built the city wall for them, he brought in the water supply for them, and he fought their battles. Then when he said to them, "May I be your king?" They said to him, "Yes." Likewise, God. He brought the Israelites out of Egypt, divided the sea for them, sent down the manna for them, brought up the well for them, brought the quails for them. He fought for them the battle with Amalek. Then He said to them, "I am to be your king." And they said to Him, "Yes, yes."

Mekhilta de-Rabbi Ishmael, Exodus 20.2[6]

Great is peace, for with regard to all the journeyings it is written, *The Israelites set out . . . and encamped* [plural] (Numbers 33.5), [the plural number implying that] they journeyed in dissension, and they encamped in dissension. When, however, they all came before Mount Sinai, they all became one encampment. This is indicated by what is written, *Israel encamped* [singular] *there in front of the mountain* (Exodus 19.2). It is written here not "Israelites encamped" [plural], but *"Israel encamped"* [singular]. Said the Holy One, blessed be He, "This is the hour at which I am giving the Torah to My children."

Leviticus Rabbah 9.9

*

* The Nations Refuse the Torah

It was for the following reason that the ancient nations of the world were asked to accept the Torah, in order that they should have no excuse for saying, "Had we been asked we would have accepted it." For, behold, they were asked and they refused to accept it, for it is said. *He said, The Lord came from Sinai . . .* (Deuteronomy 33.2).

He appeared to the children of Esau, the wicked, and said to them, "Will you accept the Torah?" They said to Him, "What is written in it?" He said to them, *"You shall not murder* (ibid. 5.17)." They then said to Him, "The very heritage which our father left us was: *Yet by your sword you shall live* (Genesis 27.40)."

He then appeared to the children of Ammon and Moab. He said to them, "Will you accept the Torah?" They said to Him, "What is written in it?" He said to them, *"You shall not commit adultery* (Deuteronomy 5.17)." They, however, said to Him that they were all of them children of adulterers, as it is said, *Thus the two daughters of Lot came to be with child by their father* (Genesis 19.36).

Then He appeared to the children of Ishmael. He said to them, "Will you accept the Torah?" They said to Him, "What is written in it?" He said to them, *"You shall not steal* (Deuteronomy 5.17)." They then said to Him, "The very blessing that had been pronounced upon our father was: *He shall be a wild ass of a man: his hand against everyone* (Genesis 16.12)."
. . . But when He came to the Israelites they all opened their mouths and said, *All that the Lord has spoken we will do and obey* (Exodus 24.7).

R. Simon b. Eleazar says, If the sons of Noah could not endure the seven commandments enjoined upon them, how much less could they have endured all the commandments of the Torah! To give a parable. A king had appointed two administrators. One was appointed over the store of straw and the other was appointed over the treasure of silver and gold. The one appointed over the store of straw was held in suspicion. But he used to complain about the fact that they had not appointed him over the treasure of silver and gold. The people then said to him, *"Reka* [good for nothing]! If you were under suspicion in connection with the store of straw, how could they trust you with the treasure of silver and gold!" Behold, it is a matter of reasoning: If the sons of Noah could not endure the seven commandments enjoined upon them, how much less could they have endured all the commandments of the Torah!

Mekhilta de-Rabbi Ishmael, Exodus 20.2[7]

When God was about to give the Torah, no other nation but Israel would accept it. It can be compared to a man who had a field which he wished to entrust to métayers. Calling the first of these, he inquired, "Will you take over this field?" He replied, "I have no strength; the work is too hard for me." In the same way the second, third, and fourth declined to undertake the work. He called the fifth and asked him, "Will you take over this field?" He replied, "Yes." "On the condition that you will till it?" The reply was again, "Yes." But as soon as he took possession of it, he let it lie fallow. With whom is the king angry? With those who declared, "We cannot undertake it," or with him who did undertake it, but no sooner that he undertook it than he left it lying fallow? Surely, with him who undertook it. Similarly, when God revealed Himself on Sinai, there was not a nation at whose doors He did not knock, but they would not undertake to keep it; as soon as He came to Israel, they exclaimed, *All that the Lord has spoken we will do and obey* (Exodus 24.7). Accordingly, it is only proper that *you* should hearken; hence *Hear ye the word of the Lord, O House of Jacob* (Jeremiah 2.4). For if you do not, you will be punished on account of your pledge.

Exodus Rabbah 27.9

*

*The Public Presentation of the Torah

The Torah was given in public, openly in a free place. For had the Torah been given in the Land of Israel, the Israelites could have said to the nations of the world: "You have no share in it." But now that it was given in the wilderness publicly and openly in a place that is free for all, everyone wishing to accept it could come and accept it. One might suppose that it was given at night, but Scripture says, *On the third day, as morning dawned* (Exodus 19.16). One might suppose that it was given in silence, but Scripture says: *there was thunder and lightning* (ibid.). One might suppose that they could not hear the voice of God, but Scripture says: *The voice of the Lord is powerful; the voice of the Lord is full of majesty* (Psalms 29.4). . . .

But what had those wretched nations done that He would not give them the Torah? *His ordinances they have not known them* (Psalms 147.20)—they were unwilling to accept them.

Mekhilta de-Rabbi Ishmael, Exodus 19.2[8]

Why was the Torah given in the desert? To teach you that if a man does not hold himself as unpossessed as the desert, he does not become worthy of the words of the Torah; and that, as the desert has no end, so with the words of the Torah: there is no end to them.

Pesikta de-Rav Kahana 107a[9]

Why was the Torah not given in the Land of Israel? In order that the nations of the world should not have the excuse for saying, "Because it was given in Israel's land, therefore we have not accepted it." Another reason: to avoid causing dissension among the tribes. Else one might have said, "In my territory the Torah was given." And the other might have said, "In my territory the Torah was given." Therefore, the Torah was given in the desert, publicly and openly, in a place belonging to no one.

To three things the Torah is likened: to the desert, to fire, and to water. This is to tell you that just as these three things are free to all who come into the world, so also are the words of the Torah free to all who come into the world.

Mekhilta de-Rabbi Ishmael, Exodus 20.2[10]

Now Mount Sinai was all in smoke (Exodus 19.18). One might think only that part of it where the Glory rested, but it says, "All of it." *For the Lord had come down upon it in fire* (ibid.) This tells that the Torah is fire, was given from the midst of fire, and is comparable to fire. What is the nature of fire? If one comes too near to it, one gets burnt. If one keeps too far from it, one is cold. The only thing for man to do is to seek to warm himself against its flame.

Mekhilta de-Rabbi Ishmael, Exodus 19.18[11]

When God gave the Torah no bird twittered, no fowl flew, no ox lowed, none of the Ophanim stirred a wing, the Seraphim did not say, "Holy, Holy," the sea did not roar, the creatures spoke not, the whole world was hushed into breathless silence and the voice went forth: *I am the Lord your God. . . .* When God spoke on Mount Sinai, the whole world became silent, so that all creatures might know that there is none beside Him.

Exodus Rabbah 29.9

*

Moses Ascends on High to Receive the Law

At the time when Moses went up to heaven to receive the Law, which the Lord, blessed be He, was giving him, the angels said, "Lord of the universe, what is a mortal man doing here in the heavens among us?" And the Lord replied, "He has come to receive the Torah." Then the angels said, "Wilt Thou hand over to man that hidden jewel which Thou hast treasured up with Thee during 974 generations, before Thou hadst created the world? What is man whom Thou hast created? Leave the Torah here and do not give it to man." Then God said, "Moses, answer the angels concerning that which they have spoken to Me." And Moses replied, "Lord of the universe, I would fain answer them, but I fear lest they burn me up with the breath of their mouths." Then God said, "Moses, take hold of the Throne of Glory and answer their speech." And when our master Moses heard this, he began to speak, and said, "Lord of the universe, what is written in that Torah which Thou intendest to give to me? *I am the Lord your God who brought you out of the land of Egypt* (Exodus 20.2). O angels, have you gone down into Egypt? Have you served Pharaoh? Then why should the Lord, blessed be He, give you the Torah? Again, what else is written in this Torah? Is it not written, *You shall have no other gods beside Me* (ibid. 3)? Are you living among heathens that you should serve other gods? It is further written therein, *Remember the Sabbath day and keep it holy* (ibid. 8), which means, rest on that day. Are you working that you should have to be commanded to rest? Furthermore, it is written therein, *you shall not swear falsely* (ibid. 7). Are you engaged in business that you should be commanded not to take a false oath? Furthermore, *Honor your father and your mother* (ibid. 12). Have you a father and a mother that you should be commanded to honor them? *You shall not murder, you shall not commit adultery, you shall not steal* (ibid. 13). Is there envy and hatred among you that you should be commanded not to do these things? Of what good, therefore, is the Torah to you?" When the angels heard this, they became friendly to Moses and every one of the angels taught him something, even the angel of death.

Shabbat 88b[12]

When Moses ascended on high he found the Holy One, blessed be He, engaged in affixing coronets to the letters [i.e., three small strokes written on top of certain letters in the form of a crown]. Said Moses, "Lord of the universe, Who stays Thy hand [i.e., is there anything wanting in the Torah that these additions are necessary]?" He answered, "There will arise a man, at the end of many generations, Akiba b. Joseph by name, who will expound upon each tittle heaps and heaps of laws." "Lord of the universe," said Moses, "permit me to see him." He replied, "Turn thee round." Moses went and sat down behind eight rows [of R. Akiba's disciples and listened to the discourses upon the Law]. Not being able to follow their arguments he was ill at ease, but when they came to a certain subject and the disciples said to the master, "Whence do you know it?" and the latter replied, "It is a law given unto Moses at Sinai," he was comforted. Thereupon he returned to the Holy One, blessed be He, and said, "Lord of the universe, Thou hast such a man and Thou givest the Torah by me!" He replied, "Be silent, for such is My decree." Then said Moses, "Lord of the universe, Thou hast shown me his Torah, show me his reward." "Turn thee round," said He; and Moses turned round and saw them weighing out his flesh at the market stalls [for R. Akiba died a martyr's death at the hands of the Romans during the Hadrianic persecution]. "Lord of the universe," cried Moses, "such is Torah, and such is its reward!" He replied, "Be silent, for such is My decree."

Menahot 29b

After God, blessed be He, had given the Law to Moses, and Moses had come down from heaven, Satan said, "Lord of the universe, where hast Thou put the Torah? To whom hast Thou given it?" The Lord replied, "I have given it to the earth." So Satan went to the earth and said, "Where hast thou put the Torah which the Lord, blessed be He, has given thee?" The earth replied, *"God understandeth the way thereof* (Job 28.23). This means that the Lord, blessed be He, knows everything. But I have not the Torah." Then Satan went to the sea and said, "O sea, where hast thou put the Torah which the Lord, blessed be He, has given thee?" The sea replied, *"The Torah is not with me* (ibid. 14)." Then Satan went to the uttermost depth of the earth and said, "Where hast thou put the Torah which the Lord, blessed be He, has given thee?" The abyss of the earth replied, *"It is not in me* (ibid.)." So Satan went all over the earth searching for the Torah, for the Lord had told him that He had given it to the earth. Then Satan went to the dead and the lost and asked them, "Where have you put the Torah which the Lord has given you?" And they replied, "Verily, we have heard of it with our ears, but we know nothing more." Then Satan came again before the Lord, blessed be He, and said, "Lord of the universe, I have searched the whole earth, but I have not found the Torah." Then the Lord said unto him, "Go to Moses, the son of Amram, to whom I have given it." Then Satan went to our master Moses and said, "Moses, where hast thou put the Torah which the Lord has given thee?" And Moses replied, "How dost thou come to ask me about the Torah? Who am I and what am I that the Lord should give me the Torah?" When the Lord, blessed be He, heard that Moses would not admit that he had received the Torah, He said, "Thou art a liar. Why dost thou deny that I have given thee the Torah?" And Moses replied, "Lord of the universe, the Torah is a desirable object, it filleth with joy him who is engaged in studying it. Thou rejoicest over it and studiest it Thyself every day. How then can I boast and say that I have received the Torah? It is not seemly for a man to boast of anything, even though he has reason to do so. On the contrary, it is better that he should be humble." And the Lord said, "Since thou humblest thyself, and dost not wish to claim the honor of having received the Torah, it shall, as a reward, be called by thy name." This is why it is written, *Remember the Law of Moses, My servant* (Malachi 3.22).

Shabbat 89a[13]

Surely, this instruction. . . . It is not in the heavens (Deuteronomy 30.11–12). Moses said to Israel, "Do not say, 'Another Moses will arise and bring us another Torah from heaven'; I therefore warn you, *It is not in the heavens,* that is to say, no part of it has remained in heaven."

Deuteronomy Rabbah 8.6

4. Moses receiving and handing down the tablets of the Law. Illuminated manuscript on vellum. Pentateuch. Germany. Circa 1300. See Chapter 8.

Now when the Holy One, blessed be He, gave the Torah to Israel, the earth rejoiced but the heavens wept. And why did the earth rejoice and the heavens weep? Consider the analogy of a king who was arranging festivities for his daughter's wedding. The city folk did not come near and did not offer praise. But the village folk came and offered praise to the king with harps and lyres and all kinds of musical instruments. A herald came forth and stood before the king and said: As things go in the world, it is city folk who know the glory of the king—it would be fitting for them to acclaim the princess.

And so it was with the Holy One, blessed be He. When He gave the Torah to Israel, the earth offered praise, but the heavens did not offer praise. The Holy One, blessed be He, said to the heavens, You who are set in the heights—you ought to acclaim My glory and My daughter more than the earth does.

The heavens replied, The earth should offer praise, for the Torah is being given to it; but we from whom it goes forth, are we to offer praise? Should we not rather be sad?

Pesikta Rabbati 20.1[14]

*

* The Lord Speaks to the People

While the supreme King of kings was yet at His table, He had already anticipated [His descent on Mount Sinai], as it says, *On the third day, as morning dawned, there was thunder . . . upon the mountain* (Exodus 19.16). He was like a king who had proclaimed, "On such-and-such a day I am going to enter the city," and as the inhabitants of the city slept through the night, when the king came he found them asleep, so he ordered trumpets and horns to be sounded, and the governor of the city woke them up and brought them out to meet the king, and the king then went before them till he reached his palace. So God came first, as it says, *On the third day, as morning dawned.* It says before this, *for on the third day the Lord will come down, in the sight of all the people* (ibid. 11). Israel slept all that night, because the sleep of Pentecost is pleasant and the night is short. R. Judan said: Not a flea worried them. God came and found them sleeping, so he began to rouse them with trumpeters, as it says, *there was thunder and lightning* (ibid. 16), and Moses roused Israel and brought them out to meet the supreme King of kings . . . and then God went before them till He reached Mount Sinai.

Song of Songs Rabbah 1.12

Moses went forth and came to the camp of the Israelites, and he aroused the Israelites from their sleep, saying to them, "Arise ye from your sleep, for behold, your God desires to give the Torah to you. Already the bridegroom wishes to lead the bride and to enter the bridal chamber. The hour has come for giving you the Torah," as it is said, *Moses led the people out of the camp toward God* (Exodus 19.17). And the Holy One, blessed be He, also went forth to meet them; like a bridegroom who goes forth to meet the bride, so the Holy One, blessed be He, went forth to meet them to give them the Torah, as it is said, *O God, when Thou wentest forth before Thy people* (Psalms 68.7).

Pirke de-Rabbi Eliezer 41[15]

You find that when Israel stood ready to receive the Torah on Mount Sinai, they wanted to hear the Decalogue from God's own mouth. R. Phinehas b. Hama, the priest, said: Two things did Israel ask of God—to see His likeness and to hear from His own mouth the Decalogue. . . . R. Phinehas b. Hama, the priest, said, Does then one comply with the request of a fool? The Holy One, blessed be He, clearly foresaw, however, that after forty days Israel would make the golden calf. Said He, "Unless I now comply with their request, they will later say: 'All we asked of Moses was that God should show us His likeness and that He should speak with us.' " In order, therefore, not to give them the excuse of saying, "Because we did not hear the commandments from God's own mouth, or see His likeness, did we make this god," God thought to Himself, "I will reveal Myself to them and also speak with them."

Exodus Rabbah 41.3

Thereupon the Holy One, blessed be He, opened the portals of the seven firmaments and appeared over them and over Israel —eye to eye, in His beauty, in His glory, in the fullness of His stature, with His crown, and upon His throne of glory. When

Israel heard *I am the Lord your God* (Exodus 20.2), their souls at once departed from them. Thereupon the Holy One, blessed be He, made descend the dew which at the resurrection will quicken the souls of the righteous, and revived them.

How did the Holy One, blessed be He, revive them? For Israel's sake He made descend to the earth one hundred and twenty myriads of ministering angels, so that for each and every one in Israel there were two ministering angels who took hold of him. One angel put his hand upon his heart that his soul should not leave him, and one lifted up his neck so that he could look at the Holy One, blessed be He, face to face.

And why did God reveal Himself to them face to face? It is as though He said to them: Behold ye! I appeared before you in My glory and My majesty. Should there be a generation that will endeavor to lead you astray, saying, "Let us go and worship other gods," say to it: We have a God whom we worship.

Pesikta Rabbati 20.4[16]

When God gave the Torah on Sinai, He displayed untold marvels to Israel with His voice. What happened? God spoke and the Voice reverberated throughout the world. Israel heard the Voice coming to them from the south so to the south they ran to meet the Voice. From the south, it changed round to the north, so they ran to the north. From the north it shifted to the east, so they ran to the east; but from the east it shifted to the west, so they ran to the west. From the west it shifted to the heavens. But when they raised their eyes heavenwards, it seemed to proceed from the earth, so they glanced to the earth. Then did the Israelites say one to another, *But wisdom, where shall it be found?* (Job 28.12). The Israelites were inquiring, "Whence cometh the Lord, from the east or south?" as it is said, *The Lord came from Sinai; He shone upon them from Seir* (Deuteronomy 33.2), and it is written *God cometh from Teman* (Habakkuk 3.3).

It says, *And all the people witnessed the thunderings* (Exodus 20.15). Note that it does not say "the thunder," but "the thunderings"; wherefore R. Johanan said that God's voice, as it was uttered, split up into seventy voices, in seventy languages, so that all the nations should understand. When each nation heard the Voice in their own vernacular their souls departed [i.e., they were in fear], save Israel, who heard but who were not hurt. . . .

Just see how the Voice went forth—coming to each Israelite with a force proportioned to his individual strength—to the old, according to their strength, and to the young, according to theirs; to the children, to the babes and to the women, according to their strength, and even to Moses according to his strength, as it is said, *As Moses spoke, God answered him by a voice* (Exodus 19.19), that is, with a voice which he could endure. Similarly, it says, *The voice of the Lord is with power* (Psalms 29. 4); not "with *His* power," but *"with power,"* i.e. with the power of *each* individual, even to pregnant women according to their strength. Thus to each person it was according to his strength.

Exodus Rabbah 5.9

The voice of the first commandment went forth, and the heavens and earth quaked thereat, and the waters and rivers fled, and the mountains and hills were moved, and all the trees fell prostrate, and the dead who were in Sheol revived, and stood on their feet till the end of all the generations, as it is said, *with those who are standing here with us this day* (Deuteronomy 29.14), and those also who in the future will be created, until the end of all the generations, there they stood with them at Mount Sinai, as it is said, *and with those who are not with us here this day* (ibid.). The Israelites who were alive then fell upon their faces and died.

The voice of the second commandment went forth, and they were quickened, and they stood upon their feet and said to Moses: "Moses, our teacher! We are unable to hear any more the voice of the Holy One, blessed be He, for we shall die even as we died just now, as it is said, *'You speak to us,' they said to Moses, 'and we will obey; but let not God speak to us, lest we die'* (Exodus 20.16). And now, why should we die as we died just now?" The Holy One, blessed be He, heard the voice of Israel, and it was pleasing to Him. . . . The rest of the commandments He spake through the mouth of Moses. . . . All that generation who heard the voice of the Holy One, blessed be He, on Mount Sinai, were worthy to be like the ministering angels.

Pirke de-Rabbi Eliezer 41[17]

*

The Children Become the Sureties

When Israel stood before Mount Sinai to receive the Torah, the Holy One, blessed be He, said to them, "Forsooth, shall I give you the Torah? Bring me good sureties that you will keep it, and then I will give it to you." They replied, "Sovereign of the universe, our ancestors will be our guarantors." He said to them, "Your ancestors themselves require sureties." They were like a man who went to borrow from the king, and to whom the king said, "Bring me a surety and I will lend you." He went and brought him a surety, whereupon the king said, "Your surety himself requires a surety." He went and brought a second surety. Said the king to him, "Your surety requires a surety." When he brought him a third surety, he said to him, "Know that for the sake of this man I lend you."

So when Israel stood ready to receive the Torah, He said to them, "I will give you My Torah, but bring Me good sureties that you will keep it and then I will give it to you." They said, "Our ancestors are our sureties." Said God to them, "I have faults to find in your ancestors. I can find fault with Abraham because he said, *How shall I know that I am to possess it* [i.e., the land—thereby showing a lack of faith] (Genesis 15.8). With Isaac I can find fault because he loved Esau though I hated him, as it says, *But Esau I hated* (Malachi 1.3). With Jacob, who said, *My way is hid from the Lord* (Isaiah 40.27). Bring Me therefore good sureties and I will give it to you." They then said, "Sovereign of the universe, our prophets will be our sureties." He replied, "I have fault to find with them, as it says, *Thy prophets have been like foxes in ruins* (Ezekiel 13.4). Still, bring Me good sureties and I will give it to you." They said to Him, "Our children will be our sureties." To which God replied, "Verily these are good sureties; for their sake I will give it to you."

Song of Songs Rabbah 1.4

*
*Israel Accepts the Torah

R. Azariah in the name of R. Judah son of R. Simon says, The matter may be compared to the case of a king who had an orchard planted with one row of fig trees, one of vines, one of pomegranates, and one of apples. He entrusted it to a tenant and went away. After a time the king came and looked in at the orchard to ascertain what it had yielded. He found it full of thorns and briars, so he brought woodcutters to raze it. He looked closely at the thorns and noticed among them a single rose-colored flower. He smelled it and his spirits calmed down. The king said, "The whole orchard shall be saved because of this flower." In a similar manner the whole world was created only for the sake of the Torah. After twenty-six generations the Holy One, blessed be He, looked closely at His world to ascertain what it had yielded, and found it full of water in water [i.e., wicked people in a wicked environment]. The generation of Enosh was water in water, the generation of the Flood was water in water, the generation of the Dispersion was water in water. So He brought cutters to cut it down; as it says, *The Lord sat enthroned at the flood* (Psalms 29.10). He saw a single rose-colored flower, to wit, Israel. He took it and smelled it when He gave them the Ten Commandments and His spirits were calmed when they said, *We will do and obey* (Exodus 24.7). Said the Holy One, blessed be He, "The orchard shall be saved on account of this flower. For the sake of the Torah and of Israel the world shall be saved."

Leviticus Rabbah 23.3

And they took their places under the mount (Exodus 19.17): R. Abdimi b. Hama b. Hasa said, This teaches that the Holy One, blessed be He, overturned the mountain upon them like an [inverted] cask, and said to them, "If ye accept the Torah, 'tis well; if not, there shall be your burial." . . . This teaches that the Holy One, blessed be He, stipulated with the works of creation and said thereto, "If Israel accepts the Torah, ye shall exist; but if not, I will turn you back into emptiness and formlessness."

Shabbat 88a

In worldly affairs, when a prince of flesh and blood issues a decree, it is doubtful whether it will be obeyed or not; and even if you say it is obeyed, it is only during his lifetime but not after his death. Whereas Moses our teacher decreed many decrees and enacted numerous enactments, and they endure for ever and unto all eternity.

Shabbat 30a

On the eve of Sabbath the Israelites stood at Mount Sinai, arranged with the men apart and the women apart. The Holy One, blessed be He, said to Moses, "Go, speak to the daughters of Israel, [asking them] whether they wish to receive the Torah." Why were the women asked [first]? Because the way of men is to follow the opinion of women, as it is said, *Thus shall you say to the house of Jacob* (Exodus 19.3); these are the women. *And declare to the children of Israel* (ibid.); these are the men. They all replied as with one mouth, and they said, *All that the Lord has spoken we will do and obey* (ibid. 24.7).

Pirke de-Rabbi Eliezer 41 [18]

Why did He command the women first?—Because they are prompt in the fulfillment of the commandments. Another explanation is: so that they should introduce their children to the study of the Torah. R. Tahlifa of Caesarea said that God said, "When I created the world, I only commanded Adam first and then Eve, too, was commanded, with the result that she transgressed and upset the world; if I do not now call unto the women *first,* they will nullify the Torah."

Exodus Rabbah 28.2

The Holy One, blessed be He, said, "When you stood at Sinai and received the Torah, I wrote that I love you, as it says, *it was because the Lord loved you* (Deuteronomy 7.8).

Exodus Rabbah 32.2

When Israel stood at Sinai and received the Torah, the Holy One, blessed be He, said to the angel of death, "Thou hast power over all the heathen but not over this people, for they are My portion and just as I live for ever, so will My children be eternal."

Exodus Rabbah 32.7

Beloved are Israel in that a desirable instrument [the Torah] was given to them. [It was a mark of] superabundant love that it was made known to them the desirable instrument, wherewith the world had been created, was given to them, as it is said, *For I give you good doctrine; forsake ye not My teaching* (Proverbs 4.2).

Avot 3.14

Great is peace, for when Israel stood at Sinai and declared, *All that the Lord has spoken we will do and obey* (Exodus 24.7), the Holy One, blessed be He, rejoiced in them and gave them His Torah and blessed them with peace, as it is stated, *The Lord will give strength* [the Torah] *unto His people; the Lord will bless His people with peace* (Psalms 29.11).

Derekh Eretz Zuta 59a–b

His truth is a shield and a buckler (Psalms 91.4). R. Simeon ben Lakish taught that God said, I provide armor for any man who gives himself to the truth of Torah. R. Simeon ben Yohai said: The truth of Torah is itself a coat of armor. R. Simeon ben Yohai also said: The coat of armor which the Holy One, blessed be He, gave to Israel on Sinai, has the Ineffable Name written upon it.

Midrash on Psalms 91.2[19]

You shall have no other gods beside Me (Exodus 20.3). Why is this said? Because it says, *I am the Lord your God.* To give a parable: A king of flesh and blood entered a province. His attendants said to him, "Issue some decrees upon the people." He, however, told them, "No! When they will have accepted my reign I shall issue decrees upon them. For if they do not accept my reign how will they carry out my decrees?" Likewise, God said to Israel, "I am the Lord your God, you shall not have other gods—I am He whose reign you have taken upon yourselves in Egypt." And when they said to Him, "Yes, yes," He continued, "Now, just as you accepted My reign, you must also accept My decrees: *You shall have no other gods beside Me.*"

Mekhilta de-Rabbi Ishmael, Exodus 20.3[20]

When they all stood before Mount Sinai to receive the Torah they all made up their mind alike to accept the reign of God joyfully. Furthermore, they pledged themselves for one another. And it was not only concerning overt acts that God, revealing

Himself to them, wished to make His covenant with them but also concerning secret acts, as it is said, *Concealed acts concern the Lord our God, but with overt acts* . . . (Deuteronomy 29.28). But they said to Him, "Concerning overt acts we are ready to make a covenant with Thee, but we will not make a covenant with Thee in regard to secret acts lest one of us commit a sin secretly and the entire community be held responsible for it."

Mekhilta de-Rabbi Ishmael, Exodus 20.2[21]

Every day a *bat kol* (a divine voice) goes forth from Mount Horeb, and proclaims: Woe unto men on account of [their] contempt toward the Torah, for whoever occupies himself not with the study of Torah is called "The Rebuked One." . . . And it says, *The tablets were God's work, and the writing was God's writing, incised upon the tablets* (Exodus 32.16). Read not *harut* [which means "incised"] but *herut* [which means "freedom"]. For there is no free man for thee but he that occupies himself with the study of the Torah.

Avot 6.2

*

Moses Breaks the Tablets of the Law

Whence is it known that the tablets [of the Law] were shattered [on the seventeenth of Tammuz]? For it has been taught: On the sixth of the month [of Sivan] the Ten Commandments were given to Israel; R. Jose says, On the seventh of the month. He who says that they were given on the sixth takes the view that on the sixth they were given and on the seventh Moses ascended the mount. And he who says that they were given on the seventh holds that they were given on the seventh and on the seventh Moses ascended the mount. For it is written, *on the seventh day He called Moses* (Exodus 24.16), and it is further written, *Moses went inside the cloud, and ascended the mountain; and Moses remained on the mountain forty days and forty nights* (ibid. 18). The [remaining] twenty-four days of Sivan and the sixteen days of Tammuz make altogether forty. On the seventeenth of Tammuz he came down [from the mountain] and shattered the tablets, as it is written, *As soon as Moses came near the camp and saw the calf . . . and he hurled the tablets from his hands and shattered them at the foot of the mountain* (ibid. 32.19).

Taanit 28b

The Holy One, blessed be He, said to Moses, "Israel has forgotten the might of My power, which I wrought for them in Egypt and at the Reed Sea, and they have made an idol for themselves." He said to Moses, "Go, get thee down from thy greatness." Moses spake before the Holy One, blessed be He, "Sovereign of all the worlds! While Israel had not yet sinned before Thee, Thou didst call them *My people,* as it is said, *I will . . . deliver My ranks, My people* (Exodus 7.4). Now that they have sinned before Thee, Thou sayest unto me, *Hurry down, for your people . . . have acted basely* (ibid. 32.7). They are Thy people and Thine inheritance, as it is said, *Yet they are Your very own people* (Deuteronomy 9.29)."

Moses took the tablets of the Law, and he descended, and the tablets carried their own weight and Moses with them; but when they beheld the calf and the dances, the writing fled from off the tablets, and they became heavy in his hands, and Moses was not able to carry himself and the tablets, and he cast them from his hand, and they were broken beneath the mount, as it is said, *He became enraged; and he hurled the tablets from his hands and shattered them at the foot of the mountain* (Exodus 32.19).

Pirke de-Rabbi Eliezer 45[22]

When Moses descended from Mount Sinai, and saw the abomination [the golden calf] of Israel, he gazed at the tablets and saw that the words had flown away, and broke them at the foot of the hill. At once he fell dumb. He could not say a word. At that moment a decree was passed concerning Israel, that they were to study these same words in the midst of sorrow and in the midst of slavery, in migration, and in confusion, in pressing poverty, and in lack of food. For the sorrow they have suffered, the Holy One, blessed be He, is destined to reward them during the days of the Messiah, many times over.

Seder Eliyahu Rabbah 19[23]

God said, "Moses, if one may say so, admonished Me because of Israel and he also reproved Israel because of Me." To Israel he said, *You have been guilty of a great sin* (Exodus 32.30); to God he said: *Let not Your anger, O Lord, blaze forth against Your people* (ibid. 11).

When Israel made the golden calf, the Holy One, blessed be He, desired to destroy them, whereupon Moses said to Him, "Master of the universe! This calf will be of great help to Thee." God then asked him, "How can it help Me?" Thereupon Moses replied, "Thou causest rain to fall, the calf will produce dew; Thou bringest out the winds, the calf will bring out lightnings." Said God to Moses, "So you also are going astray after the calf?" Whereupon Moses exclaimed before God, "Then, *let not Your anger, O Lord, blaze forth against Your people* (ibid.) [seeing that the calf is nought]." To Israel, however, he said, *"You have been guilty of a great sin* [ibid. 30]." R. Judah b. R. Simon said, This may be compared to a king who became angry with his wife and drove her out by force from his house. When the groomsmen heard of it they went to the king and said to him, "Oh, Sire, is this the way to treat a wife? What has she done to you?" They then went to her and asked her, "How long will you continue to provoke your husband? Is it your first offense? Is it your second offense?" Likewise when Moses approached God, he said to Him, *"Let not your anger, O Lord, blaze forth against your people* (ibid.). Are they not Thy children?" But when he addressed Israel, he asked them, "How long will you provoke Him? This is neither the first time nor the second time."

Deuteronomy Rabbah 1.2

R. Joshua b. Levi, in the name of R. Simeon b. Yohai, said, The Holy One, blessed be He, gave him an opening to refute [the indictment against Israel] in that He had said at Sinai, *I am the Lord thy* [singular] *God* (Exodus 20.2), [implying that He spoke] to Moses [only]. When Israel made the golden calf, Moses tried to appease God's anger, but He would not hearken unto him, for He said, "Is it possible not to execute strict justice on them for having broken the Commandment?" But Moses said, "Lord of the universe! At Sinai, Thou didst say, *I am the Lord thy God,* not '*your* [plural] *God.*' Surely Thou spakest to me but didst Thou speak to them? and have I actually broken the command?" . . . R. Simeon of Siknin said in the name of R. Levi, For this reason did God afterward write in the plural, *I am the Lord your God* (Leviticus 19.3). Henceforward does it say in connection with all the commandments, *I am the Lord* your *God,* and never again *I am the Lord* thy *God.*

Exodus Rabbah 43.5

When Israel made the golden calf, God intended to destroy them, but Moses pleaded, "Lord of the universe! Didst Thou not bring them forth from Egypt, a place of idol-worshipers? They are yet young, for it says, *When Israel was a child, then I loved him, and out of Egypt I called My son* (Hosea 11.1). Be patient with them yet awhile and go with them, and they will yet perform good deeds before Thee."

Exodus Rabbah 43.9

When he realized that there was no future hope for Israel, he linked his own fate with theirs and broke the tablets, saying to God, "They have sinned; well, I have now also sinned in breaking the tablets. If Thou wilt forgive them, forgive me also." . . . He did not budge from there before he had cleared away their sin. After he had removed their sin, Moses said, "Israel now has had one to plead for them, but whom have I to plead for me?" And he began to feel remorse for having broken the tablets, but God reassured him, saying, "Do not grieve about the first tablets. They only contained the Ten Commandments, but in the two tablets I am about to give thee now, there will also be laws, midrash, and *aggadah.*"

Exodus Rabbah 46.1

God said to Moses, "Ah! Moses, you have vented your wrath on the tablets of the covenant. Do you desire that I also should vent My wrath? You will see that the world could not endure even one hour." Moses replied, "And what can I do?" God replied, "I will impose a fine on you; you have broken the tablets and you must replace them." This is the meaning of that which is written, *Carve out two tablets of stone like the first* (Deuteronomy 10.1). . . . The Holy One, blessed be He, said to Moses, "Were not the tablets deposited with you? You broke them, and you must replace them." R. Isaac said, Moses reconciled God with Israel through the second tablets. What did Moses do? He went up to God angrily and said to Him, "Thy children have sinned, and yet Thou hast put a fine on me." He feigned anger on behalf of Israel. . . . When God saw this He said to him, "Moses! Two beings are angry, you and I are angry with them! . . . Let not the two of us be angry, but when you see Me pour hot [water—i.e., boiling with rage], you pour cold, and when you see Me pour cold, you pour hot." Moses asked, "Master of the universe, how shall this come about?" God replied, "Pray thou for mercy on their behalf." . . . He said thus to God, "Lo, they are Thy children; do Thou release them from this sin."

Deuteronomy Rabbah 3.15

When Moses went up a second time to receive the Torah, the ministering angels asked, "Master of the universe! Only yesterday, did not the people of Israel sin against the Torah in which Thou hast written *You shall have no other gods beside Me* (Exodus 20.3)?" Thereupon the Holy One, blessed be He, replied, "As accusers, you have always stood between Me and Israel. And yet when you went down to Abraham, did you not eat meat and milk together, as it is said, *Then Abraham . . . took curds and milk and the calf that had been prepared, and set these before them; and he waited on them . . . as they ate* (Genesis 18.7–8)? But even a child in Israel, after coming home from his teacher's house, will say if his mother sets out bread, meat, and cheese for him to eat, 'This day my teacher taught me: *You shall not boil a kid in its mother's milk*'" (Exodus 34.26). The angels found no answer for God. And in that instant, while the angels had no answer and no rejoinder, the Holy One, blessed be He, said to Moses, *"Write down these commandments"* (ibid. 27).

Midrash on Psalms 8.2[24]

Moses descended with the tablets, and spent forty days on the mountain, sitting down before the Holy One, blessed be He, like a disciple who is sitting before his teacher, reading the Written Law, and repeating the Oral Law which he had learned. . . .

Moses spent forty days on the mount, expounding the meaning of the words of the Torah, and examining its letters. After forty days he took the Torah, and descended on the tenth of the seventh month, on the Day of Atonement, and gave it as an everlasting inheritance to the children of Israel, as it is said, *This shall be to you a law for all time* (Leviticus 16.34). . . .

Moses said before the Holy One, blessed be He, "Sovereign

of all worlds! Pardon now the iniquities of this people." He said to him, "Moses! If thou hadst said, 'Pardon now the iniquities of all Israel, even to the end of all generations [He would have done so].' It was an acceptable time. But thou hast said, 'Pardon, I beseech Thee, the iniquities of this people with reference to the affair of the calf.' Behold, let it be according to thy words, as it is said, *And the Lord said, I pardon, as you have asked*" (Numbers 14.20).

Pirke de-Rabbi Eliezer 46[25]

Even though the Torah was given as a fence at Sinai, they were not punishable for transgressing it until it was repeated in the Tent of Meeting. This may be compared to an edict which has been written and sealed and brought into the province, but in respect whereof the inhabitants of the province are not punishable, until it has been clearly explained to them in the public meeting place of the province. So, too, with the Torah; even though it was given to Israel at Sinai, they were not punishable in respect thereof until it had been repeated in the Tent of Meeting.

Leviticus Rabbah 1.10

*

*The Ten Commandments

The second five commandments were intended to be paired off with the first five commandments.

You shall not murder corresponds to *I the Lord am your God.* The Holy One, blessed be He, said, "If thou didst murder, I hold it against thee as though thou didst diminish the image of God."

You shall not commit adultery is paired with *You shall have no other gods.* The Holy One, blessed be He, said, "If thou didst commit adultery, I hold it against thee as though thou didst bow down to another god."

You shall not steal is paired with *You shall not swear falsely by the name of the Lord your God.* In this connection R. Hiyya cited the verses *You shall not steal; you shall not deal deceitfully or falsely with one another. You shall not swear falsely by My name* (Leviticus 19.

11–12): that is, if you steal, you will go on to deal falsely, go on to lie, and end up swearing by My name falsely.

You shall not bear false witness is paired with *Remember the Sabbath day.* The Holy One, blessed be He, said, "If you bear false witness against your neighbor, I shall hold it against you as though you bore witness against Me to the the effect that I did not create My world in six days and did not rest on the seventh."

You shall not covet is paired with *Honor your father and your mother.* [Clans like] Gaius of Gadara and Lucius of Susitha would sneak into each other's homes and cohabit with the wives of the others, the others with the wives of these. In time a quarrel fell out between them, and a man killed his father, unaware that it was his father.

The Ten Commandments were intended to be paired off with the ten words [*va-yomer,* "and (God) said," occurs ten times in the story of creation] whereby the world was created.

I the Lord am your God is paired with *And God said: "Let there be light"* (Genesis 1.3), and of light Scripture says elsewhere *The Lord shall be unto thee an everlasting light* (Isaiah 60.19).

The commandment *You shall have no other gods beside Me* is paired with *And God said, "Let there be an expanse in the midst of the waters, that it may separate water from water"* (Genesis 1.6). The Holy One, blessed be He, said, "Make a separation between Me and between idolatry, which in the verse *They have forsaken Me, the fountain of living waters, and hewed them out cisterns* (Jeremiah 2.13) is implied to be stored and stagnant [water]."

You shall not swear by the name of the Lord your God is paired with *God said, "Let the water . . . be gathered in one area"* (Genesis 1.9). The Holy One, blessed be He, said, "The waters accord Me honor and restrain themselves; and will you not accord Me honor in not swearing by My name falsely?"

Remember the Sabbath day is paired with *And God said, "Let the earth sprout vegetation"* (ibid. 11). For the Holy One, blessed be He, stated that however little you feast on the Sabbath you will still be regarded as one who honors it. Remember that the world was created in the hope that man would not sin; and men can live without sinning because they can subsist if necessary only on grasses and herbs that the earth puts forth.

Honor your father is paired with *God said, "Let there be lights in the expanse of the sky"* (ibid. 14). The Holy One, blessed be He, said, "Behold, for thee I created two lights, thy father and thy mother. Take care in the honor due them."

You shall not murder is paired with *God said, "Let the waters bring forth swarms"* (ibid. 20). The Holy One, blessed be He, said, "Be not like those fish—the big ones that swallow the little ones, as is intimated in the verse *Wherefore . . . holdest Thou Thy peace . . . and makest men as the fishes of the sea?"* (Habakkuk 1.13–14).

You shall not commit adultery is paired with *God said, "Let the earth bring forth every kind of living creature"* (ibid. 24). The Holy One, blessed be He, said, "Behold I created for thee thy mate. Each and every one should cleave to his mate, to his own kind."

You shall not steal is paired with *God said, "See, I give you every seed bearing plant"* (ibid. 29). The Holy One, blessed be He, said, "Not one of you shall put forth his hand in theft of the property or the money of his neighbor—you may take only ownerless property, such as seed-yielding herbs." R. Hiyya taught, That which is guarded within a garden it is forbidden to take—the taking would be robbery; but that which is not guarded in a garden may be taken, and the taking is not robbery.

5. Moses and Aaron on either side of the Ten Commandments, inscribed in Hebrew and Spanish. Painting. 1675. By Aron de Chavez. See Chapter 8.

You shall not bear false witness against your neighbor, etc., is paired with *And God said, "I will make man in My image"* (ibid. 26). The Holy One, blessed be He, said, "Behold, for thee I created thy neighbor in My likeness. And thou, by such acts as call for punishment, wouldst swallow and make an end of thy neighbor. Do not then bear false witness against thy neighbor."

You shall not covet is paired with *God said, "It is not good for man to be alone; I will make a fitting helper for him"* (ibid. 2.18). The Holy One, blessed be He, said, "Behold, I created a mate for thee. Let each and every one of you cling to his mate. Let not a man of you covet the wife of his neighbor."

Pesikta Rabbati 21.18–19[26]

Hadrian—may his bones crumble to dust!—contrived a problem for R. Joshua ben Hananiah, saying to him: "The Holy One, blessed be He, bestowed a great privilege upon the nations of the world when He gave five commandments to Israel and offered five to the nations of the world. In the first five commandments, which the Holy One, blessed be He, gave to Israel, His name is involved with the commandments, so that if Israel sin, God raises a cry against them; but in the second five commandments, which He offered to the nations of the earth, His name is not involved with the commandments, so that when the nations of the earth sin, He raises no cry against them."

R. Joshua replied, "Come and walk about the city's squares with me." And in each and every place where R. Joshua led him, Hadrian saw standing a statue of himself. R. Joshua asked, "This object—what is it?" The emperor replied, "It is a statue of me." "And this one here—what is it?" The emperor replied, "It is a statue of me." Finally R. Joshua drew him along and led him to a privy, where he said to him, "My lord king, I see that you are ruler everywhere in this city, but you are not ruler in this place." The emperor asked, "Why not?" R. Joshua replied, "Because in each and every place I saw standing a statue of you, but a statue of you is not standing in this place." Hadrian replied, "And you are a sage among the Jews! Would such be the honor due to a king that a statue of him be set up in a place that is loathsome, in a place that is repulsive, in a place that is filthy?" R. Joshua replied, "Do not your ears hear what your mouth is saying? Would it redound to the glory of the Holy One, blessed be He, to have His name mentioned with murderers, with adulterers, with thieves?"

Pesikta Rabbati 21.2[27]

Why are these paragraphs [of the *Shema:* Deuteronomy 6.4–9, 11.13–21, Numbers 15.37–41] read daily? . . . R. Levi said, Because the Ten Commandments are included in them.

(1) *I the Lord am your God* = *Hear, O Israel! The Lord is our God* (Deuteronomy 6.4).

(2) *You shall have no other gods beside Me* = *The Lord is one* (ibid.).

(3) *You shall not take in vain the name of the Lord your God* = *You must love the Lord your God* (ibid. 5). One who loves a king will not swear in his name and lie.

(4) *Remember the Sabbath day and keep it holy* = *Thus you shall be reminded to observe all My commandments* (Numbers 15.40). This commandment of the Sabbath is of equal importance to all the commandments of the Torah. It is written, [*Thou*] *madest known unto them Thy holy Sabbath, and didst command them commandments, statutes and a law* (Nehemiah 9.14) to advise you that it [the Sabbath] is equivalent to the commandments of the Torah.

(5) *Honor your father and your mother, that you may long endure on the land which the Lord your God is giving you* = *That you and your children may endure in the land that the Lord swore to your fathers to give to them* (Deuteronomy 11.21).

(6) *You shall not murder* = *You will soon perish* (ibid. 17). He who murders is subject to death.

(7) *You shall not commit adultery* = *You should not follow your heart and eyes in your lustful urge* (Numbers 15.39). R. Levi said, The heart and the eye are the two agents of sin, as it is written, *My son, give me thy heart and let thine eyes observe my ways* (Proverbs 23.26). . . .

(8) *You shall not steal* = *You shall gather in your new grain* (Deuteronomy 11.14) and not the new grain of your neighbor.

(9) *You shall not bear false witness against your neighbor* = *I, the Lord, your God* (Numbers 15.40). It is written, *And the Lord God is truth* (Jeremiah 10.10). What is truth? R. Abbun said, It is the Living God and Eternal King. R. Levi said, The Holy One, blessed be He, said that if you bear false witness against your neighbor, I will consider it as if you claimed that I did not create the heavens and the earth.

(10) *You shall not covet your neighbor's house = Inscribe them on the doorposts of your house* (Deuteronomy 6.9), and not on your neighbor's house. . . .

Why are the Ten Commandments not read every day [like the *Shema*]? So that the heretics should not say that only these [commandments] were given to Moses on Mount Sinai.

Yerushalmi Berakhot 3c

*The 613 Commandments

R. Simlai taught: Six hundred and thirteen precepts were given to Israel through Moses, this number being the numerical value of the word *Torah.* Should you object that this is not so, since the word only amounts to six hundred and eleven, and ask where, therefore, will you obtain the other two? In answer, the Sages said, The two commands of *I the Lord* and *You shall have no other gods besides Me* were heard from the mouth of the Lord [Himself], and Moses only told them six hundred and eleven, as it says, *Moses charged us with the Teaching* [that is, Moses only commanded us Torah, the numerical value of which is 611; but together with the other two commands which God gave, the number is 613].

Exodus Rabbah 33.7

The Holy One, blessed be He, desired to make Israel worthy, therefore He gave them the Law [to study] and many commandments [to do]; for it is said, *The Lord was pleased, for his* [Israel's] *righteousness' sake, to make the Law great and glorious* (Isaiah 42.21). . . .

R. Simlai when preaching said, Six hundred and thirteen precepts were communicated to Moses, three hundred and sixty-five negative precepts, corresponding to the number of solar days [in the year], and two hundred and forty-eight positive precepts, corresponding to the number of the members [joints or bones] of man's body. Said R. Hamnuna, What is the text for this? It is, *Moses charged us with the Torah as the heritage of the congregation of*

Jacob (Deuteronomy 33.4), Torah being in letter-value equal to six hundred and eleven; *I am* and *You shall have no other gods* [not being reckoned, because] we heard from the mouth of the Might Divine.

David came and reduced them to eleven [principles], as it is written, *A Psalm of David. Lord, who shall sojourn in Thy tabernacle? Who shall dwell upon Thy holy mountain?—(i) He that walketh uprightly, and (ii) worketh righteousness, and (iii) speaketh truth in his heart; that (iv) hath no slander upon his tongue, (v) nor doeth evil to his fellow, (vi) nor taketh up a reproach against his neighbor; (vii) in whose eyes a vile person is despised, but (viii) he honoreth them that fear the Lord, (ix) he sweareth to his own hurt, and changeth not; (x) he that putteth not out his money on interest, (xi) nor taketh a bribe against the innocent* (Psalms 15.1–5). . . .

Isaiah came and reduced them to six [principles], as it is written, *(i) He that walketh righteously, and (ii) speaketh uprightly; (iii) he that despiseth the gain of oppressions, (iv) that shaketh his hand from holding of bribes, (v) that stoppeth his ears from hearing of blood, (vi) and shutteth his eyes from looking upon evil; he shall dwell on high* (Isaiah 33.15). . . .

Micah came and reduced them to three [principles], as it is written, *It hath been told thee, O man, what is good, and what the Lord doth require of thee: (i) only to do justly, and (ii) to love mercy, and (iii) to walk humbly with thy God* (Micah 6.8). . . .

Again came Isaiah and reduced them to two [principles], as it is said, *Thus saith the Lord, (i) Keep ye justice, and (ii) do righteousness* (Isaiah 56.1).

Amos came and reduced them to one [principle], as it is said, *For thus saith the Lord unto the house of Israel: Seek ye Me, and live* (Amos 5.4). To this R. Nahman b. Isaac demurred, saying, [Might it not be taken as,] Seek Me by observing the whole Torah and live?—But it is Habakkuk who came and based them all on one [principle], as it is said, *But the righteous shall live by his faith* (Habakkuk 2.4).

Makkot 23b–24a

Had Israel gazed deep into the words of the Torah when it was given them, no nation or kingdom could ever rule over them. And what did it say to them? Accept upon yourselves the yoke of the kingdom of heaven, and subdue one another in the fear of heaven, and deal with one another in charity.

Sifre Deuteronomy 32.39[28]

It happened that a certain heathen came before Shammai and said to him, "Make me a proselyte, on the condition that you teach me the whole Torah while I stand on one foot." Thereupon he repulsed him with the builder's cubit measure which was in his hand. When he went before Hillel, he said to him, "What is hateful to you, do not to your neighbor: that is the whole Torah, while the rest is the commentary thereof; go and learn it."

Shabbat 31a

*

The Transmission of the Oral Law

Moses received the Torah at Sinai and transmitted it to Joshua. Joshua to the elders, and the elders to the prophets, and the prophets to the men of the great synagogue.

Avot 1.1

The prophets received from Sinai the messages they were to prophesy to subsequent generations; for Moses told Israel, *But both with those who are standing here with us this day before the Lord our God and with those who are not with us here this day* (Deuteronomy 29.14). It does not say "that is not standing here with us this day," but just *"those who are not with us here this day"* —these are the souls that will one day be created; and because there is not yet any substance in them, the word "standing" is not used with them. Although they did not yet exist, still each one received his share [of the Torah]; for so it says, *The burden of the word of the Lord to Israel by Malachi* (Malachi 1.1). It does not say "in the days of Malachi," but *"by Malachi,"* for his prophecy was already with him since Sinai, but hitherto permission was not given him to prophesy. . . . So Isaiah said, *From the time that it was, there am I* (48.16). Isaiah said, I was present at the revelation on Sinai whence I received this prophecy, only *And now the Lord God hath sent me, and His Spirit* (ibid.); for hitherto no permission was given to him to prophesy. Not only did all the prophets receive their prophecy from Sinai, but also each of the Sages that arose in every generation received his [wisdom] from Sinai, for so it says, *The Lord spoke those words . . . to your whole congregation with a mighty voice* (Deuteronomy 5.19). R. Johanan said, It was one voice that divided itself into seven voices, and these into seventy languages. R. Simeon b. Lakish said, [It was the voice] from which all the subsequent prophets received their prophecy.

Exodus Rabbah 28.6

*

*The Oral Law

Once I was on a journey, and I came upon a man who went at me after the way of heretics. Now, he accepted the Written but not the Oral Law. He said to me, "The Written Law was given us from Mount Sinai; the Oral Law was not given us from Mount Sinai."

I said to him, "But were not both the Written and the Oral Law spoken by the Omnipresent? Then what difference is there between the Written and the Oral Law? To what can this be compared? To a king of flesh and blood who had two servants, and loved them both with a perfect love; and he gave them each a measure of wheat and a bundle of flax. The wise servant, what did he do? He took the flax and spun a cloth. Then he took the wheat and made flour. The flour he cleansed, and ground, and kneaded, and baked, and set on top of the table. Then he spread the cloth over it, and left it so until the king should come. But the foolish servant did nothing at all. After some days, the king returned from a journey and came into his house and said to them, 'My sons, bring me what I gave you.' One servant showed the wheaten bread on the table with a cloth spread over it, and the other servant showed the wheat still in the box, with a bundle of flax upon it. Alas for his shame, alas for his disgrace!

"Now, when the Holy One, blessed be He, gave the Torah to Israel, he gave it only in the form of wheat, for us to extract flour from it, and flax, to extract a garment."

Seder Eliyahu Zutta 2[29]

What is the meaning of the verse: *And I will give you the stone tablets with the teachings and commandments which I have inscribed to instruct them?* (Exodus 24.12). *Stone tablets:* these are the Ten Commandments; *the teachings:* this is the Pentateuch; *commandments:* this is the Mishnah; *which I have inscribed:* these are the Prophets and the Hagiographa; *to instruct them:* this is the Gemara. It teaches [us] that all these things were given to Moses on Sinai.

Berakhot 5a

*

* The Bringing of the Firstfruits

Some there are who bring *bikkurim* and recite [the declaration, Deuteronomy 26.5–10]; others who may only bring them, but do not make recital; and some there are who may not even bring them at all. . . .

For what reason may he not bring them? Because it is said, *The choice firstfruits of your soil* (Exodus 23.19), meaning that thou mayest not bring them unless all the produce [comes] from thy land. Tenants, lessees, or occupiers of confiscated property or a robber may not bring them for the same reason, because it says, *firstfruits of your soil.*

Bikkurim are brought only from seven kinds [for which Palestine was renowned, namely, wheat, barley, grapes, figs, pomegranates, olive oil, and date honey] but none [may be brought] from dates grown on hills, or from valley fruits [fruits grown in valleys (except dates) were not of the choice kind] or from olives that are not of the choice kind. *Bikkurim* are not to be brought before Pentecost. The men of Mount Zeboim brought their *bikkurim* before Pentecost, but they were not accepted because of what is written in the Torah: *And the Feast of the Harvest, of the firstfruits of your work, of what you sow in the field* (Exodus 23.16).

Bikkurim 1.1–3

How were the *bikkurim* set aside? A man goes down into his field, he sees a fig that ripened, or a cluster of grapes that ripened, or a pomegranate that ripened, he ties a reed rope around it and says, "Let these be *bikkurim.*" R. Simeon says, Notwithstanding this he must again designate them as *bikkurim* after they have been plucked from the soil.

How were the *bikkurim* taken up [to Jerusalem]? All [the inhabitants of] the cities that constituted the *ma'amad* [district] assembled in the city of the *ma'amad* and spent the night in the open place thereof without entering any of the houses. Early in the morning the officer [head of the *ma'amad*] said, "Let us arise and go up to Zion, into the house of the Lord our God."

Those who lived near [Jerusalem] brought fresh figs and grapes, but those from a distance brought dried figs and raisins [for fresh fruit would rot on the way]. An ox with horns bedecked with gold and with an olive crown on its head led the way. The flute was played before them until they were nigh to Jerusalem; and when they arrived close to Jerusalem they sent messengers in advance, and ornamentally arrayed their *bikkurim.* The governors and chiefs and treasurers [of the Temple] went out to meet them. According to the rank of the entrants used they to go forth. All the skilled artisans of Jerusalem would stand up before them and greet them, "Brethren, men of such and such a place, we are delighted to welcome you."

The flute was playing before them till they reached the Temple mount; and when they reached the Temple mount even King Agrippa would take the basket and place it on his shoulder and walk as far as the Temple court. At the approach to the court, the Levites would sing the song: *I will extol Thee, O Lord, for Thou hast raised me up, and hast not suffered mine enemies to rejoice over me* (Psalms 30.2).

The turtledoves [tied to] the basket were [offered up as] burnt offerings, but that which they held in their hands they presented to the priests.

While the basket was yet on his shoulder he would recite from *I acknowledge this day before the Lord your God,* until the completion of the passage (Deuteronomy 26.3–10). R. Judah said, [He would recite] till [he had reached] *My father was a fugitive Aramean.* Having reached these words, he took the basket off his shoulder and held it by its edge; and the priest placed his hand beneath it and waved it; he [the Israelite] then recited from *a fugitive Aramean* until he completed the entire passage. He would then deposit the basket by the side of the altar, prostrate himself, and depart.

Originally all who knew how to recite would recite, while

those unable to do so would repeat it [after the priests]; but when they refrained from bringing [abashed at this public avowal of their ignorance in reading Hebrew], it was decided that both those who could and those who could not [recite] should repeat the words.

The rich brought their *bikkurim* in baskets overlaid with silver or gold, while the poor used wicker baskets of peeled willow branches, and they used to give both the baskets and the *bikkurim* to the priest.

Bikkurim 3.1–8

On the way [to the Temple in Jerusalem to bring the firstfruits], they would say, *I rejoiced when they said unto me, "Let us go unto the house of the Lord"* (Psalms 122.1). In Jerusalem, they would say, *Our feet are standing within thy gates, O Jerusalem* (ibid. 2). On the Temple mount, they would say, *Praise God in His sanctuary* (ibid. 150.1). In the Temple court, they would say, *Let every thing that hath breath praise the Lord* (ibid. 6).

Yerushalmi Bikkurim 65c

It is reported that once the ruling power made a decree that Israel should not bring wood to the altar, nor bring their firstfruits to Jerusalem, and placed guards on the roads as Jeroboam the son of Nebat had done to prevent Israel from going on pilgrimage. What did the pious and sin-fearing men of that generation do? They took the baskets of the firstfruits and covered them with dried figs and carried them with a pestle on their shoulders, and when they reached the guards they were asked, "Whither are you going?" They replied, "With the pestle on our shoulders we are going to make two cakes of pressed figs in the mortar we have yonder." When they had gone away from the guard they decorated the baskets and brought them to Jerusalem.

Taanit 28a

*

The Celebration of Shavuot

Now you shall observe the Feast of Weeks for the Lord your God (Deuteronomy 16.10). What does this teach? As it has been already said, *the Feast of the Harvest, of the firstfruits of your work* (Exodus 23.16), you should not think that if there is no harvest you need not observe a festival. Therefore, it is said *you shall observe the Feast of Weeks;* for example, when Israel is in the Diaspora and has no barley sheaf to harvest even then you should celebrate Shavuot.

Pesikta Zutarta

The Boethusians held that the Feast of Weeks must always be on the day after the Sabbath [i.e., on a Sunday, at the completion of seven full weeks from the offering of the *omer* which, according to them, was offered on a Sunday]. But R. Johanan b. Zakkai entered into discussion with them saying, "Fools that you are! Whence do you derive it?" Not one of them was able to answer him, save one old man who commenced to babble and said, "Moses our teacher was a great lover of Israel, and knowing full well that the Feast of Weeks lasted only one day he therefore fixed it on the day after the Sabbath so that Israel might enjoy themselves for two successive days." [R. Johanan b. Zakkai] then quoted to him the following verse: *"It is eleven days from Horeb unto Kadeshbarnea by the Mount Seir route* (Deuteronomy 1.2). If Moses was a great lover of Israel, why then did he detain them in the wilderness for forty years?" "Master," said the other, "is it thus that you would dismiss me?" "Fool," he answered, "should not our perfect Torah be as convincing as your idle talk! Now one verse says, *You shall count fifty days* (Leviticus 23.16), while the other verse says, *You shall count* [*until*] *seven full weeks have elapsed* (ibid. 15). How are they to be reconciled? The latter verse refers to the time when the [first day of the] festival [of Passover] falls on the Sabbath, while the former to the time when the [first day of the] festival falls on a weekday.

Menahot 65a–b

Why did the Torah enjoin on us to bring two loaves on Pentecost? Because Pentecost is the season for fruit of the tree. Therefore the Holy One, blessed be He, said, "Bring before Me two loaves on Pentecost so that the fruit of your trees may be blessed."

Rosh Hashanah 16a

Abba Saul said, "Fine [weather at] the Festival of Pentecost is a good sign for [the wheat harvest of] all the year."

Baba Batra 147a

In all the other additional sacrifices the sin offering is included, but in connection with Pentecost no sin offering is mentioned, to show that at that time no sin or iniquity attached to them.

Song of Songs Rabbah 4.4

Rejoicing on a festival too is a religious duty. For it was taught, R. Eliezer said, "A man has nought else [to do] on a festival save either to eat and drink or to sit and study." R. Joshua said, "Divide it: [devote] half of it to eating and drinking, and half of it to the *bet ha-midrash.*" R. Johanan said thereon, "Both deduce it from the same verse. One says, *a solemn gathering for the Lord your God* (Deuteronomy 16.8), whereas another verse says, *You shall hold a solemn gathering* (Numbers 29.35)." R. Eliezer holds, "[That means] either entirely to God or entirely to you"; while R. Joshua holds, "Divide it: [devote] half to God and half to yourselves."

R. Eleazer said, "All agree in respect to the Feast of Weeks [the *atzeret,* solemn assembly] that we require it to be *you shall hold* too. What is the reason? It is the day on which the Torah was given. . . .

Mar son of Rabina would fast the whole year [if the occasion arose] except on the Feast of Weeks, Purim, and the eve of the Day of Atonement. The Feast of Weeks, [because] it is the day on which the Torah was given.

Pesahim 68b

SHAVUOT IN MEDIEVAL
JEWISH LITERATURE

The Middle Ages saw the creation of many Jewish classical writings that made a strong impact on Jewish thought. Selections from some of the major philosophical works of this period are cited in this chapter.

Judah Halevi (c. 1075–1141), renowned as the foremost Hebrew poet of the Middle Ages, exerted a profound influence on Jewish thinking through his *Ha-Kuzari,* a book in dialogue style written in Arabic. The title derives from the story of a disputation held before the king of the Khazars by a rabbi, a Christian scholar, and a philosopher, which resulted in the conversion of the king and his people to Judaism. Believing firmly in revelation, Judah Halevi held that Judaism does not require philosophical substantiation.

Moses ben Maimon (1135–1204), called Maimonides and Rambam, was not only a philosopher and codifier of law but also a practicing physician. In a major work, *Moreh Nevukhim* ("Guide for the Perplexed"), he sought to harmonize religion and philosophy. In response to the troubled Jewish community of Yemen, Maimonides wrote *Iggeret Teman* ("Epistle to Yemen"). In this lengthy letter, written in Arabic, he expressed the conviction that the inner strength required by the Yemenite Jews for survival was a staunch belief in the revelation on Mount Sinai.

The Aramaic *Zohar* ("Splendor" or "Light"), the basic work

of Jewish mysticism, was traditionally attributed to Simeon ben Yohai and his pupils of the second century; however, it first appeared in the thirteenth century through Moses ben Shemtov de Leon, a famous cabalist. Discursive commentaries on the Bible, parables, and discourses on mysticism are the subject matter of the *Zohar*.

The Spanish theologian Joseph Albo (c. 1380–c. 1444) authored *Sefer ha-Ikkarim* ("Book of Principles"), the last of the philosophical classics of medieval Judaism. Utilizing the works of his predecessors, he wrote in a popular vein, setting forth the basic roots or principles of religion as he saw them.

*

*The Belief in Divine Providence

JUDAH HALEVI

Although the people believed in the message of Moses after the performance of the miracles, they retained some doubt as to whether God really communed with mortals, and whether or not the Law was of human origin, only later supported by divine inspiration. They could not associate speech with a divine Being, since speech is a corporeal function. God, however, desired to remove this doubt. He commanded them to prepare themselves morally as well as physically, enjoining them to keep aloof from their wives and to be ready to hear His words. The people prepared and fitted themselves to receive prophetic inspiration and even actually to hear (in person) the words of God. This came to pass three days later, and was preceded by overwhelming phenomena, lightning, thunder, earthquake, and fire, which surrounded Mount Sinai. The fire remained visible to the people forty days; they also saw Moses enter it and emerge from it; they distinctly heard the Ten Commandments, the source and foundation of the Law. . . .

Heaven forbid that we should assume what is impossible or that which reason rejects as being impossible. The first of the Ten Commandments enjoins the belief in divine Providence; and immediately there follows the second command which forbids the worship of other gods, the association of any human beings with Him, His representation in statues, forms, and images, in general, i.e., the belief in His corporeality. We must not, however, reject the tradition concerning that apparition. We say, then, that we do not know how the idea took bodily form, or how the speech was evolved which struck our ear, or what new thing God created from nought, or what existing thing He employed; for nothing is beyond His power. Just so we have to admit that He created the two tablets, and engraved a text on them, in the same way as He created the heavens and the stars by His will alone.

Ha-Kuzari 1.87, 89[1]

*

*Strength Comes through Belief

MOSES MAIMONIDES

Put your trust in the true promises of Scripture, brethren, and be not dismayed at the series of persecutions or the enemy's ascendency over us, or the weakness of our people. These trials are designed to test and purify us so that the saints and the pious ones of the pure and undefiled lineage of Jacob will adhere to our religion and remain within the fold, as it is written, "And among the remnant are those whom the Lord shall call" (Joel 3.5). This verse makes it clear that they are not numerous, being the descendants of those who were present on Mount Sinai, witnessed the divine revelation, entered into the covenant of God, and undertook to do and obey as is signified in their saying, "We will do and obey" (Exodus 24.7). They obligated not only themselves but also their descendants, as it is written, "For us and our children ever to apply all the provisions of this Teaching" (Deuteronomy 29.28). . . .

Consequently, it is manifest that he who spurns the religion that was revealed at that theophany is not an offspring of the folk who witnessed it. For our Sages of blessed memory insisted that they who entertain scruples concerning the divine message are not scions of the race that were present on Mount Sinai (Nedarim 20a). May God guard us and you from doubt, and banish from our midst confusion, suspicion, which lead to it.

Now, my coreligionists in the Diaspora, it behooves you to hearten one another, the elders to guide the youth, and the leaders to direct the masses. Give your assent to the Truth that is immutable and unchangeable, and to the following postulates of a religion that shall never fail. God is one in a unique sense of the term, and Moses is His prophet and spokesman, and the greatest and most perfect of the seers. To him was vouchsafed by God what has never been vouchsafed to any prophet before him, nor will it be in the future. The entire Torah was divinely revealed to Moses of whom it was said, "With him I speak mouth to mouth" (Numbers 12.8). It will neither be abrogated nor superseded, neither supplemented nor abridged. Never shall it be supplanted by another divine revelation containing positive and negative duties. Keep well in mind the revelation on Sinai in accordance with the divine precept to perpetuate the memory of this occasion and not to allow it to fall into oblivion. Furthermore we were enjoined to impress this event upon the minds of our children, as it is written, "But take utmost care and watch yourselves scrupulously, so that you do not forget the things that you saw with your own eyes and so that they do not fade from your mind as long as you live. And make them known to your children and to your children's children" (Deuteronomy 4.9).

It is imperative, my fellow Jews, that you make this great spectacle of the revelation appeal to the imagination of your children. Proclaim at public gatherings its momentousness. For this event is the pivot of our religion, and the proof which demonstrates its veracity. Evaluate this phenomenon at its true importance for Scripture has pointed out its significance in the verse, "You have but to inquire about bygone ages that came before you, ever since God created man on earth, from one end of heaven to the other: has anything as grand as this ever happened, or has its like ever been known?" (Deuteronomy 4.32).

Remember, my coreligionists, that this great, incomparable, and unique historical event is attested by the best of evidence. For never before or since has a whole nation witnessed a revelation from God or beheld His splendor. The purpose of all this was to confirm us in the faith so that nothing can change it, and to reach a degree of certainty which will sustain us in these trying times of fierce persecution and absolute tyranny, as it is written, "For God has come only in order to test you" (Exodus 20.17). Scripture means that God revealed Himself to you thus in order to give you strength to withstand all future trials. Now do not slip or err, be steadfast in your religion, and persevere in your faith and its duties.

Iggeret Teman[2]

*

Moses Experiences the Revelation
MOSES MAIMONIDES

It is clear to me that what Moses experienced at the revelation on Mount Sinai was different from that which was experienced by all the other Israelites, for Moses alone was addressed by God, and for this reason the second person singular is used in the Ten Commandments; Moses then went down to the foot of the mountain and told his fellowmen what he had heard. Compare "I stood between the Lord and you at that time to convey the Lord's words to you" (Deuteronomy 5.5). Again, "As Moses spoke God answered him in thunder" (Exodus 19.19). Furthermore, the words "In order that the people hear when I speak with you" (ibid. 9) show that God spoke to Moses, and the people only heard the mighty sound, not distinct words. It is to the perception of this mighty sound that Scripture refers in the passage "When you heard the voice" (Deuteronomy 5.20); again it is stated, "You heard the sound of words" (ibid. 4.12), and it is not said, "You heard words"; and even where the hearing of the words is mentioned, only the perception of the sound is meant.
. . . There is, however, an opinion of our Sages frequently expressed in the midrashim, and found also in the Talmud, to this effect: The Israelites heard the first and the second commandments from God, i.e., they learnt the truth of the principles contained in these two commandments in the same manner as Moses, and not through Moses. For these two principles, the existence of God and His unity, can be arrived at by means of reasoning, and whatever can be established by proof is known by

the prophet in the same way as by any other person; he has no advantage in this respect. These two principles were not known through prophecy alone. But the rest of the commandments are of an ethical and authoritative character, and do not contain [truths] perceived by the intellect.

Notwithstanding all that has been said by our Sages on this subject we infer from Scripture as well as from the words of our Sages that the Israelites heard on that occasion a certain sound which Moses understood to proclaim the first two commandments, and through Moses all other Israelites learnt them when he in intelligible sounds repeated them to the people. Our Sages mention this view, and support it by the verse, "God hath spoken once; twice have I heard this" (Psalms 62.12). They state distinctly, in the beginning of *Midrash Hazita,* that the Israelites did not hear any other command directly from God. . . .

Note it, and remember it, for it is impossible for any person to expound the revelation on Mount Sinai more fully than our Sages have done, since it is one of the secrets of the Law. It is very difficult to have a true conception of the events, for there has never been before, nor will there ever be again, anything like it.

Guide for the Perplexed 2.33[3]

*
* The Torah Is Given in Public
JOSEPH ALBO

A thing perceived by an unusually popular and trustworthy person or by a number of persons of superior powers of comprehension or by an unusually large number of persons is more likely to satisfy the mind of its reality and to be firmly believed than a thing not so accredited. For this reason God desired that the Torah should be given through Moses with great publicity and in the presence of a mighty multitude of six hundred thousand people. . . .

This is the reason why the Torah was not given completely to Abraham, Isaac, or Jacob that they should command their children after them to keep the way of the Lord. For though the tradition should be handed down by them continuously from father to son, some suspicion or doubt might occur to those who came after in future generations, because those who received the law first were individuals. The case is different where the thing is clearly perceived by a very great number of persons embracing many wise and intelligent men, representing a great variety of opinions. This is the reason why the Torah was given through Moses with such great publicity, in order, namely, as I said before, that no suspicion or doubt should remain in the minds of the recipients and their associates, nor in the minds of those who came after, so that the tradition may be as firm and true as it is possible to make it.

Sefer ha-Ikkarim 1.20[4]

*
**The Two Tablets of the Law*

JOSEPH ALBO

The Ten Commandments are general rules embracing the two classes of commandments, as follows: The first tablet contains the first five commandments, which a person is obliged to follow by reason of his acceptance of the divine Being. Take the following instance: A king builds a city, then frees a body of slaves and settles them in the city, and then comes to speak to them in order to induce them to accept his lordship. Clearly, the first thing he has to tell them is that he is the master who cared for them and liberated them from bondage. This is the meaning of the first commandment in the Decalogue, "I the Lord am your God" (Exodus 20.2). It behooves you to accept My lordship because I made you free. Then he commands them that they should not give the power to anyone else, "You shall have no other gods beside Me" (ibid. 3). . . . Then it is proper to command them that they should show him honor, and not treat him with disrespect, as by swearing falsely in his name, "You shall not take in vain the name of the Lord your God" (ibid. 7). Then it is necessary that he should fix a mode of commemorating the building

6. The giving of the Torah. Woodcut. From *Sefer Minha* Amsterdam, 1723.

of the city. For in this way they will remember that they have a lord who built the city, and that they had been freed from slavery and settled therein. For this reason He commanded them to keep the Sabbath, which bears allusion to the creation of the world and the deliverance from Egyptian bondage. . . .

Then comes the commandment, "Honor your father and your mother" (ibid. 12). For it is well known that the king who built the city does not reveal himself every day to the men of the city. And while the men of that generation, who saw the king come into the city, remember that he built that city and freed them from bondage, and that they accepted his sovereignty, those who came after them, never having been slaves, and not having seen the king enter the city, may rebel, thinking that the city has always been theirs, and that they have no overlord. . . . Hence the fifth commandment, "Honor your father and your mother," teaches respect for tradition, i.e., that a person should follow the tradition of the fathers, which is a fundamental dogma of all religions. . . .

This commandment completes all those things which concern the relation of man to God, i.e., the things which the servant must do in relation to the master.

Then the Bible inculcates those general principles which men must have as social and political beings in order that the political group may be perfect. The first commandment is to preserve his fellowman's body, "You shall not murder" (ibid. 13). Then comes the command to preserve his neighbor's property, "You shall not steal," which is to be understood literally. Then comes the commandment to preserve that which is intermediate, as it were, between a man's body and his property, namely, his wife. For the wife is in a sense the man's body, as it were, and in a sense, as it were, his property—"You shall not commit adultery." Then he adds that it is not sufficient if one refrain from injuring his neighbor in his body or his property or his wife, but that he must take care not to injure him even by a word. "You shall not bear false witness against your neighbor"; nor even by a thought, "You shall not covet your neighbor's house; you shall not covet your neighbor's wife, or his male or female slave, or his ox or his ass, nor anything that is your neighbor's" (ibid. 14). This completes the general rules which are necessary for man as a being that must associate with others.

Hence the Ten Commandments were placed on two tablets, to show that though these two classes of commandments are distinct, they are necessary for human perfection, the one for the perfection of man as an individual, and the other for his perfection as being part of the state.

Sefer ha-Ikkarim 3.26[5]

*

The Decalogue Established the World

The Ten Words contain the essence of all the commandments, the essence of all celestial and terrestrial mysteries, the essence of the Ten Words of Creation. They were engraved on tablets of stone, and all the hidden things were seen by the eyes and perceived by the minds of all Israel, everything being made clear to them. At that hour all the mysteries of the Torah, all the hidden things of heaven and earth, were unfolded before them and revealed to their eyes, for they saw eye to eye the splendor of the glory of their Lord. Never before, since the Holy One created the world, had such a revelation of the divine glory taken place. . . . For on this day all the earthly dross was removed from them and purged away, and their bodies became as lucent as the angels above when they are clothed in radiant garments for the accomplishment of their Master's errands. . . . Such was the state of the Israelites when they beheld the glory of their Lord. It was not thus at the Red Sea, when the filth had not as yet been removed from them. There, at Mount Sinai, even the embryos in their mother's wombs had some perception of their Lord's glory, and everyone received according to his grade of perception. On that day the Holy One, blessed be He, rejoiced more than on any previous day since He had created the world, for creation had no proper basis before Israel received the Torah. But when once Israel received the Torah on Mount Sinai the world was duly and completely established, and heaven and earth received a proper foundation, and the glory of the Holy One was made known both above and below, and He was exalted over all. Concerning that day it is written, "The Lord reigneth; He is clothed in majesty; the Lord is clothed, He hath girded Himself with strength; yea, the world is established, that it cannot be moved" (Psalms 93.1). "Strength" signifies the Torah, as it is written, "The Lord will give strength unto His people; the Lord will bless His people with peace" (ibid. 29.11). Blessed be the Lord forever. Amen and Amen.

Zohar, Exodus 93b–94a[6]

When God created the world, it was on the condition that if Israel when they came into the world should accept the Torah, it would be well, but if not, then the world should revert to chaos. Nor was the world firmly established until Israel stood before Mount Sinai and accepted the Torah. From that day God has been creating fresh worlds, to wit, the marriages of human beings; for from that time God has been making matches and proclaiming "the daughter of so-and-so for so-and-so"; these are the worlds which He creates.

Zohar, Genesis 90a[7]

⁎

⁎The Bride and the Bridegroom

R. Simeon was sitting and studying the Torah during the night when the bride was to be rejoined to her husband [i.e., the eve of Pentecost]. For we have been taught that all the members of the bridal palace, during the night preceding her espousals, are in duty bound to keep her company and to rejoice with her in her final preparations for the great day: to study all branches of the Torah, proceeding from the Law to the Prophets, from the Prophets to the Holy Writings, and then to the deeper interpretations of Scripture and to the mysteries of Wisdom, as all these represent her preparations and her adornments. The bride, indeed, with her bridesmaids, comes up and remains with them, adorning herself at their hands and rejoicing with them all that night. And on the following day she does not enter under the canopy except in their company, they being called the canopy attendants. And when she steps under the canopy the Holy One, blessed be He, inquires after them and blesses them and crowns them with the bridal crown: happy is their portion!

Hence R. Simeon and all the companions were chanting the Scripture with exultation, each one of them making new discoveries in the Torah. Said R. Simeon to them, "O my sons, happy is your portion, for on the morrow the bride will not enter the bridal canopy except in your company; for all those who help to prepare her adornments tonight will be recorded in the book of remembrance, and the Holy One, blessed be He, will bless them with seventy blessings and crown them with crowns of the celestial world."

Zohar, Prologue 8a[8]

⁎

⁎One Day Only for the Feast of Weeks

Said R. Judah to him: "Why is it that Passover and Tabernacles consist of seven days, but not the Feast of Weeks, which really ought to more than the others?" He replied, "It is written, 'Who is like Thy people, like Israel a nation one in the earth?' (2 Samuel 7.23). Now why are Israel called 'one' here rather than in any other place? It is because the text is here speaking in praise of Israel, because it is the pride of Israel to be one. The reason is that the junction of upper and lower takes place at the spot called 'Israel,' which is linked with what is above and what is below, and with the community of Israel: wherefore the whole is called one, and in this spot faith becomes manifest and complete union and supernal holy unity. The Tree of Life [the Torah] is also called one, and its day therefore is one, and therefore we have Passover and Tabernacles and this festival in the middle, and this is the honor of the Torah that it should have this one day and no more."

Zohar, Leviticus 96a[9]

*

The Anniversary of the Revelation

MOSES MAIMONIDES

The Feast of Weeks is the anniversary of the revelation on Mount Sinai. In order to raise the importance of this day, we count the days that pass since the preceding festival, just as one who expects his most intimate friend on a certain day counts the days and even the hours. This is the reason why we count the days that pass since the offering of the *omer*, between the anniversary of our departure from Egypt and the anniversary of the Lawgiving. The latter was the aim and object of the exodus from Egypt, and thus God said that "I brought you to Me" (Exodus 19.4).

Guide for the Perplexed 3.43[10]

LAWS AND CUSTOMS
OF SHAVUOT

While there is a corpus of law governing all Jewish festivals, there are very few pertaining specifically to Shavuot. Despite its importance and sanctity the "Season of the Giving of Our Torah" did not elicit the promulgation of special commandments other than those relating to the sacrifices offered when the Temple was in existence. Besides a section on the Temple sacrifices for Shavuot, Maimonides has only a few passing references to it in his codification of Jewish laws, *Mishneh Torah.* The *Shulhan Arukh* ("Prepared Table"), based largely on Sephardic practices, was compiled by Joseph Karo (1488–1575) and supplemented with Ashkenazic traditions by Moses Isserles (c. 1520–1572), known as Rema. This authoritative code devotes lengthy sections to Passover and Sukkot but only a brief paragraph to Shavuot, headed "Order of the Prayers for the Feast of Weeks." There are, however, a number of Shavuot customs that have been well established over many generations and are now recognized as essential components of the festival.

Laws and customs that are traditionally observed are cited in this chapter. Variations of many of these usages are described in the chapter "Shavuot in Many Lands." The special foods that are customary on the festival are discussed in the chapter "The Culinary Art of Shavuot."

*

*The Period of Shavuot

Shavuot is observed by traditional Jews in the Diaspora on the sixth and seventh days of Sivan and by Reform Jews and in Israel only on the sixth day of the month.

The three days preceding Shavuot are known as *Sheloshet Yeme Hagbalah* (Three Days of Delimitation [or Preparation]), based on the biblical text "Let them be ready for the third day; for on the third day the Lord will come down, in the sight of all the people, on Mount Sinai. You shall set bounds for the people round about" (Exodus 19.11–12). As these three days are endowed with somewhat of a quasi-festive aura, the strictures governing the usual mourning practices of the period of *sefirat ha-omer* (counting of the *omer*) are abrogated.[1]

According to the law it is forbidden to fast on *Isru Hag,* the day after the festival, because when Shavuot occurred on a Sabbath during the Temple days, the slaughtering of the sacrifices was deferred to the following day.[2]

Tahanun (prayer of supplication) is not said from the beginning of the new moon of Sivan until after the day following the festival.[3]

*

*The Night of Shavuot

On the first night of Shavuot the evening service is delayed until stars appear. If the prayers were recited earlier, thus initiating the festival, there would be less than the forty-nine days of the counting of the *omer* required by the Torah: "You shall keep count until seven full weeks have elapsed" (Leviticus 23.15).[4]

It is a time-honored custom, introduced by the cabalists, to remain awake throughout the first night of Shavuot and to spend it in the study of Torah. The *Zohar* states that "the early Hasidim did not sleep on this night and occupied themselves with the Torah."[5] Another rationale derives from a midrashic statement that the Israelites overslept the night the Torah was promulgated and the Holy One, blessed be He, had to arouse them; therefore, we must rectify this indiscretion and demonstrate our gratitude for receiving the Torah by remaining awake and studying it.[6]

The night is generally devoted to the studying of *Tikkun Lel Shavuot* ("Service of the Night of Shavuot"), composed by the sixteenth-century cabalists of Safed led by Rabbis Solomon Alkabetz and Joseph Karo and later expanded by others. This book is an anthology which includes the opening and closing verses of each weekly Pentateuch portion and of every other biblical book as well as the entire Scroll of Ruth, the first and last few passages of each Mishnah tractate, and selections from cabalistic works. Some editions also enumerate the 613 commandments in the Torah. This compendium of Jewish literature was evidently intended to emphasize the indivisibility of the Written Law and the Oral Law.

*

*The Scriptural Readings

The Bible portions read on Shavuot present the historical origins and the laws pertaining to the festival. The selection on the first day deals with the revelation of the Ten Commandments; that for the second day is about the three pilgrimage festivals, read also on Passover and Sukkot. The same *maftir*, describing the Temple sacrifices on Shavuot, is read on both days. The *haftarah* of the first day describes Ezekiel's vision of heaven; that of the second day presents Habakkuk's prayer of faith in God's omnipotence.

The Book of Ruth is read on the second day (see the chapter "Shavuot in the Bible").

The scriptural readings for Shavuot are prescribed in the *Shulhan Arukh* as follows: Two Scrolls are removed [from the ark] and five men are called up [to the reading] from the first Scroll, commencing with "On the third new moon" to the end of the portion (Exodus 19.1–20.26). The *maftir* reads in the second [Scroll] from "On the day of the firstfruits" (Numbers 28.-26–31). He concludes with [the vision of] the chariot of Ezekiel and the verse, "Then a spirit lifted me up . . ." (Ezekiel 1.1–28, 3.12). On the second day [of Shavuot], "You shall consecrate to the Lord your God all male firstlings" until the end of the portion (Deuteronomy 15.19–16.17) is read. The *maftir* reads the same pentateuchal selection as on the first day. He concludes with Habakkuk from "But the Lord is in His holy temple" until "For the Leader. With my string music" (Habakkuk 2.20—3.19).[7]

The practice of having the entire congregation stand while the Decalogue is read provoked controversy. Some rabbis objected on the grounds that all portions of the Torah are of equal import; therefore no differentiation should be made. Now the rabbi is usually called up when the Ten Commandments are read, so that the congregation rises to honor him.[8]

*

*Floral Decorations

A beautiful Shavuot tradition is the adornment of the synagogue and the Jewish home with fragrant flowers, leaves, boughs, trees, and other floral decorations. Sundry reasons have been advanced for this practice. The *Shulhan Arukh* states, "It is a custom on Shavuot to spread grass in the synagogue and houses in remembrance of the joy of the giving of the Torah."[9] Also, the grass is a reminder that Mount Sinai was surrounded by green fields, for the Bible states that "neither the flocks and herds graze at the foot of this mountain" (Exodus 34.3); from this verse we learn that a pasture was there.[10]

The use of trees and branches serves to recall that, according to the Talmud, Shavuot is the day of judgment of fruit trees[11] and that we have an obligation to pray for them.[12] Elijah, the Vilna Gaon (1720–1797), opposed the use of trees on Shavuot since it became a practice among non-Jews to have trees on their festivals.[13] His interdiction was not generally accepted, for the use of floral decorations had become prevalent by the eighteenth century, and an established custom is considered as binding as a law.

This tradition was also related to Shavuot in the days of the Temple. The horns of the ox that was brought as a peace offering were wreathed with luxuriant olive leaves, and the baskets of firstfruits borne by the pilgrims to Jerusalem were also ornamented.[14]

Shavuot, being a harvest festival, is appropriate for the beautification of synagogues and homes with greenery and floral adornment. The practice also recalls that Moses was saved from drowning when his mother hid him for three months to escape Pharaoh's decree concerning newborn male children of the Hebrews; she put him in a wicker basket and placed it among the reeds by the bank of the Nile (Exodus 2.1–3). This occurred on the second day of Shavuot, for, according to tradition, Moses was born on the seventh day of Adar and three months later was the seventh of Sivan.

Roses were the most favorite among the flowers used on Shavuot. The verse "And the decree (*dat*) was proclaimed in Shushan" (Esther 8.14) was interpreted to mean that the Law was given with a rose (*shoshan*).[15]

A medieval book of customs asserts, "It is customary to scatter spices and roses on the synagogue floor for the enjoyment of the festival."[16]

The above-mentioned prohibition by Elijah, the Vilna Gaon, may account for the beautiful paper cutouts of flowers, variously called *shevuoslekh* (after the festival's name), *reizelekh,* or *shoshanta* (small roses), which were pasted on the windowpanes facing the streets. Among the intricate designs of these folk-art creations were patterns related to the Feast of Weeks and especially to roses and other blooms.

THE LITURGY OF SHAVUOT

The services for the three pilgrimage festivals—Passover, Shavuot, and Sukkot—generally follow the same structure as that of
the Sabbath liturgy, featuring the same basic elements. *Hallel*
(Psalms 113–118), the priestly benediction and *Yizkor,* the
memorial service for the deceased, are recited on Shavuot as on
the other festivals. Specific references are made to "this day of
the Feast of Weeks, the Season of the Giving of Our Law." Also
included are special *piyyutim* (liturgical hymns) pertinent to the
Feast of Weeks, particularly dealing with the revelation of the
Law on Mount Sinai. A selection of these hymns, some of which
are no longer chanted in many congregations, are given below.

*

*I Am, Thou Didst Proclaim
אנכי שמעת
SIMEON BEN ISAAC BEN ABUN

*Talmudist and poet, Simeon ben Isaac ben Abun lived in Mayence in
the tenth to eleventh centuries. This poem, recited on the first day of
Shavuot in the morning service, is a lyrical paraphrase of the Decalogue.*

Each verse begins with one or more words of the commandment it cites and ends with a passage from Proverbs 8.33—9.1.

I AM, Thou didst proclaim, and the assembly was stricken with awe. Accept My kingdom, and ye shall never fall into transgression. Hear instruction and be wise.

THOU SHALT NOT HAVE for thy hope any strange God, to corrupt thyself withal. Abate not nor annul aught of My worship.

THOU SHALT NOT TAKE to thy soul the wage of blasphemy. So shalt thou be delivered from sickness and sore disease. Happy is the man that hearkeneth unto Me.

REMEMBER AND OBSERVE the Sabbath day, and thou shalt find atonement and redemption therein, watching daily at My gates.

HONOR them that begat thee, and abide secure in My promise; for thou shalt prolong thy days and live to guard the portals of My gates.

THOU SHALT NOT MURDER the life that hath breath. So shall thy portion also be in life. For whoso findeth Me hath found life.

THOU SHALT NOT COMMIT ADULTERY, scorched with the flame of lust. He that shunneth her fires shall be filled with My delights; yea, he shall attain favor from the Lord.

THOU SHALT NOT STEAL from man the fruit of man's toil. It shall speed thine own labor to corruption. He that sinneth against Me wrongeth his own soul.

THOU SHALT NOT BEAR FALSE WITNESS, making crooked the path of righteousness. Whoso slandereth Me shall inherit the shadow of death; yea, all that hate Me love death.

THOU SHALT NOT COVET, scheming to add to thy store of treasures. Seek out prudence and bind her love about thee. Lo, wisdom hath builded her house.

Translated by Herbert M. Adler[1]

*

Loud Rang the Voice

תתו קול עז

ELEAZAR KALIR

A prolific liturgical poet in the Middle Ages, Eleazar Kalir bequeathed a rich legacy of hundreds of poems, many of which have been incorporated into Jewish liturgy. The following piyyut *is recited during the morning service of the first day of the Feast of Weeks.*

Loud rang the voice of God, and lightning spears
Pierced all the heavens; thunder shook the spheres,
And flames leaped forth; and all the angels blew
Their trumpets, and the earth was riven through.
Then all the peoples writhed, aghast and pale,
Like as a woman in her birth travail.
And lo, the mountains leaped and looked askance
On little Sinai, and began to dance,
Certain each one that it would be the place
Which God would choose to hallow and to grace.
Like calves did Lebanon and Siryon leap,
Bashan and Carmel like as frisking sheep;
Tabor, too, and each high hill; but He
Who dwells on high to all eternity
Looked not on them but on the humble mound,
And while that shame did all those hills confound,
To little Sinai bent the skies and came,
And crowned it with His mist and cloud; and flame
Of angels wreathed it. Then, amid the sound
Of thunder, under them that clustered round
Its foot gave forth His mighty voice; and they
Replied: O Lord, we hear and will obey,
And when they stood waiting, came the word,
That word that splits the rocks: I AM THE LORD.

Translated by Theodor H. Gaster[2]

*

*Before the Words of God Are Read
אקדמות מלין

MEIR BEN ISAAC NEHORAI

One of the best-known liturgical hymns is Akdamut Millin *("Introduction"), which is chanted to a traditional melody on the first day of Shavuot. Composed in Aramaic by Meir ben Isaac Nehorai, a cantor in Worms during the eleventh century, it is an acrostic of ninety lines. The initial letters of each line of the first half of the* piyyut *are in a dual alphabetical order. The acrostic of the second part spells out the author's name, followed by a benediction: "Meir son of Rabbi Isaac, may he grow in Torah and in good deeds. Amen. And be strong and of good courage." Each line ends with the syllable* ta, *the last and first letters of the Hebrew alphabet, symbolizing the continuous cycle of Torah study. On Simhat Torah the Pentateuch is concluded with a reading from Deuteronomy, and the Scroll is turned back immediately to begin anew with Genesis.*

Akdamut Millin *was originally sung as a prelude to the reading of the* Targum *(Aramaic translation) on the theophany at Mount Sinai, following the first verse (Exodus 19.1) of the scriptural reading. This accorded with the early practice of translating into Aramaic, once the lingua franca of the Jews, every few verses of the Torah reading. Later the hymn was chanted before the* kohen *begins the blessing in order not to interrupt the Torah reading.*

This piyyut *with its mystical aura is a paean to God for His creation and for His choosing the people of Israel. It also alludes to the clash between other nations and Israel, who preserve their faith inviolate despite persecutions and the allurements offered to them if they abandon it. It concludes with the promise of rich reward to the faithful in the world to come. This hymn may have been written during the Crusades to counteract the religious disputations which sought to convert Jews.*[3]

> Before the words of God Supreme
> Today are read, for this my theme
> Approbation will I seek
> These my sentences to speak;
>   Just two or three,
>   While tremblingly
> On Him I meditate:
>   The Pure, who doth bear

The world fore'er,
His power who can relate?

Were the sky of parchment made
A quill each reed, each twig and blade,
Could we with ink the oceans fill,
Were every man a scribe of skill,
　　The marvelous story
　　Of God's great glory
Would still remain untold;
　　For He, Most High,
　　The earth and sky
Created alone of old.

Without fatigue or weary hand,
He spoke the word, He breathed command;
The world and all that therein dwell,
Field and meadow, fen and fell,
　　Mount and sea,
　　In six days He
With life did them inspire;
　　The work when ended,
　　His glory ascended
Upon His throne of fire.

Before Him myriad angels flash,
To do His will they run and dash;
Each day new hosts gleam forth to praise
The Mighty One, Ancient of Days;
　　Six-wingèd hosts
　　Stand at their posts—
The flaming Seraphim—
　　In hushèd awe
　　Together draw
To chant their morning hymn.

The angels, together, without delay,
Call one to another in rapturous lay:
　　"Thrice holy He
　　Whose majesty
Fills earth from end to end."
　　The Cherubim soar,
　　Like the ocean's roar,
On celestial spheres ascend,

To gaze upon the Light on high,
Which, like the bow in cloudy sky,
Is iris-colored, silver-lined;
While hasting on their task assigned,

In every tongue
They utter song
And bless and praise the Lord,
Whose secret and source,
Whose light and force
Can ne'er be fully explored.

The heavenly hosts in awe reply:
"His kingdom be blessed fore'er and aye."
Their song being hushed, they vanish away;
They may ne'er again offer rapturous lay.
But Israel,
Therein excel—
Fixed times they set aside,
With praise and prayer,
Him one declare,
At morn and eventide.

His portion them He made, that they
His praise declare by night and day;
A Torah, precious more than gold,
He bade them study, fast to hold;
That He may be near,
Their prayer to hear,
For always wear will He
As diadem fair
His people's prayer
In His phylactery,

Wherein is told of Israel's fame
Who oft God's unity proclaim.
'Tis also meet God's praise to sing
In presence of both prince and king*
With tempestuous glee,
Like a stormy sea,
They surge and ask: "Who, then,
Is the friend of thy heart,
For whom thou art
Cast in the lions' den?

How fairer wilt thou be to sight,
If thou with us in faith unite;
Thy favor we shall always seek."
But Israel's sons with wisdom speak:
"O ye, who are wise
In your own eyes,
How can your trumpery

* This refers to the religious disputations of the Middle Ages.

At all compare
With our great share
When God proclaims us free,

And shines on us in glorious light,
While you are wrapped in gloom of night?"
His glory then will shine and gleam—
Almighty God, o'er all supreme!
His enemies,
On isles and seas,
Will suffering endure;
But He'll increase
Abundant peace
To upright men and pure.

Then perfect joy will bring our Lord,
The sacred vessels will be restored;
The exiles, He will gather them
Into rebuilt Jerusalem;
Day and night
Shall be His light
A canopy of splendor;
A crown of praise
His people will raise
To crown their Lord and Defender.

With brilliant clouds He'll ornament
Each deserving festive tent;
The pure, on stools with gold inlaid,
Before the Lord shall be arrayed;
Their countenance bright,
With sevenfold light,
Will dim heavenly sheen.
Such beauty rare
None can declare,
No prophet's eye has seen.

The joy and bliss of paradise
Have not been seen by human eyes;
There the pure rejoice and dance
In the light of His countenance;
And point: "Tis He,
We patiently
Have hoped and waited for,
To set us free
From captivity
And guide us as of yore."

You upright who heard the voice of my song,
May you merit to join this glorious throng;
In heavenly halls you shall meet them in time,
If you hearken His words, melodious, sublime.
Exalted on high,
Fore'er and aye,
Our Lord in glory and awe!
We are His choice,
Then let us rejoice
That He blessed us and gave us the Law.

Translated by Joseph Marcus[4]

⁎

⁎Introduction to Azharot

DAVID BEN ELEAZAR BEKUDA

Azharot (literally, warnings or admonitions) are liturgical hymns written by different authors for the Feast of Weeks that summarize the 613
commandments in the Torah. Such piyyutim are recited in some congregations on both days of the festival in the Musaf or Minhah services.
Azharot composed by Saadia Gaon (882–942) are divided into ten
groups, each related to one of the Ten Commandments, as the Decalogue
is said to embrace all of the 613 commandments. This has been construed
as an apologetic in reply to the Christian contention that the Ten Commandments are universal and that the other biblical laws were given to
the Jews as a punishment; hence, Christians recognize only the Decalogue
as binding on them. It is perhaps for this reason that the Ten Commandments are not included in the daily liturgy of the Jews.[5]

While Saadia's compilation of Azharot never gained general acceptance, those of Solomon ibn Gabirol (c. 1020–c. 1058) are still recited
in Sephardic congregations. His composition enumerated the 613 commandments, dividing them into two parts: 248 positive precepts recited
on the first day of Shavuot, and 365 prohibitions read on the second day.

Due to the complexity of the Azharot, introductions to them and
commentaries on them were written by Jewish poets and scholars. A
twelfth-century poet, David ben Eleazar Bekuda, wrote the following
introduction to ibn Gabirol's Azharot.

Verily is this the day on which Israel inherited the Torah
through Moses the seer, the man of God. Praise is befitting Thee,

who didst stretch forth the heavens and established the earth, O God. On Thy day of revelation when Thou didst teach Thy Law supreme, then wast Thou manifested. . . . Thy people saved from Egypt heard Thy divine word and trembled in dread before their God. Great is counsel; Thou gavest wondrous guidance to Thy people who found grace in Thine eyes. Thou didst come to them to give them the awesome heritage of the Torah, precious, beautiful, and perfect. . . .

In the ears of our multitudes Thou didst speak on Sinai—(I)I am the Lord, and (II)there is no other god. Reject estranging idol and cast it away; can man make for himself a god? (III) Dare not take in vain the name of God, for great above all gods is God. (IV)Lovingly speed to honor the Sabbath, the day of creation's perfecting and rest by God. (V)Give joy to parents with earth's best delights; so lengthen thy days before God. (VI)Cast out those who shed blood, enter not in their counsel, for man is created in the image of God. (VII)Keep far from adultery and (VIII)thieving practice, lest in retribution thou be sought out by God. (IX)Bear no false witness in quarrels, for this is one of the six things hated by God. (X)Thy brother's possessions thou shalt not covet; yea, desire not aught that is given him by God.

On hearing these words the people quaked; stricken with awe, they proclaimed the work of God. Then spoke they willingly and truly, "We shall hear and we shall do all the commands of God." Ye masses of Israel rejoice in His Law; go forward in gladness and see the work of your God. And Thou living Redeemer, uphold our hands and hasten for us Thy salvation, O God.

Translated by David de Sola Pool[6]

*

Precepts He Gave His Folk

אז שש מאות

ELIJAH BEN MENAHEM HA-ZAKEN

Elijah ben Menahem ha-Zaken was an eleventh-century liturgical poet of France who composed Azharot, *an alphabetical poem of 176 four-line strophes on the 613 commandments of the Torah that is recited on Shavuot in some communities. He also wrote the following hymn, which is chanted by the reader when he repeats the* **Musaf Amidah.**

Precepts He gave His folk, yea, thirteen more than six hundred,
Penalties fixed for breach, with rewards for rightful observance;
Pure are His words as gold or silver's seventh refining,
Hence, the beloved have kept, and they He carried have searched them,
Guarded with all their heart, explained and taught them with wisdom.
Then shall our stronghold, God, remember us in His mercy,
Gladly accept our service, gladly grant our petition.
Jubilant rang God's heights, with joy earth's depths were resounding.
Angels and men as one acclaimed the gift of the Torah.
When upon Sinai's mount that scriptured Scroll was delivered.
Like to a bride whose face appears exultant and shining,
Israel glowed that day, God's Ten Commandments receiving.

Translated by Israel Zangwill[7]

*

Thine Own Sweet Words

אם לא אמריך

SIMEON BEN ISAAC BEN ABUN

This hymn, chanted in the morning service on the second day of Shavuot, is an interpretation of the theophany on Mount Sinai.

Save that Thou wouldst Thine own sweet words unfold,
    Thou hadst not formed the earth's and heaven's ways,
Giving the least of peoples these to hold
    For love of them and memory of days
        And promises of old.

And sorely didst Thou long for them, to see
    Thy sons grow perfect, giving all their heart
And knowledge to Thy statutes, rising free

To render speech with saints of Thine apart,
And keep their troth with Thee.

When erst Thou gavest them Thy laws to hear,
They stood as one, made whole, and as the day
Beheld the secret of the angels clear
From holy heights, and cried: "We will obey,"
Before they said: "We hear."

Then spakest Thou: "O that for all their days
Their heart were so to fear Me evermore
And find their welfare, walking in My ways.
O that My people hearkened as of yore,
Blameless and full of praise!

"Soon should their haters from their face be cast!
Soon would I turn Mine hand upon their foe!
Israel would be saved of God at last,
Redeemed forever from the shame and woe
And stain of all the past."

But Thou, O Lord, the perfect Rock of old,
Still lead them by the shining of Thy face
For all time, and again for them unfold
The portals of Thy word through wisdom's grace.
Make pure their lives; let them through years untold,
Though high above the highest be Thy place,
Thee in their midst behold.

Translated by Nina Davis Salaman[8]

*

*The Myriad Angels' Songs

יציב פתגם

JACOB BEN MEIR

This Aramaic invocation on behalf of Israel is chanted on the second day of Shavuot, after reading the first verse of the haftarah. *It is written in the style of an acrostic which reveals the author's name—Jacob ben Meir Levi. It is generally assumed that he was the famous scholar and poet known as Rabbenu Tam ("Our Perfect Master") of Troyes (1100–1171).[9]*

The myriad angels' songs of praise
On high have loudly pealed;

On earth I too am glorying
God's Law this day revealed.
A stream of flame goes forth from Him
Toward the watery flood.
    A light shines on a mount of snow
    With flames as red as blood.
Creator He, He sees through dark.
He is the source of light;
    He sees afar with nought to bar;
    To Him the dark shines bright.
Approval for my song I ask
Of Him, and of those versed
    In books derived from Scripture's text
    And codes from last to first.
Guard Thou, O ever-living King,
Thy people seeking Thee;
    Make them to be as dust of earth,
    And as the sand of sea.
Yea, may their valleys shine with flocks,
Their presses flow with wine,
    And grant their prayer, and make their face
    As radiant sun to shine.
Let me be strong. Weak must they be
Whose life by Thee is blamed.
    May they be dumb as inmost stone,
    May they be ever shamed,
For Moses, meekest of all men,
Gave us Thy Torah famed.

               Translated by David de Sola Pool[10]

*

Marriage Certificate for Shavuot
כתובה לשבועות

ISRAEL NAJARA

In many Sephardic congregations, prior to the Torah reading on the first day of Shavuot a ketubah le-Shavuot *(marriage certificate for Shavuot) is read, as a symbolic betrothal of God and His people Israel. There are various versions of such* piyyutim, *nearly all similar in terminology to the traditional* tenaim *(premarital document specifying the conditions agreed upon between the two parties) or the* ketubah *(certificate the bridegroom presents to the bride at the wedding ceremony). These are hymns based on the verses: "I will betroth thee unto Me for ever; yea, I will betroth thee unto Me in righteousness, and in justice, and in lovingkindness, and in compassion. And I will betroth thee unto Me in faithfulness; and thou shalt know the Lord" (Hosea 2.21–22) and "I will make a new covenant with the house of Israel" (Jeremiah 31.31).*

Some texts describe the marriage as being solemnized symbolically between the Torah—the bride—and the people of Israel—the bridegroom. In these versions, God as the bride's father gives as dowry the 613 commandments, the Bible, Talmud, and other sacred writings. Moses presents as dowry to his son—the people of Israel—the prayer shawl and phylacteries, the Sabbath and festivals. The contracts are witnessed by God and His servant Moses.

In other versions the "Prince of princes and the Ruler of rulers" presents the Torah to the bride as dowry and in His love He gives her the Oral Law as an added portion. The bride responds affectionately, "We shall do and we shall hearken." The contract is dated the sixth day of the month Sivan in the year 2448 from the creation, which is traditionally the day on which the Torah was given. The Mishnah[11] comments that the wedding day of King Solomon (Song of Songs 3.11) refers to the day of the giving of the Torah. The heavens and the earth witness the marriage certificate.

The most widely used text of a ketubah le-Shavuot *is that of the prolific Safed mystic and poet Israel Najara (c. 1550–c. 1625). Many of his* piyyutim *are found in the liturgy of oriental Jews. A partial translation of his hymn, included in the Sephardic prayer book for Shavuot, follows.*

Friday, the sixth of Sivan, the day appointed by the Lord for the revelation of the Torah to His beloved people. . . . The Invisible One came forth from Sinai, shone from Seir and appeared from Mount Paran unto all the kings of the earth, in the year 2448 since the creation of the world, the era by which we are accustomed to reckon in this land whose foundations were upheld by God, as it is written: "For He hath founded it upon the seas and established it upon the floods" (Psalms 24.2). The Bridegroom [God], Ruler of rulers, Prince of princes, Distinguished among the select, Whose mouth is pleasing and all of Whom is delightful, said unto the pious, lovely and virtuous maiden [the people of Israel] who won His favor above all women, who is beautiful as the moon, radiant as the sun, awesome as bannered hosts: Many days wilt thou be Mine and I will be thy Redeemer. Behold, I have sent thee golden precepts through the lawgiver Jekuthiel [Moses]. Be thou My mate according to the law of Moses and Israel, and I will honor, support, and maintain thee and be thy shelter and refuge in everlasting mercy. And I will set aside for thee, in lieu of thy virginal faithfulness, the life-giving Torah by which thou and thy children will live in health and tranquility. This bride [Israel] consented and became His spouse. Thus an eternal covenant, binding them forever, was established between them. The Bridegroom then agreed to add to the above all future expositions of Scripture, including *Sifra, Sifre, Aggadah,* and *Tosefta.* He established the primacy of the 248 positive commandments which are incumbent upon all . . . and added to them the 365 negative commandments. The dowry that this bride brought from the house of her father consists of an understanding heart that understands, ears that hearken, and eyes that see. Thus the sum total of the contract and the dowry, with the addition of the positive and negative commandments, amounts to the following: "Revere God and observe His commandments; this applies to all mankind" (Ecclesiastes 12.13). The Bridegroom, desiring to confer privileges upon His people Israel and to transmit these valuable assets to them, took upon Himself the responsibility of this marriage contract, to be paid from the best portions of His property. . . .

All these conditions are valid and established forever and ever. The Bridegroom has given His oath to carry them out in favor of His people and to enable those that love Him to inherit substance. Thus the Lord has given His oath. The Bridegroom has followed the legal formality of symbolic delivery of this document, which is bigger than the earth and broader than the seas. Everything, then, is firm, clear, and established. . . .

I invoke heaven and earth as reliable witnesses.

May the Bridegroom rejoice with the bride whom He has taken as His lot and may the bride rejoice with the Husband of her youth while uttering words of praise.

Translated by Solomon Feffer

SHAVUOT IN MODERN PROSE

*
Revelation Eternal

A. ALAN STEINBACH

rabbi, poet, author, editor of Jewish Book Annual *and of* Jewish Bookland

Mount Sinai! It is relatively small when measured in terms of feet. But measured by spiritual criteria, its dimensions can be computed only through capital letters: MOUNT SINAI.

There, on the sixth day of the third month, Sivan, God delineated His architectural design for divine revelation. Because this event was significant not only to the assembled Israelites but also to subsequent generations, rabbis in the midrash indulged in the poetic fancy: "Each word uttered by God split into the seventy languages in the world" (Exodus Rabbah 5.9).

Moses ascended the mountain, while "all the people perceived the thunderings and the lightnings, and the voice of the horn, and the mountain smoking." The Bible tells us: "Moses *went up* to God." But this was only prelude. The formula needed completion: "And the Lord *came down* upon Mount Sinai." Through this mutual confrontation between man and God, between the finite and the Infinite, between human seeker and Eternal Perfection, the grand exordium of His Torah was communicated to Israel, and through Israel to the whole human race.

This initial Sinaitic revelation became the archetype for eternal, unceasing revelation. Man striving to scale his steep inner mountain ranges in an attempt to reach the loftiest peak of his spiritual self, will always find God descending to meet him. Isaiah epitomized this dichotomous pilgrimage—man upreaching for God, God downreaching for man. It is a majestic concept: "Thou shalt call and the Eternal will answer; thou shalt cry out and He will say, 'Here I am' " (Isaiah 58.9).

We reaffirm this divine charge on Shavuot. Nothing can transcend the adventure of climbing the Mount Sinai within us, knowing God will meet us if we climb high enough![1]

*

The Idea of Revelation

ABRAHAM JOSHUA HESCHEL

professor of Jewish ethics and mysticism at The Jewish Theological Seminary of America, author of books on theology and philosophy; he played a major role in the American religious scene (1907–1972)

We have never been the same since the day on which the voice of God overwhelmed us at Sinai. It is forever impossible for us to retreat into an age that predates the Sinaitic event. Something unprecedented happened. God revealed His name to us, and we are named after Him. "And all the peoples of the earth shall see that the Lord's name is proclaimed over you" (Deuteronomy 28.10). There are two Hebrew names for Jew: *Yehudi,* the first three letters of which are the first three letters of the Ineffable Name, and *Israel,* the end of which, *el,* means God in Hebrew.

If other religions may be characterized as a relation between man and God, Judaism must be described as a relation between *man with Torah* and *God.* The Jew is never alone in the face of God; the Torah is always with him. A Jew without the Torah is obsolete.

The Torah is not the wisdom but the destiny of Israel, not our literature but our essence. It is said to have come into being

7. Mount Sinai and the tablets. Torah ark curtain. Gold and silver
appliqué on violet silk. Embroidered by Simhah,
wife of Menahem Levi Meshulam. Italy. 1681. See Chapter 8.

neither by way of speculation nor by way of poetic inspiration, but by way of prophecy or revelation.

It is easy to say prophecy, revelation. But do we sense what we say? Do we understand what these words mean? Do we refer to a certainty or a fantasy, an idea or a fact, a myth or a mystery when we speak of prophecy or revelation? Did it ever happen that God disclosed His will to some men for the benefit of all men? . . .

The realization of the dangerous greatness of man, of his immense power and ability to destroy all life on earth, must completely change our conception of man's place and role in the divine scheme. If this great world of ours is not a trifle in the eyes of God, if the Creator is at all concerned with His creation, then man—who has the power to devise both culture and crime, but who is also able to be a proxy for divine justice—is important enough to be the recipient of spiritual light at the rare dawns of his history.

Unless history is a vagary of nonsense, there must be a counterpart to the immense power of man to destroy, there must be a voice that says NO to man, a voice not vague, faint and inward, like qualms of conscience, but equal in spiritual might to man's power to destroy.

The voice speaks to the spirit of prophetic men in singular moments of their lives and cries to the masses through the horror of history. The prophets respond, the masses despair.

The Bible, speaking in the name of a Being that combines justice with omnipotence, is the never-ceasing outcry of "No" to humanity. In the midst of our applauding the feats of civilization, the Bible flings itself like a knife slashing our complacency, reminding us that God, too, has a voice in history. Only those who are satisfied with the state of affairs or those who choose the easy path of escaping from society, rather than staying within it and keeping themselves clean of the mud of specious glories, will resent its attack on human independence. . . .

We must not try to read chapters in the Bible dealing with the event at Sinai as if they were texts in systematic theology. Its intention is to celebrate the mystery, to introduce us to it rather than to penetrate or to explain it. As a report about revelation the Bible itself is a midrash. . . .

For us, therefore, to imagine revelation, namely, to conceive it as if it were a psychic or physical process, is to pervert its essence and to wreck its mystery. It is just as improper to conceive revelation as a psychophysical act as it is to conceive God as a corporeal being. Few of us are able to think in a way which is never crossed by the path of imagination, and it is usually at the crossroads of thought and imagination that the great sweep of the spirit swerves into the blind alley of a parabolic image.

A Hasid, it is told, after listening to the discourse of one who lectured to him about the lofty concept of God according to the philosophers, said: "If God were the way you imagine Him, I would not believe in Him." However subtle and noble our concepts may be, as soon as they become descriptive, namely, definite, they confine Him and force Him into the triteness of our minds. Never is our mind so inadequate as in trying to describe God. The same applies to the idea of revelation. When defined, described, it completely eludes us. . . .

The dogmatic theologian who tries to understand the act of revelation in terms of his own generalizations takes himself too seriously and is guilty of oversimplification. Revelation is a mystery for which reason has no concepts. To ignore its mysterious nature is an oversight of fatal consequence. Out of the darkness came the Voice to Moses; and out of the darkness comes the word to us. The issue is baffling.

And if you ask: what was it like when the people stood at Sinai, hearing God's voice? the answer will be: Like no other event in the history of man. There are countless legends, myths, reports, but none of them tell of a whole people witnessing an event such as Sinai.[2]

*

*The Oral Tradition

SAMSON RAPHAEL HIRSCH

rabbi, statesman, philosopher, and leader of Orthodox Jewry in Germany (1808–1888) whose influence still exercises a significant impact

There is no symbol for the Torah for the same reason that there is no symbol for God: the Torah is one and unique like

God its Creator. It has nothing in common with other laws, teachings, systems, and institutions. It is so unique that it can be compared only to itself, it is something sui generis; as soon as you describe it by name and terms taken from other spheres you falsify the essence of the Torah and bar the way to its real understanding. . . .

The celebration in remembrance of the Torah, this soul of our soul, our highest good on which is based our whole existence, and without which all the precious things to which the other festivals are consecrated—freedom and soil, preservation and prosperity, purity and atonement—would lose their essence and meaning, only this celebration in remembrance of the Torah is not mentioned at all, no reference to it is made in the written word of God; it is only to the oral tradition that we owe the Festival of the Revelation of the Written Torah, and thus the first memorial of the Written Law directs us to the Oral Law, to tradition. How eloquent is this silence of the Torah concerning its own festival! The Written Law abandons itself if we deny the Oral Law; the Written Law renounces its own existence unless it is preceded by the Oral Law; the Written Law commits the very knowledge of its celebration to the living tradition of the word of mouth handed down from God. Thus the Written Law seeks to be celebrated only in a company of men who are permeated by the living breath of the Oral Law, which is divine like the written word; and in this way the Written Law itself makes it clear that its very being depends on the existence of the Oral Law. This is the second thought which the silence of the Torah with regard to the Season of the Giving of Our Torah teaches us. And indeed it is not the Oral Law which has to seek the guarantee of its authenticity in the Written Torah; on the contrary, it is the Written Law which has to look for its warrant in the oral tradition.

When we raise aloft this Torah, the revelation of which we celebrate on Shavuot, we jubilantly proclaim that it is still the same Torah which Moses brought to Israel "through the mouth of God, through the hand of Moses"—the same Torah, pure and unadulterated. When we live and die in the conviction that this precious heritage has been preserved pure and genuine amid all the tempests and vicissitudes of a history of more than three thousand years, or when we rely for the earthly welfare and heavenly salvation of ourselves and our children on the truth of this Torah, what guarantee have we for all this other than the tradition of our fathers? Yea, the selfsame fathers who, together with the Written Torah, handed down to us the Oral Law also? If our fathers have deceived us with the one, how could they be trustworthy with the other? Indeed, there is no evidence or guarantee for the truth and reality of a historic fact save our trust in tradition. All sorts of documents and monuments, all kinds of internal and external circumstances may lead you to the conclusion that it is probable or almost certain that such and such an event did really happen; but who tells you that what you consider probable or even certain has really happened? Or that the very documents from which you draw your conclusions are not in reality forged? What other assurance have you that the conclusions you draw are a safe enough basis both for your present and future course of action, if not your trust in the genuineness of tradition? The fact remains, however, that Jewish tradition—a phenomenon unique in its kind—refers us back to itself only; and that it refuses any documentation by the Written Torah which, after all, *is only handed down by that oral tradition* and presupposes it everywhere. This in itself is the most trustworthy sign of its truth—more trustworthy than any document with seven seals could possibly be. The fact is that Holy Writ contains no direct documentary evidence of this truth of the oral tradition. And yet, a whole nation has joyfully committed the preservation of its existence during more than three thousand years to the authority of this oral tradition. This shows in the most striking manner how deeply convinced all these generations were of the truth of this tradition; how sure our forebears were of the veracity of what had been handed down to them by their own fathers and would one day be passed on to the children—a truth which they themselves had sealed with their life and death. So completely assured was the people of the faithful transmission of this tradition that it required no other legitimation. . . .

If the Torah has been able to preserve our national life for more than three thousand years; if it could compensate our people for the lack of everything that to others makes life beautiful, noble, and happy; if it bestowed upon our nation clarity of mind, purity of morals, gentleness of heart, unequaled family life, a unique spirit of charity, along with an enthusiasm for all that is humane, pure, good, and noble—and, at the same time, with a courage, endurance, steadfastness, and self-sacrificing spirit that are recognized and envied by our enemies; if you praise the Torah on the festival of Shavuot for all these blessings, verily—do not deceive yourselves—it is the part of the Torah entrusted to oral tradition, to which we owe it all. . . .

That is why the Written Law needs to be brought into actual life by oral tradition only; that is why the Written Law announces itself as dependent on the Oral Law only, and that is why the commemoration of the revelation of the Written Law as celebrated by Shavuot was entrusted only to the Oral Law.

But why then is this celebration itself on so small a scale, so quiet, and restricted in the Torah to the fleeting span of but a single day? And on that day itself the celebration is marked by scarcely one positive symbol, and is expressed merely in a negative way—by abstaining from doing any work! . . .

From the very beginning it should clearly be conveyed to us that the Torah, the quintessence of all that is good and precious, is not satisfied that we devote a festival—be it a day, a week, or even a month—to it. The Torah demands of us the dedication of every hour and every moment throughout the year. . . . Because it is not the week or the month but the whole year that belongs to the Torah, and this is so because the Torah does not demand a symbol only, but life and conduct.

Translated by Isidor Grunfeld[3]

*

The Covenant at Mount Sinai

DAVID POLISH

rabbi, author, and lecturer; past president of the Central Conference of American Rabbis

Our tradition teaches us that thousands of years ago Israel entered into covenant with God at Mount Sinai. This covenant, we are told, bound the children of Israel and their descendants forever to this special relationship with God. It was a relationship in which He would be their God and they His people; in which they were to be a special kind of community, "a kingdom of priests and a holy people"; in which they committed themselves to be under the divine mandate in perpetuity. That is how the Torah describes the convenant and its meaning.

This does not necessarily mean that Israel lived in accordance with the covenant. It often violated it. It often came close to annihilating it. Yet it was always mindful of the covenant and felt subject to its authority. Even in its trespass, Israel knew that it could not be Israel without the special claim of this special relationship. From the time of Sinai, generations of Jews planted this central doctrine in the consciousness of their children; planted it with a persistence and urgency that made it part of the very psychic process of the Jew's response to his world and to his history. The event at Sinai and its consequences were the stimuli by which the Jew responded to his entire life situation. The inculcation of this awareness, this shaping of the Jewish spirit, was a continuous process for thousands of years. Thus it became part of the individual and the collective spiritual equipment of Jews. Members of closely united groups do have a common spiritual response to the central elements of their tradition. The shared faith and aspirations which are the inheritance of a society manifest themselves in critical times. . . .

Even when the religious discipline of the society has been weakened for a time, the accumulated force of the past will assert itself and stir the group and its members. The religious situation in the Soviet Union gives a striking example. Nowhere in history has religion been so systematically and effectively exorcised, not only from society but from the lives of people. Yet without any apparent outer motivation, large numbers of people still gravitate as by a common urge to their places of worship. The dynamic factor of the inner life which makes a group one being, represents the accumulated spiritual power of ages. This does not die easily.

Thus with the covenant. It is the product of a millennial cultivation of the consciousness of the Jew and of the Jewish community, and it succeeded in welding the entire community into a single spiritual organism, responding to its call. Even when individual Jews or the group did not respond adequately, this too was a response, because they were aware that there existed a reality they recognized by rejecting.

So powerful was this accumulated inheritance of the past that today, when it is manifestly much weaker and many Jews have cast it off, it still operates. It operates not only among those to whom it is still valid—in one form or another—but, more significantly, among many who believed that they had liberated themselves from it. The emancipation often proves to be more illusory than the rejected covenant. The covenant forces its way back into the lives of those who feel that they have shaken it off. They discover that it has been transmitted to them and, though dormant, has dwelt within them, to be aroused in a time of personal or group crisis. Hundreds of thousands of Jews discovered during and after World War II that the demands of the covenant pressed upward into their awareness from the hidden, unknown depths of their beings. It was Sinai at work.[4]

*

✸ *"Out of the Midst of the Fire"*

A H A D   H A - A M

pseudonym, meaning "one of the people," of Asher Ginzberg (1856–1927), essayist and philosopher who was the leading exponent of the establishment of a Jewish national spiritual center in Palestine

A people trained for generations in the house of bondage cannot cast off in an instant the effects of that training and become truly free, even when the chains have been struck off.

But the prophet believes in the power of his ideal. He is convinced that the ideal which he is destined to give to his people will have sufficient force to expel the taint of slavery, and to imbue this slave people with a new spirit of strength and upward striving, equal to all the demands of its lofty mission.

Then the prophet gathers his people at the foot of the mountain, opens the innermost heavens before them, and shows them the God of their fathers in a new form, in all His universal grandeur.

"For all the earth is Mine," so speaks the voice of the God of Israel "out of the midst of the fire." Hitherto you have believed, in common with all other nations, that every people and every country has its own god, all-powerful within his boundaries, and that these gods wage war on one another and conquer one another, like the nations that serve them. But it is not so. There is no such thing as a God of Israel and a different God of Egypt; there is one God, who was, is, and shall be: He is Lord of *all* the earth, and Ruler over *all* the nations. And it is this universal God who is the God of your fathers. The whole world is His handiwork, and all men are created in His image; but you, the children of His chosen Abraham, He has singled out to be His peculiar people, to be "a kingdom of priests and an holy nation," to sanctify His name in the world and to be an example to mankind in your individual and in your corporate life, which are to be based on new foundations, on the spirit of truth and righteousness.

"Justice, justice shall you pursue." "Keep far from a false charge." "Do not side with the mighty to do wrong." "You shall not wrong a stranger." "You shall not mistreat any widow or orphan." But neither shall you wrest justice on the side of the weak: "nor must you show deference to a poor man in his dispute." The guiding rule of your lives shall be neither hatred and jealousy, nor yet love and pity, for all alike pervert the view and bias the judgment. "Justice, justice"—that alone shall be your rule.

Did ever people hear the voice of God speaking "out of the midst of the fire" such lofty and majestic words? And the nation that has heard this message, though it may have been sunk for centuries in the morass of slavery and degradation, how can it fail to rise out of the depths and feel in its innermost soul the purifying light that streams in upon it?

So thinks the prophet; and the people confirm his belief as they cry ecstatically, with one voice, "All that the Lord hath spoken we will do."

Translated by Leon Simon[5]

*

The Source of Jewish Power

LUDWIG LEWISOHN

leading figure in American letters as novelist, essayist, and literary critic (1882–1955); professor of comparative literature at Brandeis University

The Jewish people made its historic appearance in quite a normal fashion. Yet the pattern of its history is violently abnormal. It never flourished greatly in terms of power. It knew defeat and desperate catastrophe over and over again. Yet from each historic grave it re-arose; it survived; it lived to reaffirm its changeless character and historic function.

What was the source within history of that power of survival and renewal which has taken place from age to age down to that birth of the state of Israel from the ashes of the six million martyrs, an event within the memory of the youngest Jew now living and seeking to interpret his destiny and its meaning? So far as human insight extends, the source of that perpetual life and perpetual power of rebirth must be, cannot but be, in that transcendent experience at the foot of Sinai which welded a group of rude clans and fugitives from oppression into a people whose fundamental character was stamped and molded then.

Petulant men with minds frozen thirty years ago will call this explanation "mystical" in the illiterate usage of that word as anything beyond the grasp of the most mechanical and empty understanding. Mature and unbiased reflection will show that this explanation and this alone, precisely this, like any respectable hypothesis in the sciences, serves to account for the historic phenomena which no one denies. This hypothesis alone *works*. It alone explains the character, the history, the ever-recurrent fate of the Jewish people.[6]

*

* *Why I Choose to Be a Jew*

ARTHUR A. COHEN

novelist, essayist, and theologian; author of books and articles on Jewish religious thought

Until the present day the Jew could not *choose* to be a Jew —history forced him to accept what his birth had already defined. . . .

Given the freedom to choose I have decided to embrace Judaism. I have not done so out of loyalty to the Jewish people or the Jewish state. My choice was religious. I chose to believe in the God of Abraham, Isaac, and Jacob; to acknowledge the Law of Moses as the word of God; to accept the people of Israel as the holy instrument of divine fulfillment; to await the coming of the Messiah and the redemption of history. . . .

First, I chose to believe in the God of Abraham, Isaac, and Jacob. This is to affirm the reality of a God who acts in history and addresses man. Although this God may well be the same as the abstract gods formulated by philosophers, He is still more than these— He is the God who commanded Abraham to quit the land of the Chaldeans and who wrestled with Jacob throughout the night.

The philosopher and the believer must differ in their method. The philosopher begins by examining that portion of reality to which reason allows him access. The believer, however, must at some point move beyond the limits which reason has defined. He may rightly contend that reason points beyond itself, that the rational is real, but that much in human life—evil, suffering, guilt, and love—is terrifyingly real without ever being rationally comprehensible.

Reason may thus push a man to belief, and it is inaccurate to speak of the believer as though he had deserted or betrayed reason. Informed belief demands philosophic criticism and refinement. The believer is bound to uphold his faith in things he cannot see or verify; but he is foolish if he does not try to define what that belief is and clarify the unique ways in which it makes reality meaningful for him.

For me, then, to believe in the biblical God, the God of the patriarchs, the smoking mountain, the burning bush, was not to surrender reason, but to go beyond it. More than accepting the literal word of the Bible, it meant believing in the Lord of history —the God who creates and unfolds history, and observes its tragic rifts and displacements—from the tower of Babel to the cold war; who, in His disgust, once destroyed the world with flood and later repented His anger; who, forgoing anger, gave the world counsels of revelation, commencing with the gift of Torah to Moses, and continuing through the inspired writings of the ancient rabbis; and who finally—through His involvement with the work of creation—prepares it for redemption.

It may seem difficult—indeed, for many years it was—to consider the Bible, which is the source of this belief, as more than the unreliable account of an obscure Semitic tribe. But gradually I came to discover in it an authentic statement of the grandeur and misery of man's daily existence—a statement which I could accept only if I believed in a God who could be addressed as "Lord, Lord."

My second belief is an acknowledgment that *the Law of Moses is the word of God.* The Bible tells us that the word of God broke out over the six hundred thousand Hebrews who assembled at the foot of Sinai. That word was heard by Moses—he who had been appointed to approach and receive. The word became human—in its humanity, it undoubtedly suffers from the limitation of our understanding—but it lost none of its divinity.

The Law is always a paradox: it is both the free word of God and the frozen formality of human laws. But the Law of Moses was vastly different from what we usually understand law to be. It is true that in the days before the Temple was destroyed by Titus in 70 C.E. divine law was the enforceable law of the judge and the court; but later the great rabbis who interpreted it conceived of the revelation of God to Israel, not as law in its common usage, but as Torah—teaching. . . . Broadly conceived, Torah refers to *any* teaching which brings man closer to the true God, who is the God of Israel and the Lord of history.

Torah has two aspects—the actual way of law and observance (the *halakhah,* as it is called in Hebrew) and the theology of the rabbis which interprets that way (called the *aggadah*). By means of both, according to Jewish tradition, God proposes to lead *all* of His creation to fulfillment, to perfect its imperfections, to mend the brokenness of His creatures. The Jewish people—the guardian of the *halakhah* and the *aggadah*—has been elected to be pedagogue to all the nations of the world, to become on its behalf "a kingdom of priests and a holy people."

Jews can achieve holiness—the primary objective, I believe, of their religion—neither by prayer nor meditation alone. Judaism values prayer only in conjunction with the act; it praises study only in relation to life. . . .

The third of my beliefs is, as I have indicated, simply an element of God's revelation in Torah—that *the Jewish people have been chosen as a special instrument of God.*

The Jews did not request the attentions of God. There is significant truth—truth, moreover, which the rabbis of the Talmud endorse—in the popular couplet: "How odd of God to choose the Jews." Odd, and unsolicited. The ancient rabbis disclaim particular merit. If anyone possessed merit, they repeat, it was not the generation that fled Egypt and braved the wilderness for forty years, but the generations of the biblical patriarchs—Abraham, Isaac, and Jacob. They had no organizer such as Moses, or strength of numbers, or the miracles of the well, manna, and quail. They made a covenant with God on sheer trust. The generation of Sinai was *compelled* to become the people of God or perish. A God of history grows impatient with delay. The God of Israel was profoundly impatient on Sinai.

This tradition of election should not be confused with racial pride or an attitude of arrogant exclusion toward others. The Jew believes neither that the truth flows in his blood nor that the gentile cannot come to possess it. Judaism is exclusive only in the sense that we affirm we possess important truth which is available to all—everyone can join but only on our terms.

The election of Israel is not a conclusion drawn from history—the survival and endurance of the Jews through twenty centuries of destructive persecution could be no more than blind accident. At best it could be construed as a compliment to the resiliency and stubbornness of the Jewish people. Judaism has insisted, however—not as a declaration after the fact, but as a principle of its very existence—that it is both a holy nation chosen by God to be His own and a suffering nation destined to endure martyrdom for His sake. God announces not only that "you shall be holy to me, for I the Lord am holy, and I have set

you apart from other peoples to be mine" (Leviticus 20.26) but
that "you only have I known of all the families of the earth;
therefore I will visit upon you all your iniquities" (Amos 3.2).

Israel is thus called not only to be the example to the nations,
but, being the example, is tried all the more sorely for its transgressions. To be sure, this is not a doctrine for the uncourageous.
No one even slightly familiar with the agonies of Jewish history
could claim that the election of Israel has brought with it particular reward and security. It is, however, precisely the fact of
Jewish suffering which makes its election and mission all the
more pertinent to the modern world. To have believed and
survived in spite of history is perhaps the only evidence which
Judaism can offer to the accuracy of its conviction that it is called
to be a holy community.[7]

*

* The Supreme Influence of the Decalogue

JOSEPH H. HERTZ

*chief rabbi of the United Hebrew Congregations of the British Common-
wealth of Nations, biblical and liturgical commentator and editor of* A
Book of Jewish Thoughts *(1872–1946)*

The solemn reading of the Ten Commandments in the synagogue constitutes the central part of the Shavuot service. No
religious document has exercised a greater influence on the
moral and social life of man than the divine summary of human
duty known as the Ten Commandments, or the Decalogue.
While not presenting the whole duty of man, these brief commands—only 120 Hebrew words in all—lay down in simple,
unforgettable form the *foundations* of religion and of right for all
time and for all men.

The basic importance of the Ten Commandments was ever
recognized in Israel. Their eternal and universal significance
were duly emphasized by means of parable, metaphor, and all the
rare poetic imagery of rabbinic legend. The tablets on which the
Ten Commandments were written were held to have been pre-

pared at the eve of creation—thus antedating humanity, and, therefore, independent of time or place or racial culture; and they were hewn from the sapphire Throne of Glory—and thus of infinite worth and preciousness. The revelation at Sinai, it was taught, was given in desert territory, which belongs to no one nation exclusively; and it was heard not by Israel alone, but by the inhabitants of all the earth. The divine Voice divided itself into the seventy tongues then spoken on earth, so that all the children of men might understand its world-embracing and man-redeeming message. The sixth of Sivan, the day of the revelation at Mount Sinai, was held to be as momentous as the day of creation itself; for, without the coming into existence of moral law, the creation of the material universe would have been incomplete, nay, meaningless.

It is interesting to note that for many ages the Decalogue was given equal preeminence in religion outside the synagogue. Luther summed up the opinion of Western Christendom for over 1,500 years when he declared: "Never will there be found a precept preferable or comparable to these commands." In succeeding centuries the humanists, the deists, and even the free-thinkers spoke with reverence of the Law of Sinai. Two generations ago Renan wrote: "The unique distinction which awaited this page of Exodus, namely, to become the code of universal ethics, was not unmerited. The Ten Words are for all peoples; and they will be, during all centuries, the commandments of God." And historians of civilization are generally agreed that, low as the ethical standards of the world at present undoubtedly are, it is certain that they would be even lower but for the supreme influence of the Ten Commandments.[8]

*

The Uniqueness of the Ten Commandments
ARON BARTH

religious Zionist leader, theologian, and economist (1890–1957); he was also general manager of the Bank Leumi le-Israel

Whenever we read the story of the divine revelation in the Books of Exodus and Deuteronomy, we cannot avoid feeling ourselves the trembling experienced by those at Mount Sinai, and we stand in awe and wonder at the words chosen by God for their hearing. He begins: "I the Lord am your God," and ends: "You shall not covet." He begins with the most important of fundamentals: a knowledge of God, a recognition of Him from history, the establishment of His unity, His incorporeality, the prohibition of making anything meant to be His likeness, and the prohibition of idolatry. He ends with something that no other faith or human legislation had ever dared to demand; not only does He forbid adultery, He forbids us to *covet* another man's wife; not only is it forbidden to steal, it is forbidden us even to *covet* the possessions of others. This is an example of a law that delves deeply into a region which in other nations is utterly separate from legislation. If, and we stress the "if," other cultures deal with such a question it is at best part of their moral, but not of their legal, system.

8. Moses on Mount Sinai. Copper engraving. By Joseph Herz. From *Mahzor le-Shavuot.* Sulzbach, Germany. 1826. See Chapter 8.

And between the first and the last commands there come the so-called natural laws, such as the honoring of parents and the prohibition of theft, prohibitions which are accepted by all civilized peoples—but how far are they really "accepted" and fulfilled? The commandments exactly provide for the greatest revolution in the life of a nation, the holy Sabbath. This precept embraces the *order,* "Six days you shall labor," and the *prohibition* of any manner of work on the Sabbath. This is the first prohibition of work in the history of the world, and it has remained unique in the course of many centuries. It applies alike to masters and servants, male and female, man and beast. There is one law equal for all; that all shall free themselves on one day of the week, on that day which the Lord blessed and hallowed, that all shall be free from all manner of work and from dependence on their fellows, to be as they were at the time they were created.

Translated by Haim Shachter[9]

*

Heaven and Earth

CHAIM PEARL

rabbi and author of books on the Jewish festivals

The Shavuot festival rests on two matters, viz., the commemoration of God's revelation on Sinai and the season of the harvest and the first ripe fruits. Each on its own is important enough and would provide sufficient reason for the celebration of Shavuot. However, when we hold them together it might seem that in many ways they belong to such completely different areas of thought as to be almost in opposition to each other.

The idea of revelation belongs to the highest realms of religious teaching. Its concepts are totally spiritual. Its truths point to God who created the universe and all that is in it and wills that man shall live in accordance with the highest law—God's law. He therefore made His presence manifest on Sinai in order to proclaim His word. Can there be any greater religious challenge to man? Can there be any loftier message than this, to hearken to the word of God and to live by it all one's life?

How different is the immediate picture of the wheat harvest and *bikkurim.* Here we are down to earth, surrounded by the farmer and his fields, his crops and his fruit basket, his daily worries about his material welfare and the hazards he faces in seeking some reward for his daily labors. What a contrast this is! Before we referred to God, now to the farmer; before it was heaven, now it is the earth; before it was of an eternal divine Law and now we reckon with a basket and two loaves representing the temporary material values of man's work.

Nevertheless, we can gain the full message of Shavuot through our attempt to join together these two ideas of Torah and *bikkurim.* Indeed, we might do more than that, for we might gain a clearer idea of the aim of Judaism through such an attempt. For we are meant to relate heaven to earth and to translate the divine Law in terms applicable to our daily life. It is not sufficient to acknowledge God, to hail the event on Sinai. That by itself is meaningless unless such an affirmation guides our daily life. . . . It is not in heaven that Judaism finds its greatest interest but on earth; not in life in another world but in the here and now. But just as the concept of revelation is inadequate without the idea of *bikkurim,* so *bikkurim* is of little use without the ennobling influence of revelation. The curse of modern society is its materialism. Men are too much concerned with physical well-being and materialistic progress, failing to recognize the profound spiritual truths which must bring purpose and meaning to life.

Revelation which belongs to the world of religious and spiritual truth must be made real and tangible by making it a guiding factor in our daily pursuits. *Bikkurim* which belongs to man's material world must be sanctified by the touch of religious ideals. In this way Shavuot points to a great goal indicating a perfectly integrated life in which we can aspire to the blessing of God's kingdom on earth.[10]

*

*Spring and the Feast of Weeks

MENDELE MOCHER SEFARIM

*pseudonym of Shalom Jacob Abramowitsch, who contributed volumi-
nously to both Hebrew and Yiddish literature; regarded as the "grandfather" of modern Yiddish literature (c. 1836–1917)*

How glorious is the dawn and the wonder of the morning on
this Shavuot day, the beauty and pride of Israel! As soon as the
vistas of the sky begin to brighten, the birds awaken in their
nests, sit up, and begin to chirp their morning song melodiously.
But before they have finished their songs, they begin to flutter
about their work, that of providing food for their mates who rest
upon the eggs.

Soon the blackbirds nestling in the tops of the trees will
awaken and chirp to each other with high-pitched voices and will
spread their wings to float in the atmosphere above them, which
is pure and clear as the heavens. Below them the humid air sends
forth its fragrant vapors rising from the earth like pillars of
smoke. . . .

The half circle of sun appears as the wheel of God's chariot,
as though the glory of the God of Israel came with His angels
to behold His holy people and to visit them in the spirit of love
during the holiday, during which God revealed Himself on
Mount Sinai, and took unto Himself as a bride the daughter of
Judah. On that day God shone forth as a bridegroom from
Mount Paran to take unto Himself His beloved, in justice and
righteousness; as though He would remind His forsaken one of
the days of her betrothal, and of her glory and greatness in the
Holy Land. Therefore, He is filled with love for her and brings
her greetings to the lands of the gentiles.

The break of day is pleasant to the Jews of the city who are
feasting. Many arise early in the morning to pray and to partake
of their customary Shavuot food, namely, milk and honey. They
move about to breathe the invigorating air and to indulge in
conversation; some wander into the fields, others into the gardens or into the woods; and still others stroll about the streets
and parks of the city. All rejoice and are happy, clothed in

holiday garb, as if they were continuing the ancient tradition of walking in numbers to the house of God with the fruit of their harvest to behold the face of God in Jerusalem, in uninterrupted joy as though they had never suffered.

O Israel, thou art indeed a puzzle to the nations; they do not understand! The conflicts of thy soul puzzle them. Thou art a puzzle to other nations with thy shabby clothes during the week-days and thy gay jewels and silks on the holidays! Thou art a puzzle to other nations in thy ways of thinking and thy ways of doing things. Thou art a slave and a king! Thou art repulsive and attractive, as the tents of Kadar, as the curtains of Solomon!

Thou art a puzzle, Israel, to the nations; they do not under-stand! But he who can discern the innermost depths of thy heart will find there the solution of these puzzles in thy utter devotion to God and to His teachings. Only from these wells of salvation can the Jew drink and forget his poverty, only from this source of inspiration can the Jew transcend his cares, vexations, anxie-ties; only through the purity of his soul can he shake off the bitterness of his painful conflicts and taste the sweetness of life.

Translated by Joseph Cooper Levine[11]

*

* *"The Earth Is the Lord's and the Fulness Thereof"*

MORRIS JOSEPH

British theologian (1848–1930); noted for his major work, Judaism as Creed and Life

The religious purpose served by the command ordaining the offering of firstfruits is easily perceived. The precept admonished the Israelite that all good things came from the divine Hand, even the products of the soil, though he himself might have labored for them. He had ploughed, and sown, and reaped; he had delved, and pruned, and gathered; but success had crowned his toil only because God had blessed it. He was reminded, moreover, that God is the real Master of all, that "the earth is the Lord's and the fulness thereof'' (Psalms 24.1), and that men are but stewards of their wealth. Even when he laid his gifts upon the altar he in reality only restored to God that which belonged to Him. . . .

To the Supreme he was impelled to turn in the hour of prosperity. And so it was that in the prayer which he offered when he laid his basket of firstfruits upon the altar, he remembered the low estate from which God had delivered him. He had been a slave, but the Almighty had set him free; he had been ready to perish, but the Almighty had placed him in a goodly land. And the firstfruits of that land he appropriately was giving to God in lowly gratitude. Moreover, the possessions thus entrusted to him he was exhorted to employ wisely and dutifully. Wealth implied responsibility. It was to be used temperately, for the gratification of innocent desires; it was to be used, too, for the relief of poverty and suffering, for increasing the happiness of others. . . .

The festival still continues to teach these lessons. We till the soil no more; our wealth is no longer reckoned in sheaves of corn or baskets of fruit, in flocks or herds or broad acres. But wealth we all have—even the poorest of us; and the duty of hallowing it by pious use is as imperious as ever. For there are other and more precious kinds of wealth than that which is counted in money. Health, knowledge, skill of hand or brain—these are examples. These are some of God's gracious gifts to man, gifts that may make the poorest truly rich. And each brings its responsibilities. Wealth involves the duty of philanthropy, of spending itself lavishly in the relief of human suffering, of sharing itself with poverty. "Bring the poor that are cast out to thy house," say the Rabbis, "and thou wilt offer thy choicest firstfruits to God." Upon the rich, too, is also cast the duty of seeking after that simplicity of life which scorns excessive luxury and enervating self-indulgence. And in like manner upon the healthy and the strong, the wise and the clever, is laid the obligation of dedicating their gifts to noble ends, of using their power of body or of mind in a spirit of humility and self-denial, of so employing them as to make their exercise a service of God and man. "Then you shall observe the Feast of Weeks for the Lord your God, offering your freewill contribution according as the Lord your God has blessed you" (Deuteronomy 16.10)—such is the command laid upon us by the Law. Everyone can bring such a tribute in honor of the festival. For the gift is to vary with the blessings of the heart that offers it, and there is no life that is not made bright by some gleams of sunshine. And if we can bring little else for God's acceptance, we can at least give Him the homage of our gratitude. This may be our firstfruits, and though we have nought else to offer, the Supreme, we may be sure, will accept them, for they are an offering such as He loves. "Whether we bring much or little," the Rabbis teach, "it matters not, if only we fix our heart upon the Father in heaven." Nay, Scripture said it before them: "But on this man will I look," the prophet tells us in the divine name, "even on him that is poor and of a contrite spirit, and trembleth at My word" (Isaiah 66.2) And was not the poor man's handful of meal in olden days an offering as precious in God's sight as the rich man's costly sacrifice?[12]

*

Thoughts on the Feast of Weeks

URI ZVI GREENBERG

leading Israeli poet; recipient of numerous awards and honors, including the Israel Prize, Bialik Prize, Bergen-Belsen Award, and an honorary degree from Yeshiva University. This essay was written prior to the 1967 Six-Day War, when Jerusalem was united

When I heard the report that Adolf Eichmann, he who had laid us waste, had related how he chanced to be in Lwow and how he "happened to be passing through" the slaughter field after the entombment of the multitude who had been massacred there, and how he saw a stream of blood oozing from the pit, I reexperienced the searing pain that had lacerated my flesh and my soul when I first learned about the destruction of my parents' family—my father and mother, their children, and their offspring —in the Camp of Hyanowski. Eichmann, who "happened to be passing through" and saw the blood trickling from the ditch where the dead had been buried, was already under indictment in our Jerusalem; yet he appeared in the courtroom, in his cage, like a meticulous officer entering his office with his briefcase. And no heart seemed to break—neither his nor ours, the witnesses who had the good fortune to be saved miraculously from doom and to reach Israel—to see with our own eyes Eichmann as he appeared, and to hear his plea of "not guilty" to the indictment—*im sinne der anklage nicht schuldig.*

Never again in my lifetime will I see Jewish Lwow, crowned with the tiaras of prayer shawls, steeped in Torah, in wisdom, abounding in song and warmheartedness. For how shall I tread its soil without seeing the stream of blood that murderous destroyer saw? And how can I breathe freely—in the manner of one who chances to visit his parental homestead and breathes "his own air" of childhood, adolescence and adulthood—when this air reeks with deadly poison and atomic radiation? Would I not expire there like any human being who had inhaled this air?

It is the season between Passover and Shavuot, blossomtime in Galicia. The trees in the park there, now heavy-laden with lilac, are no longer ours. "Aromas of the Garden of Eden," was how father and mother used to describe the fragrance those trees exuded while in bloom. There was a sort of nostalgia in their description for the trees of the ancient Garden of Eden. And where was this Garden of Eden if not in our own Ein Gedi, in the parks of our King? And the sweet scent from "the mount of myrrh to the hill of frankincense. . . . From Lebanon come with me, from Lebanon, my bride, with me" (Song of Songs 4.6–8)? The forest on the outskirts of the city was a replica of that goodly forest of the Lebanon! [According to Jewish tradition based on Deuteronomy 3.25, there was a forest called Lebanon in the neighborhood of Jerusalem.] Perhaps its trees were the reincarnation of that ancient forest of ours from whence the mystery of the perfumed sweetness—a sweetness almost with a *Yiddishen ta'am.* . . .

Ah! How we were intoxicated with the perfume flavor of Lag ba-Omer permeated with the aroma of a forest! During the *sefirah* days we would prepare to go out with hearts palpitating like that of a bird (which the enemy had not yet cleft . . . only later, after many, many years—down to Eichmann!) with a paper bag or a bundle containing hardboiled eggs and slices of bread, and with bows and arrows to aim at the trees in the forest! But not without trepidation prompted by the feeling that perhaps some vicious wolf would attack us in the forest—in the person of a Ukrainian or a Polish gentile lad: *that gentile lad who grew up in the course of the years and became more than the ordinary gentile—* an incarnation of the Eichmann of the future! From that forest we brought branches to cover the *sukkot* and branches for Shavuot; and from the banks of the nearby brook we plucked bullrushes for the Feast of Weeks. . . .

How well I remember the scent of the burnt resin that dripped from the numerous pines extending from Olsk and Bialikmin to the city of Brod. Brod—wise, learned, enlightened and humorous, concerned over betrothals of the community's "eligible maidens" when their dowry resources were exhausted and "they pinched their cheeks to retain their color."

For Shavuot delectable dairy dishes were prepared and fresh-baked pastries with butter and cheese, "whose rarity the kaiser himself could hardly appreciate." Do you remember, my Galician contemporaries, the appearance of the windowpanes in our houses on the eve of the festival, covered with paper cutouts of artistic design: multitudinous flowers and birds, lions and leopards, deer and rams, and all the celestial beings?

Those precious hands that decorated our windows for the Feast of Weeks were as innocent as the dove I saw fluttering at the Western Wall in Jerusalem, or like the wild doves I prefer over the tame ones. A million hands like those were ripped off like wings from their shoulders before they could grow sufficiently to be able to prepare the decorations for the holiday, or were shot down and shattered, or withered, languished and died together with their frail young bodies at the command of the obscene Eichmann. We feel the loss of those hands here among us, for they would have been occupied with work, with carving and ornamenting, with ploughing and reaping, in smithy shops and laboratories, and with weapons—they are the holy instruments in our struggle for the continued existence of this, our Holy Land. . . .

How did we, with our young and with our elders, live in Galicia and in similar lands of exile during the Shavuot festival, in our beautiful and warm synagogues, in our houses of study for the eminently pious and for the simple workingman, in the joy of song and music, full-throated and harplike, and the melodies which embodied the longings of the generations, and the scent of greenery in our nostrils, and the bullrushes and the fallen leaves on the floor under our feet? In truth, more beautiful and resplendent than the life of the Jews in the synagogues in the Diaspora was the life of the Jews during Israel's sovereignty and the Temple, during the period of the throne and altar in Jerusalem when there was neither cross nor crescent. Would that our sons and daughters might share here in the renascent state of Israel, whose Jerusalem is in the possession of an impoverished Arab king, the experience that we, the children of the exiles from Jerusalem, underwent in the Diaspora. Would that they might likewise here chant as we chanted there in the *golah* the verses of the *Akdamut,* the most sublime hymn in the world, the spacious Aramaic poem whose dulcet tones even the celestial angels must envy. . . . The vigor that emanates from those Aramaic words is like the strength of the deep-rooted trees in the forests and like the fruitful vitality in a field blessed of the Lord! They have brought of the dew of heaven and of the fat of the earth unto our Jewish existence, exiled, uprooted, tortured, exposed to cold and heat even in the month of Tammuz, terrorized by a barking dog released from its leash by its gentile master and set to prowl in our Jewish street . . . perhaps a Jew will be found there, scurrying for a local doctor for help, or for a midwife for his wife or daughter about to give birth during the night.

I remember that in 1924 I had the good fortune to go up to Mount Zion in Jerusalem for Shavuot. Together with a group of Jews, I lay down opposite the gate to the courtyard of Bet Dagani, near the entrance to the sepulcher of King David. It was a happy privilege for me to lie there in the heat of the day, in the dust of the place that belonged to me, all of it, yet was called alien teritory! I intoned some chapters of the psalms of David in the melody of simple folk, that of my father and grandfather of distinguished descent. Then there stirred within me longings and legends pertaining to this place and to the king who reposed there. The sun shone in its greatest force overhead and the dust of the place was on the roof of my mouth, yet it was as sweet as honey to me. Master of the universe! I, Uri Zvi the son of Batsheba, am here, *here!* Can the king interred in the courtyard of this house hear me, so near? Shall I, shall we Jews be worthy of crossing occasionally the threshold of King David's cave? I, and indeed all of us, have become worthy. This section of Mount Zion is the control of Israel's army; therefore it belongs to the whole nation. Whenever I come up to Jerusalem I visit there to recite psalms by the side of the king's sepulcher. Verily, "to pour out my heart" as a simple Jew. . . .

There is a wondrous fable in the treasure trove of legends: Should someone be worthy enough to reach the slumbering king's tomb and pour some water on his royal hands, the king will awake. As a child my heart yearned for this vision. Now we have at long last arrived here and shed our sacred blood, from afar and from nearby, upon the king's couch and upon this place (would that everyone would grasp the idea to which I refer), from Auschwitz even up to this sepulcher of David, to Sinai and Eilat, to the heights of Galilee and the hill country of Lebanon. Let us be the first to salute the presence of the awakening kingdom as befits us Jews, scions of the world's noblest stock: from Abraham to David, and from David to this very day—physically few in numbers, but numerous in capabilities beyond calculation and beyond measurement. *And this is the proof:* that we have again come up to Jerusalem, to have dominion within its gates, and we will go even higher! And the merit of King David will shield us on this historic road.[13]

Translated by Herbert Parzen

✳

✳The Equal Status of Ruth

GRACE AGUILAR

British Jewish author and poet (1816–1847) for whom a branch of the New York Public Library was named; despite her short career, her writings on Jewish themes were extensive, and many have appeared in several editions and some have been translated into Hebrew and German

To us, as women of Israel, the whole Book of Ruth teems with unspeakable consolation and support. It is a picture so vivid of manners, customs, aye, and even feelings of Israel at that period that even gentile writers are struck by it, and refer to it with high eulogiums on its touching beauty and impressive truth. Shall we then value it less, and refuse to draw from it the strong confirmation which it contains of our contested point—the refined and elevated position of the women of Israel themselves, and the tender yet respectful consideration with which they were regarded by their brethren? Will any one point of Naomi's character permit us to suppose that during her husband's lifetime she was merely a slave, with neither religious, moral, nor intellectual training? Had she been such in Elimelech's lifetime, such she must have remained. Instead of which, from her determination to return to her own land and worship her God once more among her own people, we perceive that she was a woman of strong mind and unfailing energy; while from the affection of both her sons' wives, and the devotion of one, we must equally infer that she possessed, and in her domestic duties must have displayed, such winning and amiable qualities, as to call such affection forth; these characteristics, and all which follow—the refined and retiring dignity, the correct judgment, and also the patient faith in her God—all were quite incompatible with a degraded position either individually or socially. It is very clear, then, that not in any received Law of Israel could the position of the women of Israel have been that which our enemies so ignorantly report. If *two* Laws were in action at this period, one must have been an exact repetition of the other, or in a book like that of Ruth, so strikingly illustrative of the national character and customs, some difference must have been discernible.

If, then, the charge on modern Judaism be really founded on apparent truth, it must be a state of things brought about by the awful horrors of persecution, and their natural effect in narrowing and brutalizing the human mind. In all that relates to Ruth too, we see the real light in which the Hebrew woman was regarded, very clearly. We should not find her filial devotion and individual goodness so appreciated by all the Bethlehemites, female as well as male, were not virtue and goodness in woman subjects of admiration, cherishing, and respect. It was not only in obedience to the Law, which commanded love and kindness to be shown toward the stranger, that Boaz so encouraged and cherished her when first gleaning in his field. He expressly states the wherefore, *because* of her devotion to her mother-in-law, and her having given up her father's gods to accept Him under whose wings she had come to trust. "A full reward shall be given thee from the Lord," he says; thus marking her as accepted and cherished by God as well as man. The most reverential yet fatherly care marks the whole of his conduct toward her; and here we see very strongly marked the obedience to the law instituted for the benefit of the stranger; he not only "showed kindness," but literally left for her the "gleanings of his field." ...

Again, in Boaz's instant pursuance of Ruth's suit, we very clearly perceive that women must have been considered of some account; and also another important point in a national view, Boaz's exact obedience to the formula of the Law, in calling the nearest kinsman to give his attention to the subject, and decide—notwithstanding his own evident anxiety to obtain Ruth as his wife—unquestionably proves that as the Law was so strictly kept in *one point,* so it would be in *all;* and consequently there could not have been, neither practically nor theoretically, any one single statute to the disparagement of woman.

The very joy of the whole people in Boaz's decision to make Ruth his wife; their hearty congratulations, and earnest wishes for his welfare, and hers, that she might be as Leah and Rachel; the delight of the women, and their joyous sympathy with Naomi at the unexpected issue to all her misfortunes; all prove the beautiful unity and love marking the people of the Lord. All seemed to vie with each other in making their respective tribes as one affectionate family, bound by the same ties, hoping the same hope, trusting the same God, weeping with those that wept, and rejoicing with those that joyed.

Such a state of things could never have existed if the women of Israel had not been morally, spiritually, and intellectually on a perfect equality with man.[14]

*

The Counting of the Omer

PHILIP BIRNBAUM

educator, translator, and editor of Jewish classical and liturgical literature

9. *Omer* calendar. Silver case, parchment with painted decoration. France. 19th century. Master: Maurice Mayer. See Chapter 8.

The counting of seven weeks from the sixteenth day of Nisan, on which the *omer* [sheaf] offering of the new barley crop was brought to the Temple, until Shavuot, serves to connect the anniversary of the exodus from Egypt with the festival that commemorates the giving of the Torah on Mount Sinai. In talmudic literature the festival of Shavuot is invariably termed Atzeret, because it is regarded as the conclusion of the Passover celebration.

Tradition has it that it was announced to the Israelites in Egypt that fifty days after the exodus the Torah would be given to them. As soon as they were liberated, they were so eager for the arrival of the promised day that they began to count the days, saying, "Now we have one day less to wait for the giving of the Torah." . . .

In a similar vein, Maimonides points out that the counting of the *omer (sefirat ha-omer)*, between the anniversary of the liberation from Egypt and the anniversary of the Torah gift, is suggestive of one who expects his most intimate friend on a certain day: he counts the days and even the hours.

The *sefirah* period between the two spring festivals, Passover and Shavuot, has long been observed through certain restraints, because most massacres recorded in Jewish history took place in the spring months, beginning with the martyrdom of Rabbi Akiva and his disciples and continuing through the three Crusades (1096–1192).

With the exception of Lag ba-Omer, the thirty-third day of the *sefirah*, the period is dedicated to national mourning in order to perpetuate the memory of the great martyrs, who might serve as an inspiration for many generations.[15]

*

The Date of Shavuot

LOUIS FINKELSTEIN

former chancellor of The Jewish Theological Seminary of America and president of the Institute for Religion and Social Studies; author of many scholarly books and contributor to theological and philosophical journals

10. *Omer* calendar. England. 18th century. See Chapter 8.

One of the most famous sectarian controversies is concerned with the date of Shavuot (Pentecost). The Pharisees observed Shavuot on the fiftieth day after the first day of Passover; the Sadducees on the seventh Sunday after the Passover week. Since all agreed that biblical law fixed the festival for the fiftieth day after the sacrifice of the first sheaf of barley cut from the fields, there was a corresponding disagreement as to the time of that offering. The Pharisees asserted that it should be made on the second day of Passover, the Sadducees on the Sunday of the Passover week.

On the surface, nothing could be more trivial than such a controversy. The biblical verses in Leviticus (23.15–21) which give the provisions of the law are concededly ambiguous. They provide that the first barley shall be cut and sacrificed on the morrow after the "sabbath," but the word may mean either the weekly Sabbath or the Passover festival. But if nothing more were involved in the issue than this, established custom or scholarly exegesis could certainly have solved the problem in early times. The difficulty lay rather in the implications of the date question. The Pharisees gave Shavuot a fixed day because, they said, it commemorated the Sinaitic theophany which occurred on the fiftieth day after the exodus. The Sadducees denied that the festival had any historical allusion or that the date of the revelation was known.

The identification of Shavuot with the season of revelation, not mentioned indeed in Scripture, was yet made in early times. Though the first talmudic sages who refer to it flourished in the second century C.E., they merely transmitted a much older tradition. The oldest portions of the liturgy know Shavuot as the "Day of the Giving of Our Torah" and, what is perhaps more important, the *Book of Jubilees,* composed early in the Maccabean age, recognizes the historical background of the festival.

Most significant of all, however, is the fact that a passage in Joshua which, however late, must be pre-Maccabean, and the Septuagint (c. 300 B.C.E.) give support to the Pharisaic teaching. The Book of Joshua clearly fixes the time when the new grain may be eaten as the second day of Passover. Speaking of the Israelites who entered Canaan on the tenth day of the first month, four days before Passover, it says: "And they did eat of the produce of the land on the morrow after the passover, unleavened cakes and parched corn, in the selfsame day. And the manna ceased on the morrow, after they had eaten of the produce of the land" (Joshua 5.11).

Moreover, the same interpretation of the passage in Leviticus is also found in the Septuagint which substitutes for the phrase, "the day after the sabbath," "the day after the first day of Passover" (Leviticus 23.15).

By removing the ambiguity of the passage in Leviticus, the Septuagint as well as the Book of Joshua adopt the view later pressed so vigorously by the Pharisees, and by implication indicate that the controversy regarding the date and significance of Shavuot had already arisen.

Why did the Pharisees and their predecessors attach such importance to the historical significance of Shavuot? Because, since they were essentially town plebeians, it had no meaning for them otherwise. Ezekiel (45.18–25), for instance, who either did not know or did not accept this explanation of Shavuot, ignores the festival altogether and omits it from his calendar.

For the farmers of the Maccabean age, Shavuot could serve as the harvest festival, as it did for their ancestors of the Davidic and Solomonic days. The joy of the harvest filled them with the desire for the festival. And the seventh week after Passover was about the time of the wheat harvest.

The inhabitant of Jerusalem was not indifferent to the question of the harvest. But he viewed the harvest from a distance; he had not ploughed; he had not watched the stalks; nor had he waited for it. If Shavuot was to have any significance for him and above all for his children, he had to find some meaning for it other than its agricultural associations.

The Pharisaic leaders, scholars and scribes that they were, had doubtless long wondered why the Sinaitic theophany, which alone gave meaning to the exodus, was not celebrated by any festival. The birth of Israel as a nation was marked by Passover. Was it possible that the incident which had established Israel as a divine people would be passed over in silence?

The Pharisees' comparative divorce from agriculture and their interest in the Law thus combined to suggest the association of Shavuot with the revelation on Sinai, just as similar conditions in urban America have practically transformed Thanksgiving Day into a historical festival celebrating the landing of the Pilgrim fathers. But this reinterpretation necessarily gave the festival a fixed date. The Sadducees, with their rural background, could see no reason for the new tradition. They found no authority for it in Scripture and denounced it as pure imagination.[16]

SHAVUOT IN ART

*

Shavuot in Art

JOSEPH GUTMANN

In Judaism the *matzah* is associated with Pesah, the *shofar* with Rosh Hashanah, the *lulav* and booth with Sukkot, but no particular symbol is linked exclusively with Shavuot.

According to rabbinic interpretation, Shavuot is the "Season of the Giving of Our Torah." Many illustrations have come down to us, especially from medieval Hebrew manuscripts, highlighting this supreme moment in Israel's history. One fine example is a page from a south German *mahzor* of around 1320 containing the *piyyut* beginning with *Adon* ("the Lord has faith in me"), recited during the *yotzer* of the first day morning service of Shavuot. Between the Hebrew letters is a man lifting a sword to kill a ferocious lion. In the lower margin a bearded Moses (the Hebrew script above his head reads "Moses, our teacher") is standing on a small mountain, handing an open book to a man with outstretched hands, who is followed by three other men. All wear the pointed medieval Jew's hat (fig. 1).

Another south German *mahzor* miniature of the same period depicts the theophany at Sinai below the word *Adon.* A beardless young Moses kneels at the foot of the mountain as two rectangular inscribed tablets of the Ten Commandments are handed to him. *Shofars* and trumpets emerge from the sky, alluding to the biblical passages that "the whole mountain trembled violently. The blare of the shofar grew louder and louder" (Exodus 19. 18–19). Behind Moses stands Aaron, hands folded, wearing the miter of a medieval bishop. The men and women of Israel are assembled reverently in separate groups to witness the revelation at Sinai (fig. 3).

A full-page miniature in a Pentateuch, also from early fourteenth-century southern Germany, depicts Moses atop a fiery mountain. Above him are seven colored arcs, alluding perhaps to the seven legendary heavens. Moses is seen handing the inscribed tablets—one at a time—to the waiting Israelites, who receive them eagerly and assemble them at the foot of the mountain (fig. 4).[1]

An unusual oil painting also prominently features the two rounded tablets of the Law with the Ten Commandments written in gold letters in Hebrew and Spanish. The tablets are flanked by Moses and Aaron; a *shofar* and lightning can be seen issuing from the clouds. Painted in 1675 by Aron de Chavez, the painting originally hung above the *hekhal* (Torah ark) in the Portuguese synagogue in Creechurch Lane, London, England. The placing of the Ten Commandments within the synagogue, a practice now generally accepted, was strongly condemned by the rabbis and is clearly due to Christian influence (fig. 5).[2]

A beautiful Italian Torah ark curtain, made in 1681 by Simhah, the wife of Menahem Levi Meshulam, features the theophany at Sinai. Decorated with gold and silver appliqué and embroidery on violet silk, it features Mount Sinai with clouds above it. Emerging from the clouds are hands holding the tablets of the Law. Below is the walled city of Jerusalem encircling the Temple. Biblical inscriptions drawn from Deuteronomy 5.4, Exodus 19.9, and Psalms 68.17 and 137.6 accompany the depiction (fig. 7).[3]

The 1826 copper engraving by Joseph Herz in the popular Sulzbach *mahzor* shows Moses enveloped in a cloud at the very peak of Mount Sinai. A multitude of Israelites crowd around the mountain and raise their hands in jubilation. A fence placed

11. Israel pursued by enemies. *Worms Mahzor.*
Illuminated manuscript on vellum. Germany. 1272.

around the mountain prevents the Israelites from ascending or
drawing near (Exodus 19.23); it may also allude to the rabbinic
injunction to make a fence about the Torah (fig. 8).[4]

The giving of the Torah by God and its acceptance by Israel
imposed certain obligations upon the latter. These obligations
are conveyed symbolically by special marriage contracts which
record and seal the union of God or the Torah as the bridegroom
and Israel as the bride. Such contracts were read during the
Shavuot services in some Italian and Sephardic congregations.
An unusual contract from eighteenth-century Italy has illustrations of the life of Moses in its upper and lower borders. The text
of the contract itself is flanked by large figures of Moses with the
tablets and Aaron in his priestly garments. Inscriptions drawn
from Isaiah 61.10 ("I greatly rejoice in the Lord"), Exodus 24.7
("We will do and obey"), and the Song of Songs 3.11 ("O
maidens of Zion, go forth") frame both the figures of Moses and
Aaron and the contract text.

Shavuot is also traditionally the day on which Jewish children
are initiated into the study of Torah. An interesting German

Jewish Torah initiation custom of the Middle Ages is illustrated in an early fourteenth-century south German *mahzor* (in the *yotzer* section of the first day morning service). We see in the center of the marginal illustration a child, wrapped in a mantle or *tallit,* being brought by his father to the synagogue or the house of his teacher. To the left the teacher is seated on a bench holding the child in his lap. In the child's hands are an egg and a honey cake. The final act of the ceremony was for teacher and pupil to walk along a river together, as we note on the right side of our illustration. This symbolic act was to impress upon the child that the Torah is like a river, in keeping with Proverbs 5.16: "Let thy springs [=teachings] be [like streams] dispersed abroad." After this ceremony the egg and honey cake, which are still held aloft by the child in our illustration, were eaten (fig. 13).⁵

Acceptance of Torah also implied acceptance of the trials and tribulations to which Israel might be subjected. This fate is symbolically conveyed in *mahzor* illustrations accompanying the passage "the gift of Sinai is like a loving hind," recited in the morning service of the second day of Shavuot. The hind represents faithful Israel, who, because of loyalty to Torah, is pursued by enemies—hounds and hunter. An instructive depiction is found in the late thirteenth-century Worms *mahzor.* Under the word *ayyelet* ("hind"), hunting dogs are seen snapping at a fleeing hind, while an evil-looking hunter blows his horn to signal the attack (fig. 11). A miniature from an early fourteenth-century south German *mahzor* has many dogs attacking the hind, while two hunters in open doorways blow their horns (fig. 12).⁶

The original agricultural nature of the biblical Shavuot—one of the three pilgrimage festivals—was not forgotten by the rabbis in synagogal celebrations.

The Book of Ruth was read during the morning service of the second day of Shavuot. The reasons for its adoption for the holiday are many and varied. One of them may have been that the story takes place during the grain harvest and deals with the treatment of the impoverished during the harvest season. Unlike the Scroll of Esther, the Scroll of Ruth never received lavish ornamentation. Only isolated scenes from medieval manuscripts exist in addition to those made by contemporary artists of Jewish origin. A splendid Gothic miniature from a south German *mah-*

אֵילַת

אֲ הָבִים מִתַּנַת   סִינִי

אֲ מִן שֶׁעֲשׁוּעִים מֵיֹרַשְׁהַם סִינִי

בְּ אֹור תְּנֹורַת אֹור קְדֹושַׁת סִינִי

בָּ הֶחֱרֶד עִם סְבִיבֹות   סִינִי

הִשָּׁמְרוּ עַם בְּלִי נַגַּע בְּהַר וְעָנָן כְּבֵד
עַל הַהַר קֹלֹות וּבְרָקִים מִזֶּה
הָהַר שָׁמְעוּ נִצָּבִים בְּתַחְתִּית הַהַר יֹוצֵר
אֹור בְּעָטְפֹו יִבְדֹּור   קֹדֶשׁ

גֵּ בְּרַחֲבֶם עָלָה לְ סִינִי

גֵּ אַהֲרֹב בְּכֹחֹו שָׁבַן בְּ סִינִי

הֵ תְמַשְׁחַקְת יֹום יֹום לְ סִינִי

דֵּ עַת מִזְנֵה הָאִירָה לְ סִינִי

12. Israel pursued by enemies. *Mahzor.* Illuminated manuscript on vellum. South Germany. Circa 1320.

zor, dated around 1320, has scenes of Ruth amid the reapers of the harvest. Whether the animal heads of some figures are rooted in medieval Jewish mysticism or are attributable to the prohibition of images has yet to be determined (fig. 2).

The contemporary Israeli artist Jacob Steinhardt shows Ruth gracefully gleaning in the fields while Boaz looks on. With an economy of line, Steinhardt touchingly renders the mood of the encounter (fig. 23).

Jossi Stern, another Israeli artist, lyrically illustrates a contemporary Israeli practice in his *Hag ha-Bikkurim.* Israeli youth once again, as in biblical times, bring the firstfruits of the harvest as an offering (fig. 22).

The synagogue itself was decorated on Shavuot with green twigs, shrubbery, and flowers in commemoration of the agricultural bounty and the fact that Mount Sinai greened on that day. Special green Torah curtains and mantles were sometimes made for Shavuot and the silver Torah shields, executed by master craftsmen, carried the name of the holiday on their interchangeable plates (fig. 16).

Bodenschatz reveals to us what a German eighteenth century synagogue looked like on Shavuot. He has also illustrated, in the cartouche at the bottom of the engraving, a German Jewish custom performed on the day prior to Shavuot. Jews are seen standing outdoors in a cold body of water, beating their breasts while reciting prescribed penitential prayers (fig. 18).[7]

The popular nineteenth-century German painter Moritz Oppenheim depicts the rabbi after he has removed the Torah from the ark. He is standing on the *bimah* under festoons and is surrounded by green shrubbery. His eyes are uplifted sentimentally in praise of God. Children who have rushed forward have strewn the steps of the *bimah* with flowers (fig. 19).

A favorite custom in many congregations during the Shavuot festivities was to distribute fruits and sweets to the children, as we can witness in the eighteenth-century woodcut from the *Sefer Minhagim* (fig. 20).

Beginning with the second night of Passover, the observant Jew counts in the home and synagogue the days of the seven-week period culminating in Shavuot. On the second day of Pesah, the *omer* (the first sheaf of the harvest) used to be offered at the Jerusalem Temple. To simplify the counting, *omer* calendars were fashioned. At times they were simple, unadorned tablets or books; at other times they were cases with adjustable rollers inside. One such case with adjustable rollers was made by Maurice Mayer, a French mid-nineteenth-century goldsmith. The silver case is topped by the tablets of the Commandments and is adorned with scrolls, coral pendants, and semiprecious stones (fig. 9). A painted *omer* calendar—known as an "Homer board"—was probably made for the eighteenth-century Baron Ephraim de Aguilar of London. It records on a parchment strip, which was adjusted daily by rollers, the *omer* count, the number of weeks and days which had elapsed since Passover. The letters H, S, and D on the *omer* calendar designate the *omer* count ("Homer"), weeks ("Semanas"), and days ("Dias"), respectively (fig. 10).[8]

Silver *Kiddush* cups were fashioned to celebrate the holiday both in the home and the synagogue. A handsome specimen from 1773 Nuremberg has the words of Deuteronomy 16.9: "You shall count off seven weeks . . ." engraved on the cup (fig. 21).

The glass windowpanes of Jewish homes, especially in nineteenth- and twentieth-century Poland, were once gaily decorated on Shavuot with Jewish paper cuts—patterns cut out of paper, frequently tinted and mounted on a layer of different colored paper. Called *shevuoslekh,* they employed geometric forms, animals, plants, and, of course, biblical figures (fig. 27).[9]

The artistic remnants discussed, though few in number, vividly capture beautiful and fascinating Jewish customs of a world gone by, and are precious documents of a sacred heritage.

SHAVUOT IN MANY LANDS

*

*The Bringing of the Firstfruits during the Second Commonwealth

SOLOMON ZEITLIN

The Festival of Weeks, also called the Festival of the Firstfruits, was really a harvest feast for the farmers to celebrate. Only those who possessed land—not tenants—could bring the firstfruits. These were brought from the following products: wheat, barley, grapes, figs, pomegranates, olive oil, and honey.

A spectacular parade accompanied the bringing of the fruit to the Temple. The men of the smaller towns gathered in the town of the *ma'amad* to which they belonged and spent the night in the marketplace. Early in the morning the appointed supervisor called out, "Arise and let us go up to Zion to the house of the Lord our God." An ox, its horns overlaid with gold and a wreath of olive leaves on its head, walked at the head of the procession. It was given this prominent position because it alone shared with the farmer in the toil of cultivating the land and of the threshing the wheat and other grains. The donkey and the camel were largely involved in transportation, while the horse was employed mostly in wars and occasionally for speedy travel.

Flutes played at the head of the parade. The people, bearing decorated baskets of firstfruits, sang as they marched, "I rejoice when they said unto me, 'Let us go unto the house of the Lord.'" When they approached Jerusalem, they sent messengers ahead to announce their coming. The elite of the city came forth to meet them. The parade entered Jerusalem singing:

Our feet are standing within thy gates, O Jerusalem;
Jerusalem, that art builded as a city
    that is compact together;
Whither the tribes went up, even
    the tribes of the Lord,
As a testimony unto Israel, to give thanks unto the name of
    the Lord.
For there were set thrones for judgment,
The thrones of the house of David.

Pray for the peace of Jerusalem;
May they prosper that love thee.
Peace be within thy walls, and prosperity within thy palaces.
For my brethren and companions' sakes,
I will now say: "Peace be within thee."
For the sake of the house of the Lord our God
I will seek thy good. [Psalms 122.2–9]

When they passed through the streets of Jerusalem, all the craftsmen stood up to greet them, saying, "Brethren, men of such and such a place, peace to you." When they reached the Temple mount each one took the basket and put it on his shoulder. Later there was a proverbial saying that even King Agrippa would carry his own basket on his shoulder. On entering the Temple mount, they sang:

Hallelujah. Praise God in His sanctuary;
Praise Him in the firmament of His power.
Praise Him for His mighty acts;
Praise Him according to His abundant greatness.
Praise Him with the blast of the horn;
Praise Him with the psaltery and harp,
Praise Him with the timbrel and dance;
Praise Him with stringed instruments and the pipe.
Praise Him with the loud-sounding cymbals;
Praise Him with the clanging cymbals. [Ibid. 150.1–5]

When they reached the *azarah* they sang:

> Let everything that hath breath praise the Lord.
> Hallelujah. [Ibid. 6]

while the Levites sang:

> I will extol Thee, O Lord, for Thou hast raised me up,
> and hast not suffered mine enemies to rejoice over me.
> [Ibid. 30.2]

These canticles became a part of the Book of Psalms.

With the baskets on their shoulders, the celebrants read the account of the sufferings of the Israelites in Egypt, which concludes with the following verses:

> He brought us to this place and gave us this land, a land flowing with milk and honey. Wherefore I now bring the firstfruits of the soil which You, O Lord, have given me. [Deuteronomy 26.9–10]

Originally, those who could read recited these verses and the priests read them for those who could not read. This embarrassed those unable to read and they refused to bring the firstfruits. It was then ordained that the priests should recite the portion from the Pentateuch regardless of whether those bringing the firstfruits could read or not. The pilgrims then took their baskets with the firstfruits from their shoulders and the priests placed them at the side of the altar. The baskets as well as the fruit were normally given as part of the offering. However, the baskets which were of gold or silver were returned to their owners.

Besides bringing the firstfruits, sacrifices were offered in the Temple and two wave loaves, baked with leaven from fine flour of the first harvest, were also brought.[1]

*

*The Voice of Simeon Bar Yohai

ZEV VILNAY

Rabbi Isaac Heilo of Spain, who was in Palestine in 1333, relates of the city of Etam which was fortified by Rehoboam, the king of Judah: "Today it is deserted, and there are no inhabitants other than a few poor Jews who watch over the old synagogue of Etam. It is said that this is one of the seven synagogues which existed in the days of Rabbi Simeon, the son of Yohai. One of the guardians of the synagogue said to me: 'During every feast of Pentecost, the time of the giving of the Law, one can hear a voice proceeding from the ark of the Law, saying: Ye children of Israel, study the Law, as a reward for which the Lord will console you and bring about your deliverance. All your troubles have come unto you because your forefathers abandoned the study of the Law.' This is the voice of Simeon, the son of Yohai, who returns each year to this synagogue."[2]

*

*Karo and Alkabetz Hold a Tikkun Shavuot in Salonika

SOLOMON LEVI ALKABETZ

Let it be known to you that the Hasid [Joseph Karo (1488–1575), author of the *Shulhan Arukh*] and I, his and your servant, decided to remain alone during the night of Shavuot and abstain from sleep. Praise the Lord that we succeeded, for we did not cease [reciting the Bible] for a single instant. . . . And then we studied the order Zeraim of the Mishnah. . . . And when we finished two tractates our Creator made us worthy of hearkening to the voice that spoke within the mouth of the Hasid. It was a loud voice and clearly articulate. . . .

"My friends, you who are the zealous of the zealous, my beloved ones—peace be unto you! . . . The voice of your study of the Torah and the breath of your mouth have risen to the presence of the Holy One, blessed be He, and pierced many heavens and many atmospheres while ascending. Angels became silent and Seraphim kept quiet; the [heavenly] beasts ceased to move; and all the hosts of heaven and the Holy One, blessed be He, listened to your voices." . . .

When morning came we performed ritual immersion, as we had two days before, and there we found scholars who had not been present with us that night, and we rebuked them and told them of the favor God had bestowed upon us. And their hearts ceased beating within them and they stroked their own faces and broke out in lament. And we too were harsh to them; because of them [i.e., because of their absence] we did not merit more [uplift] as mentioned before. And they said, "Tonight we shall join together and there shall be ten of us." . . . And though the night before we saw not a moment of sleep, during the following day we were not permitted to sleep because the Hasid [i.e., Karo], may God preserve him and help him, delivered his sermon after the noon prayer and we were present there. We nevertheless girded our loins with fortitude and we spent the second night as we had the first night.

Translated by Hirsch Loeb Gordon[3]

*

*Shavuot among the Samaritans

BINYAMIN TSEDAKA

On this festival, as on *Hag ha-Matzot,* the Samaritans make a pilgrimage to Mount Gerizim. The holiday is celebrated on the fiftieth day of *sefirat ha-omer* [counting of the *omer*] which is on a Sunday. The Samaritans divide the period of the *sefirah* into seven weeks, and on each of the Sabbaths during the period they devote the service to one of the seven stations the children of Israel passed on their exodus from Egypt until they arrived at Mount Sinai: the (Red) Sea (Exodus 14.26—15.21); the second Sabbath is called *Shabbat Marah* (ibid. 15.22–26); the third Sabbath is called *Shabbat Elim* (ibid. 15.27—16.3); the fourth Sabbath is *Shabbat ha-Man* (ibid. 16.4–36); the fifth is *Shabbat ha-Zur ba-Horev* (ibid. 17.1–7); and the seventh *Shabbat Amalek* (ibid. 17.8–17).

On the fourth day after the sixth Sabbath of *sefirat ha-omer,* the Samaritans celebrate the day of standing at Mount Sinai. According to their tradition, the Pentateuch was given to the children of Israel from above Mount Sinai on this day. They pray and read from the Pentateuch from the middle of the night until the following evening. The seventh Sabbath during *sefirat ha-omer,* the forty-ninth day of the period, is called the Sabbath of the Ten Commandments (ibid. 19.1—20.14).

The pilgrimage on the festival of Pentecost begins early in the morning, and during the processional all the places holy to the Samaritans that are situated on the peak are visited: Givat Olam, on which Moses' tabernacle stood; Isaac's altar, the spot where Abraham bound his son; and the site of the twelve rocks that Joshua placed before erecting Moses' tabernacle, according to Samaritan tradition.[4]

*

*Shavuot as Celebrated by the Jews of Kurdistan

ERICH BRAUER

The Jews of Kurdistan call the festival of Shavuot, the second of the three pilgrimage holidays, *Ziyara* ("Making a Pilgrimage") for this festal day is set aside for the visitation of holy places. The most important of these sites is the tomb of Nahum the prophet in Alkush, near Mosul, since there they also carry out the symbolic ascent on Mount Sinai. They likewise visit the graves of Hazan David and Hazan Joseph of the Hazanai family in Amadiyah; the tomb of Rabbi Nataniel Halevi Barzanai in Barazan; the Cave of Elijah in Bitanura, and the sepulcher of Daniel near Kirkuk. . . .

The custom to eat on Shavuot dairy foods is also widespread among the Kurdistan Jews. Consequently, most of the preparations for this holiday involve large quantities of butter and cheese. The Jews who have businesses in distant villages exchange their wares at this season principally for dairy products. On Shavuot evening the dinner is not much different from the customary evening meal; however, in Gila, Rican, and several other places they eat on this evening a sort of milky food which is known as *madira,* made of crushed wheat boiled in sour milk, with *kutalai,* dumplings stuffed with a filling of butter and flour instead of meat, as is usual.

After the meal the people go to the synagogue for the *Hatimat Ziyara* (the end of the *Ziyara*), as they call the prayers on the first night of Shavuot. This service of worship at which they use the Baghdad edition of *Seder Kriah Moed* is more important to the Jews of Kurdistan than even the night of *Hoshana Rabbah.* The men likewise gather in the homes of mourners, where, according to tradition, are also invited a quorum of ten scholars to offer prayers in honor of the departed.

While in Zakho only a small number of elderly women come to the synagogue, in Amadiyah almost all the women and young maidens go to the synagogue to participate in the evening religious service; some of the women also attend the prayers in the mourners' homes.

In the synagogue hundreds of candles are alit, for every individual kindles a candle in honor of his deceased. Today candles are generally made from oil with wicks. However, there are settlements where wax candles are lighted.

In memory of their dead, families bring to the synagogue dishes full of fruits in order to make a blessing over them. If a close relative died during the course of the year, the mourners make every effort to obtain new fruits of various kinds, as far as possible, to recite the blessing *Sheheheyanu;* and the rich import fruits from Baghdad for this purpose.

In the morning the devout go to the river for immersion, for they want to greet the presence of the Torah like bridegrooms who bathe ritually before the marriage ceremony.

In Zakho, the *gevir* (rich man of the community) is honored with being called up to the reading of the Torah portion which contains the Ten Commandments. In Amadiyah, in the past, this honor was given to the man who succeeded in buying the fourth *aliyah* for the entire year. Today, however, they sell this *aliyah* separately in Amadiyah and Seneh. Formerly, this honor was also awarded to the *gevir.*

In Amadiyah, when the service is over, the women bring *yiprakh,* that is, arak, and three-layered cakes, known as *kadai,* from the homes of the mourners and present them to the head of the "fellowship" (in charge of taking care of the dead bodies until interment) for these are gifts associated with the dead. The head divides the *yiprakh* among the "fellows" exclusively; but the rest of the congregation may also receive some of the *kadai.* . . .

The great significance of the festival of Shavuot for the Jews of Kurdistan is derived from the pilgrimages to the holy places. To these shrines stream, on this holiday, crowds of Jews from nearby and far off.

In Amadiyah, for the pilgrimage to the sepulcher of the Hazanai family masses of Jews gather, and the local Jews are obliged to provide shelter for the visitors. Often one family shelters not less than fifteen pilgrim families. The *ziyara* (pilgrimage) of the males takes place on the first day after the religious services, and the one for the women on the second day. Before they visit the graves the pilgrims immerse in a ritual bath and put on new clothing. Then they pass in a procession before the grave and every person kisses it.

On the second day, especially, during the *ziyara* of the women, there is great rejoicing. The women dance and sing, and the maidens bring with them their own swings. The *gabbai* sits at the entrance of the shrine and distributes wine or sherbet to the pilgrims. They approach the grave, kiss it, deliver their petitions, and distribute their money, which they saved for this purpose during the entire year, among the various charity boxes. Afterwards, the women reassemble to sing and dance and to wish each other a blessed pilgrimage *(ziyara berikha).*

The holy shrine which attracts the largest crowds is the tomb of the prophet Nahum at Alkush. Annually, thousands of Jews come here from Mosul, Baghdad, Basra, and from all areas of Kurdistan. An idiosyncratic detail of this *ziyara* is "the ascent on Mount Sinai," which takes place on the two days of the festival. Near the sepulcher is a hill which is called Mount Sinai. The men climb up this mount and recite the Ten Commandments [from the Torah] as they stand on the summit. Every community does this separately. The *aliyot* are sold at a public auction. Frequently the price is very high since individuals from other communities participate in the auction; it is indeed regarded as a shame for a community to permit an outsider to acquire any of the *aliyot.*

After the Torah reading the crowds descend with joy and jubilance. Bands accompany them and the strongest men at their head perform a sword dance.

On the second day they again ascend Mount Sinai and read the Torah on the summit. On the third day they also pass before the tomb, give charity, and receive from the *gabbai tubarkai* some fruits and sweets that were lying on the grave throughout the whole night.

After the morning prayer service and the *ziyara* following it, the men return to their homes to eat the Shavuot meal. In Amadiyah this feast consists of *kadai,* butter, and drinks prepared from honey and milk. However, in the provincial villages the women cook *madira.*

After the feast everybody goes to the home of the man who was honored with the *aliyah* of the Ten Commandments. There they dance and sing and are served arak and *maza* plentifully. These foods they consume without waiting the two hours, as is customary with them, between dairy and meat foods. In many places, the person who receives the honor of "going up" for the reading of the Ten Commandments gives a banquet for the prominent people of the community. On this occasion the men sing "hallelujah"—psalms of praise—and, in addition, indulge in merriment and amusing witticisms: "Hallelujah, hallelujah, let us eat boiled eggs and roasted beef."[5]

Translated by Herbert Parzen

*

*Shavuot at the Tomb of the Prophet Nahum

JOSEPH ISRAEL BENJAMIN II

From Tanura I went to Alkush [Iraq], where I arrived in 1848, two days before the Feast of Weeks.

Alkush is situated in a very unfruitful neighborhood. The town is inhabited only by Armenians, and appears to be very ancient. The houses, which stand single, are like fortified towers, rising at the foot of the mountains. Several Israelites and Kurds accompanied me to Alkush, in order to attend the ceremonies here, which take place at the tomb of the prophet Nahum. Quite close to one of the mountains is a large court, in the middle of which stands a spacious building, consisting only of one room, capable of containing about one thousand persons. There are two entrances into this building, which was intended for a synagogue; but, standing as it does without a community, it presents but a strange appearance. In this desolate temple on a spot, parted off by railings, is a catafalque, covered with tapestry worked in gold, and ornamented with various coins, above which is a costly canopy. This is said to be the tomb of the prophet Nahum. The Jews from Mosul, Aruel, Arbil, Kirkuk, from the Kurdistan mountains and from a still farther distance of eight days' journey round, annually assemble a week before the Feast of Weeks for a ceremony, at which they spend fourteen days in religious exercises. . . .

The pilgrims bring their manuscripts of the Law with them, and deposit them in the holy shrine of the temple. The women then enter the chamber of the prophet; and after this the service begins. First the Book of Nahum is read aloud from an old manuscript, which is laid upon the catafalque; when this is finished, they make a solemn procession seven times round the sacred shrine, singing sacred songs. After the seventh round, a hymn is sung addressed to the prophet, the chorus of which is "Rejoice in the joy of the Prophet Nahum!" . . .

On the first evening of the Feast of Weeks, the sixth of Sivan, they assemble in the synagogue, which is lighted by about one thousand lamps, and enter the chamber of the prophet, when service begins. . . . As soon as it is over, they go without further ceremonies into the sacred house, where a festive and general entertainment takes place, at which coffee is plentifully served. At break of day the morning prayer is recited; and then the men, bearing the Pentateuch before them, go, armed with guns, pistols, and daggers, to a mountain in the vicinity, when, in remembrance of the Law, which on this day was announced to them from Mount Sinai, they read in the Torah and go through the *Musaf* prayer. With the same warlike procession they descend the mountain. The whole community breaks up at the foot, and an Arabic fantasie, a war performance, begins. The picturesque confusion, the combatants, their war cries heard through the clouds of smoke, the clashing of weapons, and the whole mimic tumult presents a fantastic spectacle, which is not without a certain dignity and makes a strange impression on the spectator. This war performance is said to be a representation of the great combat, which, according to the belief in those parts, the Jews, at the coming of the Messiah, will have to maintain against those nations who oppose their entrance into the promised land, and the formation by them of a free and independent kingdom. The women, who remained behind in the town, come, singing and dancing to the accompaniment of a tambourine, to meet the men, and they all return together. . . .

I was at first almost stunned by the tumult and excitement of the noisy crowd; but later became quite meditative, when I saw to what a degree ignorance and custom can deface a religious festival, and injure even the most essential principle.

Several parts of these ceremonies are doubtless of foreign origin, and give evidence of Arabic custom. I therefore thought it well to address some words on this subject to my brethren in the faith, who testify great respect to Jewish European travelers, and consider their opinion as especially important. It was explained to me that these customs have been held in respect since ancient times, and that they must be kept up until the coming of the Messiah.

The return to the synagogue took up nearly half a day, as they often stopped by the way and renewed their warlike games. When at length they reached the synagogue, the Pentateuch, which they had taken with them, was replaced to the holy shrine; after which began near the catafalque the usual service for the prophet. That finished, all returned to the town, to rest themselves after the exertions of the day.[6]

*

*Among the Jews of Algeria
NAHUM SLOUSCHZ

On the evening of the eighth day of Passover the Jews [of Tlemcen, Algeria] buy green corn from the Arabs, which they suspend in their houses from the ceiling. There they let it hang until the Feast of Weeks, and during the [counting of the] *omer* they all eat of the corn, together with a sort of pancake, first dipping both of these in milk. On the day after Shavuot is the "Feast of Waters," when the Jewish women besprinkle each other. This festival is also observed at Tripoli and elsewhere. . . .

The morning after Shavuot the Jews of Mzab in the Sahara have a peculiar festival which they call ironically: "The Taking of Ghardaia by the Jews." All the Jews unite in the open oasis and, mounted on mules and donkeys and bearing long branches of palm, make a triumphant entry into the city.[7]

*

*The Torah's Marriage in Gibraltar

CECIL ROTH

The account which follows is based on personal observation at Gibraltar, during an unforgettable, exquisitely enjoyable Pentecost in 1929. The neighboring communities of North Africa, of course, follow the same practice and it is to be traced also farther East in the Mediterranean world.

In these communities, then, one of the features of Pentecost is the solemn celebration of the espousals of Israel with the Torah. The parallel is carried out as exactly as possible. In front of the ark burn bridal torches, surrounded with bouquets. The Scrolls of the Law are decked in white vestments, like a bride. When the ark is opened, special hymns are sung. And then comes the climax. The reader unrolls a parchment, illuminated in color as all *ketubot* (marriage contracts) should be; from it he reads, in the characteristic chant reserved for such occasions, the contract of marriage. Its form is exactly the same as that which serves on all similar occasions—though with a few poetic embellishments.

On Friday . . . the sixth day of the month of Sivan, on the day when the Lord came from Sinai and shone forth from Seir . . . in the year 2448 from the creation of the world, according to the reckoning which we here reckon in gladness and song, in this lovely and glorious land, and great and awesome wilderness. Then came before us the prince of princes and noble of nobles who is named Israel . . . and said to the dear and pleasant child of many qualities, the perfect Law of God . . . be unto me as wife, thou who art lovely as the moon, and I will betroth thee unto me for ever. . . . By the bidding and with the help of heaven I will cherish and honor thee all the days, forever and forever. I will give unto thee moreover as the price of thy maidenhood an ear that hears and an eye that sees, which may have abundant fruit. And this bride, the holy Torah, was willing and became his wife, engraven on the tablet of his heart; and he placed the crown of sovereignty on her head.

There is a good deal more in the same hyperbolic language. When the recital is finished, the Scrolls are taken up to the reading desk, preceded by a boy bearing a bouquet of flowers. The greatest *mitzvah* of the day is that of holding the mantle during the procession—accompanying the bride, as it were, to the espousals. Meanwhile, the usual psalm is sung to the melody generally reserved for the marriage hymn.[8]

*

*The Jewish Child's Initiation into School

HAYYIM SCHAUSS

In the Middle Ages, the elementary Jewish school was an old established institution behind which was a history and tradition of over a thousand years. Every boy began school at the age of five or a little later, depending on the health of the child. Among the Franco-German Jews, the day on which the boy began school was celebrated as a great event in his life.

The little boy was washed and dressed in his best clothes. Three eggs were cooked for him, and three honey cakes were baked, the dough kneaded by an innocent virgin. Apples and other fruits were brought to him. In some communities school began on the new moon of the month of Nisan. In other communities this great event took place on Shavuot.

The Festival of the Giving of Our Law was selected as the day when the child should begin his study of the Torah.

ה גֵּג' לָארֹשׁ ה מֻוִּיקֵק לְפָרֹשׁ ה נֶפְלָא לַחֲרֹשׁ
נְפְלְהֵי מֵרֹאשׁ

ו אֶהֶיֶה בְּעֶרֶץ ו שֶׁעְשׁוּעֵי יַדֶן ו קַרְמֵנִי בְּמֶרֶץ
מֵהֶרְמֵי אֶרֶץ

ז יָהַד נְכַלְלְהִי ז כֵּיהַ נְכַלְלְהִי ז אַה נְתַהֲלֵלְהִי
בְּרֵי לְהַרְמַת וְלַלְלְהִי

ח קֵר עֵינֶנּוּה ח לֵּל וּמֵעֵינֶנּוּה ח קַקְבֵּי עֵינֶינֶנּוּה
מָאוּ מֵעֵינֶנּוּה

ט פּוּחֵי שָׁמַיִם ט פַּסֵר אֶשִׁימִים ט וּדַמֵּנִי יָמַיִם
בְּעֶרֵי מַיִם

י קָרוּהָדִי נִבְעַר י רְשׁוּתְהִי הֻבְעַר י תִּדֵוֵהִי נִקְבַּע
בְּטוּבַךְ חַיִךְ אֻבְעַר

כ לְלֹה נְכַלְלְהִי כ וּפֶרְט נְפַלְלְהִי כ מֵיהַדִי נְגַלְלְהִי
לְפֵי נִעֵמַת הַיַּלְלְהִי

ל יָשֵׁת מוֹעֵצֶנּוּה ל דוּזִי בְּרֵינֶנּוּה ל עַל לֹא עֶשֵׂה קַנֶנּוּה
אֶרֶץ וְרֵיצֶה

מ יַנוּתִי לְקַבֵּל מ נֶה וְהַכֵּל מ הֻדְקַיֵב לֹא אֶגֹּל
מֵרֹאשׁ עֲפָרֹת הַבֵּל

נ רֵישַׁלְשִׁים וְשׁ נ וַעֵם נְתֵיבֹתֵים נ יָהַרְכֵּי שְׁפָתֵים
בְּתַלְמֵ שְׁפָתֵים

ס פּוֹנֶה הֶרֹאנִי ס סוֹדֵי קְרָאנִי ס מֵד לְגֹאוֹנִי
שֶׁשׁ אֹנִי

ע צֵדֵי הַתְהַג ע עֹלֶב נְהֹג ע יַכֵּר בְּמֵיהַג
בְּקֵיקֵר הַתְהַג

פ צְמֵיהַלֵיהֶם פ קֵר קוֹרְוֵיהֶם פ יֵלֵךְ לְתַהֵיהֶם

13. Initiation of children into the study of Torah. *Mahzor Lipsiae.*
South Germany. Circa 1320. See Chapter 8.

At daybreak, the child was taken to the synagogue or to the house of the teacher by a pious and learned man of the community, who hid him under the skirts of his coat in order that an evil eye should not injure him. The teacher who was in charge of his instruction handed him a slate on which the Hebrew alphabet was written forward, from *alef* to *tov,* and backward, from *tov* to *alef.* The following verses were also written on the slate: "The Law which Moses commanded us is the inheritance of the congregation of Jacob." "The Torah will be my occupation." "And the Lord called unto Moses and spoke unto him out of the Tent of Meeting, saying." As the teacher read the words and letters on the slate, the little pupil repeated them after him. Then a little honey was spread on the slate, which the child licked off. The custom was based upon the verse in Ezekiel in which the prophet states he felt God's words in his mouth "as honey for sweetness." Next, a honey cake was brought, on which were inscribed several sentences of the Prophets and the Psalms, the import of which was the praise of God's words and His precepts. The teacher read, and the little boy repeated after him each word of these verses. Following the cake, a cooked egg was brought, on the shell of which was inscribed the verses: "From all my teachers have I learned wisdom," and "How sweet are Thy words unto my palate! Yea, sweeter than honey to my mouth!" These verses were also read by the teacher and repeated by the child.

The lesson was now finished and the child was given the cake, the egg, and the fruit to eat. Then he was led back home again, concealed under the skirts of the coat of an adult.

That night, at home, the parents of the boy entertained many guests at a festive meal in honor of the occasion. It was the custom for everyone participating in the celebration to bless the child with the words "May God enlighten thine eyes with His Torah."

In the earlier Middle Ages, names of angels were inscribed upon the honey cakes, and amulets attached to them, but this custom was later discarded.[9]

*

Shavuot in Eastern Europe

HAYYIM SCHAUSS

Shavuot does not give Jewish children as many days of freedom as does Pesah, but the Hebrew school is open only half days from the beginning of the month of Sivan. *Rosh Hodesh*, the first day of the Jewish month, was always considered a semiholiday in Jewish schools; since there are only four days after that till the coming of the festival itself, these are also minor holidays. The three days before Shavuot are marked as the days during which the Jews were forbidden to approach close to Mount Sinai. The one day that remains, the day after the New Moon, also becomes a semiholiday, and is called *Yom ha-Meyuhas*, "Choice Day." Its exclusiveness, it is claimed, lies in the fact that on that same day of the week Yom Kippur is bound to fall. But what do children care for the importance ascribed to those days? They are satisfied that they are free and attend school for only half the day. . . .

Even in school the instruction is festive and breathes the spirit of the holiday. The children are taught the Book of Ruth. So clear is the imagery thereof that they are carried back to the days of old, when Jews reaped the harvest of the fields of their own land.

The older children sit around a long table with the teacher and study the Book of Ruth. But their thoughts are not on their studies; they are thinking of Bethlehem, the town where David was born and spent his childhood. They imagine they are standing at harvesttime in the fields that surround the town. Gentle breezes blow from the hills of Judah. The fields are filled with the freshly cut sheaves. They hear the whir of the reaping scythe, and the song of the workers in the fields. And everywhere is the pleasing aroma of the newly fallen gleanings which Ruth is gathering in the fields. . . .

[On Shavuot eve,] after feasting the congregation goes to the *bet ha-midrash*, the house of study, to spend the entire night reading *Tikkun*. The children, alas, must go to bed. They are extremely envious of their older brothers and their parents who stay awake all night in the synagogue and pray at the earliest service in the morning. . . .

Only half of the second evening of Shavuot is spent in the

synagogue. But this time the congregation recites, not *Tikkun,* but the psalms of David. The practice of staying awake in the synagogue on this night is not bound up with the giving of the Torah, as is the first night, but with a tradition that King David died on Shavuot.

On the long table in the house of study burns a great memorial candle. Around the table sit pious Jews, dressed in their holiday best, holding copies of the Psalms in their hands. The flame of the candle, large enough to last twenty-four hours, flickers above them as they read and chant the psalms, the songs of David, king of Israel, and in this manner observe the anniversary of his death.

Translated by Samuel Jaffe[10]

*

Pentecost in Svislovitz

SHMARYA LEVIN

Clear in my memory is the first Pentecost of my *heder* years and the preparations for it. My mother told me for the first time of the giving of the Torah to the children of Israel: of Mount Sinai, wrapped in sheets of fire, and clouds of smoke; of the tablets of the Law, engraved with exactly the same letters as I was learning to read in *heder,* telling the Jews forever and ever what they might and what they might not do. Her voice was proudest and happiest when she told me of that *rebbe* of old, the teacher of the whole Jewish people, Moses: how he delivered us from the hands of the gentile, how he divided the sea for us, so that the waters stood up on either side like the fir trees on the royal road that led from Svislovitz to Pinsk and Bobrusik. So dry was the passage left between that the children of Israel did not even have to take their shoes off. Then she told me how Moses had led us through the wilderness abounding in scorpions and snakes, with the pillar of fire before us on the march. She explained the incident of the wilderness very simply: Moses wanted to teach us, during those years, all of his Five Books, the Pentateuch, just the ones I was learning in *heder.* And the wilderness was good because no gentiles were there to interrupt the lessons.

Mottye the *melamed* told us the same story, but Mother's way of telling it was better, heartier, tenderer. When the *rebbe* told the story I just listened; when Mother told it my heart began to beat, and my imagination to burn with bright fires of its own. I looked before me, not at the walls of the room, but at scenes so distant that my eyes hurt. I dreamed: perhaps some day the Svislo would rear into walls, and sheets of flame and billows of smoke would encircle Castle Hill. There, on the highest story, Moses would appear, and the letters of the Law would be engraved on the four wings of the mill, telling us again of the things we might do and the things we might not do.

Translated by Maurice Samuel[11]

*

* *Shavuot in Vamia, Hungary*

BENJAMIN SCHREIBER

The *shul* is decorated with green foliage on Shavuot because the Midrash states that, when the Torah was given, all herbs, flowers, grasses, and trees crowded each other for a seat on Mount Sinai to witness the unique event. In our small *shul,* too, we received the impression that all the plants and flowers were competing for space. The *almemor,* centrally located like the altar in the holy Temple, was embellished with bouquets and surrounded with fragrant greens. It was a reminder of the day when the whole people of Israel similarly surrounded the mountain of God. The rabbi's seat was decorated with flowery festoons. Beautiful bouquets, arranged with much good taste, hung over the ark. As Shavuot is the birthday of the Torah, the decor took on a festive air. Even the Torah Scrolls had been decorated with flowers. . . .

This particular Shavuot promised to be especially interesting. Our community was looking forward to a great event, for on the first day of Shavuot, a new *Sefer Torah,* which had been penned by Reb Shimon, a respected member of the community, was to be ceremoniously presented to the congregation. As Reb Shimon had no children, this *Sefer Torah,* as he used to say, was to be his *"Kaddish."* Shavuot was quite a fitting occasion for this dignified celebration, and a rich impressive program had been carefully planned. The holy Scroll was to be conducted to the *shul* under a canopy in a solemn procession, to reach the *shul* just before the reading of the Torah. The *Sefer,* preceded by the rabbi, was carried by its donor from his house to the *shul,* winding through the whole town. Like a bride, the *Sefer* had been covered with a white veil and was adorned with myrtle twigs. It was to be met by another solemn procession, led by the cantor, which would include a number of rabbis from other towns who had been invited for the occasion. This procession was to leave the synagogue with another *Sefer Torah* to welcome the new one. The children, too, had been dressed up. They were to form the tail end of the procession, carrying lighted *Havdalah* candles.

Everything went according to plan. The new Scroll of the Law was inaugurated, in its being used for the Torah reading that day. . . .

The rabbi explained, I remember, that the special celebration of the day was appropriate, although it might be seen as competing with the Shavuot festival. He was concerned with the rule: "One may not mingle one celebration with another." The rabbi demonstrated that this principle applies to physical enjoyment only, wherein two rejoicings cannot be fully appreciated simultaneously; for spiritual enjoyment, however, no such rule applies.

The celebration was conducted with special psalms recited by the cantor, supported by the improvised choir. Everything came off with dignity.

Translated by Paul Forchheimer[12]

*

When Lilacs Bloomed in Bohemia
VOJTECH RAKOUS

Shavuot. . . . All work ceases and you notice in everything, in things as well as in people, that there is a holiday—a great holiday. Our two cows and our two goats also celebrated this holiday with us. Today they do not have to go out to pasture, today they are fed at home and they can eat as much as they want to—just like us children and anything else that lives and breathes in the house. Even the old plough out in the yard takes part in the celebration. It rests and shines in the bright sunshine as if it were made of pure silver. And throughout, even to the remotest nook or cranny, the hut is filled with the fragrance of lilacs . . . the sweet fragrance of lilacs.

Of course our hut hasn't got its festive appearance overnight. A full week before the holiday, the preparations began by white-washing the living room. . . .

Two days before the feast the baking started. "Horns" of dark, soft flour were baked, and cakes of finest wheat flour. The cakes were baked in our own oven, but only at night. All the neighbors' wives were invited for the baking, not because our people could not have finished the work without them, but because to them it was an honor, which the neighbors regularly repaid to my mother.

On the eve of Shavuot we children went into the neighbors' gardens to collect "greens"—fresh lilac branches and young lilac blossoms. On this day our living room looked like a blossoming grove. Wherever there was the smallest free space along the walls, there were always fresh branches and fresh blooms.

There were blossoming lilacs everywhere. Over the door, over the mirror, between the windows—even the many photographs on the living-room walls were decorated with lilacs. The pictures of old aunts in their crinolines and hoop skirts and old-fashioned bonnets looked strange under their new spring dress. The fragrance of the lilacs filled the entire hut and we breathed this fragrance for two days and two nights.

Translated by K. E. Lichtenecker[13]

*

Letters from a Desert in North Africa
MOSHE MOSENSON

June 1, 1941

My little girl,

Tomorrow is the Festival of the Firstfruits. You will probably have a fine celebration and you will write me all about it. Here we are in a desert, with sandstorms that sweep over our camp, and so we can't celebrate. What can we bring in our baskets? The dust storm? Or shall we fill our baskets with our longings for home? Nevertheless, we shall have a holiday meeting in the evening and afterwards each one of us will cover himself with his blanket and will dream about Palestine. That's how it will be.

Thank you for the names of the birds that you studied at Maoz. Here, in the desert, there are great birds flying overhead, at whom we shoot. May these birds never reach you at home. How noisy they are. Do you know their name, too?

June 2, 1941

In spite of everything we did celebrate Shavuot. The whole company, both officers and men, gathered together in a deep gully. One of the officers made a speech about the meaning of the holiday and one of the men got up and added something to this. . . . But I felt very sad, nevertheless. This is the fourth holiday for me away from home. Hanukkah I was in the training camp at Sarafand. Purim I was in Africa, and on the *seder* night I lay at the battlefront, in the front lines—and now it is Shavuot.

A Jewish legend tells about Shavuot that there is an hour during the night of the holiday when the heavens open and he who is fortunate to strike the right time can ask for all the wishes of his heart. There were days when our eyes were raised to the sky in childish faith and innocence. . . . But today the heavens do not open for us. They are closed securely against us. When they open, it is only to rain down death and destruction. And this holiday is after all the holiday celebrating the giving of the Law, the Torah, that is so sharply opposed to everything that is happening in the world today. But if the heavens were to open for me, after all, on the night of Shavuot, I should ask but one thing —that Nazism be destroyed and that a new world should arise after that, a world in which we, too, will be given the chance to build our home, a home for the most wretched of nations. And when this day comes, and it is bound to come, even if after much blood and tears and suffering, *then* I shall return home. . . .

May 22, 1942

This is the second Shavuot that I have spent in the army. Did you celebrate the Festival of the Firstfruits at Naan? We wondered for a long while about how we would celebrate it here—

for how can we bring the firstfruits of the season in the desert?
We whitewashed our dining room—the large tent—and decorated it with greens that we brought from a nearby town. In the
center we hung an inscription: "Those who sow with tears will
reap in gladness." We read the passages in the *Aggadah* that
relate to the holiday and someone played the flute while we sang
in chorus. It looked as if this was a party in the kibbutz, instead
of a party of soldiers. At the end there was a farewell speech by
the commanding officer, who is going on a short leave. He said
some very moving things, about his feelings among us on this
holiday and about how proud he was to be with us. At the end
we broke into a *hora* just the way we do at home. Outside, in the
moonlight, we formed a circle and even A——, from Kfar
Giladi, danced with us, in spite of the fact that his position as
sergeant major embarrasses him not a little.

Translated by Hilda Auerbach[14]

* *The Torah Is Accepted Again in Buchenwald

S. B. UNSDORFER

Strangely enough it was on the pyre of the camp, in that hellhole
of Buchenwald, that I received my first injection of vitamin R—
Religious Revival.

A few days before our scheduled departure for Czechoslo-
vakia, the camp loudspeakers blazed out an announcement that
the Jewish chaplain to the U. S. forces would be conducting
religious services in the evening to mark the festival of Shavuot
—the anniversary of the receiving of the Law by the Jewish
people on Mount Sinai.

Having lost my handwritten diary, as well as my *Haggadah,*
during the march from Nieder-Orschel to Buchenwald, this announcement came as a pleasant yet disturbing surprise.

Since my childhood I had always looked forward eagerly to the
arrival of our wonderful and inspiring festivals, and particularly
so in the tragic war years. But I wondered whether we weren't

being put to a test too soon. Who among those thousands of physical and mental cripples would want to attend services and prayers so soon after their tragic experiences? The Festival of the Receiving of the Torah! Within a few weeks after liberation, religion, which had seemed to do so little for us, was now challenging us and our loyalties.

But just as you cannot measure the physical strength of an oppressed people, so you cannot gauge its spiritual wealth and power.

On that evening, Buchenwald staged a fantastic demonstration of faith and loyalty to God. Thousands upon thousands of liberated Jews crowded into the specially vacated block for the first postwar Jewish religious service to be held on the soil of defeated Germany. The *Mussulmänner,* the cripples, the injured, and the weak came to demonstrate to the world that the last ounce of their strength, the last drop of their blood, and the last breath of their lives belonged to God, to Torah, and to the Jewish religion.

As Chaplain [Herschel] Schacter intoned the evening prayers, all the inmates in and outside the block stood in silence, reaccepting the Torah whose people, message, and purpose Hitler's Germany had attempted to destroy. Jewish history repeated itself. Just as our forefathers who were liberated from Egypt accepted the Law in the desert, so did we, the liberated Jews of Buchenwald, reaccept the same Law in the concentration camps of Germany.[15]

*

* *Shavuot in the Soviet Union*

JOSHUA ROTHENBERG

While Shavuot is from the religious point of view as important and meaningful a holiday as the other two festivals of Sukkot and Passover, it is not associated with symbols and symbolic rites such as the *matzah, etrog,* and Sukkot booths. The decorating of houses and synagogues and eating of dairy dishes on Shavuot is an observed custom but has not the power of a religious injunction. For that reason Shavuot has not attracted as much attention from

Soviet authorities or Soviet antireligious propagandists as have other Jewish holidays.

Attendance of worshipers at the Shavuot prayers is, as a rule, not very large, except on the second day of the holiday when *Yizkor,* the prayer for the departed, is recited (any occasion when *Yizkor* is said attracts many worshipers). Whereas 400 to 500 persons was the average number of worshipers on the first day of Shavuot in the large synagogues of Moscow and Leningrad, the number of worshipers in the Moscow synagogue on the second day of Shavuot was 2,500 [in 1964], as reported in the Israeli press.[16]

*

*Shavuot Services in Newport, R. I., May 28, 1773

EZRA STILES *

Pentecost. Went to the Synagogue at ix h[ours] A.M. At reading the Law the Rabbi [Haijm Isaac Karigal of Hebron] was desired and read the Ten Commandments. But before reading the Law and the Prophets the Rabbi went to the Desk or Taubauh and preached a Sermon about 47 minutes long in Spanish. It was interspersed with Hebrew. His Oratory, Elocution, and Gestures were fine and oriental. It was very animated. He exhorted them not to perplex themselves with Traditions and Criticisms, but to attend to certain capital points and principal points of Religion —he expatiated upon the Miseries and Calamities of their Nation in their present Captivity and Dispersion and comforted them under their Tribulations by the assured Prospect of the Messiahs Kingdom—he exhorted them not to be discouraged but persevere &c—he showed that Calamities and sufferings were not Evidence of their being forsaken of God—that Adversity and Judgments were the common Lot of all Nations Kingdoms and Countries—and instanced in the Desolation made by the Eruption of Mt. Vesuvius near Naples in Italy which he said he had seen, and beheld the Deluge of liquid Matter, flowing and carry-

* Minister in Newport who later became president of Yale University.

A
SERMON

PREACHED AT THE

SYNAGOGUE,

In NEWPORT, *Rhode-Ifland,*

CALLED

"The SALVATION of ISRAEL:"

On the Day of PENTECOST,

Or FEAST of WEEKS,

The 6th day of the Month *Sivan,*
The year of the Creation, 5533:
Or, *May* 28, 1773.

Being the ANNIVERSARY
Of giving the LAW at *Mount Sinai:*

BY THE VENERABLE HOCHAM,
THE LEARNED RABBI,

HAIJM ISAAC KARIGAL,

Of the City of HEBRON, near JERUSALEM,
In the HOLY LAND.

NEWPORT, Rhode-Ifland: Printed and Sold by
S. SOUTHWICK, in Queen-Street, 1773.

---

4. Title page of sermon preached by Rabbi Haijm Isaac Karigal
on Shavuot, 1773, at the synagogue in Newport, R. I.
Newport. 1773. The first sermon
both preached by a rabbi and printed in the United States.

ing all before it, overwhelming Villages, Houses, Temples, people &c—yet Christians did not consider this as an Evidence against their Religion; neither was the Destruction of the Temple and the City of Jerusalem by the Romans &c any argument against the Truth of the Jewish Religion. They were chastised for their Sins, but not forsaken of God, who was the common Parent of all mankind, while he had chosen Israel his peculiar Treasure. Then he enlarged with Fervor on the Divine Benevolence and seemed to be elevated with very sublime Ideas of the divine Benevolence Mercy and Love; which he converted into an argument for their loving one another, which he earnestly pressed upon them—and closed with a serious Prayer. The Affinity of the Spanish and Latin enabled me to understand something of the Discourse—but after all I have but an imperfect Idea of it. He wore Spectacles thro' the whole Sermon, and frequently looked down on the Desk before him as if he had the Discourse written, but I don't know that he had any Writing. The Jews intend to print it. He was dressed in his Fur Cap, scarlet Robe, green silk Damask Vest, and a chintz under Vest,—girt with a Sash or Turkish Girdle—besides the Alb. with Tzizith. The Jews don't admire his *reading* (the X Commandments) and indeed he speaks off with much greater Fluency and Ease than he reads, tho' he reads correctly. There was Dignity and Authority about him, mixt with Modesty. After the Sermon, two Rolls of the Law were brought forward with great Solemnity, and after Elevation the parasang [*parashat*] including the xxth Chapter of Genesis [sic] was read as usual: at reading the X Commandments the whole Congregation rose up and stood. After which Mr. Rivera's little son 8 or 9 aet. read the first Chapter of Ezekiel—then prayers for all Nations, for the Jews, for the King and Royal Family, for the Magistrates of Rhode Island.—The Law was then returned in solemn procession singing the usual Psalm: then Alms Prayers and Singing concluded the Whole. The Synagogue was decorated with Flowers &c. About the Time the Rabbi began sermon which was a few minutes before Xh three of the Commissioners came in, viz. Gov. Wanton & Judge Oliver and afterwards Judge Auchmuty and were seated in the Seat of the Parnass or President of the Synagogue. The whole service ended a quarter after twelve.[17]

*

The First Confirmation in New York

HYMAN B. GRINSTEIN

In 1846, Max Lilienthal introduced in his union of German synagogues a custom previously unknown in the United States: the confirmation of both boys and girls on Shavuot. Twice a week, during the five months preceding the festival, he gave instruction to all children over twelve concerning the attributes of God, the Ten Commandments, the holidays and fast days, Jewish ceremonies, and one's duties towards oneself, one's parents, and others. Each teaching was accompanied by the memorization of a short biblical statement in Hebrew. On Shavuot in 1846 this first group was confirmed in Anshe Chesed synagogue on Henry Street in the presence of members of the three synagogues, the parents of the confirmands in special seats of honor, and the teachers of the various congregational schools. The program included the singing of psalms by the confirmands, an examination of their readiness for confirmation, an exhortation to them to keep the faith, delivered by the rabbi, the reply of the confirmands solemnly promising adherence to Judaism, the distribution to them of a printed biblical verse, and the blessing of the confirmands by their parents and by the rabbi.

This novelty evoked considerable criticism from the Orthodox. There is no telling how much more objection would have been forthcoming if the boards of the German synagogues had acceded to Lilienthal's proposal that both boys and girls should be called as a group *(im kol ha-nearim)* to the reading of the Torah on the second day of Shavuot as a part of the confirmation ceremony. It should be pointed out, however, that Lilienthal intended the confirmation as a supplement to, rather than a substitute for, the traditional *bar mitzvah* ceremony for boys.

When the union of German synagogues collapsed, the Shavuot confirmation ceremony was abandoned by the three German congregations until after 1860. Temple Emanu-El, however, instituted the custom in 1852. Although the program of instruction and the nature of the actual ceremony of confirmation in the 1850s are not known, this synagogue seems to have held confirmations every year after the custom was started.[18]

*
*Shavuot on a Farm in Connecticut

ISRAEL KASOVICH

Our first holiday on the farm was Shavuot. All around us was a sea of verdure and everything was in bloom. I told my children that this holiday commemorates the giving of the Torah to the children of Israel at Sinai—a Torah which teaches us to live on fair and brotherly terms with our fellowmen; and who could do this so well as the farmer with his unique mode of life? I described to them how our ancestors, the Jewish farmers of Palestine, used to go to Jerusalem for Shavuot, bearing the fairest fruits as offerings to the Temple; how the hills of Judea would resound with the sweet Hebrew songs of the brave, proud Jewish farmers; and how the priests and leading men of Jerusalem would come out to meet their brothers, whose labor fed the whole nation, and escort them with great pomp to the Temple. And I related to them how, when I was a little boy and went on the eve of Shavuot to other men's fields to pluck some blades of grass and twigs with which to decorate our house for the holiday, gentile peasant boys threw stones and set their dogs at me. And now we were living in a free country among our own green fields and woods, and I was proud to hold our Torah in one hand and a plow in the other.

Translated by Maximilian Hurwitz[19]

*
*The Festival in Haifa

GERSHON AHITUV

The preparations for the great day were noticeable in Haifa on the eve of Shavuot. The streets and the houses were decorated

with greenery and national flags. Crowds of people in festive
mood, including groups of youth and children who had come
from other parts of the country in order to take part in the
festivities, filled the streets and the festival atmosphere permeated the city. On both sides of the streets leading to the square
on which the ceremony was to take place, two large gates were
erected, adorned with the inscription *Barukhim ha-baim* (Blessed
are they who come). One gate took the shape of two winged
lions, and the second was in the form of a gigantic bunch of
grapes with two doves stretching their wings on both sides.

The platform for the bearers of the firstfruits was set up in the
courtyard of the Technion. It was ornamented with symbols
connected with the festival and a representation of the Temple.
The celebration began with the procession of the bearers of the
firstfruits. All the villagers of the Valley of Jezreel, the Valley of
the Jordan and the Galil were represented, each village trying to
bring forth the best that it had produced in the past year. There
were carts laden with hay, barley, wheat, vegetable crops, chickens, sheep, and calves. The offerings, which in ancient days were
brought to the priest and the Temple, were now made to the
Keren Kayemet le-Yisrael (Jewish National Fund).

After passing through the streets of the city the celebrants
reached the platform and were received with loud applause by
the thousands of people who crowded both sides of the streets,
and the roofs and balconies of the houses.

On the platform there took place a pageant of the bringing of
the firstfruits in ancient days, showing the men of the Galil
leaving their villages to go up to Jerusalem, being met by men
of the Negev and Gilead on the way, and forming with them one
great procession, composed of large numbers of people with
their cattle, their donkeys and their camels, laden with sheaves
of corn and baskets of fruit. Next the spectators could see the
men of Jerusalem, headed by the priests, coming out to meet
them, welcoming them with singing and dancing and escorting
them with rejoicing to the Temple.

The children also played their part in the festivities. Thousands
of children garlanded with leaves and flowers walked in procession between the rows of spectators, bringing their offerings.
Fourteen boys, clad in white clothes, and fourteen girls, dressed
in blue robes, representing Levites, received the firstfruits from

15. A *bikkurim* festival in Kibbutz Gan Shmuel, Israel.

the children. The "Levites" sang and declaimed the formula beginning "My father was a wandering Aramean," continued with singing of biblical verses connected with the occasion, and concluded with the "Dance of Sheaves."

In 1932 when Menachem Ussishkin, at that time at the head of the Keren Kayemet, accepted the firstfruits brought forth by the children of Israel, he emphasized the importance and significance of the festival in the following words:

"You, children of Israel, have brought the firstfruits of your soil, the fruits of your toil, to the supreme body for the redemption of the land of our fathers. Our forefathers two thousand years ago also brought forth firstfruits on Shavuot, but then they brought their firstfruits not to Haifa, the City of the Future, but to Jerusalem, the Eternal City; not to Mount Carmel, but to Mount Moriah. And they gave the fruits not to the Jewish National Fund, but to the holy Temple.

"Nevertheless, I have consented to accept from you your firstfruits in the form in which you have brought them today for this reason: the same form was customary in that period when our people lived as a free nation in its own homeland. Our times today are not the same as that period, to which we aspire, which we hope to attain, for which we long. Our redemption is still not the complete redemption, but the beginning of the redemption.

The Messiah has still not come. There are only the agonies of the Messiah. Therefore the form of renewal of our lives and the bringing of the firstfruits is still not complete. It accords with this period; it is only the beginning of the ancient form, which will be complete when the redemption is complete. . . .

"Let us not forget that the national chain of the people begins with the festival which we are celebrating today, the festival of Shavuot. This was not only a festival of nature, the Festival of the Firstfruits of soil and toil. This is the day of the 'Giving of the Torah,' and on that day we became a nation. We cannot separate these two festivals. In one day we were created a nation and became a people tilling its land with the sweat of its brow."[20]

*

*Bikkurim *in Kibbutz Matzuba*

GERSHON AHITUV

The sea is wide and still during the hot month of Sivan. From behind the copse that faces the road there approaches a red tractor, pulling a wide platform laden with freshly cut fodder. Aboard are a host of little children wearing their holiday clothes, decorated with greenery. Immediately following you see a procession of people attired in holiday costume, some walking, others traveling in vehicles.

The entire cavalcade is decked out in fresh foliage. They move slowly, the tractors and machines, the horse- and donkey-drawn wagons. The wagons are filled with workers in high spirits, dressed in their working clothes, carrying their tools and the fruits of their labors. There are broad-shouldered plowmen; workers from the orchards and vineyards wearing their wide-brimmed hats; sun-tanned vegetable gardeners and poultrymen carrying baskets of chickens and eggs; drivers and beekeepers.

Among them on foot are the dairy workers and the fodder-men pulling a little bull calf. There are those who work in the banana orchards, two of them carrying a weighty bunch of ripe bananas, fastened to poles; the landscape gardeners adorned in flowers; the mushroom growers with their produce. Following on their heels, gaily singing, are the workers from the laundry, the carpentry shop, and the looms, the builders, and those who do the sewing and work in the kitchen. A band accompanies the procession and song after song spontaneously breaks forth. "Open the way for us, we bring the *bikkurim!*" . . .

The cavalcade reaches the reaped fields. On their faces you can see their pride as workers on the soil. In festive spirit they enter a square through seven gates which are crowned with the seven kinds of produce with which the Land of Israel was blessed.

One after another, the workers of the various branches approach the stage and offer, with the appropriate blessing, the firstfruits contained in their straw baskets. Seven *haverim* and *haverot* stand on the decorated stage and accept the baskets, containing the produce of the fields and the garden. . . .

Those who accept the *bikkurim* answer with festive greetings, and the leader of the ceremony totals up the income, which is dedicated to the Jewish National Fund. The children, who have also brought their firstfruits, proudly present recitations and songs. A group performs a play about the story of Ruth. The choir accompanies them with songs and special harvest dances. The time spent in the fields is enjoyed by all; the *haverim* and the children sing and dance together, there in the fields as in the days of yore. Before everyone starts back home, the sun begins to sink into the sea, the young *haverim* pass around biscuits coated with honey and glasses of milk. Thus the biblical saying is fulfilled in Matzuba: "He brought us to this place and gave us this land, a land flowing with milk and honey" (Deuteronomy 26.9).[21]

＊

＊Tikkun Lel Shavuot *at* Yifat

MEIR EYALI

One of the contributions of the kibbutz movement toward a new Judaism—and this in spite of its generally secular ideology—has been the revival of the festivals. How charming to see the children gathering the *omer,* or bringing their firstfruits, to the accompaniment of music and dance! But in thus celebrating nature and the seasons, without the religious content, there is a danger of what might almost seem a return to paganism, which is an enemy of true culture. At Shavuot, the Festival of the Giving of Our Law, the specifically religious and Jewish aspect is usually omitted altogether.

To correct this, we decided two years ago to revive the old custom of all-night study on Shavuot. Some seventy took part: former students of the high school at Yifat, teachers and members of Yifat and neighboring kibbutzim. Roughly two hours were devoted to Talmud (Sanhedrin): examination of witnesses, "there is no deputy for an illegal act," "who saves a single soul, saves a whole world," leading up to discussion of current issues involved, e.g., the trial of war criminals. After a short break, a philosophical lecture on "The Moral Autonomy of Man" was followed by discussion. Lastly, there was a lesson on "Honor thy father and thy mother," with the reading of texts from the Bible and *Aggadah.* By that time, it was already dawn, and the "students" dispersed to their homes, carrying with them the memory of a true spiritual experience.

The *Tikkun* could not be conducted last year on account of the Six-Day War; but this year we are holding it again.[22]

*

*At the Western Wall

YAACOV LURIA

For this holiday [Shavuot] we return from Tel Aviv to Jerusalem, which is after all where the great holidays were meant to be celebrated. Waiting at dusk for evening services to begin at the Western Wall, one can with no great effort of imagination picture the scene two thousand years ago. Then as now there were the dark shadows of birds flying across the face of this outer wall, and a great horde of people assembled with the coming of evening. Cut into the rock to the left of the exposed part of the Wall is a series of cavelike rooms, one of which contains a deep well. Here surely some of the multitudes which came to Jerusalem on foot crowded for shelter.

Our sages tell us that there was always room, no matter how many came. A remarkable thing about the Wall today is that it seems to have room enough for everybody. Though there may be dozens of *minyanim* at prayer simultaneously, none seems to interfere with the others. Each *minyan* has its own style: black-garbed Hasidim pray with zeal, raising their voices toward God with force and resonance. The oriental Jews pray more quietly, as if to impress their Father through understatement. The boys from the beautiful newly built Yeshivah Hakotel sing and dance in a circle, then bow away facing the Wall. Finally they dance their way up the hills toward the *yeshivah,* their white skullcaps and shirts receding in a billowing stream into the night. The tourists gather in knots to watch at the low stone fence at the approach to the Wall and store up impressions; on holidays and *Shabbat* they may not use cameras here. And somehow it all fits together in a single harmonious setting to which the massive Wall is the eternal backdrop.

Jerusalem in May is hot, dry, and exhausting, and we are in bed by ten o'clock that night. We fall asleep quickly, for our room is in a quiet street off Zion Square. At midnight we are awakened by the sound of singing and dancing, lusty enough for a regiment. This, apparently, is not a night for sleeping, not in Jerusalem at any rate. I dress quickly and look outside for the revelers, but they have disappeared. I walk back to the Wall through dark, silent streets. Anywhere else I would be uneasy; in Israel one loses his fear of walking alone at night.

Close to the Jaffa Gate light gleams from the windows of a tiny Kurdish synagogue. A man makes room for me on his bench when I enter, and for a long while I join the congregants in chanting *Tikkun Lel Shavuot.* As I leave, they motion for me to take some *kibbud* from a table laden with cake, fruit, and chick-peas.

By now there is a steady flow of people through the steep narrow walls of the Old City toward the Wall. The Hasidim have left no one at home; entire families are here in their holiday clothes, earlocked children not even sleepy-eyed, infants cradled in the arms of parents. The stalls of the Arab market are padlocked, but the daytime smells linger. The cool night air is redolent of coffee and pepper, cabbage and scallions, and uncured sheepskins. Aroused by the shuffling of hundreds of shoes, hens in a live poultry market cackle behind a wire enclosure.

At the Wall there is no night. Light highlights the rough-hewn Herodian bottom stones, but it floods the entire square. Everywhere, in the open and in the cavernous rooms at the side, men are bent and swaying over the *Tikkun*. Some, having apparently completed the *Tikkun,* are reading Psalms or studying Talmud. By three o'clock the crescent moon has vanished and the first glimmerings of dawn appear in the sky.

The square is as full as I have ever seen it. Prayer shawls are draped over thousands of heads, thousands of voices rise in prayer. Across the millennia I hear the echo of voices at Sinai. "We will do and we will listen." All my intellectual reservations fall away. From under a heap of prayer books I dig up an old prayer shawl and enfold myself in it. A *minyan* is just beginning the service, and my voice is one among many. "How goodly are thy tents, O Jacob, thy dwelling places, O Israel!"

It is broad day when I return to our room. I try to sleep, but there are still voices vibrating within me. I sleep very little, but I am exhilarated, not exhausted, that entire day. Miriam marvels over that and remarks, "There must be something in the air here."

"There always has been," I say.[23]

SHAVUOT IN POETRY

*

*Sinai

JUDAH HALEVI

*physician, philosopher, and the foremost Hebrew poet of the Middle Ages
(c. 1085–1142)*

When Thou didst descend upon Sinai's mountain,
　　It trembled and shook 'neath Thy mighty hand,
And the rocks were moved by Thy power and splendor:
　　How then can my spirit before Thee stand
On the day when darkness o'erspread the heavens
　　And the sun was hidden at Thy command?
The angels of God, for Thy great name's worship,
　　Are ranged before Thee, a shining band,
And the children of men are awaiting ever
　　Thy mercies unnumbered as grains of sand;
The Law they received from the mouth of Thy glory
　　They learn and consider and understand.
O accept Thou their song and rejoice in their gladness
　　Who proclaim Thy glory in every land.
　　　　　　　　　　　Translated by Alice Lucas[1]

*
* The Law

ABRAHAM IBN EZRA

a Hebrew scholar and poet of Spain who wrote Bible commentaries; some of his poetry is included in the traditional liturgy (c. 1092–1167)

My help, my hope, my strength shall be,
Thou perfect Law of God, in thee!

My faith shall be my rock of might,
Its Law my portion and my right,
Its testimonies my delight,
And day by day, my voice I raise
In song and hymn to chant their praise.

How did th' angelic hosts lament
When from their midst, by God's intent,
The holy Law to earth was sent.
"Woe that the pure and sanctified
Should now on sinful lips abide."

The people trembled when they saw
Approaching them the heavenly Law—
Their voices rose in joy and awe:
"Thy covenant, O Lord, fulfill,
Declare it, we will do Thy will."

Great wonders He on Sinai wrought,
When unto us His Law He taught,
Wherefore to praise His name I sought;
But what am I what my words
Before the almighty Lord of lords?

Hear Thou Thy people's prayer, O King,
When like the heavenly host they sing
Thrice Holy, Holy—uttering
Sweet hymns and songs of pleasantness
With joy and awe Thy name to bless.

                              Translated by Alice Lucas[2]

*

* The Giving of the Law

NINA DAVIS SALAMAN

a British Jewish essayist and poet who translated many liturgical selections (1876–1925)

When the Holy One came to give life, to reveal the great
light of His Law,
All His wonder of worlds grew silent in sudden, unspeakable awe,
More tense than the stillness ere dawn riseth up in a burst
of gold,
Every quiver and pulse, every breath of the world caught
fast in His hold.
No twitter of bird, no soaring of wings made stir in the air,
And the oxen that lowed from the fields were mute as if
death passed there;
And in heaven the Ophanim paused in their flight through
the limitless space,
And the Seraphim, singing Thrice Holy, grew still in their
glorious place.
Full of the storm and the swell of the tide, an immovable sea
Lay dumb with the hushing of lips, with a pausing eternity;
Till the life-giving voice should thrill, and the imminent call
be heard,
A marvel, absorbing the sound of all spheres, the Ineffable
Word;
Until God in His wonder of worlds, the Holy One, blessed
be He,
Should set His creation athrob with the light and the life to
be.
Lo! who could endure to stand on the terrible day when He
came,
In a universe full of His voice, grown thunderous with
sound of His name?
Lo! He struck the high seas with terror, He saw the mountains quake,
And the stars in His heaven paled, "and my soul went forth
when He spake."
And from stars to the shaken earth where the trembling
footsteps trod,
One voice fell—one, tremendous: I am the Lord thy God.[3]

16. Torah shield with Shavuot plate. Silver, repoussé.
    Master: M. Wolff. Augsburg, Germany. 18th century. See Chapter 8.

*

The Ever-living Moses

A. ALAN STEINBACH

rabbi, author, and editor; recipient of many poetry awards and of the National Jewish Welfare Board's Frank L. Weil Award for distinguished contributions to the advancement of American Jewish culture

The heavens have their span and earth its measure,
The stars their galaxies, the tides their flow;
But who can fathom boundaries for the treasure
In a heart that radiates faith's lambent glow?
O saintly soul, with wisdom's crown bejeweled,
Transcendent prophet of the true and good,
Through you our Torah's *Ner Tamid* was fueled
With love divine enkindling brotherhood.

You are not dead! We sense your spirit treading
Within the temples of our wounded age,
We feel your benedictive hands upspreading,
Beckoning homage to our heritage.
You taught us, Moses, how to spurn earth's clod,
To mount life's balustrades that lead to God.

*

The Vision of Moses

ISRAEL M. LASK

author of poems and stories in Hebrew and English who achieved recognition for his excellent translations of Hebrew works

Akiba the sage was gnarled and hoar,
Akiba was fragrant with our fathers' lore
As acacia and jasmine blooms that pour
Their scents in the night—like storming of hail
That scatters in pattering hurricane
And rattles again in pelting rain—
And rend the veil of the heavens to glow
With the incense-flare of the wavering air
Mounting the perfumed skies to bear
Its daily offering, the flower-drenched gale

Fanning the Seraphim to blow
The flame of their song to the very rim
Of our dim hearing as our bodies hymn
    The Ancient of Days in the dance. . . .
Akiba expounded Torah before
His forty thousand students and more
And his teaching forsook his mouth to soar
To the boundless light where Moses saw
Rabbi Akiba teaching the Law.

    And Moses quivered and Moses shook,
And scarcely a moment did he dare to look
Or hearken to Akiba's rede.
And he cried to the Lord, "I am lost indeed;
Where did the harvest ripen to feed
Such famine for vision? And who this seer
And shepherd feeding my flock without fear
Of Israel's foes? Whence comes his clear
Spring of the Torah that glows as it flows?"

    And the Lord replied, "From every tittle
And jot of each letter of the Torah he will whittle
A law like rock from a quarry. Little
He needs to stablish and buttress the brittle
Power of Yeshurun. From every stroke
Of the letters of the Torah he fashioned a cloak
For Israel's faith; he fashions a wall
Of deeds round the Torah to flame through the night
Of Israel in exile. Eyes grow dim
As they gaze at the brightness surrounding him,
And ages will come to renew their sight
Within the buttresses and bastions of might
He raised round the Torah never to fall
But rearing through the ages, rising over all."[4]

*

* *The Ten Commandments*

RUTH F. BRIN

short-story writer, poet, and interpreter of Jewish liturgy

And the words which were spoken to the people
from the fiery mountain were ten.

In Egypt the priests were powerful and rich
because they knew the secrets of the Book
of the Dead;

In Greece the oracles revealed the fates
determined by capricious gods for princes
or warriors;

In Babylon the priests taught each other
mysteries too deep for ordinary men to fathom.

But in Israel there is no secret and privileged
priesthood, but a holy people.

In Israel the heart of the mystery is the Ten
Commandments, so easy to understand a child
can recite them as he counts on his fingers.

In Israel we pray for God's help
when we make the difficult effort
to perform His commandments.[5]

*

Where Is That Mountain?

CHARLES REZNIKOFF

a native New Yorker who writes fiction, drama, and verse and has served as editor of the Jewish Frontier *and as a contributing editor of the* Menorah Journal

Where is that mountain of which we read in the Bible—
Sinai—on which the Torah was given to Israel?
Perhaps it is in Egypt
Where the wild Israelites left the little idols
Of the sons of Jacob, the little idols
which stood in the corners of the tents
and rode with the rider
under the saddlecloth; perhaps it is in Egypt—
a land of such affliction
three thousand years or so afterwards
we speak of it to this day.
Blessed are You, Lord, God of the universe,
Who has kept us alive.

Where is that mountain of which we read in the Bible—
Sinai—on which the Torah was given to Israel?
Perhaps it is in Palestine;
for Sinai was built out of skeletons
of much suffering,
in which the lives of the Israelites
were like the sands—
that become in the centuries rock, ledges of rock,
a mountain, and at last
the Law,
cut into tables of stone.
Blessed are You, God, King of the universe,
Who has kept Israel alive.[6]

*

**Sinai*

NELLY SACHS

winner of the coveted Nobel Prize for Literature; reported to be "the
greatest writer of verse in the German language" who, in her own words,
represented "the tragedy of the Jewish people" (1891–1970)

You ark of starry sleep
broken open in the night,
where all your treasures,
the petrified eyes of the lovers,
their mouths, ears, their putrefied happiness
moved into glory.
Smoking with memory you struck out
as the hand of eternity turned your hourglass—
as the dragonfly in the blood-ironstone
knew the hour of its creator—

Sinai
down from your peak
Moses bore the opened sky
on his forehead
cooling step by step
until they who waited in the shadow
were able to bear, trembling,
what shone beneath the veil—

Is there still an heir
to the succession of them that trembled?
Oh, may he glow
in the crowd of them that do not remember,
of the petrified!

Translated by Ruth and Matthew Mead[7]

*

*Dead Men Don't Praise God

JACOB GLATSTEIN

an American Yiddish poet, novelist, and journalist who was the recipient of several awards for his creative writing (1896–1971)

We received the Torah on Sinai
and in Lublin we gave it back.
Dead men don't praise God,
the Torah was given to the living.
And just as we all stood together
at the giving of the Torah,
so did we all die together at Lublin.

I'll translate the tousled head, the pure eyes,
the tremulous mouth of a Jewish child
into this frightful fairy tale.
I'll fill the sky with stars
and I'll tell him:
our people is a fiery sun
from beginning to beginning to beginning.
Learn this, my little one,
from beginning to beginning to beginning.

Our whole imagined people
stood at Mount Sinai
and received the Torah.
The dead, the living, the unborn,
every soul among us answered:
we will obey and hear.
You, the saddest boy of all generations,
you also stood on Mount Sinai.
Your nostrils caught the raisin-almond fragrance of each
word of the Torah.

It was Shavuot, the green holiday.
You sang with them like a songbird:

I will hear and obey, obey and hear
From beginning to beginning to beginning.
Little one, your life is carved
in the constellations of our sky,
you were never absent,
you could never be missing.
When we were, you were.
And when we vanished,
you vanished with us.

And just as we all stood together
at the giving of the Torah,
so did we all die together in Lublin.
From all sides the souls came flocking,
The souls of those who had lived out their lives, of those
who had died young,
of those who were tortured, tested in every fire,
of those who were not yet born,
and of all the dead Jews from great-grandfather Abraham
down,
they all came to Lublin for the great slaughter.
All those who stood at Mount Sinai
and received the Torah
took these holy deaths upon themselves.
"We want to perish with our whole people,
we want to be dead again,"
the ancient souls cried out.
Mama Sara, Mother Rachel,
Miriam and Deborah the prophetess
went down singing prayers and songs,
and even Moses, who so much didn't want to die
when his time came,
now died again.
And his brother, Aaron,
and King David
and the Rambam, the Vilna Gaon,
and Mahram and Marshal
the Seer and Abraham Eiger.
And with every holy soul
that perished in torture
hundreds of souls
of Jews long dead died with them.

And you, beloved boy, you too were there.
You, carved against the constellated sky,
you were there, and you died there.
Sweet as a dove you stretched out your neck
and sang together with the fathers and mothers.
From beginning to beginning to beginning.

Shut your eyes, Jewish child,
and remember how the Baal Shem rocked you
in his arms
when your whole imagined people
vanished in the gas chambers of Lublin.

And above the gas chambers
and the holy dead souls,
a forsaken abandoned Mount Sinai veiled itself in smoke.
Little boy with the tousled head, pure eyes, tremulous mouth,
that was you, then—the quiet, tiny, forlorn
given-back Torah.
You stood on top of Mount Sinai and cried,
you cried your cry to a dead world.
From beginning to beginning to beginning.

And this was your cry:
we received the Torah on Sinai
and in Lublin we gave it back.
Dead men don't praise God.
The Torah was given to the living.

Translated by Ruth Whitman[8]

*

*Song of Adorning

ABRAHAM SHLONSKY

Hebrew poet, literary editor, and translator of classics from several languages; a major contributor to modern Hebrew literature and recipient of significant awards (1900-1973)

Clear the way, behold, we're nearing!
Festive throngs all singing, cheering.
The fruit festival is this day,
Garden, orchard, field are gay.
From the fields come boy and maiden,
With firstfruits their baskets laden.

Baskets with our land's fruit laden,
Come, let's wreathe them, youth and maiden!
Let us garland them with posies:
Fully blown and fragrant roses.
Come, our baskets let's adorn
With firstfruits on this bright morn!

Translated by Harry H. Fein[9]

17. Bringing the firstfruits in the Bessie Gotsfeld
Children's Village (Kfar Batya), Israel. 1948.

SHAVUOT IN THE
SHORT STORY

*

*Epilogue to the Book of Ruth

HAYYIM NAHMAN BIALIK

most eminent of modern Hebrew poets and leader of the Hebrew literary renaissance who also edited Jewish legends (1873–1934)

Ruth clave continually to the seed of the pure and holy people, as it is written in the Book of Ruth. And Ruth waxed old and full of days, yet she continued fresh and buxom. Her hands never wearied in sowing righteousness, mercy, and compassion upon them that were round about her. And she beheld children's children, and children to the third generation—all of them mighty men and such as feared God.

And at the end of her days, on her knees was born a son to her grandson, Jesse, in his old age, and his name was called David. And the child grew and God blessed him, and he was ruddy, of a beautiful countenance and goodly to look upon, courageous in spirit and steadfast in deed. He taught his fingers to play upon the harp, and he was a sweet singer and skilled in music. When he tended his father's flock he fought doughtily against wild beasts, and smote the lion and the bear and delivered the prey out of their mouth. The sound of his sweet songs filled the hills, and pervaded earth and heaven.

But, in the land of the Philistines, Orpah shriveled from old age and became shrewish and wayward. All day long she sat at crossroads and street corners like any wanton, spinning flax and toying with the spindle-whorl. She, too, beheld children by her giant husband, to the third generation. Among them were Goliath and Yishbi, his brother. In their childhood no hand ruled them and they grew up to be violent and lawless men. They were tall and terrible in appearance, and like their forefathers they clothed themselves in iron and brass; and from their youth up they learned slaughter and murder. Whenever they went out marauding they were like wolves from the wilderness and they drenched the land with tears and blood.

As is the tree so is the fruit thereof, and the fruit of the fruit; for the vigor of the fathers continueth forever in their seed after them.

And when the time was come about, the Philistines gathered together in their camp to fight against Israel, and they stood on the mountain on the one side, and Israel stood on the mountain on the other side, and there was a valley between them. And there went out a champion from the camp of the Philistines whose height was six cubits and a span, and he had a helmet of brass upon his head, and he was clad with a coat of mail. And the weight of the coat was five thousand shekels of brass. And he had greaves of brass upon his legs and a javelin of brass between his shoulders, and the shaft of his spear was like a weaver's beam, and the blade of his spear weighed six hundred shekels of iron, and his shield-bearer went before him, and the Philistine stood and defied the armies of the living God.

He was Goliath, a Philistine from Gath, the great-grandson of Orpah.

And from the ranks of Israel there came out to meet him a youth, ruddy and of a beautiful countenance and goodly to look upon. He had neither weapons nor armor, and nothing in his hand save his staff and his sling, and five smooth stones in his wallet, and on his lips the name of the living God.

He was David, a shepherd from Bethlehem, the great-grandson of Ruth.

A Philistine giant and a Hebrew boy, offspring of the Moabit-
ish sisters, they stood opposite one another in the valley; and in
their eyes burned a deadly enmity, the enmity of one nation and
its god against another nation and its God.

Translated by Herbert Danby[1]

*

*Tikkun Lel Shavuot

DAVID FRISCHMAN

*author of numerous stories and feuilletons, both in Hebrew and Yiddish,
and translator into Hebrew of many works of the great European writers
(1861–1922)*

The month of Sivan, the night when the festival was hallowed
—when the evening stars sang together.

Who has heard the song which the stars sing at night? Who has
listened to the voices of these torches hanging—suspended on
nothing—over our heads? Often do I walk alone through the
streets of the city on summer nights, my ears wide open and
straining for a sound that does not come other than the sound
of my footfalls. I then count my steps, one, one and one, one and
two. . . . I go on counting unconsciously. All around me are the
pure warm breezes, above me a sweet light spread from one end
of the heavens to the other. Gradually these penetrate into me
and touch my very soul, and I tremble and feel agitated from
delicateness and tenderness. Then my heart is roused and it longs
and yearns for that which it has not, and a spirit, the source of
which I know not, enwraps all that is before me. Who does not
know those sacred and lofty moments? Upon whom has this
great and overpowering hand not been laid? In those moments,
man becomes uplifted and exalted, magnified and sanctified, and
his eyes see divine visions, and his ears hear wonders without
number. In such moments, I, too, have suddenly heard the voice
of song that traversed the skies from end to end, and my soul
knew full well who it was that gave forth music at night. . . . Many
a time have I walked alone on summer nights through the city's
streets, but the memory of one of those nights will never forsake

me. It was a night of clear skies, the night when the feast of Shavuot was hallowed. And with the hallowing of the festival, the ground under my feet, too, became holy, and I walked along solemnly, listening intently as the stars above were singing.

Arise all that is around me, come, sing with me, for my lips, too, are filled with song!

"Hallelujah!"

Who is that? Someone has just sung out "Hallelujah." I heard the word distinctly uttered by a human voice. I turned all around me to see who it was that called out, but I could not find the person. Perhaps that was the voice of a man sitting over the Torah all night, reading the book *Tikkun Lel Shavuot.* As I looked around again I discovered that I was not mistaken. I looked through a window and beheld a distinguished-looking aged Jew, sitting at a table reading now softly, now loudly. That man's face will not pass from my memory as long as I live.

Arise, sing ye at night—lo! the glory of the Lord fills all the earth—my lips, too, are filled with song. . . .

"Hallelujah."

The candle in the silver candelabrum had not yet gone out, and the old man was still sitting at the table. The other occupants of the house were already abed, and he was left alone. It was the night of Shavuot, and he had to read the Torah all through the night. The occupants of the house were asleep—but what would they have mattered to him even had they been awake and stayed up with him all night? His sons had gone forth from him, his daughter was not, his wife had died; the people in the house were only strangers with whom he lodged, he had nothing in common with them. The old man roused himself—that day was a festival unto the Lord, and sadness of heart was sinful—he therefore passed his hand over his forehead to shake off, as it were, with outstretched arm, his troublesome thoughts, and took the book up from the table to concentrate the more intently and deeply upon its contents; perchance those verses of Holy Writ would create within him a pure heart and a new spirit. But he read the verses with his lips only, his heart and mind were not there. Various pictures passed before him, while he was entirely unconscious of the words that he was uttering with his lips. One page after another he read off, but he was not aware of it. . . .

What is the latter end of man whose way is hidden?

"And we said unto my lord: we have a father, an old man, and a child of his old age, a little one; and his brother is dead, and he alone is left of his mother, and his father loveth him."

And he, had he not loved him? Had he not loved the son of his old age, the little one, as his own soul, and guarded him as the apple of his eye? Why, he himself had been old and full of days, and he, too, had had a son of his old age, a little one, of whom he had made more than of all his brothers. Of course, it was true he had loved all his children with an exceeding great love, but they had angered him with their vanities, and had embittered his life, and only his youngest son was left unto him. Yes, yes, his older sons refused to go in his ways, and turned away from the trodden path upon which all the loyal and faithful of Israel went, and they followed after the stubbornness of the evil hearts. . . . No, not after the stubbornness of their hearts did they go, for one cannot call it stubbornness when one chooses a new way for oneself that suits one's taste and accords with one's spirit; therefore, of his sons, too, it cannot be said that they went after the stubbornness of their hearts, but only that they chose new ways for themselves in accord with their own spirit. He had set his heart upon leading them to the fountain-springs of the Torah, and to make of them "children taught of the Lord," but they turned very soon from that way, and they chose for themselves other studies; and even when they did that, it was not their own transgression, nor their own sin. It was the transgression of the generation, and the sin of the many; for a new spirit had passed over the land, and had gathered his sons up, too, in its folds. In those days seminaries [for secular education] had been established in Vilna and Zhitomir, and the Jewish youth from many cities flocked to them, and his two elder sons also went. Until that very day he did not know whither they went, whether to Vilna or Zhitomir. He would never forget that day when, on getting up in the morning, and calling his sons to receive their lesson from him, he had got no reply, and on walking into their room, found it empty, but for a short note on the table from both of them that that night they were taking their bundles on their shoulders and going to learn "Haskalah," to seek "Enlightenment." Then he flew into a rage, and his heart ached and ached. . . . Though there came times when he forgave them for what they had done to him, yet their action had set up a lasting antipathy between him and them, and so, even when he pitied them as a father having compassion with his children, his heart was not whole with them, as it had previously been. Thus had his older sons treated him. But the youngest, the child of his old age, was still left to him, and he loved him more than all royal treasures—nay, even this day he loves him as he ever has done. . . .

"Visiting the iniquity of fathers upon children, upon the third generation, and upon the fourth generation, unto those that hate Me, and doing kindness unto thousands, unto those that love Me and unto those who observe My commandments."

Wherein had his forefathers sinned that God should have been visiting their sins upon him and upon his children? See, God doth kindness unto thousands to all who love and to all who observe His commandments, but where was the kindness He had shown him? God does kindness unto the thousands, but does He act thus also to the individual? Why, every man, when he is all by himself and friendless, knows in his heart that he has pursued goodness and kindness all his life, and has never succeeded in obtaining them for himself. How many lonely men turn upon their couches in the night, knowing in their innermost souls that they love God and observe His commandments, but that they had never enjoyed goodness? How many righteous and upright-hearted men read and know that God is one who does kindness unto thousands, but know no one to whom the kindness is done? How many are there who call and are not answered, who cry and are not saved, who keep the commandments and are not kept, who love God and are not loved? Wherever one turns, one sees the righteous man with whom it goes ill, and the wicked man who prospers. Shall the righteous ever perish in their righteousness and the wicked live long in their wickedness?

Sh! The clock strikes. It is midnight. . . .

"Ye shall fear every man his father and his mother, and yet shall keep My Sabbaths."

But his sons had not feared their father or mother, so they got up and went away. They had gone to a strange city and engaged in strange work. Who could know whether in those cities they did not desecrate the Sabbaths? Still, the third son, the youngest, the child of his old age, remained, and him he loved more than all royal treasures. Indeed, that boy was the pick of the brothers

—cleverer than they, and he had made excellent progress in his studies. Why, the boy had been only twelve years old when he delivered a learned discourse to a large congregation in the Great Synagogue, to the wonderment and amazement of all. Yes, he had been only twelve then and his name had come in for praise and for blessing, and all the families of the city blessed themselves with him. When he had been sixteen years old, it was generally known that there was not his equal anywhere, and that soon his seat would be firmly established among the rabbis, and his father would see it all with his own eyes and hear it with his own ears. Then evil had descended suddenly. One morning, this son had approached him saying: "Father, let me go, I desire to take a course at one of the seats of learning in one of the big cities. Let me go, and bless me father. . . . Surely you will not deal harshly with me, nor will you hide yourself from your own flesh!" Such words were spoken to him by his son, the son of whom he used to say to himself that he would live under his roof, and that he would be as one who restoreth the soul unto him, and a compensation for his brothers who had gone away, and now belonged to strangers.

He would never forget that night when he lay upon his bed after having heard those words from him who was the delight of his life. He would never forget the struggles he then waged within his soul that night, or the tears with which he made his couch to melt away. He would never forget his meditation and musings, both spoken and unspoken. As the morning approached, however, his soul had attained rest and he knew what he had to do. In the morning he had called into his son's room and said to him in a calm but loud voice: "Go, my son, go whithersoever your spirit leads you, and may God be with you whithersoever you go. Do I not see that a new spirit is abroad, and who am I that I should boast that I can restrain that spirit. . . ."

"And they shall speak and say 'Our hands have not shed this blood, neither have our eyes seen it. Forgive, O Lord, Thy people Israel whom Thou hast redeemed and suffer not innocent blood to remain in the midst of Thy people Israel,' and the blood shall be forgiven them. . . ."

O Thou mighty God! How shall this blood be forgiven him which his own hands had shed and his own eyes had seen? Would he ever have forgiveness? Had he not with his own eyes suffered innocent blood in his own house and in the midst of his own people? Had he not with his own lips said to his son: "Go, my son, whithersoever thy spirit leadeth thee"? Could he then complain against his son if he did go whithersoever his spirit carried him, and turned aside from the way in which his forefathers had gone from generation to generation?

"And this people will rise up and go astray after the foreign gods of the land, whither they go to be among them and will forsake Me and break My covenant which I have made with them. . . ."

All these words had come about in their fullness, not one of those terrible words failed. Till that very day he could not quite make out exactly what had happened with his son, who had always been very careful and circumspect, and how it was that the evil spirit had entered into him that he should suddenly have turned after the gods of the heathen of the land, to do according to their deeds. Still it was so. In the early days his son had used to write to him from the city of _____ at regular intervals, but afterwards the letters became rarer and rarer, and after a time they ceased altogether, and he heard nothing more either good or bad. Suddenly a terrible piece of news became known throughout the length and breadth of the land. A revolt had been discovered. The youth of Poland had risen up against their monarch. It was the year 1863. Then came the bitter day, and he witnessed it. It was a Friday afternoon and many people had been hurrying to the market square, he among them. When he got there, a terrible sight met his eyes: a high gallows set up in the middle of the market square, with an executioner hauling up, with a rope, youth after youth, strangling them, one by one, unto death. Then he saw the last of these young men . . . and a terrible cry escaped his lips and he fell to the ground and saw no more. . . .

But now other pictures began to pass before him. He saw now neither his older sons nor even his youngest. He only saw his wife as she was lying on the floor with a black cloth covering her, candles burning at her head and her feet toward the door. All he remembered was that it had been the day after that Friday. She, too, must have learnt of the terrible happening, and she too had evidently fallen to the ground like him, but unlike him she did not rise again. . . . After three days, she was committed to Jewish burial with marks of great respect. . . . But all these memories are as nothing, they were vain, they were empty, only one vision stood before him. He was unable to remove it from before his eyes. He could not deface or destroy its marks and its impressions. That would have been as much as his life was worth.

But why was he sinning and not reading the verses as he ought? Why, he was a man who had never in his life transgressed even a minor commandment.

He grasped the book and read on. Page followed page, verse followed verse, and chapter followed chapter . . . but the apparition still stood before him as when it first rose before him. . . .

"And Ruth said 'Entreat me not to leave thee, to turn back from accompanying thee, for whither thou goest I will go, wheresoever thou lodgest I will lodge, thy people shall be my people, and thy God my God, where thou diest will I die, and there will I be buried; the Lord do so to me, and more also, if aught but death part me and thee.' "

Yes, only death parted her and him! Ruth the Moabitess, had, of course, been very beautiful, but sevenfold more beautiful was his daughter. Besides, there had been no girl anywhere so pure-hearted and upright of spirit. Verily, the Almighty had produced a wonderwork when He made her. Indeed, He seemed to have created her for the specific purpose that all who would see her should fall at her feet and worship her; and, in very fact, all who beheld her did kneel and prostrate themselves before her; among them, also, the young Christian druggist from the dispensary facing his house; and his daughter had used to treat him in quite a different manner to that with which she treated other gentiles, for she used to vex, and even anger him, to show him, now and again, how she despised and abominated him, whereas other gentiles she neither vexed nor angered, for she treated them with complete indifference. Who knew how the unfortunate girl strained her very being, and how heroically she fought in defense of her soul to curb the innermost yearnings of her heart, and to subdue them with all her strength. It cannot be that at the last she had neither spirit nor strength left, and she had, therefore, said to him, "Whithersoever thou goest I will go, and wherever thou lodgest I will lodge," and she arose and went whither he went, and they went, both of them together, until they came unto a place where the waters of the river were deep, and there they would sleep where no one would ever wake them. And on the following day the rushing waters washed ashore the body of the young man and the body of the girl. . . .

Sh. The old man is weeping like a little child.

It is morning.

It is a festival unto the Lord today, and Israel's children are walking in a throng to the house of God. They walk with firm steps, their faces are bright with joy, and their garments are their choicest.

Through his window peers an old man, watching the growing festive procession. He cannot take his eyes off the scene. Gradually his mood changes, one by one the wrinkles on his forehead pass away and disappear, and his face, too, beams. Why, it is a festival unto the Lord today, and sadness of spirit is a sin!

Such is the power that the Jew possesses. . . .

Holy is this day unto the Lord; do not grieve!

Translated by J. Israelstam[2]

*

Another Page to the Song of Songs
SHOLOM ALEICHEM

(pseudonym of Shalom Rabinowitz), the great humorist of Yiddish literature; born in 1859 in Russia and died in 1916 in New York; a most prolific writer known as the "Jewish Mark Twain," his masterful stories were extremely popular among the Jewish masses and have been translated into many languages

"Bessie, Bessie! Quicker, quicker!" I caught hold of little Bessie's hand, and together we began to run up the hill. This was the day before Pentecost. "Come, Bessie; the day won't wait for us, little goose, and look what a big hill we've to cross! And on the other side of the hill is a river, and over the river is stretched a wooden bridge. And the water runs and the frogs croak and the planks of the bridge all creak and shake. And when we get to the other side of the bridge we get to the real, real paradise, Bessie. That's where my estates begin!"

"Your estates?"

"I mean the meadow—a big, big field. It stretches and stretches away without an end. And it's all covered with a green blanket, and on the green blanket are scattered specks of yellow and shoots of red. Oh, and you should smell the air—the most beautiful spices in the whole world! And you should see my trees —trees, I tell you, without number—great high trees, branching outwards. And I've got a hill there on which I sit down. I mean to say, if I wish to, I sit on it, but if I don't, well, I just sit down on my magic carpet and I fly away, like an eagle, high above the clouds and mists, over field and forest, over ocean and desert— until I come to the other side of the dark river." . . .

But you ought to know who Bessie is. I think I've already told you once, but I suppose you've forgotten, so I'll tell it to you again.

I had a big brother once—Benny was his name—and he was drowned. And he left behind him a water mill, a young widow, two horses, and a baby. We left the mill there; we sold the two horses; the widow married someone who lived far away; and we kept the baby.

That was Bessie.

Sometimes I really have to laugh. Everybody thinks that Bessie and I are sister and brother. She calls my mother "Mamma," and she calls my father "Papa." And the two of us live together like brother and sister, and we love each other like brother and sister.

Like brother and sister? Then why are you sometimes so shy with me, Bessie? . . . Whenever I speak of Bessie I remember the Song of Songs.

Oh, what was I telling you? Oh, yes, the day before Pentecost. We're just running downhill; first Bessie and I after her. . . . And now we have reached the bridge. . . .

The meadow is green. It stretches and stretches far without an end. And it is all covered with a green blanket and on the green blanket there are scattered specks of yellow and shoots of red. And the scents of the meadow are those of the most beautiful spices in the whole world. And we two walk here with our arms around one another. Just we two, we two alone in this paradise.

"Sammy," says Bessie, looking straight into my eyes and nestling still closer to me, "When shall we begin to gather greens for Pentecost?"

"There is still plenty of time, little goose," I say, and my face burns. I do not know where to look—shall I look into the great blue covering of the sky, or shall I look at the green blanket of the broad field, or shall I look away to the end of the world yonder, where heavens come down to meet the earth? Or shall I look at Bessie's bright face, into her beautiful wide eyes, which seem to me to be deep, deep as the heavens, and sorrowful, sorrowful as the night? A great sorrow lies hidden in them, and a quiet sadness veils them in a mist. I know what the sorrow is that lies hidden in them; I know the reason of her sadness. And I feel a silent anger rising in me against her mother, who married a strange father, and left her forever, forever, just as if they had been strangers. In our house the name of her mother is forbidden, as if Bessie never had a mother. My mother is her mother, my father is her father. And they love her as one of their own children, give her whatever her heart desires. Bessie says she wants to go with me to gather greens for Pentecost (that is why we have come to this field together), and father turns to mother, and says, "Well?" and he looks over the silver rims of his glasses and strokes the silver threads in his beard. And a discussion arises between them as to whether Bessie should go with me out of the city and gather greens for Pentecost.

Father: What do you think about it?

Mother: What do you think about it?

Father: Shall we let them go together?

Mother: Why shouldn't we?

Father: I didn't say we shouldn't let them go.

Mother: Well, then, what do you say?

Father: I simply said, shall we let them go?

Mother: Why shouldn't we let them go?

And so on. I know what there is at the back of their minds. About a dozen times Father reminds me—and Mother repeats it after him, that over there, on the way, there is a bridge, and under the bridge there is running water . . . a river . . . a river. . . .

There, on the little hill, we sit, Bessie and I, and we have not even begun to gather greens for Pentecost. We tell stories, that is to say, I tell stories, and she listens to them. And I tell her of

that which is to be in the days to come, when I will grow into
a man, and she into a woman, and we will marry each other.
. . . We will take our places on the magic carpet and rise above
the mists and clouds, and then commence to fly over the whole
earth. First we will go to all the countries which Alexander the
Great visited; then we will go to Palestine. We will visit the hills
where spices grow, fill our pockets with figs and dates and almonds and then fly on and on. And wherever we will come we
will play different tricks, for of course *nobody* will be able to see
us. . . .

"Will *nobody* be able to see us?" cries Bessie and catches hold
of my hand.

"Nobody, nobody at all. We will see *everybody* and *nobody* will see
us."

"Well, Sammy, I want to ask you a favor."

"A favor?"

"One little favor."

But I know well enough what the favor is to be. She wants us
to fly to the faraway city where her mother married a second
time, and play some kind of a trick on her stepfather.

"Certainly, why not?" I answer her. "With the greatest pleasure. You may depend on me. I will play them such a trick that
they will remember me forever."

"Not them; only him, him alone," she begs of me. But I am
not so easily persuaded. It is no safe matter to trifle with my
temper. Does Bessie think I am going to forgive her mother?
That slut of a woman! Fancy having the impudence to marry
another father, and go away with him somewhere to the other
end of the earth—and leave her child—never even write her the
shortest note! Now I ask you, have you ever heard anything like
it, in all your born days?

But I lost my temper in vain. I regret it, regret it bitterly; but
it is too late. Bessie has put up both her hands to her face. Is she
crying? I want to kick myself. What on earth did I want to open
her wounds afresh for? I call myself all the names I can think of
—"Donkey! idiot! ass! chatterbox!" I move up to her. I take her
hand. "Bessie! Bessie!" I want to speak to her in the words of
the Song of Songs: "Let me see thy countenance, let me hear thy
voice."

And then, suddenly—where did they spring from?—my father
and mother.

My father's silver-rimmed glasses twinkle from afar. The silver threads of his beard float in the gentle wind, and my mother beckons to us with her shawl. Both of us, Bessie and I, remain sitting as though turned to stone. What are they doing here, my father and mother?

They have come to see that we are quite safe, to make sure that nothing has happened to us—God forbid. Heaven knows what might have happened . . . a bridge . . . a river. . . .

Queer folks, my father and mother.

"And where are the greens?"

"What greens?"

"The greens for Pentecost you went to gather?"

The two of us, Bessie and I, look at each other. I read her eyes and I understood her looks. And she seems to speak to me in the words of the Song of Songs:

"Oh, that thou wert unto me as a brother. Why wert thou not a brother unto me?"

"Well, well, I suppose our greens for Pentecost will come in their own good time," says my father, and smiles above the silver threads of his beard that gleam in the golden sunlight. "Thank heaven nothing has happened to the children."

"Thank heaven!" repeats my mother, and with her shawl wipes her red, perspiring face.

And both of them look at us and their faces begin to beam. . . .

Queer folks, my father and mother.

Translated by Maurice Samuel[3]

*

* "We Will Do and We Will Obey"

S H O L O M   A S C H

Yiddish novelist and playwright whose controversial works on Judaism and Christianity, translated into English, became best sellers (1880–1957)

The beautiful holiday which commemorates the receiving of the Torah arrived, and with it spring came to the steppe. Zlochov was inundated by a sea of moist, green, velvety grass, which streamed from the steppe into the town. The vegetation sprouted wherever it could get a foothold, and not only was the earth green with the moist plants but the roofs of the houses seemed to blossom, and even the walls. The houses looked as if they grew up out of the earth, decked out and beflowered as they were with the wild vine, which clambered all over the walls. And above the low roofs spread the sheltering branches of the linden trees which bent toward each other, became entwined, and hung over the houses like a canopy. Every gutter in Zlochov was transformed into a row of flowers, and every marsh was covered with forget-me-nots. Golden yellow daisies twinkled on the moss-covered roofs. Tall bushes of jessamine looked into every window of Zlochov, and the fragrance of white lilac filled the little rooms.

And the breezes of spring which came from the steppe began to sweep through Zlochov, blowing from the welling waters which had been liberated from the ice, winds from the great green sea, which flowed around Zlochov in waves of hills and dales of blooming forests and flowered steppes. And the twilights came when trees and shrubs became wrapped in dark shadows, and Zlochov seemed threatened to be wholly engulfed in the steppe and never more to emerge from it.

The day before Shavuot, as the children of Zlochov were playing at the log near the public well in the marketplace, there arrived in town a little old Jew with a round white beard, a big sack slung over his shoulder, and a stick cut from a branch in his hand. The children looked eagerly at the stranger, for it was seldom that Zlochov had a visitor. Suddenly a boy with curled earlocks and bare feet jumped from the log and cried:

"There goes the little tailor, there goes the little tailor!"

The children recognized the little tailor and ran to meet him, shirts and trousers askew, and faces smeared over with the juice of berries.

"Little tailor, little tailor, hurrah!"

"Keep away, away!" The little tailor waved his stick.

"Come to my home, little tailor."

"To mine, to mine!"

"No, to mine! You will sleep on the sleeping-bench."

But the little tailor had his own lodgings in town, in the

18. Shavuot scenes. (Upper) Services in a synagogue
decorated with trees and flowers; (lower) recitation of
penitential prayers while standing in a cold stream. Copper engraving.
From *Kirchliche Verfassung der heutigen Juden,*
by Johann C. G. Bodenschatz. Erlangen, 1748. See
Chapter 8.

vestibule of the synagogue. The children followed him gleefully. In the vestibule he put down his sack and took from it gifts of all sorts for the children. To one he gave a whistle carved out of a twig; another received a honey cake saved from the previous town; and a third, who was already able to read, got a little book. And, as there was still time before going to the bath, the children gathered around him and he taught them a fine song for the holiday.

At night after the services, the householders of Zlochov quarreled as to which one of them should have the honor of entertaining the little tailor. Each of them was anxious to observe the sacred duty of hospitality, for it was very seldom that they had the opportunity of fulfilling this duty in Zlochov.

The first day of the festival he ate in Mendel's home, this honor being the special prerogative of Mendel, as *parnas.* At the table the little tailor was very jolly, he sang and talked, a thing which he was not in the habit of doing. He was greatly rejoiced over Shlomele because of the young man's return from the *yeshivah* of Lublin, and demanded tuition money from him for having taught him to read his prayer book, and Shlomele rewarded him with a cup of ale. As the little tailor drank the ale, he sighed:

"Behold Zlochov grown to be 'a city and a center in Israel,' the pity of it!"

But no one understood his sighing and his "pity of it." They marveled over it, but no one questioned him, for the ways of the little tailor were indeed wonderful.

Very early the following morning, the second day of the festival, Shlomele was sitting in his room studying his portion of the Talmud. The little window was open, and the trees which grew behind the window looked into the low-ceiled room. The sweet singing of birds could be heard outdoors, and a sweet scent of honey was wafted from the honeyflowers of the steppe, and filled the low, little room of the young husband and bride. The young wife was standing over the chest and taking out her fine dresses and jewels with which she decked and embellished herself to go to the synagogue with her mother-in-law. A great charm rested on her that spring holiday morning. Her cheeks were tender, the bliss of the night still lingered on them, and her large eyes were veiled with a brilliant dew as though they were not yet awake from the dream of the night. And a great love for his wife was kindled in the heart of the young man, and he felt for her a great pity and tenderness. And her heart also was filled with love toward him, for his Torah chant that holiday morning sounded as sweet in her ears as the singing of happy birds. For they loved each other very much as is usual with young people just after the wedding. And he could not continue his studying, so he placed his fur hat on the Talmud folio, and paced up and down the room. And she, his young wife, decked and embellished herself before him in her finery. And when she was very beautifully adorned, she rose up from before the chest and approached her husband that he might bless her before she set out for the synagogue. And he laid both his hands on her beautiful head and spoke as follows:

"May your loveliness remain ever with you as with our mother Rachel."

And the young woman took her large prayer book with the covers of silver which her father-in-law had given her, and with a great flourish, decked out in her holiday finery, she set out for the synagogue.

The people were gathered in the synagogue. The women, dressed in their holiday best, are standing in their separate section, and through the curtained railing look down into the section for the men. Between her mother and her mother-in-law stands Deborah, beautiful in her new, jeweled headdress which her father-in-law had given her when she had presented herself before him in honor of the holiday, wearing the golden slippers which Shlomele had brought her from the *yeshivah*. She looks down through the railing and sees Shlomele, wrapped in a long prayer shawl, standing on the pulpit, holding a Scroll of the Torah in a loving embrace, and singing a song in glorification of the festival. Like a songbird he caresses with his sweet voice the melody of *Akdamut,* imparting to each word all the beauty of the chant. And as Deborah listens to Shomele's voice, sweet thoughts come to her and course through her soul like music, thoughts that softly steal their way in and raise a tender blush on the young woman's cheeks and a moist, bashful look in her eyes. She hides her eyes in the palm of her hands as though afraid lest her mother read in her face the sweet thought that she is thinking.

Still as in a dream sounds the music of her husband's voice, when a violent noise from the street breaks in and drowns the holiday song. No one at first dares put away his prayer shawl and step out to see what has happened. And Shlomele strives to raise his voice and to add more sweetness to his singing, but the tumult of the street comes nearer to the synagogue and banishes the holiday. Here and there, one and another slip out of the synagogue. The *parnas* is banging on the platform table, and the next minute a crowd of men, women, and children break into the synagogue and a murmur rises up:

"Messengers are coming."

"Two messengers from Karsoon."

"They've come on horseback; desecrated the holiday."

"It's a matter of life and death!"

No one now listens to Shlomele's trilling; the holiday song is silenced. Mendel is striking the platform table, the people are running in and out of the synagogue.

All at once there is heard the sound of weeping.

"What has happened?"

"Silence! Silence!" Mendel strikes the table.

Just then the door of the synagogue is opened violently, and a frightened voice calls out:

"Jews, flee for your lives!"

On the synagogue platform, decorated with holiday greenery, among the Scrolls of the Torah in their mantles of silver cloth stand two Jews in their weekday clothes, covered with the dust of the road, who had arrived on horseback in despite of the holiday.

The wicked Chmelnitzki has defeated the two Polish generals Pototzki and Kalinowski, the Jews report, and he is advancing with his armies on the whole of the Ukraine. The khan of the Tatars has joined him. The *kehillah* of Karsoon has already been utterly destroyed. Many Jews have perished. Only they, the riders, have saved themselves, and galloped to Zlochov, desecrating the holiday, in order to inform their fellow Jews of Zlochov that the danger is very great, that despite the holiday they must flee for their lives, because Chmelnitzki with his cossacks and Tatars is advancing on their city.

Thereupon a panic arose in the synagogue. Mothers snatched up their little ones and ran without knowing whither. Some shouted that the horses should at once be harnessed to the vans and all escape from the city despite the holiday. But no one dared do it. They could not imagine that their lives could be cut off so suddenly. No one found it in his heart to move a single object on that beautiful holiday. In the meantime more and more men, women, and children came running to the synagogue, as if seeking a place of hiding in the house of God. No one remained at home, all felt that they must be together in the synagogue.

And Mendel the *parnas,* looking very pale, stepped up to the platform and striking the table, spoke as follows:

"Jews, let us not leave this place. We have built up a settlement, a synagogue—in whose hands are we going to leave all this? It cannot be that a whole world should be destroyed. Another day or two and help will come. The lord Vishnewetzki will arrive with Polish soldiers, other nobles also. In the meantime we will hide, lock ourselves in the synagogue. And it may be that Chmelnitzki has turned aside with his armies toward Chihirin, where he lives. What has he against us? We have done him no harm. To take a city and destroy it deliberately, to abandon everything to rack and ruin—no, we will not go!"

Many were reassured by Mendel's words. The Jews who had been there from the beginning, when the settlement was first built, were so deeply attached to Zlochov that they seized upon the ray of hope which the *parnas* offered them in the possibility that Chmelnitzki had turned toward Chihirin because his home was there. The calamity befell them so suddenly, so unexpectedly, that they were unable to realize the danger. And soon there gathered round Mendel a group of Jews, manual laborers, horse dealers who used to travel about among the cossack camps and trade with the cossacks, often at the risk of their lives. They were men of strength and courage, their faces tanned by the sun of the steppes, with strong, black beards and bushy brows, Jews with broad shoulders and large heavy hands, hands that had built up cities. And they were in accord with the *parnas.*

"Whoever wishes to go, let him go. We stay with our *parnas.*"

"We stay with our synagogue."

"The synagogue! In whose care will you leave the synagogue? The cossacks will burn it!"

Silence fell upon the assembly. The rabbi arose, stepped up to the platform, and struck the table:

"Jews must not risk their lives to no purpose. 'And thou shalt preserve thy life' is written in the Torah. And he who destroys himself knowingly has no portion in the world to come. And the saving of life takes precedence over the Sabbath, even over the Day of Atonement. Therefore, as rabbi I command the *parnas* of the community to be the first to harness his van and leave the city at once, for the danger is very great."

The *parnas* did not stir. He remained seated on the platform.

"Whoever wishes to go, let him go. I will stay here with the synagogue. God has built a synagogue and He will protect it. Abandon a city to rack and ruin—I will not do it."

The people, seeing that the *parnas* stayed, were in no hurry to obey the rabbi's command. Around Mendel gathered the butchers, the horse dealers, the camp traders, and no one dared to be the first to desecrate the holiday.

A dead silence fell upon the synagogue. All looked to see what the rabbi would do. The rabbi said not a word, but stepped up to the ark, took up two Scrolls of the Torah in his outstretched arms and started out of the synagogue.

"Jews, save the Torah Scrolls!" the rabbi said.

But he need not have said it. Seeing the rabbi carrying the Scrolls out of the synagogue, the people broke into loud wailing. Only then did thy realize the catastrophe. They recalled the time when the Scrolls were installed, and they wept frantically. No one could speak or think. The Scrolls of the Torah were taken up, and the people trooped out of the synagogue after the rabbi.

Old Reb Shmuel was no longer alive, so another Jew took his little Scroll under his arm and left the synagogue with it.

And the rabbi exclaimed:

"Jews, you may profane the holiday, I command it! Harness your wagons and save whatever you can. I will do the same."

The people hastened from the synagogue after the rabbi. There was a running to and fro. Here and there horses were being harnessed to the vans. They pulled them up in front of the houses, helped in the little ones, and began dragging out their belongings, especially books and bedding. Some pulled out of their houses the chests in which they kept their precious articles, harnessing themselves into the leather belts and dragging the trunks on wheels through the streets toward the cemetery. Others snatched up whatever first came to hand—a dish, a garment, a piece of furniture. Some still had on the prayer shawls they wore in the synagogue. Thus the people of Zlochov followed their rabbi out of the city and on the road to Nemirov. . . .

Shlomele stood near his father. He agreed with the rabbi that the saving of life takes precedence over everything, and he begged his father to leave the synagogue and go with the rest. But his father continued to sit immovable as a rock.

"God built a synagogue, and He will protect it," he mumbled in his beard.

Seeing his father bent on staying, he stayed with him. And together with him were Deborah and the rest of Mendel's family. . . .

The noise and tumult outside began to subside. Zlochov became drained and empty. The synagogue became silent. Cold drafts seemed to be wafted from its dark corners. Through the two red-and-blue windows in the ceiling brilliant pencils of light entered and zigzagged across the synagogue, lighting up the open ark and the stars which were painted on it. In front of the pulpit burned a solitary candle which the sexton had lighted for the holiday services. Around the railed platform still hung the rushes and other greenery, for it was the custom so to decorate the homes and synagogues in commemoration of Mount Sinai. On the platform sat the silent guard, the *parnas* and his companions, who remained with him to defend the synagogue.

Suddenly some one rose up from a corner and approached the platform. It was the little tailor. No one had until then noticed him where he sat in a corner, singing his psalms. Mendel and the others were surprised to see him. The little tailor looked hard at them and then spoke as follows:

"You are guarding the synagogue? What will you defend it with? Force? Is God in need of your force? Is not a stone, a piece of wood stronger than you are? Does God lack force?"

No one answered him.

But suddenly, in the corner from which the little tailor had emerged, a pale flame was seen to shoot up. The fire seized upon the curtain which hung in front of the ark near by. And the next moment the oil-soaked pulpit stand was ablaze.

"Fire! Fire! The synagogue is burning!"

"Who did it?" And the men jumped up to run to the fire.

"Wait, I did it!" And the little tailor kept the people back.

"When the Lord of the universe wanted to banish the Jews from Eretz Yisrael, says the Talmud, they had all incurred the penalty of death. But God poured out His wrath upon stones and sticks of wood. He burnt the Temple and saved the Jews. Are you going to be better than the Lord of the universe? What is it that you were going to protect? Stones and sticks of wood! Save your strength; God will require your strength for a higher purpose, when the time will come and we shall be privileged. Save your lives, they do not belong to you, they belong to God!"

The Jews were awed by the voice of the tailor. One by one they began to slip out of the synagogue. Moreover, there was nothing left to defend. The curtains and furniture, covered with oil and tallow, burned like kindling wood.

"Better so! We've burnt it ourselves before the *goyim* could desecrate it. Come, brothers, let us harness our horses," the *parnas* cried, and together with the members of his family, he left the synagogue. . . .

And as the *parnas*'s van was leaving the city, the last in the procession, Mendel turned and looked for the last time on Zlochov. He saw the synagogue burning alone and it reminded him of a candle that burns for one that is dead.

Long caravans of covered wagons wound across the steppe, filled with women, children, and bedding, converging from the entire neighborhood toward Nemirov. At night, afraid to proceed on account of wild beasts, they halted near a river. The women and children fell asleep and the men mounted guard in order to protect the wagons against wild beasts and wicked Tatars.

They built a fire, and the old Jews sat around it, devoutly chanting psalms, while the younger men stood guard.

It was the night of the second day of the festival of Shavuot, when Jews ordinarily rejoice in the Torah. The pious little tailor would not allow the people to fall into melancholy.

"Jews, let us rejoice in the Torah!"

The people made no answer. Each one was preoccupied with his own affairs. Their grief in having left their city was very great, and they forgot the holiday, they forgot their faith in the Lord of the universe. And that was why no one answered him.

"Poor Jews, at the very first trial you lose your faith," someone remarked.

"And perhaps this is His way. He wants to see the Jews rejoice in the Torah, not in the houses of cities or in synagogues, but in the open field."

"And the Jews who received the Torah from Mount Sinai had no cities or houses either, and no synagogues as yet. They were encamped in the open field even as we are, nevertheless they said: 'We will do and we will obey.' "

"We will do and we will obey!" someone exclaimed.

And it was as if a great consolation had come upon the people, as if a spark of hope had kindled their hearts and caused their faith to blaze up. They began to understand, to perceive the reason of it, and soon one of them took out the little Scroll, the Zlochov Scroll which accompanied the Jews into exile, and exclaimed in a loud voice: "We will do and we will obey!"

And the people responded lustily:

"We will do and we will obey!"

Someone began to sing the psalms from the *Hallel,* and the people after him. The children woke up and saw the great fire burning in the steppe and the Jews dancing around it with their Scrolls.

"We will do and we will obey!"

And the steppe was transformed into a Mount Sinai—loud the fire crackled, and far and wide resounded across the steppe the cry of the Jews, dancing with their Torah Scrolls around the fire:

"We will do and we will obey!"

Translated by Rufus Learsi[4]

*

The Address to the Sixty

MARTIN BUBER

German Jewish theologian, founder of neomysticism, Zionist thinker, and professor at the Hebrew University; prolific author who wrote extensively on Hasidic lore (1878–1965)

"Behold, it is the litter of Solomon," it is written in the Song of Songs, "three-score mighty men are about it, of the mighty men of Israel. They all handle the sword and are expert in war:

every man has his sword upon his thigh, because of fear in the night."

Rabbi Israel ben Eliezer, the Baal Shem Tov, said in his time: "My soul was unwilling to descend into this world, for it was of the opinion that it would not be able to prevail against the consuming snakes which exist in this generation." For that reason sixty heroes, the souls of *tzaddikim,* were given the soul of the Baal Shem Tov to protect it. These sixty were his disciples, through whom his good tidings went forth among men and renewed the community of Israel. The greatest of his disciples was Dov Baer, the *Maggid* of Mesritsh, whose disciple in turn was Rabbi Jacob Yitzhak, the Seer of Lublin.

Seven weeks after the Passover, on Shavout, the Feast of Weeks, the Festival of the Firstfruits and of the revelation of the Torah, there sat about the Seer's table, having come thither from near and far, the chosen disciples who had gathered about him in the space of thirteen years. He counted them and said: "My sixty heroes."

They had all donned white garments on this day, even David of Lelov. Only at the foot of the table there sat one, not known to all, who wore a short, dark coat of Western European cut. His hair and beard were also trimmed in Western fashion. He was somewhat older than the Yehudi. This was Simhah Bunam, the apothecary. Considering how highly esteemed he was by all the *tzaddikim* whom he sought out, his previous calling had been no less curious than his present one. He had been an exporter of timber to Danzig and had even visited the fair at Leipzig. Thereafter he devoted himself to the study of pharmacy; he passed his examinations in Lwow, received the grade of a master of that art, and, about a year ago, opened an apothecary's shop in the town of Pshysha. For a long time his devotion had been given to the *Maggid* of Kosnitz. In recent years he had from time to time visited Lublin. Like the Yehudi, he had first been brought here by David of Lelov. The Seer set great hopes upon him. Once he studied a section alone with him. Then he said: "Now you are my pupil and I am your teacher." Among those present, Naftali alone paid any particular attention to Bunam—an attention similar to that which quicksilver, had it the power to attend, would pay to silver.

It was the interval between the temporary victory of the Polish rebellion and its collapse. To be sure, the Russians had evacuated both Warsaw and Vilna some weeks before. But in the very hour during which the "sixty heroes" were sitting around the table in Lublin, the great little *mujik,* Suvarov, was already drawing up, on the Russo-Turkish frontier, the plan of attack for his beloved bayonets, although he could not yet have had the slightest suspicion that midsummer would bring him the command to attack. One of the older disciples had a son whom he sought in vain to persuade not to join the Polish rebels, relying upon a saying of the Seer to help him.

The house of study, in which this time, too, the table had been set, was radiantly green, as it always was on this day. Green branches covered the floor and green trees stood against the walls. It was no mere decoration; the Polish forest itself had entered the Jews' *shul.*

The rabbi, who conversed not only with those nearest him but also with those across the table, used more frugal gestures and a more emphatic voice than at other times. It was as though he had made a decision which was now to be executed. His eyes, too, had a sharper glance than was their wont. No one would have thought that he was nearsighted.

In the course of the meal Bunam whispered to David of Lelov: "Do you know who will be permitted to say grace today? I. Look how the rabbi regards each one of us. It is an examination which fills one with dread. Who can stand up under it? Neither you nor anyone whom he knows intimately. I am the only one whom he does not know so intimately."

In point of fact, the rabbi, as soon as he grasped the beaker at the end of the meal, asked: "Who will say grace?" And immediately with a smile upon his face, but with inexorable clarity, he passed in review each of those present. The faults and errors of each one, some of those things that had either seemed scarcely to have been noticed or else had long been thought forgotten, were not expressed. What was expressed was only the ultimate cause of those actions to which a human eye had penetrated and which human lips now translated into words. No one was wounded; no one could be. David of Lelov nodded as though in gratitude; the Yehudi reflected long over each syllable; even the sensitive Naftali laughed as at a good joke and, to the astonishment of all, even the austere Jehuda Loeb of Zakilkov replied to the Seer's smile with a smile, thin though it was, of his own. The end of the address was: "The wise Rabbi Bunam will say grace."

When, later, the Seer began to speak, they were all aware that something had grown ripe for the harvesting. He did not speak, as was his custom, from a great depth, but authoritatively and commandingly.

This time, too, he began by an exegesis of a scriptural saying. It was the introduction to the Ten Commandments, which he had read to the congregation in the middle of morning prayers. Next he proceeded with the significance of the customs of this festival.

"Why," he asked, "do trees cover the walls of this house and of our dwelling houses today? And why do green boughs cover the floors? Because we commemorate the revelation. But God revealed himself to Israel not in a house but on a mountain, and round about the mountain grew trees and grass. As it is written: 'Neither shall your sheep and your goats nor your cattle seek pasturage in the direction of the mountain.'

"We do not place this greenery round about us in commemoration of a revelation which took place once upon a time. Revelation *is;* it lives and lasts. It is not something that happened once upon a time and lives now only in our memory. That which has happened happens; it happens *now.* We are not building us an image of something that once was. We, ourselves, create the place of revelation; we, ourselves, wait to be sanctified.

" 'If a man,' the Rabbi of Berditchev once said, 'is worthy of it, he hears on every Feast of Weeks the Voice which says: I am the Lord thy God.' If we are worthy thereof, we hear it now and here. If we are prepared to hear, we will hear. How could the Voice deny Itself to us? It is addressed to us and seeks us out! 'Where are you?' the Voice asks. 'You, whose God I am? Are you there? Are you still there?'

"It is written: 'And Mount Sinai, the whole of it, smoked because the Lord descended upon it in fire; and the smoke thereof ascended as the smoke of a furnace, and the whole mount quaked greatly.' The world of the peoples is the mountain upon which in this hour the Lord descends in fire, and the mountain begins to smoke; it begins to quake greatly. We, however, stand at the foot of the mountain and behold the first cloud of smoke; we feel the first quaking in our own members. But do we also hear the Voice which speaks to us from the top of the mountain: 'I am the Lord thy God'? If we are prepared to hear it, we shall. . . .

"Look you, all this is nothing but the smoke of the mountain of this world. It smokes, because in this hour the Lord descends upon it in fire. He, the Ever-living speaks: 'I am the Lord thy God.' To whom does he address that 'thou'? To him who hears it. Open your ears, Hasidim; open your ears, Israel; open your ears, peoples of the world. It is He who leads from servitude to freedom and reveals Himself to the free."

The rabbi paused. When he spoke again his voice was brighter still and hard as steel.

"The world of the peoples," said he, "is in tumult and agitation. Nor can we desire this thing to cease, for not until the world is broken by conflict do the birth pangs of the Messiah begin. Redemption is no ready-made gift of God handed down from heaven to earth. The body of this world must travail as in birth and reach the very edge of death before redemption can be born. For the sake of redemption does God permit mortal forces to rebel against Him more and more. But it is not yet inscribed upon any scroll in heaven at what time the great conflict between light and darkness will enter its final phase. This is a thing which God has placed within the power of his *tzaddikim,* and this it is concerning which we have the saying: 'The *tzaddik* decided and God fulfills.' But why is this so? Because God would have redemption be our own redemption. We ourselves must strive to heighten earth's conflict to the plane of the messianic birth pangs. The clouds of smoke about the mount of the world's peoples are still small and transitory ones. Greater and steadier ones will come. We must wait for the hour in which the sign will be given us to influence them in the depths of mystery. We must keep wakeful our inner strength against the hour in which the dark fire will dare to challenge the power of brightness. It is not for us to extinguish; our task is to kindle. It is written: 'The mountains melt before the Lord; that is Sinai.' Wherever the mountains melt and the wonder comes to pass, *there* is Sinai."

When he had finished speaking there was silence. None addressed another as the sixty went their ways.

Translated by Ludwig Lewisohn[5]

*

Shavuot among Brothers and Friends

SHMUEL YOSEF AGNON

*born in Galicia and after 1924 a resident of Jerusalem; master of an
original style and a prolific pen, he authored several novels, hundreds of
short stories, and anthologies of Jewish folklore; recognized as the foremost
modern Hebrew writer, he received the Nobel Prize for Literature, the
first author writing in the holy tongue to be so honored (1888–1970)*

On the first of the Three Days of Delimitation before the
festival of Shavuot, two young men came to the *bet ha-midrash.*
A young man in the *bet ha-midrash* is a novelty; all the more so
two. I believe that since I returned no young man has entered
the *bet ha-midrash.* The young men came up and greeted me, and
said they had come only for my sake. Why for my sake? Because
in a certain village near our town there was a little group of six
young men and two young women, who had abandoned the
occupations of their fathers and were cultivating the soil to prepare themselves to work in the Land of Israel. They were earning
a livelihood by the labor of their hands, by their work in the
fields and the cowsheds with the peasants. And since they had
heard that I came from the Land of Israel, they had come to ask
me to stay with them for the festival.

When the young men came in, I was engrossed in study. I said
to myself: Not only are they making me neglect the Torah, but
they are giving me the trouble of going to them. I looked at them
like a man who is sitting on top of the world, when someone
comes to tell him to undertake some sordid task.

The young men lowered their eyes and said nothing. Finally
one of them—Zvi was his name—took heart and said, "I thought
that since you've come from the Land of Israel, sir, you would
be glad to see young men and women working in the fields and
the cowsheds for the sake of the Land." "My friend," said I,
"why do you tell me tales about preparing yourselves for the
Land of Israel? So did Yeruham prepare himself for the Land,
and he went and stayed there for a few years. And what was the
end of him? In the end he came back here, and now he decries
the Land and its people."

"If you are thinking of Yeruham Freeman, sir," Zvi replied, "you have reason to be angry, but there was another Yeruham, called Yeruham Bach, who was killed in guarding the Land, and I believe you have nothing against him. And if we are fated to share his end, we shall willingly accept the Almighty's decree." I took Zvi's hand in mine, and said, "When would you like me to come?" "Any time," said both of them together, "whenever you come we shall welcome you." Said I, "You invited me for the festival, didn't you? Well, I shall come for the festival of Shavuot."

On the eve of the festival, after midday, I hired a cart and set out for the village. Before I could find the comrades the whole village knew that a guest had come to the Jewish lads. Immediately some of the villagers ran on ahead to let them know, and some walked in front of the cart to show me the way.

In a farmer's house, or rather a hut, the six young men and two young women had made their home. The house was half in ruins and the furniture was in pieces. In all the villages the farmers have broken-down houses, but the youthful grace of those who lived here glorified the place and its furnishings.

In honor of the festival the young men had stopped work about two hours before nightfall and I did not see them at work in the fields, but I saw the girls in the cowshed milking the cows. For many days I had not seen a cow, or a girl either, and suddenly it came about that I saw both at the same time. . . .

The sun had almost set. The girls came back from the cowshed bringing the milk, went into their room and washed, and put on holiday clothes; then they set the table and lit the candles. The young men went out to the spring, washed, and dressed themselves. We went into the room and welcomed the festival with prayer. A fine smell rose from the gardens and fields and vegetable plots, driving out the smell of the pigs who grunted from the nearby houses. After we had finished our prayer we recited the blessing over the wine, broke bread, and ate what our comrades had prepared. Between one dish and the next they sang songs sweet as honey, and I told them something of the Land of Israel.

Shavuot nights are brief, and our comrades had not heard their fill of the Land before night came to an end. We said grace, rose from the table, and set out for the nearby town to pray with the congregation and hear the reading of the Torah.

We walked among the fields and gardens, vegetable patches and hedges, along crooked and winding paths. This world, which I had thought was still by night, was busy with a thousand labors. The heavens dropped down dew, the earth brought forth its grasses, and the grasses gave out fragrance. Between heaven and earth was heard the voice of the angel of night, saying things not every ear can hear. But the higher ear can hear, and the heavens answer that angel's voice. And down below, between our feet, played little creeping things, which the Almighty has abased to the dust, but His merciful eye watches over them even in their abasement, so that they should not be crushed. While we were walking the dawn began to break, and the town appeared out of the pure mists, which divided, then separated, then came to-gether again as one and covered the town, until in the end town and mist were absorbed in each other, and the rooftops seemed like fringed sheets. Few are the hours of favor when this man rejoices, but this was one of them. Finally, the whole town was submerged in a white mist and all that was in the town was submerged. At that moment the cocks crowed and the birds began to twitter, to tell us that everything was in order, and that He who in His goodness continually, every day, renews the work of creation had renewed His world on that day too. At once, a new light shone, and the forest, too, which had been hidden in darkness, emerged and revealed all its trees. And every tree and branch glistened with the dew of night.

The morning of the festival had left its mark on every house; even the streets looked as if this were a special day for Israel and they need not be in a tumult as on all other days. When we entered the synagogue the congregation was in the middle of the *Musaf* service, and a second quorum was beginning to collect for prayer. The synagogue was adorned with branches and green-ery, and its fragrance was like the fragrance of the forest.

The *kohanim* went up to the pulpit and blessed the congrega-tion with the *Shlaf-Kratzel* melody, like men who are seized by sleep and want to arouse themselves. The other worshipers, too, still had the night in their eyes. They finished their prayer and we began ours.

The cantor chanted the "Great Love" prayer with the special melody for Shavuot and dwelt upon the verse "And to fulfill in love all the words of instruction in Thy Law." And when he came to the verse "Enlighten our eyes in Thy Law," he seemed like one who wanders alone in the night and entreats the Almighty to be merciful and lighten his darkness.

More beautiful was the melody of the *Akdamut* hymn; even more beautiful was the reading of the Torah. This was a little town and the professional cantors did not reach it, so the ancient melodies were preserved and not mingled with foreign tunes. After the prayer we went out into the street. All the houses in the town were small and low, some of them actually down to the ground, and their roofs were made of straw. Some of the windows were ornamented with rosettes of green paper, in memory of the revelation on Mount Sinai, as our forefathers used to do in honor of Shavuot.

At the doors of the houses the women stood and watched the young men, who plowed and sowed and reaped like gentiles, but came to pray like Jews. One woman pointed at me, mentioning the Land of Israel. My comrades were delighted and said, "Now that they have seen a man from there they will no longer say that the whole business of the Land is sheer wishful thinking." In the big cities, where emissaries frequently come from the Land, the arrival of a man from there makes no impression; in this small town, to which no man from the Land had come before, even a man like me made an impression.

Meanwhile, a number of the townsfolk came along and invited us to say the *Kiddush* with them, but the two girls were furious and would not let us go, because they had prepared a fine feast in honor of the festival and wanted us to start the meal hungry, so that our enjoyment might be doubled.

Most of the townsfolk went along with us on our way to hear something about the Land of Israel. To please the old men, I told them about the Wailing Wall of the Temple, and the Cave of the Patriarchs, and the Tomb of Rachel, and the Cave of Elijah, and the Tomb of Simon the Just, and the tombs of the Great Sanhedrin and the Lesser Sanhedrin, and the Lag ba-Omer celebrations at Meron, and all the other holy places. What did I tell and what did I not tell? May the Almighty not punish me if I exaggerated somewhat and went a little too far; after all, it was not for my honor that I did so, but for the honor of the Land of Israel, whose glories it is meritorious to relate even when it is in ruins—to make it beloved of Israel, that they may take to heart what they have lost and turn again in repentance. . . .

Finally I took my leave of them and they took their leave of

19. Shavuot. By Moritz Oppenheim (1800–1882). Painting. See Chapter 8.

me. They went back to their town and we went back to the
village. The earth that the Holy One, blessed be He, has given
to the sons of man is full of boundaries. It is not enough that he
has set a boundary between the Land of Israel and the Exile, but
even this Exile is made of many exiles, and when Jews meet
together, in the end they must leave each other.

Silently I walked after my comrades, meditating to myself.
When I was a child I used to beseech the Holy One, blessed be
He, to reveal to me the magic name by which one could go up
to the Land of Israel. Something like this request I made at that
moment, not for myself but for those weary of exile, weary of
hoping.

Said one of the comrades, "We should not have refused them
like that; when they asked us to come in and recite the *Kiddush*
with them, we should have gone in." Another replied, "On the
contrary, we should have gone back to the village immediately
after the service to sit down to our meal. After all, we have not
had a good meal since Passover, and now, when the girls have
taken the trouble to prepare a big meal, we must eat at our own
table."

And here they revealed the secret of the girls, who had prepared not one meal but two, one of milk dishes and one with
meat—one for the first day of the festival and one for the second,
besides a big cheesecake with butter and raisins.

The sun shone over the earth and hunger began to torment us.
The young men took long strides so as to reach home quickly.

We reached the village and went into the house. The girls
were quick to set the table and arrange the dishes, and each of
us came and sat at his place.

One of us spoke up first and said, "The Sages were right when
they fixed a short *Kiddush* for the festival, especially for those
who have a cheescake ready and waiting." Another spoke up and
said, "Why are the girls taking so long?" He jumped up and
went into the kitchen. When he did not return, another jumped
up and went in after him. Very soon they had all got up and gone
into the kitchen.

I sat alone, before the laid table. My hunger hurt. I took out
a cigarette and began to smoke. In the meantime the young men
came back with gloomy faces. It was clear that something bad had
happened.

What had happened was this: when the girls had gone into the kitchen they found the food cupboard open and the lock broken; no wine for *Kiddush,* no cake, no food at all, not even a morsel of bread was left. While we had been in the town, evil neighbors had come and taken away all that the comrades had prepared in honor of the festival.

What could be done? One of the girls went to the farmer's house to ask for something to eat, but she found his door locked. She went on to another farmer, but none of the household were at home, for that day the chief priest of Szibucz had come to a neighboring village and they had all gone to hear him preach.

The girls thought of going to the cows to get some milk, but all the cows were out to pasture, and there wasn't a drop of milk to be had. We wanted to make tea, but could not find even a pinch of tea. Those who had taken the food had taken the tea and the sugar. What could be done? They took the tea leaves that were left in the kettle from yesterday, put the kettle on the fire, and made some tea.

Close to nightfall the farmers came home and the cows returned from the meadow. The farmers' wives had pity on us and gave us what they gave. We sat and ate and drank. The meal was not large, but the joy was not small.

When the first day of the festival was ended and the eve of the second day had arrived, I said to my comrades, "I will go to the town and bring you bread, tea, and sugar, and any other food you need." "Heaven forbid," they said, shocked, for they did not wish me to travel on the holy day. "I belong to the Land of Israel," I reminded them, "and I intend to go back there, so the observance of the second day of the festival does not apply to me." "But what will people say?" they said.

After we had eaten, drunk, and said grace, the young men consulted and decided that two should go to the town and bring food. It took an hour to go and an hour to come back, and they spent an hour there; they brought loaves and butter, cheese and sardines, tea and sugar, a little bottle of wine, and two candles. The girls set the table and lit the candles; we recited the *Kiddush* over the wine and had our supper. At intervals in the meal the boys and girls sang songs sweet as honey, and I told them a little about the Land of Israel, until morning came on the second day of Shavuot.

We intended to go to town to pray with the congregation and hear the reading of the Torah, but one of the group said, "We cannot all go, in case what happened yesterday happens again; some of us will go and some will stay at home to watch the house." It was hard for some to give up their praying together with the congregation and the reading of the Torah, and it was hard for the others to bear the discomfort of their comrades who would remain in the village on the festival. Said I, "You go, and I will stay here, for I belong to the Land of Israel and I have to put on the *tefillin*, as on a weekday, which I cannot do in public." "When you have come to visit us, can we leave you alone and go?" they said. "What else do you want to do?" I said. One of them jumped up, took the festival prayer book, and began to recite the prayers, and all the others took up theirs and prayed with him. They recited the festival prayers and I the prayers for weekdays. I wore my *tefillin* and used the ordinary prayer book, while they prayed from the festival book.

After the service, the girls set the table and we had our meal, though not with meat and fish and other festival dishes. The comrades bantered, calling the sardines fish, the bread meat, the butter compote, the cheese cake, and the tea wine, for they had brought sugar from town and we had sweetened the tea. Between courses, the boys and girls sang songs sweet as honey, and I told them a little of the Land of Israel. The farmers and their women stood in front of the window, pointing to me and saying, "That man has been in Jerusalem and Palestine." They think that Jerusalem and Palestine are two different places, and anyone who has been in one of them is a somebody—all the more if he has been in both. Thus we sat until evening approached and it was time for the afternoon service. I recited the weekday prayers and they the festival prayers. Then we danced and sang, "Thou hast chosen us from all the peoples," until the day departed and the trees and bushes were wrapped in shadow.

Night was falling, the shadows of the trees and bushes stretched gradually toward the East. I am not a sentimental man, but at that moment I said to myself: Trees and bushes, which are inanimate objects, turn to the East, and I, who was in the East, have turned here instead. I rose and stood beside the window, looking outside. A little hedgehog was running about in the garden in front of the house, carrying some blades of grass between its prickles, for itself—and perhaps its mate—to lie on. As I stood there, looking, the moon shone into the window. We recited the evening service, and after the closing blessing the comrades sat down and arranged their work for the following day.

So I spent the two days of the festival and the day after with my comrades in the village. I saw them at home and outdoors, in the field and the cowshed. May the Almighty give them strength to face all the trials they bear every day and every hour, for while their fellows go idle, they stand in the sun and the wind and the rain, and when their parents scold them for leaving their shops and taking up farming they redouble their work to win bread from the soil. I heard that all the gentiles praised them; some of them told me that these young men flinch at no hard work, that there are some tasks which the farmers avoid but they perform out of love.

Shortly before sunset I hired a wagon to go back to town. The boys and girls accompanied me to the outskirts of the village, and one of them, called Zvi, went with me to town to buy food.

When I took my leave of them, they asked me to write down their names in a notebook, so that if we should meet in the Land of Israel I should remember them. "Brothers," I replied, "I have already engraved you in my heart; I have no need of a notebook."

This Zvi, who traveled with me, was as handsome as his name, which means "beautiful" in Hebrew, and lovable—a handsome young man, of fine appearance, and alert and sharp. On the way he said to me, "I will not stay here, each day I spend in exile is a pity." "Have you an immigration certificate?" I asked. He laughed and said, "I myself am my own immigration certificate." For some reason I do not know myself, I did not ask him what he meant.

Translated by Misha Louvish[6]

A SHAVUOT SHEAF

*Nomenclature

Shavuot is known by more different names than any other festival. Five names are in general use: *Hag ha-Katzir* (Feast of the Harvest), *Hag ha-Shavuot* (Feast of Weeks), *Yom ha-Bikkurim* (Day of the Firstfruits), *Atzeret* (Concluding Festival), and *Zeman Mattan Toratenu* (Season of the Giving of Our Law). The first three designations are found in the Pentateuch.

"And the Feast of the Harvest, of the firstfruits of your work, of what you sow in the field" (Exodus 23.16) alludes to the completion of the reaping of the wheat that takes place at this time and is celebrated with a festival.

"You shall observe the Feast of Weeks, of the firstfruits of the wheat harvest" (Exodus 34.22) and "You shall count off seven weeks. . . . Then you shall observe the Feast of Weeks for the Lord your God" (Deuteronomy 16.9–10) indicate the relationship of Shavuot to Passover, when the *omer*-counting commences. It is written: "From the day after you bring the sheaf [*omer*] of wave offering, you shall keep count [until] seven full weeks have elapsed: you shall count fifty days, until the day after the seventh week" (Leviticus 23.15–16). Hence it is denominated the Feast of Weeks.

The designation of Shavuot as the Day of the Firstfruits is found in the verse: "On the day of the firstfruits, your Feast of Weeks, when you bring an offering of new grain to the Lord, you shall observe a sacred occasion" (Numbers 28.26). In his commentary on this verse, Rashi states that Shavuot is called Firstfruits of the Wheat Harvest.

The Talmud as well as Josephus called this festival *Atzeret,* or *Atzarta* in Aramaic. While the precise meaning of *Atzeret* is uncertain, the Bible associates it with the seventh day of Passover (Deuteronomy 16.8) and the eighth day of Sukkot (Leviticus 23.26), where it is translated as "solemn gathering." It is also interpreted to mean "concluding festival." Just as the eighth and concluding day of Sukkot is named *Shemini Atzeret* so, the rabbis deduced, Shavuot should be considered the eighth and concluding day of Passover, therefore it was called *Atzeret.* It was later expounded that the exodus from Egypt, celebrated on Passover, was not fully consummated until the Law was given on Mount Sinai, commemorated on Shavuot.

The above four appellations are basically related to the agricultural aspects of the festival. It was not until the second century C.E., after the destruction of the Second Temple, when firstfruits and sacrifices were no longer brought to Jerusalem, that Shavuot became identified with the theophany at Mount Sinai (Shabbat 86b). In the festival liturgy it is called *Zeman Mattan Toratenu* (Time [or Season] of the Giving of Our Torah), or by the designation *Yom Hag ha-Shavuot ha-Zeh Zeman Mattan Toratenu* (Day of This Feast of Weeks, Time of the Giving of Our Torah). "Time" or "season" is used, rather than "day" or "days," to imply that Torah acquisition requires a long period of study.

In Judaic-Hellenistic literature the Greek term *Pentecost,* meaning fiftieth, is used, since the festival is celebrated on the fiftieth day after the first day of Passover.

In Babylon the Feast of Weeks was called the Feast of Visitation, derived from the custom of visiting the traditional grave sites of noted ancestors on the festival. The same tradition was maintained in Kurdistan, where Shavuot was named Pilgrimage.

In Italy Shavuot was known as the Feast of Roses and in Persia as the Feast of Flowers because of the floral decorations associated with the festival.

The Privileged Day

The second day of the month of Sivan is called *Yom ha-Meyuhas* (Privileged or Choice Day). It falls between the New Moon and the Three Days of Delimitation preceding Shavuot (Exodus 19. 12); as it occurs between two festive days, it is also considered as a festival.

In addition, according to the Talmud, on the second day of Sivan God told the children of Israel "you shall be to Me a kingdom of priests and a holy nation" (Exodus 19.6); thus their distinguished genealogy was established.[1]

The Bride Sabbath

Every Sabbath is figuratively called the "bride" of Israel, as is indicated in the well-known Friday evening hymn by Solomon Alkabetz, *Lekhah Dodi Likrat Kallah* ("Come, beloved Israel, to greet the bride; let us welcome the Sabbath"). In this vein, the Sabbath preceding a wedding, on which the bridegroom is honored by being called up to the reading of the Torah, is designated *Shabbat Kallah* (Bride Sabbath) in honor of the bride. It is also customary to call the Sabbath before Shavuot *Shabbat Kallah,* since, according to Jewish legend, it preceded the day of the nuptials between the Torah and Israel or, according to one version, between God and Israel.[2]

Numerology

The sum of the Hebrew letters in the Ten Commandments, excepting the seven in the last two words, *asher le-reekha* ("that is your neighbor's"), is 613, corresponding to the 613 commandments in the Torah. Some rabbis explained that the last seven letters correspond to the seven Noachian laws which obligate not only Jews but also "your neighbor." Others interpreted these extra letters as referring to the seven days of creation, to teach that the whole universe was created on the merit of the Torah.[3]

The appropriateness of reading the Book of Ruth on Shavuot is attested to by the fact that the numerical value of the Hebrew letters in her name totals 606—the number of precepts Ruth accepted as a proselyte on her conversion to Judaism. These 606 commandments plus the seven Noachian precepts that were previously incumbent on her equal all the 613 laws of the Torah.

The *gematria*—numerical equivalent—of *keter* (crown) is 620, the same as the number of letters in the Decalogue, symbolizing that the Ten Commandments are the crown of the Torah.

The liturgical poems read on Shavuot which enumerate or summarize the 613 commandments of the Torah are called *azharot* (warnings) as this Hebrew word is numerically equal to 613.

When *Tikkun Lel Shavuot* is read in a quorum of ten male adults, the *Kaddish* (the prayer for the sanctification of God) may be recited thirteen times, once after each major section of the *Tikkun*. This serves as a reminder of the thirteen attributes of God's love.

*

King David's Yahrzeit

On Shavuot, the anniversary of King David's death, visits are made to his traditional tomb on Mount Zion in Jerusalem. In other communities his *yahrzeit* is commemorated with reading the Book of Psalms, since the authorship of many of the psalms is ascribed to David. In one Polish congregation 150 memorial candles were lit, corresponding to the 150 psalms.[4]

*

The Baal Shem Tov's Yahrzeit

It is reported that the Baal Shem Tov (Master of a Good Name), founder of the Hasidic movement, spent the night of Shavuot in

1760 in study with his congregation. Although he had been ill since Passover and it was difficult for him to speak, he delivered an address on the theophany on Mount Sinai. The next day he died. To commemorate the anniversary of his death, Hasidim light candles and engage in study on Shavuot.[5]

The Origin of Yizkor

The origin of *Yizkor,* the memorial service recited on Yom Kippur and on the last days of the three major festivals, is associated with Shavuot. The early communal memorial prayer, *Av ha-Rahamim* (Father of Mercy), composed for those martyred during the Crusades, was originally recited on the Sabbath before Shavuot. According to Dr. Solomon B. Freehof, "the butchery of Rhineland Jewry (especially the large communities of Mainz, Speyer, Worms and Cologne) took place around Shavuot, as the dates in the memor-lists indicate. It was not deemed proper to set the memorial on the holiday itself. To do so would disturb the joy of the festival (which was mandatory) and therefore they fixed it on the Sabbath before the holiday. This Sabbath was suitable for memorial since it was part of the *omer* period which was associated with the massacre of the disciples of Rabbi Akiba. Thus the Sabbath before Shavuot became set after the Crusades as the special memorial Sabbath at which the lists of the martyrs were read and the prayer *Av ha-Rahamim* recited." As a later development, the memorial prayer was recited for individual family members.[6]

The Confirmation Ceremony

The confirmation ceremony was the first religious innovation by Reform Judaism. In 1810 a confirmation ritual was conducted for boys in Cassel and in 1817 for girls in Berlin. Five years later the first class of boys and girls was confirmed at the Hamburg Temple. Although Israel Jacobson confirmed his son at a Reform service in Berlin on Shavuot in 1815,[7] the original practice was to conduct the confirmation rite on the Sabbath of Sukkot, Passover, or Hanukkah.

While Orthodox rabbis were opposed to this new ritual, it was surprisingly the Orthodox Rabbi Samuel Eger who set the example for confirmation on Shavuot in 1831, when he instituted this practice for boys and girls at the Brunswick synagogue. The Festival of the Giving of Our Law was considered most appropriate for the ritual. According to Max Landsberg and Kaufmann Kohler: "As it [Shavuot] celebrated the occasion when the Israelites on Sinai, of their own free will, declared their intention to accept the obligation of God's Law, so those of every new generation should follow the ancient example and declare their willingness to be faithful to the religion transmitted by the Fathers."[8] The prevailing contemporary practice in Reform and in many Conservative congregations is to conduct the confirmation ceremony on Shavuot.

*
The Bene-Israel and Shavuot

For many centuries the Bene-Israel of India did not observe the Feast of Weeks as there were no visual symbols associated with the festival and they did not possess a copy of the Bible to remind them of it. Not until the beginning of the nineteenth century, when a synagogue was erected in Bombay, was Shavuot observed by these oriental Jews who had long been separated from the mainstream of Jewish life.[9]

*
*Dialogo dos Montes

Dialogo dos Montes (The Controversy of the Mountains), a play written by Rabbi Rehuel Jessurun in Portuguese, was first performed in the Sephardic synagogue of Amsterdam on Shavuot in 1624. According to the title page of an edition published in 1767, the drama was "Performed with Great Pomp and Circumstance by the Author and Eight Other Learned Gentlemen, Including the Hazan, in the Amsterdam Synagogue of BETH JAHACOB, During the Celebrated *Festival of Sebuot.*" The drama depicts the ancient legendary rivalry among the mountains—Sinai, Zion, Nebo, Gerizim, Carmel, and Zetin—to become the locale of the theophany; the conflict is resolved by King Jehosaphat, chosen to be the judge. In his decision, he judiciously declares:

> All of you are holy, all beloved
> Of your Creator, who with the kindnesses
> He showered upon you with a generous hand
> Honors and enriches you, and with
> The miracles performed upon your peaks
> Has made you famous throughout all the world,
> Of which you all deserve to be the heads.
>
> But who disputes the clear preeminence
> God gave to Sinai, giving upon him
> A Law which offers peace and joy to the world,
> A joyful wedding on him celebrating,
> A happy and propitious marriage bond
> To the people whom He dedicates to serve Him,
> Whom to this end He freed
> From the tyrannical and infamous yoke
> Of cruel Egypt, stern, implacable;
>
> Wherefore, like a bridegroom, by His train
> Accompanied, innumerable hosts
> Of angels who assist Him,
> All ready to obey Him at a sign,
> He wished to display the greatness of His power,
> Of which this day is glorious evidence,
> Eternally recurring year by year
> Throughout the revolutions of all time.
>
> Translated by Philip Polack[10]

*

*Gathering Pomegranates and Apples

Targum Sheni, a commentary on the Book of Esther, and also other midrashim narrate that when Haman accused the Jews of Persia "whose laws are different from those of any other people and who do not obey the King's laws" (Esther 3.8), he said: "In the month Sivan they keep a feast of two days, in which they go into their synagogues . . . and call it the day of convocation. Then they go up to the roof of the house of their God and throw down pomegranates and apples, and then collect them and say: 'Like as we gather these pomegranates and apples, so may their sons be gathered out from among us.' They also say: 'This is the day in which the Law was given to our fathers on Mount Sinai.' " The throwing of fruit from the roof of the synagogue was a custom in Babylonian and Persian communities and their gathering a symbolic act to express the hope of the ingathering of the scattered Jewish exiles from among the nations. This Shavuot custom is no longer observed; in the course of generations, it was transferred to *Simhat Torah,* when apples and nuts are tossed to the congregants.[11]

20. Distribution of fruit and sweets to children on Shavuot. Woodcut. From *Sefer Minhagim.* Amsterdam. 1723. See Chapter 8.

*

*The Martyrdom of a Righteous Proselyte

Abraham ben Abraham was a nobleman named Count Valentine Potocki before he became a *ger tzedek* (righteous proselyte). He is reported to have taught that when God offered the Torah to the nations of the world and they refused to accept it, there were individuals among them who were prepared to receive the Law; from them descended converts whose souls were present at Mount Sinai. As a consequence of his conversion to Judaism, he was publicly burned at the stake in Vilna on the second day of Shavuot, May 24, 1749. It became a custom to memorialize him on the anniversary of his martyrdom in the main synagogue of Vilna. Rabbi Hirsh Levinson would interrupt the rejoicing on Shavuot to relate how Abraham ben Abraham Potocki became a Jew and how he died for the sanctification of His name on the day of the giving of the Torah.[12]

*

*Mob Revenge

During the Crusades an old Jew in Cologne was tortured until he lost consciousness and was then baptized. When he became aware of what had happened, he drowned himself in the Rhine River. In revenge, a mob invaded the synagogue and desecrated the Scrolls of the Law on the day the Jews were celebrating the giving of the Torah—Shavuot—May 30, 1096.[13]

SHAVUOT WIT AND HUMOR

*The Wrong Season

A merchant had engaged a coachman to transport a case of dishes to a neighboring town. It was winter. Snow, slush, and ice covered the ground and rendered the roads dangerously slippery. As a result, the coach toppled into a ditch along the road and the dishes were smashed.

When the coachman returned and reported the accident to the merchant, the latter hailed the unfortunate driver before the rabbi, requesting payment for the breakage. The rabbi adjudged that the coachman was obligated to pay for the loss in accordance with the laws of the Torah. The poor man bitterly contested this decision. While the rabbi sympathized with him, he felt duty bound to uphold Jewish law.

The shrewd coachman, seeking to discover a loophole, asked the rabbi:

"When was the Torah given?"

"On Shavuot, of course."

"During which season of the year does Shavuot occur?"

"During the summer."

"You see, rabbi," the coachman argued, "when the Torah was given to the children of Israel it was summer and there was no snow or ice on the roads; therefore, the law is understandable. Now, don't you believe that if the Torah had been given in the winter, when the roads are dangerous, the law would not hold me responsible for the damage?"

*
*Our Torah

One Shavuot Reb Hayyim was called to the reading of the Torah. As he recited the benediction, "Blessed art Thou, O Lord our God, King of the universe, who hast given unto us the Torah of Truth . . . ," he pronounced "unto us" with deep fervor. In reply to the rabbi's inquiry as to the reason he had emphasized that particular phrase, Reb Hayyim explained:

"I am grateful to God that He gave the Torah to the Jews and not to any other people. Can you imagine what would have happened if He had given it to the Russians? They would have punished us even for the minutest violation of a commandment. However, we Jews among ourselves will always be able to get along."

*
*The Priority of Judaism

A king ordered the Jews and the Karaites of his country to designate representatives for a disputation in his presence so that he could determine which religion was established first.

The Karaites sent their most learned sage, attired in beautiful garments of silk, while the spokesman for the Jewish community appeared to be an unobtrusive person dressed in everyday clothes.

When the Jewish representative appeared in the king's throne room, he removed his shoes and held them under his arm, and barefooted, he approached the monarch. The king became exceedingly angry at this strange behavior. This reaction was not unexpected by the Jew who said meekly:

"Your Royal Highness, permit me to explain. When the Jews

wish to honor the King of kings they remove their shoes, as it is written in the Bible 'Remove your shoes from your feet.' "

"But why do you carry the shoes under your arm?" the king inquired quizzically.

"We learned this practice from a sad experience," the Jew explained. "Before we approached Mount Sinai to receive the Torah, we took off our shoes, but when we returned they were gone. The Karaites had stolen them."

The elegantly clad Karaite spokesman, prepared to debate on the subject for which he had been invited, was shocked to hear this false accusation. Unable to restrain himself, he interrupted the conversation between the king and the Jew, shouting:

"That's a lie! When the Torah was given on Mount Sinai there were no Karaites in the world."

"We need go no further, Your Majesty," the Jew said casually. "You heard even this Karaite admit that the religion of the Jews preceded that of the Karaites."

*

*United as One

Rabbi Elijah, the Vilna Gaon, interpreted as follows the verse "All the people answered as one, saying, 'All that the Lord has spoken we will do' ": "The reply of the people to Moses indicates that it is feasible to obey the Lord when all Israel are united as one in their own land and not scattered among the nations of the world."

*

*Selling Books

It is told that Rabbi Jacob Joseph of Polnoye published a book and went to Berditchev to sell it. Arriving at the inn, he waited in vain for buyers to purchase copies. Finally he went to the town rabbi and complained: "I came here to sell a book containing the teachings of the Baal Shem Tov and no one has come to purchase it."

The local rabbi, with a smile on his lips, said to Rabbi Jacob Joseph: "Why are you surprised? You know that God was also the Author of a Book and His Book was certainly not worse than yours. Nevertheless, the midrash tells us that the Almighty went from one nation to another offering each one the Torah and not one of them accepted it."

*The Ugly Are Despised

An aged woman appeared before a rabbi and poured out her tale of woe:

"My husband hates me. He keeps telling me I'm ugly."

The pious sage, not daring to look at the woman's face, reluctantly queried:

"Maybe you are really ugly."

"I don't know, rabbi," the anguished woman cried. "When my husband married me he called me beautiful. Now, I've become ugly in his sight."

The rabbi, a staunch defender of his people, attentively followed the woman's argument, then raised his eyes heavenward and said: "O God, this woman is undoubtedly right. Also we, the children of Israel, have a justifiable complaint against You. When we stood at Mount Sinai You chose us from among all the nations. You praised us and we agreed to accept your contract —the Torah. But now that we have become ugly from many generations of persecution You do not want to save us from our troubles!"

*The Golden Calf

Two *yeshivah* students were studying the Torah portion which recounts that, while Moses tarried on Mount Sinai, where he went to receive the tablets of the Law, Aaron had collected golden earrings from the Israelites and with them he had fashioned a golden calf.

At this point one of the students remarked:

"I don't understand why Aaron made a calf. If he collected so much gold, he should have had more than enough for an ox."

The other promptly countered:

"You should know better! Aaron ordered collectors to gather the golden earrings from the people. It is really a wonder that the collectors turned in enough to make even a calf."

*
* *"We Repair Faded Letters"*

Two old Hasidim, emissaries of the preceding Lubavitcher *rebbe,* Rabbi Joseph Isaac Schneerson of sainted memory, once visited a wealthy man in an American city in a campaign to raise the level and standard of Jewish education in the United States. Noting that they had not come for funds, he questioned them as to their purpose. One of them replied: "Do you recall the scribes in Europe who traveled from village to village, correcting errors or rewriting faded letters in the Torah Scrolls of synagogues? We are like those scribes. There were 600,000 Jews at the giving of the Torah, and the Torah itself has 600,000 letters—one for every Jew. If one Jew had been missing at Mount Sinai, the Torah would not have been given. Should even one letter become faded or illegible, the whole Torah Scroll is prohibited from use in the synagogue. Similarly, if even one Jew becomes 'faded' and 'worn' in his observance of Judaism, the whole of Jewry suffers. So we travel from place to place, encouraging Jews to return to Torah and *mitzvot.* We repair faded letters!" The wealthy man was moved by the parable.

When the two Hasidim related the incident to their *rebbe,* he remarked: "The parable is not quite accurate. Jews are not like letters of ink on parchment that can fade, God forbid. They are like letters engraved on stone. Such characters never fade; they may accumulate dust and become unrecognizable. But all one needs to do is to disperse the dirt, and the full letter is restored as it was originally—clearly engraved!"[1]

*
* Commandments for Rich and Poor

A rabbi who loved his poor congregants had little respect for the wealthy ones. On Shavuot morning, using the Ten Commandments as the theme of his sermon he told the following story:

"When Moses appeared at the foot of Mount Sinai, he carried the two tablets on which the Ten Commandments were engraved. The tablets were also studded with precious jewels. As Moses saw the Israelites worshiping the golden calf, he shattered the tablets. The rich Jews, who naturally were standing near the leader, immediately hastened to pick up the larger pieces of the tablets in order to acquire more of the precious jewels. When they had selected the choicest pieces, the poor people came forward from the rear and collected the remaining fragments. On the large pieces there happened to be engraved the words 'You shall . . . murder,' 'You shall . . . commit adultery,' 'You shall . . . steal,' 'You shall . . . bear false witness.' On the small fragments appeared only the word 'not.' That is why the rich are permitted to murder, to steal, and to bear false witness while the poor are forbidden to do anything."

*
* Witnesses

It is told that the late Rabbi Stephen S. Wise attended a public dinner where he was seated next to a prominent woman. In an effort to impress the rabbi, the lady remarked that one of her ancestors was present at the signing of the Declaration of Independence. Rabbi Wise quickly retorted: "My ancestors witnessed the giving of the Ten Commandments."

*
Violation of a Commandment

On the eve of Shavuot a thief who had stolen a pair of silver candlesticks was brought before the rabbi. The sage reprimanded the culprit:

"Today you should be preparing to receive the Torah. Instead you have violated one of the commandments of the Torah—'You shall not steal.' "

The thief, who appeared unabashed at his crime, replied:

"Believe me, rabbi, I seriously considered what I was doing before I stole the candlesticks. I was faced with a dilemma: either to violate the commandment 'You shall not steal' or 'You shall not covet.' As both commandments are of equal importance, I realized that if I were to violate the commandment 'You shall not covet,' I would sin and have nothing. Now, I have violated only one commandment but at least I have the candlesticks."

*
A Consolation

On Shavuot the rabbi appropriately preached a sermon on the Ten Commandments, emphasizing the importance of each. Noah listened attentively and was truly conscience-stricken. After pondering the enormity of his sins, he consoled himself with the thought:

"At least I have never made a graven image."

*
Upholders of the Law

On entering a synagogue in Berlin, a Polish Jew was overwhelmed by the palpable disregard of Jewish traditions. Noticing the beautiful ark of the Law upon which were set two tablets with the Ten Commandments supported by two lions, he thought to himself:

"Apparently the only ones in this congregation who uphold the Ten Commandments are the lions."

*

"Keep the Commandments . . ."

During the week preceding Shavuot, a rabbi visited a number of his prominent congregants to solicit flowers and plants to adorn the synagogue during the festival.

When he presented his request to one of his members, a nouveau riche, the latter, seeking to vaunt his erudition and his generosity, boasted:

"Instead of giving flowers in honor of Shavuot, I will present the synagogue with the tablets of the Ten Commandments."

The rabbi retorted:

"It would be better that you *keep* the commandments and give something else to the synagogue."

*

Reciting Tikkun Lel Shavuot

On the first night of Shavuot, Rabbi Aaron Karliner entered the synagogue where many Jews were reciting the *Tikkun Lel Shavuot.* He interrupted them by calling out: "Give merchandise! Give merchandise!"

In reply to the perplexed looks on the faces of the assemblage, he explained:

"Pious Jews need to learn from businessmen. They employ salesmen who carry samples of their merchandise to show customers. When the salesmen accept orders, they know that they can be filled from the stocks in their employers' stores or warehouses. Needless to say, if a salesman displays samples for which there is no stock he must be either a cheat or a fool.

"The same principle applies to the recital of *Tikkun Lel Shavuot.* On this night when we celebrate the Season of the Giving of Our Torah, we take samples from the vast warehouse of

Jewish literature and study them. If, however, we do not possess a wider knowledge of Jewish lore, if we are not well versed because we have neglected to study the Torah throughout the year, we are either cheats or fools. And so I say, 'Give merchandise and not just samples.' "

*A Pious Thief

Rabbi Isaac Levi of Berditchev was spending Shavuot night in his study reading *Tikkun Lel Shavuot.* Hearing a noise in the living room, he peeked in and saw a Jew who had entered through an open window and was stealing a pair of silver candlesticks and a Bible.

The Berditchever would not disturb the thief and thus embarrass him. He thought to himself: "The Jewish people are truly pious. If a Jew is a thief, God forbid, what does he steal? A Bible to study God's commandments and candlesticks so that he can read the Holy Book on Shavuot night."

*Milk for Infants

Rabbi Mendele Kotzker explained the reason for eating milk products on Shavuot: "When the Jews received the Torah they were considered as newborn infants who are only able to drink milk."

*The Pleasure of Blintzes

Hayyim learned that on Shavuot the well-to-do Jews ate *blintzes.* While he had always eaten only dairy foods on this festival, in accordance with the Jewish custom, he never had tasted this delicacy. Anxious to observe the holiday punctiliously, he requested his wife, Sarah, to make *blintzes* for Shavuot.

"To make *blintzes* I need eggs," the spouse replied.

"Make them without eggs," Hayyim suggested.

"Cheese is also needed for *blintzes*."

"If there is no cheese, we can have *blintzes* without cheese."

The dutiful wife, eager to please her husband, made *blintzes* without eggs and cheese.

When Hayyim returned from the synagogue on Shavuot night, he recited the festival *Kiddush* and proceeded to savor the pièce de résistance. As he ate the *blintzes,* a look of pain and confusion spread over his face. Turning to Sarah he said with a deep sigh:

"I fail to see why rich Jews enjoy *blintzes*."[2]

THE CULINARY ART
OF SHAVUOT

Rabbi Solomon ben Isaac (1040–1105), the perceptive and erudite Bible and Talmud commentator known as Rashi, said of Shavuot: "One should rejoice on it by eating and drinking to demonstrate that this day on which the Torah was given is acceptable to him."[1] A folklorist opined: "Shavuot is really far superior to the other festivals. On Passover we are not permitted to eat what we want; on Sukkot we cannot eat where we want; but on Shavuot we may eat what we want, where we want, and even when we want." Accordingly, certain culinary customs have evolved to give due honor to Shavuot.

Dairy dishes characterize the Shavuot meals served on the first day of the festival celebrating the revelation on Mount Sinai. Various reasons have been advanced for this tradition. The Bible itself compares the Torah to milk and honey. The verse "honey and milk shall be under your tongue" (Song of Songs 4.11) implies that the words of the Torah shall be as dulcet to your heart and ear as milk and honey are sweet to your tongue. The psalmist declared that "the precepts of the Lord are . . . sweeter than honey and the honeycomb" (Psalms 19.9–11). Hence it is obligatory to partake of honey on Shavuot.[2] Another rationale for eating these foods on the Feast of the Harvest derives from the biblical description of the Land of Israel as "a land flowing with milk and honey" (Exodus 3.8).

Rabbi Moses Isserles (c. 1520–1572) states: "It is a universal custom to eat dairy food on the first day of Shavuot. The reason appears to be that just as on the night of Passover two cooked dishes are taken in remembrance of the paschal sacrifice and the festival offering, so one should eat a dairy dish and then a meat dish [as a reminder of the two sacrifices offered on Shavuot]. It is also necessary to have two loaves of bread on the table [since it is forbidden to eat milk and meat with the same loaf], the substitute for the Temple altar. These are a reminder of the two loaves of bread [made from the first ears of the new wheat] that were offered on the day of the firstfruits."[3] A further caution was voiced to avoid mingling meat and milk foods: "Since one eats dairy foods and also necessarily partakes of meat, for it is a duty to eat meat in honor of every festival, one should be scrupulous not to violate a prohibition."[4] On Shavuot the usual six-hour waiting period to partake of dairy dishes after eating meat was waived in some communities.

Other commentators maintain that, prior to their receiving the Torah, the children of Israel were permitted to eat nonkosher meat that was not ritually slaughtered. However, when the Torah was given on Shavuot, they were thenceforth obligated to adhere to the laws pertaining to ritual slaughter and to forbidden foods. All their cooking utensils and eating vessels were forbidden: they could not be purged because it was on a Sabbath and a festival that the Torah was given. Thus they had no alternative but to eat dairy foods, which were relatively easy to prepare.[5]

The custom of indulging in dairy fare on Shavuot is also derived from this biblical verse: *Minhah hadashah la-Adoshem be-Shavuotekhem* (your Feast of Weeks, when you bring an offering of new grain to the Lord [Numbers 28.26]). The initials of the four Hebrew words spell *me-halav* (from milk), implying that foods made from milk are acceptable on Shavuot.[6] Mystics see a reason in the fact that the numerical equivalent of *halav* (milk) is forty—the number of days Moses tarried on Mount Sinai. Others find an explanation in the tradition that the infant Moses refused to suckle from anyone but a Hebrew nurse. Finally, in Psalm 68, which is read on Shavuot, the mountain on which the Divine Presence rested is called *Gavnunim*, a word akin to *gevinah*, the Hebrew for cheese.

Perhaps the most delectable of Shavuot foods are *blintzes*,

21. *Kiddush* cup for Shavuot.
Engraved silver. Master: G. N. Bierfreund.
Nuremberg. 1773. See Chapter 8.

rolled pancakes filled with cheese. Among other tempting tid-
bits are cheese *knishes,* butter cakes and cheesecakes and
cheese *kreplakh.* The *kreplakh* are three-cornered, a shape
based on the talmudic statement: "Blessed be the Merciful
One who gave the threefold Law [Torah, Prophets, Writings]
to a people comprising three classes [Kohen, Levi, Israel],
through a thirdborn [Moses, the third child of his parents], in
the third month [Sivan]."[7]

Jewish women in oriental countries took pride in baking for
Shavuot a seven-layer cake called *Siete Cielos* (Seven Heavens),
symbolic of the traditional seven celestial spheres God traversed
to present the Torah to Moses on Mount Sinai.[8] Fashioned in
seven circular tiers, one smaller than the other with the smallest
on top, it was decorated with various symbols such as a star of
David, the rod of Moses, the two tablets of the Law, manna,
Jacob's ladder, and the ark of the covenant. Others topped the
cake with a seven-rung ladder to recall Moses ascending Mount
Sinai. Similar elaborate pastries called Sinai Cake alluded to the
mountain. A large cake or bread with raisins, generally known

as *pashtudan* or *floden* when baked for Shavuot, was also called Sinai. Some oriental Jewish women baked *baklava*—a very sweet cake made with nuts, sugar, and honey.

Jews of Kurdistan prepare large quantities of butter and cheese for the festival. Their special dish was ground wheat cooked in sour milk with dumplings of butter and flour. Jewish housewives in Tripoli baked wafers in various shapes: a ladder, to recall that Moses went up Mount Sinai; a hand, denoting hands extended to receive the Torah; the two tablets of the Law; eyeglasses, to see the words of the Torah, and other symbolic forms.[9]

In some communities it was customary to serve *matzah* remaining from Passover as a reminder that Shavuot is the culmination of the exodus from Egypt. In North Africa the *matzah* was shredded into bowls of milk and honey.

Some baked long loaves to denote the broad scope of the Torah, regarding which Job said, "The measure thereof is longer than the earth" (Job 11.9). The long *hallah* sometimes had four heads to signify the four methods of Torah study: *peshat*, the literal meaning; *remez*, interpretation by intimations; *derush*, the homiletical explanation; and *sod*, the mystical meaning.[10] Others baked loaves with seven rings to symbolize the seven celestial spheres mentioned above.

Pious Jews herald Shavuot with an all-night vigil devoted to study of *Tikkun Lel Shavuot,* and partake of cheesecake and coffee to refresh themselves. Yemenite Jews read the *Tikkun* in the synagogue on the second night of Shavuot. Each brings a choice delicacy such as spiced coffee or candy to share with those spending the night in study.

Shavuot was considered the most appropriate season to initiate children in the study of Torah. To endear studying to the children, Hebrew words and letters were written on a slate spread with honey. The children were encouraged to lick the honey and thus sense the Torah's sweetness. At the end of the lesson honey cakes decorated with biblical verses were distributed to the newly initiated pupils.

*

*Recipes for Shavuot
HANNA GOODMAN

*BLINTZES

2 eggs
dash of salt
1 cup flour

1 cup water
1 tablespoon oil
butter or margarine

FILLING
1/2 pound farmer cheese
1/2 pound cream cheese
2 egg yolks

vanilla or lemon flavoring
1 1/2 teaspoons farina
sugar to taste

Beat the eggs well with a mixer. Add the salt and flour, and slowly add the water, continuing to mix. Add the oil. The batter will be thin. Let it stand at room temperature for 2 hours. If preferred, use a blender.

To make the filling, mash the farmer cheese well; add all the other ingredients and mix well.

Heat a 7-inch frying pan, and grease lightly. When the frying pan is hot, add two tablespoons of the batter, tipping the pan so that the batter covers the surface of the pan. Cook on one side only, until the top is dry. Turn out, bottom side up, on a clean towel. Continue the process with the rest of the batter. (Two frying pans speed up the work.) When all the pancakes have been made, fill each one with a tablespoon of the filling. Fold over the sides, and then roll the *blintzes* as you would roll a jelly roll. Fry in butter or margarine.

Serve the *blintzes* with sour cream, fresh or frozen berries, or other fruits.

The *blintzes* can also be baked by placing them on a well-greased foil-lined baking sheet and brushing the top of the *blintzes* with butter or margarine. Bake in a 400° oven until golden brown. Do not overbake. 8 to 10 *blintzes*.

*CHEESE AND SPINACH PASTRY

2 packages frozen chopped
  spinach
1 medium onion, chopped
3 tablespoons butter or
  margarine
1/4 cup dill, chopped
1/4 cup parsley, chopped

2 scallions, chopped
salt and pepper to taste
6 strudel leaves*
4 tablespoons butter or
  margarine, melted
6 ounces cream cheese

Defrost the spinach, and cook without water until soft.

Sauté the onion in 3 tablespoons of butter, but do not brown. Add the dill, parsley, and scallions. Add the spinach and let cool. Season with salt and pepper.

In a 8 × 10-inch well-greased pan lay 1 strudel leaf, folding if necessary. Brush generously with some of the melted butter. Add 2 more leaves, brushing each with melted butter. Put the spinach mixture on the top of the leaves, and scatter the cream cheese over the spinach. Put the other 3 strudel leaves over the cream cheese and spinach. Brush with the rest of the butter.

Bake for 30 minutes in a 350° oven. Serve hot or cold. 6 servings.

*NOODLE AND CHEESE PUDDING

1/4 pound medium or fine
  noodles
1/2 cup butter
2 eggs
1/3 cup sugar
1/2 cup sour cream

1/4 pound cream cheese
1 teaspoon vanilla
1/4 teaspoon salt
1/4 cup white raisins
1/4 cup cornflake crumbs
1/2 teaspoon cinnamon

Cook the noodles according to directions. To the hot cooked noodles, add 1/4 cup of butter.

Beat the eggs with the sugar. Add the sour cream, cream cheese, vanilla, salt, and raisins. Pour the mixture over the noodles and mix well.

*Available in Greek grocery stores and gourmet food shops.

Melt the remaining 1/4 cup of butter in a 9 × 9-inch baking dish. Pour the noodle mixture into the dish.

Mix the cornflake crumbs with the cinnamon, and sprinkle all over the pudding. Bake in a 350° oven for 40 minutes. Serve hot or cold. 8 servings.

*CHEESE STRUDEL

1 pound farmer cheese
3/4 cup sugar
2 egg yolks
1/2 cup golden raisins
1 teaspoon vanilla
1/2 cup butter, melted

6 strudel leaves
1 cup cornflake crumbs or
  bread crumbs
1 cup almonds, chopped
confectioners' sugar

Mix the cheese, sugar, egg yolks, raisins, and vanilla.

Spread some melted butter over three of the strudel leaves. Sprinkle with half the cornflake or bread crumbs and half the chopped almonds. Spread half the cheese filling across one end of the strudel, a few inches from the edge. Fold the dough over the filling and roll up the strudel.

Place the filled strudel on a well-greased cookie sheet, brush with melted butter, and sprinkle with sugar. Cut the strudel in portions but do not cut all the way through. Repeat the process with the other three strudel leaves.

Bake in a 375° oven until nicely browned. Cool and cut the strudel in portions. When cold, sprinkle with confectioners' sugar. 10 servings.

*CHEESECAKE

CRUST

1 2/3 cups graham cracker, zwieback,
  or vanilla cookie crumbs

1/2 cup brown sugar
1/2 cup butter

FILLING

1 1/2 pounds cream cheese
1 cup sugar
4 eggs
1 cup sour cream

1/4 cup flour
juice of 1 lemon
grated rind of 1 lemon

Mix the crumbs with the brown sugar and butter. Line a 9-inch springform pan with the crumb mixture.

With a mixer, beat the cream cheese until soft. Add the sugar. Add the eggs, one at a time, beating well. Add the sour cream, flour, lemon juice, and lemon rind. Mix well.

Pour the cheese mixture in the crumb-lined springform pan. Bake the cheesecake in a 325° oven for 1 hour. Turn off the heat, and allow the cake to remain in the oven until cool. Refrigerate.

*PINEAPPLE CHEESECAKE

CRUST

1 2/3 cups graham cracker crumbs	1/2 cup butter, melted
1/3 cup brown sugar	1/2 teaspoon cinnamon
	1/2 cup walnuts, chopped

FILLING

1 cup heavy sweet cream	1/2 pound cream cheese
1 cup confectioners' sugar	1 can pineapple pie filling

Mix the graham cracker crumbs with the brown sugar, butter, cinnamon, and nuts. Spread the crumbs in a flat 11 × 13-inch pan. Bake the crust in a 350° oven for 8 minutes, and then allow to cool.

Whip the sweet cream until thick. Mix the confectioners' sugar and the cream cheese, and stir into the whipped cream. Pour into the cooled graham cracker crust.

Cover with the pineapple pie filling. (Any pie filling may be used.) Refrigerate the cake overnight.

*BUREKAS

1/2 cup butter or margarine	1 1/2 tablespoons white vinegar
1/2 cup oil	1/2 cup cold water
3 cups flour	1 egg, beaten with a teaspoon
1 teaspoon baking powder	of water
1 teaspoon salt	sesame seeds

Mix the butter or margarine and oil together with the flour, baking powder, and salt. Add the vinegar with the water, and mix well.

Roll out the pastry very thin on a piece of wax paper. Cut into circles. Put some of the filling on each piece, and fold in half, pinching the edges together with a fork. Lay the *burekas* on a greased foil-lined baking sheet. Brush with the beaten egg, and scatter sesame seeds on top. Prick the top of each *bureka* with a fork. Bake in a 375° oven until nicely browned.

CHEESE FILLING

1 pound farmer cheese　　　　　　*1 cup mashed potatoes*
2 egg yolks　　　　　　　　　　　*salt and pepper to taste*

Mash the farmer cheese. Add the egg yolks, potatoes, and salt and pepper, and mix well.

COTTAGE CHEESE MOLD

1 pound cottage cheese　　　　　*2 tablespoons lemon juice*
1 cup heavy sweet cream,　　　　*2 tablespoons candied ginger,*
　whipped　　　　　　　　　　　*cut fine*
3 tablespoons confectioners'　　　*fresh strawberries*
　sugar

Mash the cottage cheese. Add the whipped cream to the confectioners' sugar. Mix the cottage cheese with the lemon juice and candied ginger; add the cream, mixing lightly. Pour the mixture into a greased mold or a bowl, and refrigerate overnight.

Unmold on a serving dish. Place the strawberries around the mold and serve. (Any fresh berries or fruit go well with the mold.) 6 servings.

ROGELACH

1 package dry yeast　　　　　　　*1/4 cup sour cream or orange*
1/4 cup warm water (105°–115°)　　*juice*
1/2 cup butter or margarine　　　　*3–3 1/4 cups flour, sifted*
1/3 cup sugar　　　　　　　　　　*1/2 teaspoon salt*
2 eggs　　　　　　　　　　　　　*butter or margarine, melted*
　　　　　　　　　　　　　　　　1 egg white, beaten

FILLING

1/2 cup sugar	1 teaspoon cardamom or cinnamon
1/2 cup nuts, chopped	1/2 cup raisins

Mix well the four ingredients for the filling.

Dissolve the yeast in the water.

Cream the butter or margarine with the sugar; add the 2 eggs, sour cream or orange juice, and yeast. Add the flour and salt, and mix well. Knead the dough until it is smooth and does not stick to the hands. Use more flour if dough is sticky. Put the dough in a greased bowl. Cover with plastic wrap, and refrigerate overnight.

Divide the dough into 6 or 8 parts. Roll out each piece of dough into a thin circle. Spread melted butter or margarine on the dough and sprinkle with some of the filling. Cut each circle of dough into 8 wedges. Roll up tightly each wedge of dough from the outer edge of the circle. Place the *rogelach* on a greased baking sheet. Brush the tops with the egg white. Sprinkle with sugar. Let rise in a warm place until double in bulk.

Bake in a 350° oven until nicely browned. Do not overbake. Baking time depends on the size of the *rogelach*. 48 large or 64 small *rogelach*.

*BABKA (Yeast Cake)

1 package dry yeast	1/4 pound butter or margarine
1/4 cup warm water (105°–115°)	3 eggs
3/4 cup sugar	1/2 cup white raisins
1/4 teaspoon salt	1 teaspoon vanilla
3 3/4 cups flour, sifted	butter or margarine, melted
3/4 cup warm milk or water	

Dissolve the yeast in 1/4 cup of warm water. Add 2 teaspoons of sugar and the salt. Mix 1 cup of flour with 3/4 cup warm milk or water, and add to the dissolved yeast. Beat well with a wooden spoon and let it rise until double in bulk.

Cream the butter or margarine with the rest of the sugar until fluffy. Add the eggs, one at a time. Mix in the yeast batter with the rest of the flour and the raisins. Add the vanilla. Mix well by hand or with a wooden spoon. The batter will be thick. Cover the batter with a towel, and let the dough rise until double in bulk (2 to 3 hours).

Spread half the batter in a well-greased angel cake pan, and sprinkle with half the filling. Spread the rest of the batter on top of the filling. Brush the top with melted butter or margarine, and sprinkle with the rest of the filling. Let the *babka* rise again, uncovered, until the dough reaches to the top of the pan. Bake the *babka* in a 375° oven for 40 to 45 minutes.

FILLING

4 tablespoons butter or
    margarine
4 tablespoons flour

3/4 cup sugar
1 teaspoon cinnamon
3/4 cup nuts, chopped

Mix together all the ingredients.

*MOUNT SINAI CAKE

SPONGE CAKE

5 eggs
1 cup sugar
3 tablespoons white wine

1 cup flour, sifted
1 teaspoon baking powder

WINE SAUCE

9 eggs, separated
3 cups white wine
3 teaspoons vanilla

1 cup sugar
1 cup pineapple juice

FILLING

1-pound can pitted dark
    cherries
1-pound 4-ounce can pineapple
    slices, cut up

1-pound 4-ounce can pie-sliced
    apples
1 cup sliced almonds

Bake the sponge cake a day before assembling the "mountain."

In a medium mixing bowl, beat the eggs with the sugar on high speed until very thick and lemon-colored. Add the wine, and beat a few more minutes.

Reduce the speed of the mixer and slowly mix in the flour sifted with the baking powder.

Line the bottom of a 9-inch springform pan with lightly oiled wax paper. Pour the cake batter into the pan.

Bake the cake in a 350° oven for 30 minutes or until done. Remove from oven, and allow the cake to cool. When cold, run a knife around the cake form, release the spring, and remove the cake. Remove the wax paper.

Drain the fruits for the filling well, saving 1 cup of the pineapple juice for the wine sauce.

To make the wine sauce, put the egg yolks, wine, vanilla, sugar, and pineapple juice in the top of a double boiler, and place over hot but not boiling water. Cook the wine sauce, stirring constantly, until the sauce thickens and coats the spoon. Sauce will be thin. Allow the sauce to cool.

Cut the sponge cake vertically in half, and then cut each half vertically into 6 pieces, each about 3/4" wide.

Lay 5 of the longer slices of the cake side by side in an oven-proof dish. On the cake put some of the pineapple, cherries, and apple slices. Pour some of the wine sauce on top, and scatter some almonds. Make a second layer with 4 other slices of cake, some of the fruits, and add some of the wine sauce and almonds. On top of this put 2 of the smaller pieces of the cake, and more fruits, wine sauce, and almonds. Put the last piece of cake on top, and pour the rest of the wine sauce all over the cake and fruits. The cake should resemble a mountain.

Beat the egg whites until very stiff and dry. With a spatula cover the cake with the egg whites, and scatter some of the almonds on the bottom part of the mountain only.

Bake in a 250° oven for 10 minutes just to dry the egg whites. After 10 minutes place a piece of foil on the top part of the cake to keep it from browning. Bake for 10 more minutes until the bottom is a light brown (the top should remain white). The egg whites should resemble snow, and the almonds, stones. Turn off the heat, and leave the cake in the oven for 1 hour. Remove the cake from the oven, and allow to cool at room temperature.

If the cake is to be served the next day, it is advisable to refrigerate it.

Cut a piece of white cardboard into the shape of the two tablets for the Ten Commandments, and place on top of the cake.

CHILDREN'S STORIES
FOR SHAVUOT

*

*Shavuot

CHARLOTTE BRONSTEIN

active as a teacher, actress, writer, director of theater groups, and author of scripts and a book on the Jewish holidays

(age level four to seven)

On the sixth day of the moon month of Sivan it is time for another holiday. This lovely holiday is called Shavuot. Shavuot is a Hebrew word which means "weeks." You see, Shavuot comes just seven *weeks* after the second day of Passover. Now it is time to climb up into the sky on the moonbeams. You are going to make two trips, so hold on tight and away you go!

Such a fast ride to the long-ago! You are sailing right over the Temple in the city of Jerusalem. You see many people there. Some are carrying two loaves of bread made from the first ripe wheat, and others carry baskets of the first fruit to ripen on the trees. Some of the baskets are silver and gold; others are made of willow twigs. All the people will spend the night outside the Temple. In the morning they will bring their fruit and bread into the Temple so they can thank God for their good harvest.

Now the moon starts to spin. It is sailing back, farther back, in time. You are with the Israelites who fled from the land of Egypt.

While the people rested at the foot of Mount Sinai, God told Moses He would give the Jewish people some laws. God had chosen the Jewish people because they were the only people on earth who said they would obey Him. God then said that when the Jewish people learned to obey these laws, they would go to a land of their own.

God commanded Moses to go back to his people and to tell them to wash their clothes, to bathe themselves, and to clean their tents. After all this was done, the people were to pray for three days. Then God would speak to them from the top of Mount Sinai.

The people did as God commanded. On the third day they looked up, and they trembled at what they saw. A large black cloud of smoke covered the top of the mountain. It looked as though the mountain itself were on fire. Thunder roared and lightning flashed and the sound of a trumpet rang out.

Suddenly the trumpet stopped, the thunder was still, the birds stopped singing, and even the rivers stopped flowing. All was quiet, and out of the stillness came the voice of God.

"I am the Lord thy God, who brought thee out of the land of Egypt, out of the house of bondage."

Then the Voice spoke again:

I. Thou shalt have no other Gods before me.

II. Thou shalt not pray to any images or statues.

III. Thou shalt not take the name of the Lord thy God in vain.

IV. Remember the Sabbath day to keep it holy.

V. Honor thy father and thy mother.

VI. Thou shalt not murder.

VII. Thou shalt not do any wrong act.

VIII. Thou shalt not steal.

IX. Thou shalt not lie or say anything untrue about people.

X. Thou shalt not want anything which belongs to someone else.

Those are the Ten Commandments, or laws, which God gave to the Jewish people.

When the voice of God was no longer heard, the people were still frightened, and they said to Moses:

"After this you speak to God for us and tell us what He says. We are afraid of God."

Moses told his people not to fear God, because God loved them. But the people were still afraid and they backed away from the mountain. So Moses left the people with Aaron and he went up to Mount Sinai and stayed there for forty days and forty nights. On the mountain God gave Moses two stone tablets on which were written the Ten Commandments. Moses brought the tablets to his people. They called the Commandments the "Holy Law," and they were proud that God had chosen them as His people.[1]

*

*How K'tonton Wished a Wish on Shavuot Night

SADIE ROSE WEILERSTEIN

author of eleven books for children in a successful writing career, and twice the recipient of the Jewish Book Council's Juvenile Award

(age level four to seven)

K'tonton was going to the country for Shavuot.

"It's a dairy holiday," said his mother. "We'll be able to get such nice cheese and butter for the *blintzes.*"

"And the woods are there," said Father. "Think of the branches for Shavuot greens!"

"The country! Shavuot greens!" K'tonton was so happy he turned three somersaults, one after the other. Suddenly a thought popped into his mind and he sat up straight.

"And sky!" he said. "Sky!"

He climbed up into his little garden on the window seat and stood looking out of the window. His eyes were far away and dreamy.

"Sky!" he said. "Lots and lots of it! Not just a little bit between tall buildings! I'll do it! I'll do it! I've always wanted to and now I will."

What was it that K'tonton wanted so much to do?

I won't ask you to guess because I'm sure you couldn't.
HE WANTED TO SEE THE SKY OPEN!

You see, every year on Shavuot exactly at midnight, the sky opens. It opens up for one second and you can see right inside —provided there aren't any tall buildings or chimneys to hide it, and provided you are wide awake. If you closed your eyes for one minute or gave as much as a wink, you might miss it all. But the most wonderful part is this. If you make a wish while the sky is open, the WISH COMES TRUE.

Well, Mother made K'tonton a wee pair of overalls and Father bought him a farmer hat just his size, and off they went to the country. An old mother cow nodded to them over the fence. It had a wobbly young calf nuzzling up to it. Yellow chicks were running about the lawn. There was a big barn and a rooster on a straw stack, and SKY, sky everywhere. It dipped over to the cornfields at one end and down to the hills at the other. There were fluffy clouds in it, "like angels' wings," K'tonton thought.

K'tonton slipped into his overalls and the farmer said: "So this is the new hired man, is it?" and took him out to the barn. It was milking time and the cows were standing in a row waiting to be milked. The little calf's mother wasn't there. She was out in the pasture with her baby. She never left her baby for a minute.

Squirt! squirt! squirt! went the milk into the pail. The farmer gave K'tonton a thimbleful, warm and bubbly.

How busy K'tonton was all that day and the next! He rode up and down on the dasher of the farm wife's churn. She was making butter to fry the *blintzes* in. He went to the woods for greens with his father, and came swinging home on the slender branches.

But mostly he sat on the fence watching the mother cow and her calf and thinking of the wish he would make when the sky opened. It was such a tremendous wish that he held his breath just to think of it. He was going to wish that he knew the whole Talmud by heart, every word of it, all the sixty-three tractates from cover to cover. He could see his father's face when the wish came true. "Father," he would say, opening up the Talmud, "put your finger somewhere on this page." Then without looking he would tell his father exactly what was written on that spot, ten pages, or twenty pages, even fifty pages further. How astonished his father would be!

K'tonton thought of it as he got into his holiday suit, as he recited his prayers with the wind blowing sweet smells through the window, as he listened to *Kiddush.* He even thought of it as he ate his cheese *blintzes,* crispy brown ones covered with sour cream.

At last the eating and the singing and praying were over. Mother carried K'tonton upstairs and tucked him into bed.

"Good night, little son," she said. "Don't lie awake for Father. He won't be home until almost morning. He has to say *Tikkun* tonight."

K'tonton watched her as she left the room. "She calls me little son," he thought. "She doesn't know that by morning I'll be a great scholar, a learned man, a *talmid hakham.*"

He kicked off the covers and climbed out of his bed to the windowsill.

"I must keep awake," he said. "I mustn't let my eyes shut one minute."

A breeze was blowing through the strings of the morning glory vines that climbed past his window. It made him think of David's harp.

"I'd better say psalms," he said.

He sang one psalm, another and another. He recited his *Shema.* He repeated all the passages he knew—from the Torah, the Prophets, the midrash, the Talmud.

Back and forth K'tonton swayed reciting his verse, each in its proper tune. All the while his eyes were fixed on the dark sky. Mountains of clouds were hurrying across it. "I will come to you in a thick cloud," God had said to Moses.

"Perhaps God is hiding behind those clouds now," K'tonton thought. "Perhaps He is getting ready to open up the heavens and give me my wish. It's so still. It's as still as when God gave the Torah."

He peered into the darkness and repeated softly, "No bird sang, no ox lowed, not a creature uttered a sound."

As he said the word "sound," out of the night a sound did come. It wasn't a loud sound, just a soft plaintive lowing "Moo-Moo!" But it brought K'tonton to his feet.

"It's the calf," he said. "It wants its mother. Where is its mother? What has happened to its mother?"

He took hold of a morning glory vine, and before you could wink, was sliding to the ground.

"Moo! Moo!" came the sound across the pasture. Now there was an answering call "Moo—oo!" The mother cow! K'tonton hurried across the lawn so fast his bare feet twinkled in the grass. Through the barnyard he went to the fence. Over in the pasture stood the wobbly calf shivering and frightened, and in the barnyard stood the poor mother cow. Oh, how distressed she was with two fences and a lane between her and her baby! K'tonton understood in a minute what had happened. In his hurry to get ready for the holiday, the farm boy must have driven the cows into the barnyard and left the calf behind. He would open the gate at once and let the mother through.

K'tonton climbed up the wire gate, but it wasn't so easy to open as he had thought. He tugged at the great iron hook and tugged at it. His cheeks grew red and his heart beat fast with exertion, but the hook refused to budge.

"Moo! Moo-oo!" lowed the young calf pitifully. K'tonton could not bear to hear it. It made him think of the time he had been lost in the forest far away from his mother.

"I must help it! I must!" he said, tugging away.

He was so busy thinking about the calf he had forgotten all about his wish. Suddenly his eyes glanced upward and there in the sky was—a split! Yes, a real split—right in the clouds. A heavenly light was shining through it.

"I wish," said K'tonton, "that the little calf could be with its mother this minute!"

As he spoke, the hook gave a scraping noise and sprang back. The mother cow pushed against the gate and passed down the lane into the pasture. The next minute she was licking her precious calf with her tongue.

Suddenly K'tonton remembered his great wish! He couldn't make it now. It was too late. When morning came he wouldn't be a *talmid hakham,* a great man, a learned scholar. He would still be an ordinary little *heder* boy.

K'tonton walked slowly across the barnyard, across the lawn. Slowly he climbed up the strings of the morning glory vines to his room. He entered at the window as Father entered at the door.

"K'tonton," said Father, hurrying across the room and picking him up in his hand, "What are you doing up so late?"

K'tonton buried his face in his father's neck and told him the story.

"And, Father," he said between sobs, "if it hadn't been for the calf I'd be a scholar now, what you said you wanted me to be, a *talmid hakham.*"

But Father only smiled a big comforting smile.

"Don't you remember what the Rabbis say: 'Not learning but doing is the chief thing'? I'd rather have you show tender mercy to God's creatures than be the greatest scholar in the world."[2]

*

*A New Commandment

MORRIS EPSTEIN

editor of World Over, *a magazine for Jewish children, and professor and chairman of the Department of English at Stern College for Women of Yeshivah University (1921-1973)*

(age level six to nine)

"You know what, Mom?" said Gita, smiling her prettiest smile.

Mother looked at Gita. Now she would find out why Gita had been so silent during dinner. The family was gathered in the living room. Gita had been staring out of the window, quiet as a mouse. Mother knew that *something* was brewing in her daughter's mind. She put down her mending and said, "What is it, dear?"

"I think I ought to stop going to school. The term is almost over anyway. I could stay home and help you shop and . . . and . . ." She broke off; Father had that certain look in his eye, even though he wasn't saying anything.

Mother picked up one of Father's socks and the darning needle. "Did anything happen in school today, Gita? Anything unusual, I mean?"

"N-o-o-o," replied Gita slowly, slowly, "except . . ."

"Except what?" Father prodded.

"Except, if I go back to that old school, I'll keep my mouth tight shut and never say a single word!"

"Gita, what on earth happened?" Mother was really concerned now.

"Well," said Gita, "we were playing Going to Jerusalem and

I told the teacher that it must be a Jewish game, because our ancestors used to go to Jerusalem three times each year. They went on Passover, Shavuot, and Sukkot. We just studied it in Hebrew school, because Shavuot is coming next week."

"How wonderful!" beamed Mother, and Father relaxed, too. "The teacher must have been proud of you."

"She was *too* proud," pouted Gita. "She said that it would be very interesting for the whole class to hear about Shavuot. She said I could give a report on it tomorrow. Oh, why did I have to open my mouth!"

Father said, "I think it's a grand idea for you to tell the class about Shavuot."

"But I don't know much about it," complained Gita. "We didn't finish studying Shavuot in Hebrew school. All I know is that Moses brought the Ten Commandments down from Mount Sinai and . . . O-o-o-h! I've got an idea. Daddy! Why don't *you* tell me a story about Shavuot?"

Father smiled. "The *best* story is told in the Bible itself," he said. "It's very exciting, too. Can you imagine Moses leading our people through the hot desert after they had left Egypt? Just shut your eyes and think how it must have felt to face the blinding sun and burning sands each day on the long march to the promised land!

"Think of Moses, a proud leader, approaching Mount Sinai. He tells his people that he will climb that mountain to get the Ten Commandments for them. The Commandments would teach them to worship God, and to be kind and honest.

"Up he goes, higher and higher. At last he is hidden by the clouds covering the top of Mount Sinai. The people wait many days, watching for the return of their beloved leader.

"And then he comes down, holding the two tablets on which the Ten Commandments are written. He teaches the laws to his people, and they learn to worship one God, to be kind to each other, to be honest, to rest on the Sabbath, never to steal or kill. The children are taught to honor and obey their parents.

"That was only the beginning. When the Jews reached Eretz Yisrael, they became farmers. They built homes and tilled the soil and planted barley and wheat. They planted vineyards and olive trees, tall palms and cypress trees. In Jerusalem they built a Temple where they could worship God.

"And each year, when the grain harvest was ended, the Jews

22. *Hag ha-Bikkurim.* By Jossi Stern. Color lithograph.
See Chapter 8.

would celebrate the holiday of Shavuot. Then the farmers would take barley and wheat and baskets of fruit that had ripened first to the city of Jerusalem as a thanks offering to God. That is why Shavuot is sometimes called *Hag ha-Bikkurim,* the Festival of Firstfruits.

"Picture that scene! Jerusalem, the sun shining on its domed roofs, the pilgrims traveling from every corner of the land, on donkeys, on camels, or on foot. And then, after the celebration, returning home to till the soil and plant and reap again.

"That is the historical story of Shavuot. Years later, our people were forced to leave Palestine. But we have never failed to celebrate Shavuot. We decorate our homes and synagogues and schools with flowers and green branches. We eat cheese *blintzes* and honey cake to remind us that the Torah is sweet as honey and as nourishing as milk to those who study it and keep the Commandments."

"And we read the Book of Ruth," said Mother.

"Just like a woman, speaking up for other women," smiled Father. "Yes, we read the Book of Ruth in our synagogues. Ruth was a girl of Moab who came to Palestine with Naomi, her Jewish mother-in-law. Ruth became Jewish and accepted the Torah, just as our ancestors had accepted it. Ruth was a poor girl, and she gathered sheaves of wheat in the fields of a rich man called Boaz. Later Boaz married Ruth and they were very happy together. One of their descendants was famous King David."

"So you see, Gita," said Mother, "Shavuot is really two holidays in one. It is a harvest holiday and it is the Ten Commandments holiday. And we always try to make Shavuot as happy a festival as the pilgrims did when they came with their firstfruits to the city of Jerusalem."

It was very quiet now in the living room. Suddenly Father rose and walked over to the window and pulled aside the curtain. "See the twinkling stars?" he said to his family. "There is a beautiful legend about the stars and the Torah.

"They have been up there in the sky for a very long time. They saw, with their eyes of light, the giving of the Torah on Mount Sinai. 'Do not give the Torah to the earthmen,' they pleaded with God. 'Let it stay with us in heaven, where all is bright and cheerful. The earth has little light and warmth, and many people there are wicked.'

"Morning came and the stars stopped twinkling. The voice of God was heard: 'The earth is cold and dark. Therefore I am giving it the Torah, so that it may be light and warm. It has no stars. The people will study the Torah and wise, learned men will bring light and wisdom to them. Then the cold dark earth will be as warm and bright as the sun and stars in heaven.'

"Then Moses went up on Mount Sinai and brought down the two tablets of the Law on which the Ten Commandments were written. And since that time, those very stars you see now look down upon the earth every night with sadness and longing. They long for the light of the Torah."

Mother turned to Gita and said, "Do you think you'll be able to tell the class about Shavuot now, dear?"

Gita didn't answer. She had a faraway look in her eyes. She said, "You know, Mom, if God wanted to make sure we'd be good, there really should have been *eleven* commandments instead of ten."

Mother looked startled. "Why, what would the eleventh commandment be?"

"Keep the other ten!" cried Gita, skipping out of the room.[3]

*

Not a Chirp Was Heard

LEVIN KIPNIS

a pioneer and a popular Israeli author of children's stories, legends, poems, and plays, many of which have been translated into English

(age level seven to ten)

One day Moses was following his sheep in the desert near Mount Sinai, when he suddenly saw a bird circling a burning bush and screeching desperately. Moses became curious and ran to the bush. He found between the branches of the smoldering bush a bird's nest with several young birds in it, stretching their necks and chirping pitifully. Without any hesitation Moses stuck his hand into the fire, brought out the nest with the birds, and placed it on another bush. The mother bird flew with a loud shriek into the nest.

* Copyright © by the author.

Moses returned to his sheep and sat down to bandage his burned hand. The mother bird came and settled on the palm of his hand twittering softly as though thanking him for saving her babies. Moses fondled the bird and threw it into the air.

The mother and her young became attached to Moses and followed him wherever he went, chirping and twittering. Soon Moses learned their language. The news about his friendship to birds spread to other regions and many birds left their nests and came to settle in the desert. They filled the desert with their twitters and songs.

Sometime later Moses saw another bush burning in the desert. He approached and heard a voice coming from the fire:

"Moses, I saw you bringing the birds out from the fire. Go now and bring out the children of Israel from Egypt!"

Moses left the desert, the sheep and the birds and went to Pharaoh. The children of Israel soon were freed from bondage in Egypt and Moses led them to Mount Sinai. The birds of the desert greeted Moses and the liberated slaves with joyful twittering and loud singing.

Then one of the Israelites saw a mother bird sitting on her young in a nest and took the mother away from her babies. The birds of the desert raised a great commotion and decided to bring their complaint against the Israelite to Moses, but they were afraid to approach him. He appeared to them not the same Moses they had known as a shepherd. That Moses was jolly and enjoyed their company. The present Moses had a serious look, was always busy, and had no time even to look at birds.

Meanwhile, the children of the Israelites looked for bird nests. Wherever they found one, they took away the mother from her young. The birds quickly left their nests and built new ones on the top of Mount Sinai, where no human hand could reach them. Only the mother birds remained with their young in the desert to wait until they grow wings.

Soon the birds heard the news that Moses was about to give the children of Israel the Torah. They immediately chose a delegation and sent it to Moses. The delegation found Moses on Mount Sinai with a chisel in his hand, engraving the Ten Commandments on the two stone tablets.

"Moses, what is written in the Torah which you are about to give to the children of Israel?" the birds of the delegation asked.

"Thou shalt not kill!" Moses told them.

"Moses, do you know that the Israelites have taken mother birds out from their nests and killed them and left their young orphaned?" the birds continued.

Moses was silent.

"You are silent, Moses, but we birds do not intend to remain silent. We will raise such a noise with our wings and with our screeching voices that your Torah will not be heard by your listeners unless you insert a commandment for the protection of birds."

Moses thought for a moment. Then he raised his eyes to the birds and said:

"You are right! I will!"

The reassured delegation brought the glad news to those who had sent them.

Three days later the children of Israel stood at the foot of Mount Sinai and watched thousands of birds hovering in the air above the mountain. Moses read the commandments one by one. He lifted his sparkling eyes to the birds and read:

"If you find a bird's nest on a tree or on the ground, do not take the mother from her young!"

The birds hovered above, but—*not a chirp was heard.*

Translated by Israel M. Goodelman[4]

*

**At Sinai*

DEBORAH PESSIN

author of Jewish children's books and recipient of the Juvenile Award of the Jewish Book Council of the National Jewish Welfare Board

(age level seven to ten)

Reuben lay on his back before the tent and blinked up at the hot blue sky. Throwing one leg over the knee of the other, he moved his sandaled foot up and down. Slowly he turned his head and looked at Mount Sinai. Its peak was hidden in soft gray clouds.

Somewhere among those clouds was Moses, gone many days now. Reuben sat up, his face troubled.

"Reuben," his mother's voice came from the tent, "it is too hot to lie out there."

Reuben got to his feet. His short tunic clung damply to his body. He did not take his eyes from the mountain that squatted in the hot sands. Sometimes he kept watching it all day and late into the night, when it was swallowed by the heavy darkness.

"Still worried about Moses?"

He turned. His mother had come to the door of the tent, an earthen jug in her hand.

"Yes," said Reuben, "he has been up on the mountain many days alone. Do you think—"

"Tomorrow," said his mother, "he will return. It is forty days that he is gone." She held out the jug to him. "Run to the well and get some water."

Reuben trotted off, the jug on his shoulder. He made his way in and out between the scraggly rows of tents. Groups of men stood about, talking of Moses. Reuben knew they were restless for Moses' return. He knew by the way they kept turning and looking at Sinai.

The well was behind a cluster of trees at the very edge of the encampment. Jacob and Naphtali were sitting there, scraping pictures in the sand with sharp sticks. They looked up as Reuben came up to them.

"Tell us, Reuben," Jacob grinned at him, "how many days is it that Moses has been gone?"

Reuben said nothing, He lowered the jug into the well and drew it up again, filled with cool sparkling water. Jacob nudged Naphtali with his foot. "He can think of nothing else since Moses went up on Sinai."

Naphtali turned his suntanned face to Reuben.

"Have you ever seen Moses?" he asked.

"N-no," said Reuben. He shifted the brimming jug to his shoulder. "I have never really seen him. Only from the distance. I saw his head, and when I came closer he was gone."

"I was in his tent once," Jacob said proudly. "It was three days before he went up on Sinai for the Commandments."

"What is he like?" asked Reuben eagerly.

"He has a white beard," said Jacob, "and he seemed tired."

"And—" Reuben prompted him.

Jacob shrugged his shoulders.

"It is hard to describe him," he said. "Perhaps you will see him when he comes down from Sinai."

"I am going to get up early," said Naphtali, stretching his long arms over his head. "I'll be one of the first to get there. Then I'll be sure to see him."

Reuben turned to go. Everyone would be at Sinai when Moses returned, and perhaps he would not see him then, either.

Reuben could not sleep that night. The camp had buzzed all evening with talk about Moses, about the Commandments he would bring. No one really knew what they would be, but Caleb thought there would be one about God, and another about the Sabbath. Everyone had tried to guess, talking eagerly near the campfires. At last the fires died down, and the people had gone into their tents to sleep. But Reuben could not sleep.

For a long time he tossed and turned restlessly on his mat. Then he rose, listened for a moment to the deep, quiet breathing of his father and mother, and crept out of doors. A bright moon hung over the silent tents, and from the distance he heard the braying of a donkey. Tonight Mount Sinai was clear under the moonlit sky. Somewhere on the lonely mountain Moses sat. Reuben began to walk toward Sinai. The sand was still hot under his feet, though the sun had gone down many hours before.

When Reuben reached the end of the encampment, he stopped. It was still a great distance to Sinai, and there were no guards posted beyond the tents. Dan had told him only yesterday that he had seen a mountain lion.

Reuben fingered the sharp knife in his belt, swallowed hard, and walked on. His feet moved noiselessly over the ground. This time he would see Moses. He turned quickly as he heard the patter of feet behind him. Joshua, one of the guards, came up to him and peered into his face.

"Where are you going, lad?" Joshua asked him curiously.

"To Sinai."

"But Moses will not return till morning. Then we will all go."

"If I wait till morning I may not see him," Reuben explained eagerly. "There will be too many."

The guard looked at him. He seemed to hesitate.

"Do not go too near to the mountain," he said at last.

And he turned and walked back to the encampment, while Reuben continued on his way. He would see Moses. He would be the first one. A cloud moved over the moon. Perhaps the guard was right. Perhaps he should have waited till morning. Reuben jumped, then stood frozen to the ground. A shadow fell along the ground before him. He shifted his eyes from side to side. The shape of a rock loomed up on his left, its shadow slanting toward Sinai. Reuben sighed with relief and hurried on.

The moon sailed out from under the cloud and hung over Mount Sinai. Reuben stopped and looked up. The pearly gray clouds over the peak of Sinai had become black and heavy, and a strange rumbling sound seemed to shake the mountain from its core.

"Moses," whispered Reuben, "come quickly. I am afraid here in the dark. . . . And I have never seen your face."

A gust of wind swept down from the mountainside. Reuben drew his tunic closer about him, clutched his knife in his hand, and stretched out on the sand. The mountain rumbled. Then all was quiet.

Reuben felt a stab of light in his eyes. He opened them and looked about. The bright morning sunlight was streaming over the mountain. He sat up with a start, then scrambled to his feet.

The next moment he saw him.

Moses stood alone on the mountainside, and it seemed that his face was made of light and the light reached up and streamed out in two beams from his silvery hair. He stood motionless, a tall figure dressed in white, looking out over the sleeping encampment. Far above his head the shrouded mountain rumbled and roared. But Moses did not stir. The two tablets of the Law in his hand, he stood waiting.

"Moses," whispered Reuben. He took a step toward the lonely figure whose face he could hardly see for the light upon it. "Moses, you have come."

Then Moses turned and saw the boy. Slowly he began to descend the mountain. Reuben stood rooted to the spot, unable to move. It was toward him that Moses was coming. He waited, his heart beating. Then he felt Moses' hand upon his shoulder.

"What is your name, lad," he heard Moses ask.

"Reuben," the boy stammered.

"I am glad it was you I saw first from the mountain," Moses

spoke again, "the young and eager, who waited for my return. It is for those who are anxious to learn that I remained for forty days on Sinai. For you, Reuben. . . ."

The sharp blast of a trumpet was heard from the mountain, so loud that it shook the ground beneath their feet. But Reuben was not afraid.

Standing there beside Moses and watching the people hurrying toward them from the encampment, Reuben's heart sang. For Moses' hand was upon his shoulder and his voice rang in his ears.[5]

*

* *Who Will Be My Surety?*

SEYMOUR ROSSEL

Jewish educator, short-story writer, and editor

(*age level nine to eleven*)

When Moses went up Mount Sinai to speak with the Lord, the people of Israel waited below for him to return.

The people of Israel were very anxious. They wondered what the Lord would say to Moses. Then they saw Moses coming down the mountain. They turned to him eagerly and, as they looked at his face, they saw that he was sad.

"What has happened?" they asked him.

Moses spoke to them and said, "The Lord wishes to give us a most wonderful gift, a precious thing."

Excitedly, the people asked, "What is this gift?"

"It is called the Torah," Moses said. "In its words the light of truth shines like pearls in the dark seas. In the Torah there are stories which teach us how God wishes us to live.

"There are laws in it also, laws which teach us how to live peacefully with our neighbors so that a man will love his fellowmen. The Torah will teach us how to live as free men, so that we will never be slaves again."

The people remembered Egypt where they were slaves of the

Pharaoh. They did not wish to be slaves again. They wanted to be free. They wished to live in peace. Truly, they thought, God's Torah is a great gift.

But Moses was still sad.

"Why are you unhappy, Moses?" the people asked.

Moses sat upon a rock at the foot of the mountain. "God will not give us this gift of Torah unless we promise Him something in return. We must offer him a surety."

Then the people too were sad. "What have we to offer in exchange for such a precious gift?" one man asked another. "A gift like this is worth empires, and we are a poor people in the desert. Now we will never have the gift of Torah."

But the women of Israel came to Moses and said, "We have bracelets with rubies and rings with diamonds. We have precious necklaces and pins. We will give them all to the Lord in exchange for the Torah."

So Moses went up the mountain again and spoke with the Lord. But when he returned, he was still sad.

"The Lord has said that His Torah is more precious than all the rubies and diamonds in the world. The Torah is so bright that it will light the souls of men. Not even a thousand diamonds can do that!"

Then the people sat on the sand of the desert and thought.

All night long the people thought, and when the sun came up they had an idea. "We will offer the Lord our great leaders, Moses and Aaron, as surety for the Torah. Surely the Lord will accept the loyalty of Moses and Aaron in exchange for His wonderful gift."

So Moses went up Mount Sinai to the Lord again. But again he was sad when he returned.

"The Lord has spoken and told me that He cannot accept Moses and Aaron as surety. They are already His; they have already pledged their loyalty to the Lord."

Now in the camp of the Israelites there was an old man whose wisdom was very great. When this wise man heard Moses' words, he rose and spoke to the people.

"God has offered us *His* most precious possession, the Torah. Now we must offer God *our* most precious possession. If a man could choose only one thing in all the world to be his own, would he choose precious jewels? No. Would he choose an honored leader? No. Would he choose money? No. What would he choose if he had only one choice?—his children!"

Then the people turned to Moses. "Yes!" they cried out. "We will offer our children as surety for the Torah. If God will give us His Torah, we will teach it faithfully to our children. And our children will teach it to their children. What could be a better surety?"

So Moses went up the mountain again to speak with the Lord. And when he came down, he was carrying the tablets of the Law, the Torah which God had given him.

Moses stood before all the people of Israel and said: "The Lord has given us the Torah. Our children will be His surety. For the Lord has said that all men are His children, and the children of all men are precious to Him."

Then the people of Israel thanked the Lord by studying His Torah, and they have kept their promise by teaching the Torah to their children from that day until this.[6]

*

*Play for Shavuot

SYDNEY TAYLOR

author of the popular series of children's books, "All-of-a-Kind Family," and winner of the Charles W. Follett Award and the Jewish Book Council Juvenile Award

(age level ten to thirteen)

Ella loved dramatics, so she threw herself wholeheartedly into directing plays at Sunday school. For every important Jewish holiday she had the children present a play. Now she was rehearsing the biblical story of Ruth and Naomi for Shavuot, the Feast of Weeks.

Shavuot, which comes seven weeks after Passover, commemorates a festival that was held in Palestine in ancient times when the Jews were farmers. At this season of the year, they had finished gathering in their crops. Rejoicing in the harvest, they celebrated by making a pilgrimage to Jerusalem. Each one

brought to the Temple the firstfruits of his crops, wheat or barley, dates or figs, olive oil, grapes, and pomegranates. This was
to remind them that everything on the earth belongs to the Lord
and that man is but the caretaker.

At Shavuot, those who had rich fields were expected to share
with the poor and the stranger. The needy were allowed to
follow after the gleaners so that they might pick up the fallen
grain, or to cut the grain in a corner of the field that was set aside
especially for them.

But even more important—Shavuot is the birthday of the Jewish religion. It was at this time that Moses received the Ten
Commandments from God on Mount Sinai to give to His people.

One Sunday the children came home from Sunday school,
fluttering with excitement. "Mama," Gertie cried, "guess what!

23. Ruth gleaning in the fields. Woodcut. By Jacob Steinhardt.
From *The Book of Ruth*. Woodcuts by Jacob Steinhardt.
Calligraphy by Franzisca Baruch. See Chapter 8.

You know the play we're rehearsing with Ella? Well—we're going to charge admission and give the money to the Red Cross!"

"That's very good," Mama said. "Whose idea was that?"

"Henny's!" Sarah told her.

"I asked permission from the principal," Henny said proudly, "and he said yes."

"But now that it's all settled," Ella chimed in, "I'm scared to death. Suppose it doesn't turn out well?"

Mama smiled. "It will."

The next three weeks were crowded with preparations for the big event. Ella's guiding hand was in everything. Other teachers did the sewing, but it was Ella who designed the costumes. The scenery was being put together by the older boys, under Ella's watchful eye, and with Ella doing much of the painting. It was Henny who worked out the dances, but it was Ella who offered suggestions. Sometimes she came home in high spirits. Everything was going along fine. Sometimes she despaired of everything. "Mama," she complained, "that girl who's playing Ruth —she's a good actress, and she certainly looks beautiful on the stage, but she'll never be able to sing Ruth's song. I'm going crazy trying to teach her, but it's just no use. She just hasn't got the voice for it."

"Don't take it so to heart," Papa consoled her. "I'm sure no one expects her to be an opera singer. Besides, it's a friendly audience, just the parents and relatives and neighbors. Ten years from now, who'll remember who sang?"

Henny clapped her hands. Her eyes sparkled. "That's it!" she shouted. Rushing over to Ella, she whispered excitedly into her ear. Ella's face lit up.

"What is it? What is it?" the sisters clamored. But neither Ella nor Henny would tell.

Then Shavuot was here. Friends and relatives brought gifts of plants and fruits and shared in the eating of the customary dairy foods that were served for this holiday.

On the Sunday afternoon of the performance, the Hebrew school auditorium was packed. The Healys had been invited to see the play they had heard so much about. They sat in the same row with Papa, Mama, Charlie, Lena, Uncle Hyman, and Mrs. Shiner.

Backstage was bedlam. Ella and Henny rushed about pinning squirming youngsters into their costumes, putting makeup on their faces, giving last-minute instructions, and, in between, hissing: "Shush! They'll hear you outside!"

At the very final moment, Ella yanked away from the curtain a small boy who was peeping out and waving to his mama and papa.

The curtain went up. A spotlight revealed a little girl standing at one side of the stage. She began to read:

"And it came to pass that there was a famine in the land of Judah. And a certain man of Bethlehem went to live in the fields of Moab, he and his wife, and his two sons. And the man was named Elimelech and his wife was named Naomi. . . .

"Elimelech died. And the two sons took wives of the women of Moab—the name of the one was Orpah and the name of the other Ruth, and they dwelt there about ten years. And the sons died and the three women were left widowed. Naomi wished to return to the land of her fathers, and Ruth and Orpah went with her through the fields to the road that led to Bethlehem. . . ."

"Isn't that from the Bible?" Mrs. Healy whispered to Papa.

"Well, it's not exactly like we read it in the synagogue. I suppose they made it simple so the children would understand."

The reader closed her book and disappeared. The stage lights brightened.

"See, Charlie," Mama said softly, "that's Ruth, and that's Orpah, and there is Naomi."

Charlie scoffed. "Nah! That's not Naomi. That's Sarah. She's dressed up like an old lady."

Naomi stretched out her arms and began to speak in a broken voice. "Alas, soon it will be dark. Return you now to your homes."

And Orpah, weeping bitterly, embraced Naomi and departed.

Then Naomi said to Ruth, "Dearest Ruth, go you too as Orpah has done. I am an old woman, but you are still young. Your husband is dead, but here in the land of Moab you have many relatives and friends. You will find happiness with them again."

But no matter how much Naomi urged, Ruth would not leave. Lifting her head, she began to sing. The audience grew still under the spell of the lovely voice, so full and strong, yet so tender.

Papa and Mama exchanged bewildered glances. The voice—they knew it so well! But how could it be? There was the girl on stage singing the role of Ruth. Her mouth moved in song. Her whole body seemed alive with the music. They listened intently. "It *is* Ella singing!" Mama whispered.

"No mistake about it," Papa whispered back.

They marveled how cleverly it was being done. Ruth's lips moved perfectly in time with Ella's backstage singing. Pure and clear were the beautiful words of devotion that have come down through the ages:

> Entreat me not to leave thee
>   And to return from following after thee
> For whither thou goest, I will go
>   And where thou lodgest, I will lodge
> Thy people shall be my people
>   And thy God my God.
>
> Where thou diest, will I die
>   And there will I be buried
> The Lord do so to me
> And more also
>   If aught but death part thee and me.

The curtain was lowered, and the applause rang out. Murmurs of admiration swelled from all sides of the auditorium. "Such a wonderful voice!"

Mama and Papa smiled at each other.

Grace leaned over and touched Mama's hand. "You know, I would have sworn that was Ella singing."

Mama's eyes twinkled. "You think so?"

Act two began almost immediately. Once again the reader stood in a circle of light. . . .

"Now it happened that Ruth and Naomi came to Bethlehem at the time of the harvest. There was a man called Boaz, kinsman to Naomi, and he had many large fields. And Ruth joined the poor who followed after the gleaners in the fields of Boaz, for it was known that he was kind and generous. . . ."

Bright light flooded the stage, and sighs of delight rippled through the audience, so charming was the picture. The golden fields filled with cut sheaves seemed so real that one could almost smell the fallen gleanings. Slowly the gleaners moved across the stage gathering up the grain. Ruth was among them, and the others gazed at her and whispered about her great beauty.

Boaz appeared. "Who is this maiden?" he asked of his gleaners.

"She is the daughter-in-law of thy kinswoman, Naomi. They have just come from the land of Moab."

"Ah, yes, so I have heard. They have suffered much and are in great need. See that you let many stalks fall in the maiden's path."

Then Boaz addressed himself to Ruth. "I bid you welcome. Come to my fields as often as you like for the grain with which to make your bread. You shall eat with my workers when you are hungry, and if you are thirsty, they will draw water for you to drink."

"Why are you so kind to me?" Ruth asked.

And Boaz replied, "It has been told to me all that you have done for Naomi. Who deserves kindness more than you who have been so loyal and generous to an old woman?"

Soon the harvest gatherers laid aside their scythes and sat down to eat and drink and make merry. "Come, let us dance!" cried one, and in a moment a small group leaped to their feet. Among the dancers were Gertie and Charlotte.

The piano gave forth a rollicking tune, and the gleaners burst into song, clapping their hands in rhythm. Skirts billowing gracefully, heads proudly raised, the little dancers circled about. "Did you ever see a prettier sight!" exclaimed Mrs. Healy.

Caught up in the happy beat of the music, the audience began clapping their hands and stamping their feet. Backstage, Ella and Henny hugged each other. "They like it! They really like it!"

Hopping and skipping for all she was worth, Gertie was leading the line of dancers when suddenly she heard—snap! The safety pin holding her skirt band flew open! She could feel the skirt beginning to slip down the back. Desperately she clung to it with one hand, trying to face front all the time. Already some people in the front row were tittering. Oh, dear, what should she do? She turned her head toward the wings, sending appealing glances for help.

Frantically, Ella beckoned to her. Gertie started to dance sideways, forcing herself to smile. But before she could reach the wings, the droopy skirt was trailing on the floor. The titters grew into boisterous laughter. Gertie's face puckered up. She ran sobbing off the stage.

Ella caught her. "It's all right, Gertie. They're not laughing at you. They're laughing with you!" Quickly she pinned the unruly skirt back into place. "Go on back!" and she gave her a little push.

Sniffling a little, Gertie skipped back to her place among the dancers. The audience applauded loudly.

"They're clapping for you," Charlotte murmured to Gertie as she danced by.

"Honest?" Gertie asked, and her eyes glowed.

Without further mishap, the play went into act three. Boaz, the rich landowner, grew to love Ruth; they were married and lived happily ever after. Thus the play ended. Everyone agreed that it had been a huge success.

That night the family sat around the table eating the traditional *blintzes,* the pancakes filled with sweetened cheese that everyone loved. The talk was of nothing but the play. "Just think," Ella said, "besides all the fun we had, we made one hundred and twenty-five dollars for the Red Cross!"

"Ella, I thought you said the girl who played Ruth couldn't sing a note," Papa remarked, merry crinkles showing around his eyes.

Laughter rolled around the table. "Wasn't it amazing the way it was done?" Sarah said, enthusiastically. "The audience never even guessed."

"It was Henny's idea," Ella put in. "You were really smart, Henny."

"Nope. Not at all," replied Henny. "Actually it was Papa who gave me the idea."

Papa looked puzzled. "Who? Me?"

"Don't you remember, Papa? You said, 'Ten years from now, who'll remember who sang? That's when it came to me like a flash!"

"Well, so I'm the smart one!" Papa exclaimed, looking pleased at everyone.[7]

*

Mountains of Blintzes

SYDNEY TAYLOR

(age level ten to thirteen)

Danny snuggled happily beneath the coverlet. It was story time. He felt comfy-cosy, and drowsy, and full to bursting. "Daddy," he murmured, "Shavuot's a swell holiday 'cause Mommy always makes lots of cheese *blintzes.*"

"I know," replied Daddy, laughing. "You ate enough *blintzes* tonight to make a mountain."

Danny grinned and patted his stomach. "It feels like a mountain."

"Want to hear a Shavuot story about mountains?"

"Uh-huh!" Danny flip-flopped on his pillow a couple of times, getting settled. "All right, Daddy. I'm ready."

"Well, after the Jews left Egypt, they wandered about in the desert for seven weeks. One day they came to a mountain, and it was here, the Bible tells us, that Moses went up to receive the Ten Commandments from God.

"The Commandments are God's laws. They teach us how to be good. To remember this wonderful gift God gave us, we celebrate Shavuot.

"Now when the mountains first heard about this, they began to quarrel. Each mountain wanted the Law to be given on its peak.

"Mount Tabor spoke up proudly. 'I should be the favored one, for I am the tallest! In the time of Noah, when the great floods came, all you other mountains were covered up by water. Only my head remained safely above!'

"That made Mount Hermon very cross. 'Huh! Just being the biggest doesn't count! You've got to do something important! Like me, for instance!'

" 'And what did you do that's so important?' asked Mount Tabor.

"Mount Hermon huffed and puffed with pride. 'When the Jews fled from Egypt, the waters of the Red Sea divided. I got down between the two shores so the Jews could cross over safely.'

"Meanwhile foxy Mount Carmel plopped itself down near the sea. 'If I stay right here I'll surely be the lucky one. For if God wants to give the Law on the sea, then I am on the sea! If on land, then I am also by the land.'

" 'Stuff and nonsense!' shouted the other mountains.

"But little Mount Sinai said nothing. *I'm so very little,* he sighed. *Nothing wonderful ever happens to me.*

"Suddenly a voice rang out of heaven. 'The Lord will not choose any of the tall, proud mountains that boast and quarrel. The Lord chooses a humble mountain—Mount Sinai!'

"And that's how little Mount Sinai became the place where the Ten Commandments were given to the Jews."

Danny yawned sleepily. "I'm glad God picked Mount Sinai, Daddy. All the other mountains were so stuck on themselves."

"Good night, Danny," Daddy whispered, kissing him.

Danny lay quietly in the soft darkness thinking about the mountains. All at once his bed started to quiver and shake! Danny sat upright. What was the matter? He stared around. The walls were moving away! Danny jumped out of bed and raced after them, trying to catch up. It was too late! They were gone!

Danny stopped running. He felt all mixed up. He was outdoors! All around him were big rolled-up yellow things, and from their tops oozed squashy, creamy stuff. "Ooh! They're *blintzes!* Mountains and mountains of *blintzes!*" yelled Danny. But as he spoke, the shapes changed. No, they were really mountains! Mountains with faces, all angry and scowling! Now they were galumping toward him, groaning and muttering.

"So!" roared one of them, "you think we're stuck up, do you?"

A second mountain swept its head back and bellowed. "Look at the size of him! And he dares to criticize us! Ha! Ha! Ha!"

"He thinks 'cause he's so full of *blintzes,* he's as big as we are!" shouted another.

"Say, Mount Carmel, let's have a little fun with this *Blintze Boy!*" yelled a medium-size mountain. It bent its crown and suddenly Danny was lifted high. "Catch!" cried the mountain. WHOOSH! . . . Danny flew through the air. Smack! He landed sprawling atop Mount Carmel.

"Oh, please, please Mister Mountain!" he gasped. No one paid him any attention. "Your turn, Mount Hermon!" screamed

24. Children in Tel Aviv bearing firstfruits.

Mount Carmel, shaking Danny like a small puppy. WHOOSH!
. . . He whirled into space again! Crash! He was flat on his face
atop Mount Hermon!

"This is fun! Send that *Blintze* Boy on to me!" And Mount
Tabor set its peak all ready for the catch.

"Oh please, Mount Tabor! I'm sorry for what I said. I didn't
mean . . ." The only answer the mountains gave was WHOOSH
. . . WHOOSH . . . WHOOSH! Danny was being tossed back and
forth like a rubber ball.

Danny's stomach began to hurt terribly from all the shaking.
"Oh please! Stop!" he cried.

Suddenly as he flew over Mount Carmel, Danny spied a low
mountain waddling toward him. It had a kind face and was
smiling. "Danny," it called out, "I'm Mount Sinai! I'll save you.
Quick, land on me! I'll send you straight on home again!"

With his heart in his mouth, Danny twisted and turned until
he toppled right onto the peak of little Mount Sinai. "Good boy!
Now, hold on tight!" Mount Sinai took a running start. "One-
two-three! Let go!"

Danny felt himself falling and falling. From far away, he could hear Mount Sinai calling after him. "Remember Danny, remember! If you ever come to Israel, come and visit me! Don't forget! Don't forget. . . ."

There was the sound of running feet. Danny blinked his eyes wonderingly. He was stretched out on the floor of his own little bedroom! Over there was his bed and here were Mommy and Daddy standing over him.

"Danny, you fell out of bed!" Mommy's voice sounded a little alarmed. "Are you hurt?"

"Oh no!" Danny tried to explain. "I didn't fall. It was little Mount Sinai that threw me home."

Mommy and Daddy looked at each other. "Oh, it was only a bad dream," Daddy said.

"I warned him not to eat so many *blintzes,*" Mommy added, laughing.

And they all laughed together.[8]

*

*King Agrippa and the Firstfruits
SAMUEL SHIHOR

an Israeli journalist, editor, and writer on many subjects

  (age level ten to thirteen)

The dew glistened on the vine, and Uriel's hand trembled as he prepared to use the pruning knife. Would his *bikkurim* be accepted?

Last year, when he was ten, his father had promised that he could join the Shavuot *bikkurim* procession when he was one year older. Now the time had come. But Uriel would carry the basket without his father.

His father's vineyard belonged to someone else. Only one vine remained, and it was Uriel's.

Uriel knew just what to do. When his father was alive, he had gone with him to the vineyard to choose the ripest clusters. Father would tie them with a string and say, "These will be our *bikkurim*—our firstfruit offering."

Uriel only had twelve bunches on his vine. He tied the finest. "This cluster is to be for *bikkurim*," he repeated over and over again.

Uriel went into the house, and decorated his basket with dates and figs. The willow basket had three compartments. The *bikkurim* were in the center; on each side was tied a white dove, a gift for the *kohanim*, the priests.

When all was ready, his neighbor Haggai came to take Uriel along on his donkey. Uriel kissed his mother, and they joined the company of other travelers who were going to Jerusalem.

Uriel's village of Avihiel was a small one, but its *bikkurim* caravan was beautiful. The ox that led the procession was large and strong, with gilded horns and a crown of olives on his head.

Elimelech, the oldest inhabitant, rode behind the ox. He turned to Haggai, saying, "There is no need to hurry. We will arrive at our post when day is done. In the torchlight our caravan will appear the finest of all."

The "posts" were cities near Jerusalem where the pilgrims gathered just before Shavuot. At daybreak they proceeded to Jerusalem without confusion or crowding. The post assigned to Uriel's village was the city of Betar.

In the afternoon the caravan reached the Orchard of Pomegranates. The orchard-keeper welcomed the travelers. The pilgrims gratefully fanned out under the trees and quenched their thirst with cooling drinks offered by the owner of the orchard.

After lunch the elders lay down to nap, but the younger people started to dance. Only when the sun had set did the caravan continue on its journey to Betar. The torches were lit, and the procession wound its way through the mountains.

The inhabitants of Betar spread out mats for the guests, and again the youth from all the communities that gathered in Betar danced and sang far into the night.

At dawn Uriel was abruptly awakened by a cry: "Children of Israel, pilgrims of the Post of Betar, arise and let us go to Zion!"

Rubbing the sleep from their eyes, the pilgrims took their baskets and formed caravans again. At the head of each caravan marched the flute-players, and drummers walked at the sides.

At the gate of Jerusalem, a committee came out to meet them and formed two rows on both sides of the gate. When it was the turn of Uriel's caravan to enter, the citizens of Jerusalem cried in the ancient way of greeting the pilgrims, "Our brothers from the village of Avihiel, enter the city of Zion in peace!"

In answer, the drums beat and the flutes played, and the procession entered Jerusalem with rhythmical dancing. At the Temple each man lifted his basket and put it on his shoulder, and the chief singer of the village chanted: "Praise God in His Temple . . ." until they reached the Temple court and they heard the voices of the choir of Levites.

Uriel's heart beat faster as he gripped the basket and raised it to his shoulder. They moved into the Temple court in single file. The *kohanim* were in the aisles, ready to receive the *bikkurim.* Louder and louder sang the Levite choir, and the sound of musical instruments was heard from the Temple.

A whisper rippled through the crowd. "Here comes Agrippa! Here comes the king!"

Uriel saw the king.

Agrippa was dressed in a cloak of dazzling white. His golden crown was on his head, and on his shoulder he bore a *bikkurim* basket made of beaten gold.

Uriel wondered aloud: "Does the king carry the *bikkurim* by himself?"

"That's right, my son," whispered Haggai. "Even the king must fulfill the *mitzvot,* the laws of our Torah."

All at once, a resounding cry burst from the throats of the great assembly of pilgrims. It echoed again and again, drowning the voices of the Levite choir, "Long live Agrippa our king!"

Now it was the turn of Haggai and Uriel to enter the Temple court. The king was still approaching.

"Do as I do!" Haggai whispered. With both hands, he lifted the basket from his shoulder and gave it to the priest, saying: "Behold, I have brought the first of the fruit of the land." And soon as Haggai finished, Uriel started to do the same.

"How old are you, my child?" the priest inquired.

"Eleven," said Uriel.

The priest patted Uriel's head and smiled. "You are too young. The Torah does not require you to bring *bikkurim.* I cannot accept them from you."

Uriel grew very sad. The happy holiday feeling which had filled his heart disappeared. His eyes brimmed with tears.

"Please, dear *kohen,*" he pleaded. "My father died but five months ago. His last words were, 'Uriel, do not forget to bring *bikkurim* in from the vineyard.' But things went badly, and my mother was forced to sell the vineyard."

"Then the vineyard is not yours," said the priest. "And *bikkurim,* you know, must be brought from one's own land."

"But this branch, O *kohen,* is mine," cried Uriel. "The day we sold the vineyard I uprooted this vine and planted it in our yard. The elders of our town told me that it is my vine, and the firstfruits must be taken from it! I did everything to fulfill my father's last wish, everything, and now you forbid me . . ."

A choking feeling in his throat stopped the flow of Uriel's words. Big tears splashed on his beautiful cluster of grapes. The pair of doves blinked at him. Everyone turned to look at him. Even the priest brushed away a tear. "Wait, my child," he said. "I will ask the opinion of the older *kohanim.* This has never happened before."

Then Uriel heard a deep, soft voice at his side. King Agrippa was standing next to him.

"Do not cry, boy. As king of Israel I return to you the vineyard which belonged to your father. From now on it is yours. The man who owns it now will be paid from the king's treasury. *Kohen!* Accept the child's *bikkurim.*"

Uriel looked up gratefully at King Agrippa. He lifted his basket, gave it to the priest, and turned to bow to the king. Instead, King Agrippa stopped and lifted Uriel into his arms.

"Do not bow before a man of flesh and blood," he said. "Although I am king, remember that you stand in the house of Almighty God, King of kings!"

Uriel buried his head in the folds of the king's robe and wept with happiness.[9]

*

*Shavuot in Modern Israel

DOROTHY F. ZELIGS

a psychologist who received a doctorate in education, and the author of a series of Jewish history texts and other children's books

(age level ten to thirteen)

Emil looked forward eagerly to the next holiday, the festival of Shavuot. For some time in advance the children had been holding meetings at which they discussed their plans for the celebration of this important holiday. Emil gladly volunteered to be one of the committee responsible for decorating the various buildings of Ben Shemen with flowers and green branches.

In ancient biblical days, the Jewish farmers of Palestine used to journey to the Temple in Jerusalem to lay their firstfruits upon the altar. Now, in Israel, Shavuot has again become a Festival of Firstfruits, known in Hebrew as *Hag ha-Bikkurim.* The Jewish farmers bring their products of the soil as an offering to the Jewish National Fund. These products are sold and the money is used to redeem more land for the Jewish people.

The children of Ben Shemen were going to take part in the ceremony of *Bikkurim.* When the day came, they carefully selected the best fruits, vegetables, and eggs which their farm and dairy yielded. These were attractively arranged in large baskets. Then the children, dressed in costumes of ancient biblical days, journeyed to Tel Aviv, one of the centers where the ceremony of giving the firstfruits was held. Many people from the surrounding colonies flocked to Tel Aviv for this occasion. There was a parade of gaily decorated automobiles, trucks, and wagons laden with offerings. Tel Aviv was in a holiday mood and crowds of people thronged the streets.

The children from Ben Shemen formed part of the parade to the open square where a large platform had been set up. It was beautifully decorated with flowers and green branches. On the platform were seated the leaders of the city and officials of the Jewish National Fund. Someone led the entire assembly in the singing of songs. These songs expressed the joy of a nation reborn and the determination of the people of Israel to live and labor, and to continue with the task of rebuilding and re-creating the land of their fathers. Then representatives from each of the nearby colonies came forward and presented their offerings. An official of the Jewish National Fund received these.

The gifts were then offered for sale and the money became a part of the Jewish National Fund. After this part of the ceremony, a group of children from Tel Aviv gave a play dealing with the biblical story of Ruth. There was more spirited singing and the dancing of the *hora* before the happy occasion ended. As Emil journeyed homeward with the other children of Ben Shemen, he felt that he had never known before what a beautiful festival Shavuot was and how much meaning it had.

Several days later, Emil received an enthusiastic letter from his brother Albert describing how the Festival of Firstfruits had been celebrated in the Emek. The farmers of the Jezreel Valley had gathered in Ain Harod and presented their offerings there. The children, carrying flowers and singing songs, had a large part in the festivities.

But it is at Haifa that the largest Shavuot celebration of the land is held. Just as Tel Aviv is famous for its Purim carnival and Jerusalem is the center of the Passover pilgrimages, so Haifa is known for its celebration of *Hag ha-Bikkurim.* Emil heard all about it in a letter from Ben David, who had gone to Haifa for Shavuot. There, in a large open-air theater, a great pageant was held, showing how the firstfruits were brought to the Temple in biblical days. Ben David described the stream of vehicles that rolled through the main streets of the Hadar Hacarmel on the way to the ceremony. The automobiles, trucks, wagons, and even bicycles were decorated with wreaths and flowers. Many had large posters on which were inscribed some quotation from the Bible or Talmud. The children paraded through the streets singing songs. They were dressed in white and wore wreaths upon their heads.

The ceremony in the huge open-air theater had been a thrilling one, Ben David wrote. He, too, understood better what the ancient festival of Shavuot meant to the new Jewish farmers of Israel.[10]

*

The Ten Commandments of Helm

(age level ten to thirteen)

In the city of Helm there dwelled Lemech, a teacher, and his wife, Leah, a peddler. Both were advanced in years. Both worked hard and together eked out the bare necessities of life. The Passover festival had passed and their thoughts naturally turned to the next holiday—Shavuot.

Lemech said to Leah:

"Leah, although God has granted me a lengthy and full life, I've never eaten *blintzes* on Shavuot. Do you think we can do anything about filling this obvious void?"

Leah was most sympathetic to the need of overcoming this lack which she, too, had experienced. Possessed of as much wisdom as her husband, the teacher in Israel, she proposed a unique scheme to enable them to realize their ambition of eating *blintzes* on Shavuot.

"Listen to me, Lemech," she said. "Let's take the large trunk with wheels that my parents gave us as part of my dowry. We'll make two small holes in it, one at each end. Every evening I'll insert a coin from my earnings in one hole and you'll do likewise in the other hole. On the eve of Shavuot we'll open the trunk, take out the money, and use it to buy what is required to make *blintzes*."

Lemech was joyfully amazed at the ingenuity of his wife and readily agreed to adopt her plan. No sacrifice would be too great for the sake of eating *blintzes* on Shavuot!

On the first evening that the couple were to initiate their self-imposed savings plan, Leah took out a coin to insert in the trunk. As she was about to do so, a brilliant stroke of genius smote her. She thought to herself:

"I need my meager earnings to buy food for our daily sustenance. Let Lemech save his money for the *blintzes!*"

When Lemech arrived home, he promptly approached the trunk with the good and sincere intention of putting in a coin. Removing the money from his pocket, he was about to drop it into the trunk when his hand suddenly became paralyzed, as if an angel were holding it fast, and this warning was revealed to his inner consciousness:

"Lemech, you, as a teacher in Helm, are engaged in a holy occupation. Let not your sacred earnings be used for such mundane matters as *blintzes*. Let Leah save from the money she earns by peddling earthly wares."

Let the truth be told! Lemech did not require much coaxing, and he accepted the chiding of the hidden voice that called to him.

25. Bringing firstfruits to the Jewish National Fund in Jerusalem.

The eve of Shavuot arrived. Leah brought forth the key to the trunk and, in the presence of Lemech, with adequate preliminary fanfare, she inserted it in the lock and turned it. Graciously, she gave the honor of raising the cover of the trunk to her beloved husband. In great anticipation, Lemech laid both hands on the cover and, with a prayer in his heart, raised it.

First, Leah looked in the trunk. Second, Lemech looked in the trunk. Then, both together, they looked at the emptiness of the trunk. Leah looked at Lemech; Lemech looked at Leah. They looked at each other. But not for long!

She grabbed his beard. He grabbed her hair. She pulled. He pulled. She screamed. He screamed.

Leah and Lemech screamed so that their voices were heard throughout the streets of Helm. This commotion failed to interfere with the people of Helm who were deeply engrossed in the preparations for Shavuot. Anyway, screaming was a favorite method of the Helmites to win an argument and its frequent use never disturbed the populace.

Pulling each other before the open trunk, Leah and Lemech lost their balance and fell, head over heels, into the empty trunk. This sudden movement brought down the cover into its place and closed in the couple.

The vibrations caused by the still struggling pair speeded the trunk on its wheels through the open door that was without a threshold, down the steep hill, at the foot of which was the synagogue. The trunk wended its way to the house of worship, whose doors were always open. With a complete lack of deference for the holy place, the trunk rode on into the synagogue and came to a halt only when the impact, physical rather than spiritual, of the holy ark faced it.

The rabbi, the sexton, and the trustees, assembled in the synagogue to decorate it with greens in honor of Shavuot, were horror-struck at the sight of the trunk that did not fear to stand, defiantly, before the holy ark. It did not take long for the rabbi and the trustees to arrive at a brave decision. They courageously ordered the sexton to open the trunk so that they might see what had been sent to them from on high for Shavuot. The sexton girded himself with *tefillin* and *tallit,* recited the prayer of confession before death, and, with *Shema Yisrael* on his lips, opened the trunk.

The synagogue dignitaries were astounded to look upon Lemech and Leah, completely exhausted and barely conscious. After helping the couple get out of the trunk, they queried them. Learning what had happened, the rabbi and the trustees promptly decided to promulgate rules and regulations to avoid similar occurrences in the future.

The following morning at the Shavuot services, after the Ten Commandments were read in the Torah, the rabbi read another set of ten commandments that are a heritage of the Jews of Helm for all generations.

And the rabbi spoke all these words, saying:

1. I am the rabbi of Helm, who brought thee out of the lands of wisdom, out of the houses of learning.

2. Thou shalt have no other rabbis before me.

3. Remember the days of Shavuot, to keep them holy.

4. Honor thy husband or thy wife, that thy days may be long in the city of Helm.

5. Thou shalt not pull hair, neither the hair of a head nor the hair of a face.

6. Thou shalt not make unto thee a trunk with wheels.

7. Thou shalt place thresholds on thy doors.

8. Thou shalt keep the doors of the synagogue closed.

9. Thou shalt not save money.

10. Thou shalt not covet *blintzes,* neither for Shavuot, nor any festival, nor any day; thou shalt not covet *blintzes* of cheese, nor of potatoes, nor of any thing which is good to eat.[11]

CHILDREN'S POEMS
FOR SHAVUOT

*
Lifting of the Torah
JESSIE E. SAMPTER

an American poet who settled in an Israeli kibbutz (1883–1938)

At Sinai we received the Law
In earthquake, storm, and flame:
We stood to hear the Voice of Awe
Our tasks and duties name.

To Sinai still we turn our eyes,
Obedient to His voice;
Before His Law in homage rise
The people of His choice.[1]

*
The First Shavuot
SADIE ROSE WEILERSTEIN

devoted to Jewish children's literature, she has written many widely disseminated books

When God gave the Torah the whole earth heard;
No birdling chirruped; no creature stirred,
There wasn't a bleat, a lowing, a purr,
   A stir of feather or fur.

The word had gone forth, "Prepare! Prepare!"
Each mother washed her child with care;
And the unborn souls all fresh and new
   Bathed in heavenly dew.

Even the kitten heard in awe
And licked itself from head to paw;
While birds flew off to a mountain spring
   And dipped and shook each wing.

Oh, the earth was clean and hushed in awe
When God proclaimed His holy Law,
The Law that brings life to man and beast,
   To the great, the wise—and the least.[2]

*

*The Pledge of Israel

LOUIS I. NEWMAN

*rabbi and communal leader in New York, he authored several books
including plays, cantatas, and poetry (1893–1972)*

"If I should give to you the Law, my sons,"
Said God at Sinai's Mount to Israel;
"What sureties can you provide to me,
To testify that you will guard it well."

The Israelites replied: "O Mighty Lord,
Our ancestors will vouch for us today."
But God declared: "Your ancestors themselves
Need sureties which they may too display."

Then said the Israelites: "O God of Truth,
Our prophets' word can prove we will obey."
But God declared: "Your prophets, stern and wise,
Are not sufficient bond for you to pay."

At last the Israelites exclaimed: "O Lord,
Our children come as pledges without flaw."
Then God replied: "Your children please me well;
On their account, I give to you the Law."[3]

*

But God Chose Sinai

LOUIS I. NEWMAN

When God proclaimed: "I now will give my Law;
To Israel the Torah will be sent";
Behold, the mountains came to Him in awe,
And each a prayer with hope and longing blent.

"O Sovereign of the boundless universe,
Be gracious; let Thy splendor fall on me;
Upon me place Thy blessing, not Thy curse;
And from my summit, set Thy Torah free!"

"Choose me," said Hermon, "Royal is my blood;
I tower loftiest amid my kin;
And as my brow emerged from the flood,
The Law will rise triumphant over sin."

"Choose me," said Carmel, "Beauty without flaw;
My gardens know Thy firmament's caress;
And plant on me the garden of Thy Law,
To make the soul like Eden's loveliness."

"Choose me," said Lebanon, "A hymn of praise;
My cedars sing Thy grandeur, tree to tree;
Amid their voices, let Thy Torah raise
A hymn to make man's life a hymn to Thee."

But God chose Sinai, saying: "On thy stone,
The tablets of the Torah shall be read;
For in the desert thou dost stand alone;
In solitude thou liftest up thy head.

"As Israel My people is alone,
Amid the desert of a world perverse;
As I the Lord am lonely on My throne,
Amid the desert of the universe."[4]

*

Heroes of the Law

ABRAHAM BURSTEIN

*rabbi, author, and editor who penned a book of Jewish verse for children
(1893–1966)*

When Moses brought the tablets down
From Sinai's mist-encircled crown,
He bore us from the heights he trod
The love of Israel and of God.

And long the Torah's words have made
The Jewish spirit unafraid;
The glorious precepts that it taught
Of feeble men have heroes wrought.

Our priests and prophets, armed thereby,
In time of strife could do and die.
No threat of torture or disgrace
Could Israel's faith of soul efface.

Heroes are our eternal need—
Men like Akiba, strong in deed.
Would that such souls today might rise
To still our bitter, martyred cries![5]

*

*The Ten Commandments

ILO ORLEANS

*a lawyer and a prolific author of verse for children whose poems have been
included in anthologies and in textbooks and music books*

The Father of all
the Lord is one—

Seek no strange gods
For there are none.
'Tis wrong to bend
The knee, or pray
To gods of wood
Or stone or clay.

Be reverent!
Keep out the shame
Of speaking evil
In God's name.

Find rest upon
The Sabbath day.

Thy parents, honor
and obey.

'Tis wrong to take
A human life,

Or cause a rift
'Twixt man and wife.

'Tis wrong to steal,
Mark well the line,
Dividing what
Is "mine" and "thine."

'Tis wrong to lie.
Good living starts
With truthful words
And honest hearts.

Don't gaze with eyes
Of jealousy
Upon your neighbor's
Property.
These rules of life
We must obey.
From these commands
'Tis wrong to stray![6]

*

The Feast of Weeks

PHILIP M. RASKIN

a lifelong Zionist and prolific poet who created in English, Hebrew, and Yiddish (1878–1944)

We have an ancient custom
    Surviving from the East,
To decorate our dwellings
    With flowers for the feast.

How quaint the age-old custom
    From East to exile brought!
But why does it awaken
    In me such gloomy thought?

I see the flower-bearers
    'Mid ghetto's rush and strife,
And in my mind is woven
    A dream of vanished life.

A land of hills and valleys
  Begilt by the golden morn,
And forests of mighty cedar,
  And fields of waving corn.

And mountains trimmed with olives,
  And vales with lilies decked,
And peasants proud and sturdy,
  With heart and head erect.

Each garden, field and vineyard
  In tones of beauty speaks,
God's earth is celebrating
  Its glorious Feast of Weeks.

The men as strong as cedars,
  The women fair as palms,
Their festal hymns are chanting,
  Their soul-inspired psalms.

Their children—sons of freedom—
  Arrive in long array,
Luxuriant laurels bearing
  In honor of the day. . . .

My phantom views are vanished;
  Around, alas, I see
A sordid, gloomy ghetto—
  No trace of field or tree.

I see through noisy alleys
  A Jew his flowers bring,
To decorate his dwelling
  In memory of spring.

For since he left in sadness
  His flower-jeweled home;
His cruel exile taught him
  From town to town to roam.

No longer a Judean—
  A weary wandering Jew;
In ghetto he is praying
  For endless rain, and dew. . . .

I see him bent and crouching—
  O God, how sad it is!—
How long will he pluck flowers
  From fields that are not his?

And prayingly I murmur:
  "O Israel's Rock and Shield,

Bring back Thy exiled people
   To garden, wood, and field.

That they uphold the custom,
   Surviving from the East,
With sweat-reared, toil-raised flowers
   To celebrate their feast."[7]

*

The Midnight Wish

MYRIM

Danny heard in school one day
The legend—so the people say—
That if a boy on Shavuot night
Kept his eyes unclosed and bright,
Exactly at the midnight hour
He'd see a most angelic power
Split wide the skies
And with sharp eyes
The boy might see for one brief minute
The open heaven and all that's in it.

And if he then a wish pronounced
But not to anyone announced
What he had wished—an angel band
Would take him gently by the hand
And lead him to his heart's desire
Safely through both flood and fire.

Dan at once made up his mind
That unless his eyes went blind
He would watch the skies that night
Waiting for the flash of light
That showed the miracle time was here
When angels his wish would gladly hear.

The weeks went by and Danny wondered
What he would wish when the sky sundered.
Of toys and games he had so many,
Of all good things he lacked not any.
What could a boy
Of years eleven
Ask with joy
Of the open heaven?

The weeks went by and the great day came.
The first few hours seemed very tame
To Danny who waited impatiently
For the time to come when he could see
The annual miracle of the sky
And make his wish—and so would I!

The hour grew late—
Wait, Danny, wait.
Bedtime passed
And soon, at last,
'Twas ten o'clock
And then eleven. . . .
Tick-tock, tick . . . tock. . . .
Danny looked at heaven.

He crawled into bed—
But laid his head
Where he could see
What was to be
In the skies—
But his sleepy eyes
Winked . . .
And blinked. . . .

A roar
And flash—
A roar
And c r a s h—
And Danny clearly saw the sky
Burst open, and with a startled cry
He looked into God's home on high.

Quick!
Now pick
The best of wishes you can make,
Now is the time your choice to take.

Suddenly Danny knew what to choose:
"Angels above, there's no time to lose.
Give me—if I can have anything—
Not the ransom of a king,
Not riches or wealth
Nor even health—
But give me this, I beg of you:
To grow to become a citizen true.
Keep my country of Israel strong
Now and forever, and all my life long
Let me do what I can to keep it so.

Let me live so that I may know
That whatever I do, wherever I go,
Will make me feel both proud and glad
That I am an Israel citizen-lad."

No sooner had Danny spoken out
Then he saw beyond a shadow of doubt
Hundreds of angels, thousands, millions
(Later he said there were nine quadrillions)
Trooping out of the open sky,
Marching in orderly ranks on high
Right along the Milky Way
Which became as bright as the brightest day.

Each came to him, bent over his bed,
Rustled his wings, and whispering said:
"As you've made your choice
So shall it be.
God hears your voice—
As you will see."

Danny heard the sound of bells
And the singing of the song that tells
That angels have been on earth again
Walking among the mortal men.

But all grew suddenly dark around
And daylight came—and with a bound
Dan sprang out of bed, and began to recall
That before the hour of midnight could fall
His head had nodded, his eyes grown dim—
Had angels really visited him?

Whether the angels did or not,
This is surely a comforting thought:
   That the secret of the Feast of Weeks
   He will find who but well seeks.[8]

*

* For Shavuot

JESSIE E. SAMPTER

My heart is blossoming like a flower
   On Sharon's harvest field,
My heart is burning like the star

That shines on David's shield.
Because once more I see God's Law
To Israel revealed.[9]

*

✻My Garden's Firstfruits

AHARON ZEEV

one-time editor of an Israeli children's periodical and for many years head of the cultural services of the Israel Defense Forces, he penned many children's stories and poems

Not very large is my garden,
Not very big—
A green bed and a pathway
And a budding twig.

26. The dance of the firstfruits.

But small gardens too have sun and dew,
And the fruits grow true.
The firstfruit festival is come anew—
And to my garden too.

What shall I give—who knows?
But I took it into my head
To give the twig and the petals of rose
And all from my one green bed.

The children bring their baskets
As the flute notes fall and rise.
Wreaths of green adorn their heads
Joy fills their shining eyes.

They look into my basket
And question, "Is that all?"
"My garden's very small,"
I say, "but I have given all—
I have given all—my all."

Translated by Myrim[10]

*

*The Radish and the Cucumber

ANDA AMIR

a prolific Israeli author of popular children's stories and poems

The Radish and Cucumber
Almost went to war:
Each claimed that in the garden
He'd been ripe before.
Said Radish to Cucumber,
"I was ripe here first."
Said Cucumber to Radish,
"Of liars, you're the worst.
I was first here to be ripe,
I'm oldest—smoke *that* in your pipe."
Radish face took on a flush,
Cucumber grew as green as plush
And who knows what might then have been
If Lettuce hadn't soon stepped in.

"Dear Radish and good Cucumber,
There's no need to fight.
Each of you in his own group
First came to see sunlight.
You're both the first, and now be good
And go and join the brotherhood
That's celebrating the right way
The yearly Firstfruits Holiday."

Radish wore a white frock,
Cucumber a green,
And they went along, arm in arm,
With only love between.
In the air there is a hum—
All the garden "firsts" have come.
Hand in hand, and arm in arm,
Marching proudly from the farm:

Tomatoes, carrots, red beetroots,
Eggplant, spinach, onion shoots,
Garlic, cabbage, peas, and beans,
All the family of greens
Marching gaily on parade,
Making the gifts that are always made
In festive spirits, high and gay,
On the Firstfruits Holiday.

Translated by Myrim[11]

*

*A Shavuot Offering in Exile

ABRAHAM NATHAN PERLBERG

a teacher of Hebrew literature at the Yeshiva University Teachers Institute, he wrote plays, poems, and stories for children (1889–1934)

I came to a field and I saw it was blessed,
    I filled with its flourishing produce my hand;
I picked fragrant flowers. I thought for a while
    My nostrils were filled with the scent of "our land."

I came to a dale and lay down on its bed;
    On my mother's warm lap I was lying meseemed.
I slept and I dreamed that in Sharon was I,
    The Sharon still verdant, the Sharon redeemed.

I woke. It was late—time for *Minhah* had come—
I put in a basket the flowers in haste,
And brought to the synagogue, thinking that I
In Solomon's Temple an offering had placed.
Translated by Harry H. Fein[12]

PROGRAMS AND PROJECTS

*

*BIKKURIM *FESTIVAL*

In remembrance of the bringing of the firstfruits to the Temple in Jerusalem, an elaborate ceremonial procession can be enacted by children, preferably outdoors in a natural setting. The participants, dressed as farmers and laborers and wearing flower garlands, carry baskets of fruits and vegetables. They may also carry homemade products of their own craftmanship. Floats can be easily devised with children's wagons, automobiles, and bicycles abundantly decorated with crepe paper, posters, flags, flowers, twigs, and leaves. The procession may be led by a toy band or it can proceed with the marchers singing Shavuot songs. The festival is concluded with each participant placing his or her "firstfruits" on a stage or platform. The children's offerings can then or subsequently be auctioned or sold with the proceeds donated to the Jewish National Fund for planting trees in Israel. Further ideas for this commemorative program can be gleaned from "The Bringing of the Firstfruits during the Second Commonwealth," by Solomon Zeitlin, pages 145–147, "The Festival in Haifa," by Gershon Ahituv, pages 172–175, and "*Bikkurim* in Kibbutz Matzuba," by Gershon Ahituv, pages 175–176.

*FIRSTFRUITS FESTIVITY

An informal party may center around Shavuot as its theme. Invitations in the shape of the two tablets of the Ten Commandments may request guests to bring as *"bikkurim"* a can of fruit or vegetables. The cans may be collected in a large basket or bin, tastefully decorated, and later donated to an institution or a needy family. A suitable atmosphere will be created by decorating the room with flowers, plants, leaves, and the like.

The table setting should present a festive atmosphere. One or more of these items may be placed on ferns adorning the tablecloth: a Bible open to the pages with the Ten Commandments, a miniature Torah Scroll, a cake decorated with Shavuot symbols, and a floral arrangement. For the centerpiece, a pyramid of fruit in token of Mount Sinai can be built by using a styrofoam cone wrapped in foil. Set the cone on lettuce leaves and attach the fruits —dates, figs, orange segments, grapes, strawberries, cherries— with toothpicks. Fill in the empty spaces with parsley sprigs and place an illustration of the tablets of the Law on the crest.

Refreshments can also be served at a "milk bar," featuring milk, cheese *blintzes,* cheesecake, an assortment of Israeli cheese and crackers, Israeli honey, and fruits. See chapter 14 in this book, "The Culinary Art of Shavuot."

*DECORATION OF HOME AND SYNAGOGUE

For Shavuot, it is customary to decorate Jewish homes and synagogues with beautiful flowers, colorful leaves, and fragrant foliage. Sundry floral arrangements can be devised to enhance the beauty of the home and synagogue. Some congregations use a special Shavuot *parokhet* (ark curtain) made of a green fabric and arrange a canopy of flowers for the Torah reading.

Jewish schools and community centers can also ornament their buildings with floral decorations in honor of the festival. In addition, they can hang chains of paper flowers, murals, friezes, and posters.

*TIKKUN LEL SHAVUOT

The traditional *Tikkun Lel Shavuot* is recited in some congregations throughout the first night of the festival. Others devote the all-night session to the study of other Jewish books. There are periodic coffee breaks with light refreshments, including cheesecakes.

A "Shavuot Read-In," patterned on the traditional observance, may be held for young people on Saturday night prior to the festival. The entire night might be devoted to Bible study, utilizing selected biblical texts, films, filmstrips, stories, and songs. Local rabbis and educators can be scheduled at intervals during the night to teach or lead discussions. The session can be concluded with morning prayers at sunrise, followed by breakfast.

An original *Tikkun Lel Shavuot* may be created by culling and copying on loose-leaf paper selections from the Bible, legends, poems, and other items from literary sources available in this book. Original essays, poems, and stories can be included. The book can be artistically illustrated with drawings, photographs, and pictures from periodicals. An attractively designed title page should be prepared. All the sheets should be placed in a loose-leaf binder. This *Tikkun* can be read at the "Shavuot Read-In" or on other appropriate occasions.

*INITIATION CEREMONY

On Shavuot it was customary for children to begin their religious schooling (see "The Jewish Child's Initiation into School" by Hayyim Schauss, pages 157–159). It is therefore fitting to conduct an initiation ceremony for children who are about to enter a religious school. This ceremonial can be held during or even following the Shavuot morning service. Each child can be given a miniature *Sefer Torah* to hold aloft as he marches in a procession to the front of the synagogue. The rabbi will greet the children as a group and hand each one a bag of sweets.

LECTURE AND DISCUSSION THEMES

The significant historical background of Shavuot and its profound contemporary relevance suggest a wide variety of subjects for both lectures and discussions. Following are a number of pertinent themes:

Shavuot: Birthday of the Jewish Religion
The Festival of Revelation
Moses the Lawgiver
The Ten Commandments: Cornerstone of Civilization
The Covenant at Mount Sinai
The Torah and Its Meaning to Israel
The Source of Jewish Power
The Struggle for the Preservation of the Torah in All Ages
The Torah: Our Spiritual Rampart
Torah: The Means of Jewish Survival
Pilgrimages of the Children of Israel
Harvest Gleanings: The Jewish Concept of *Tzedakah*
The Offering of Firstfruits
Ruth the Convert
The Position of Women as Reflected in the Holy Scriptures

EXHIBITS

A book display can feature a Scroll of the Law, the Scroll of Ruth, a variety of Bibles, illustrated editions of the Book of Ruth, and books with Shavuot illustrations. The illustrated books should be open to pages pertaining to the festival.

An exhibit of a variety of Torah accouterments—crowns, finials, shields, pointers, wimpels, mantels—can be enhanced with detailed explanatory labels describing each object.

A collection of Israeli stamps and first-day covers issued for Shavuot could be borrowed from a philatelist for display.

A series of original dioramas can constitute an attractive exhibit. The three-dimensional scenes might depict Moses giving the Law to the children of Israel, a pilgrimage to Jerusalem, the Temple, harvesting, and episodes from the Book of Ruth.

*DRAMATIZATIONS

A pageant can be based on the legends about the giving of the Torah or dramatic scenes from the Book of Ruth, utilizing dances, songs, and readings interrelated by a narration.

A puppet or marionette show featuring Ruth, Naomi, and Boaz can present the story in the Bible. Two scenes may be sufficient—Ruth and Naomi on the road and the field of Boaz. Much of the dialogue can be culled from the text of the Book of Ruth.

Improvisations can be based on the Shavuot legends and stories in this volume. See chapters 3, 11, and 15, "Shavuot in Talmud and Midrash," "Shavuot in the Short Story," and "Children's Stories for Shavuot."

*GAMES

Pilgrimage to Jerusalem: One player begins by saying, "I am making a pilgrimage to Jerusalem. The firstfruits I am bringing are dates." The second player must repeat what the first one said and add another fruit or a vegetable; for example, "I am making a pilgrimage to Jerusalem. The firstfruits I am bringing are dates and oranges." Each player in turn must repeat the preceding sentences, adding another fruit or vegetable. If a player omits any of the fruits or vegetables, or does not recite them in the original sequence or fails to add a new item, he is eliminated from the game. The game continues until only one player remains.

Gleaners: Barley stalks, either real or made with construction paper, are scattered on the floor. There should be one less barley stalk than the number of gleaners (players). The gleaners walk in a circle around the room to the music of a Shavuot harvest song. When the music stops, the gleaners stoop to harvest the barley stalks. The one who fails to pick up a stalk is eliminated. Before the music starts again, a stalk is removed so that there is always one less stalk on the floor than the number of players still in the game. The game continues until only one gleaner remains.

Moses: This game is played with a Bible. Each player is given the opportunity to open the Bible without looking at it. If the name of Moses is found on the top line of the right-hand page at which he opened the Bible, he receives 100 points. If there is an M on the top line, he earns 50 points and for each of the other letters —O, S, E—10 points. After one or more rounds, the player with the highest score is declared the winner.

A Shavuot Story: The storyteller relates the biblical account of the giving of the Ten Commandments which may be interspersed with legends. Each player is assigned the name of a character, place, object, or quotation that will appear in the story —for example, Moses, Aaron, children of Israel, Mount Sinai, Ten Commandments, tablets of the Law, Torah, "Honor your father and your mother," and "You shall not steal." As the storyteller narrates, each player must rise, call out "Shavuot" and turn around in his place as his assumed name is mentioned. When the storyteller mentions Shavuot, all the players must respond in the same manner. A player who fails to respond promptly and properly is eliminated from the game. The story of Ruth may also be used with the assignment of these names: Ruth, Naomi, Elimelech, Orpah, Boaz, Moab, Bethlehem, harvest, and gleaners.

Charades: Players can be assigned to small groups of three to six persons. The groups are allowed a few minutes to plan and rehearse a scene associated with Shavuot. Each group is then called to perform the scene in pantomime, while the others try to guess its subject. Scenes may depict the legendary dispute among the mountains, Moses giving the Ten Commandments to the children of Israel, Moses breaking the tablets of the Law, a pilgrimage to Jerusalem, Ruth and Naomi, Ruth gleaning in the fields of Boaz.

Questions: While one player absents himself from the room, the other players select a word or term associated with Shavuot, for example, Ten Commandments, confirmation, *blintzes, Tikkun,* harvest, Moses, Ruth. The absent player then returns and he must guess the word or term selected by posing questions beginning with "Who," "Why," "What," "When," or "Where." All questions must be answered accurately by the other players. The player whose answer leads to the correct guess is the next one to leave the room.

*ARTS AND CRAFTS

Motifs: There are many illustrative motifs identified with Shavuot which can be utilized in various arts and crafts media. Among them are the following: Moses receiving the tablets of the Law on Mount Sinai, the Ten Commandments, the Torah, pilgrims ascending to Jerusalem, bringing firstfruits to the Temple, the Scroll of Ruth, Ruth gleaning in the fields of Boaz, the harvest in Israel, *Hag ha-Bikkurim* in modern Israel, the seven species, fruits and flowers, confirmation, and synagogue and home floral decorations. For other motifs, see chapter 8, "Shavuot in Art" by Joseph Gutmann.

Omer Calendar: As a daily reminder for counting the *omer* for seven weeks from the second day of Passover to Shavuot, a special calendar may be made. Such a calendar can be easily constructed with a rectangular sheet of poster board. The top of the board should contain the blessing recited on the counting of the *omer.* The balance of the space, which should be a square, is divided into forty-nine small boxes. The number of the week (first to seventh) is written on the top of each vertical column. The small boxes are numbered from one to forty-nine, starting from the top in the column of the first week. A cardboard arrow, moved daily to the number being counted, can be attached with a heavy pin or a thumbtack. The calendar can be decorated with barley sheaves and relevant biblical quotations. For ideas for more elaborate *omer* calendars, see illustration figures 18 and 19.

Torah Scroll: To make a Torah scroll, take shelf paper or paste sheets of construction or parchment paper end to end. The scroll can be inscribed with the Ten Commandments and other biblical verses pertinent to Shavuot, and then illuminated with appropriate illustrations and decorative designs. The ends of the scroll can be stapled, tacked, or glued to dowels, which serve as the scroll rollers. The dowels should be long enough to protrude one or two inches over the top and bottom of the scroll. The protruding ends of the sticks may be shaped and then painted or shellacked. If woodworking tools are available, four wooden disks with holes in the center can be made to accommodate the dowels. When the scroll is rolled up, it can be tied together with a ribbon.

A very small scroll can be made by using two empty film rolls or cotton spools. Four wooden pegs can be whittled to fit snugly into the top and bottom holes of the spools.

Torah Mantle: Using a regular Torah mantle as a model, make a pattern on wrapping paper to fit the miniature scroll. Adhering to the pattern, cut a piece of satin, velvet, felt, or some other fabric. On the front of the mantle, embroider an appropriate design or legend with gold or silver thread and sequins. Ribbon or braid may also be used. Stitch or glue with rubber cement a piece of heavy cardboard to the inside of the mantle top. Cut two holes in the top so that it can slip over the protruding ends of the rollers.

Torah Accouterments: A pointer can be whittled or carved from a piece of wood or cut out from a sheet of aluminum, 1/16″ copper, or heavy plastic. Heavy silver thread inserted through a hole near the top of the pointer may serve as a chain so that the *yad* can hang on the Torah staves.

A breastplate for the Torah can be made by stippling a design on a sheet of copper. Puncture two holes near the top and insert a piece of chain or a strip of braid for hanging the breastplate.

The Ten Commandments: The Ten Commandments on two tablets can be executed through one or more of the following craft techniques: tooling on copper foil, tin, or leather; stippling on metal; carving on wood or on a large rectangular cake of white soap; woodburning on plywood; molding with clay; block printing with linoleum; and needlework.

Depending on the size of the tablets, they can be inscribed with the complete or an abbreviated text of the Ten Commandments in Hebrew or English, the first two Hebrew words of each commandment or the Hebrew or Roman numerals from one to ten.

Scroll of Ruth: On a long sheet of shelf paper, write selected passages from the Scroll of Ruth, allowing space for illustrations of the quoted texts and decorative designs. The illustrations and designs may be made with paint or crayons. Take a dowel or a rolling pin, about four inches longer than the height of the shelf paper; this will allow about two inches of the dowel or rolling pin to protrude on each side. Paint or lacquer the two ends of the dowels. Glue, tack, or staple the end of the paper scroll to the dowel. Roll the scroll on the dowel and tie with a ribbon.

Shevuoslekh: The making of *shevuoslekh,* paper cutouts for Shavuot that are hung on windowpanes, is an old folk custom (see figures 21a, 21b, 21c, and 21d). These adornments, usually with designs of flowers, animals, stars of David, or the tablets of the Law, can be made in a variety of ways. Each method may require a certain amount of experimentation.

Using a 8½ × 8½-inch sheet of white or colored paper, make four folds as follows: fold in half to form a rectangle; fold in half to form a square; fold in half to form a triangle; fold in half to form a right angle. Draw a design with a pencil on one side of the paper. The design should be made so that it reaches the three edges, allowing some paper on the folds which will not be cut. Shade the pieces to be cut out. Use a sharp scissors, knife, or razor blade to cut the shaded parts that are to be excised, making sure to cut through all the layers of paper. Unfold and paste on a windowpane.

A similar cutout with a symmetrical design can be made in the following manner. With a pencil, draw an outline of a design on half a sheet of white paper. Use linking lines to keep the cutout together when unfolded. The outline should extend to the center of the paper so that it will touch the half which has no design. Mark the pieces to be cut out by shading them. Fold the sheet in half so that the design is on top. With a knife, razor blade, or some small sharp scissors, excise all the shaded pieces beginning on the fold. When unfolded the images will be back to back, facing opposite directions. Paste the cutout on colored tissue paper or cellophane so that light can shine through it.

If a square sheet of paper is folded three times and then cut, symmetrical figures will appear in each of the four corners. If a

27. *Shevuoslekh.* Paper cutouts used as window decorations on Shavuot. See Chapter 8.

long rectangle is used, it can be folded two, three, or four times the short way, and then cut on the last fold.

It is possible to create an attractive design without a preliminary sketch.

Another type of window display can be made with two sheets of construction paper or cardboard and colored cellophane. Draw a design on a sheet of dark construction paper or poster board, marking clearly the pieces to be cut out. Place it on top of the second sheet and cut through both sheets at the same time so that they are identical. Paste colored cellophane, tissue paper, or crepe paper between the two sheets of paper or borders so that when placed on a window or in front of a light bulb the colored design will be seen. Different colored cellophanes or crepe paper may be used to create an unusual effect.

Silhouettes of black construction paper can also be used as *shevuoslekh.*

Flowerpots and Vases: Ordinary flowerpots or boxes can be fittingly decorated for use as Shavuot adornments. Take a piece of paper large enough to cover the sides of the pot or the box and draw a floral design. An appropriate quotation (see "Posters and Murals" below) can be included. Trace the design and the quotation on the pot or box and paint with poster colors. When the paint is dry, coat with shellac.

Tin cans, bottles, and jars can be converted to beautiful vases by decorating them with enamel, raffia, or crepe paper strips. If tin cans are used, coat the inside with asphalt paint to prevent rusting.

The cans can be made suitable for hanging plants in the following way: punch three holes, evenly spaced, near the top of the can; attach a wire from a coat hanger to each hole; bend the upper ends of the three wires to form a hook.

Baskets: Baskets for "firstfruits" can be woven with reed and raffia. They can also be made with cardboard cartons on which handles are placed. For handles, twist crepe paper strips into ropes and attach with heavy staples. Adorn the baskets with colorful crepe paper. The completed baskets may be filled with live or artificial flowers, fruits, and vegetables or used to enclose flowerpots.

Garlands: Secure flowers to an ordinary hair band or arrange them on wire, using fine wire or string to attach them. Artificial flowers, made with wire and liquid plastic or paper, can also be used for garlands.

Posters and Murals: Posters can be made with slogans and symbols pertinent to the festival. Friezes may be executed by a group, with each participant painting one of the scenes. Ideas for motifs are suggested above. The following are suggested legends or slogans for posters: Shavuot: The Birthday of Judaism; "The choice firstfruits of your soil you shall bring to the house of the Lord" (Exodus 23.19); "You shall rejoice before the Lord" (Deuteronomy 16.11); "The gleanings of your harvest you shall leave for the poor and the stranger" (Leviticus 23.22); *Hag Sameah!* Joyous Festival!; The Festival of Firstfruits; and Season of the Giving of Our Law.

18.

MUSIC FOR SHAVUOT

COMPILED AND EDITED BY PAUL KAVON

*Torat Emet

We received the true Torah from the hands of Moses, God's faithful prophet.

Liturgy

Composer unknown
Arrangement: Harry Coopersmith

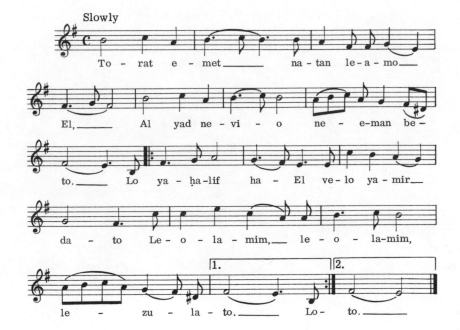

Slowly

To - rat e - met____ na - tan le - a - mo__

El,____ Al yad ne - vi - o ne - e-man be -

to.____ Lo ya - ḥa-lif ha - El ve - lo ya - mir__

da - to Le - o - la - mim,__ le - o - la-mim,

1.

2.

le - zu - la - to.____ Lo - to.____

Tanu Rabanan
(Our Saintly Rabbis)

Our saintly rabbis sing praises to God who gave the Torah.

English verse: Jacob S. Golub   Folk Song
                              Arrangement: Harry Coopersmith

(Sung as a round. Group 2 begins when Group 1 repeats the stanza.)

*Kabbalat ha-Torah

"If I have Torah, I have light . . . everything I have."

Isaac Katznelson

Music: Gershon Ephros
Arrangement: Samuel E. Goldfarb

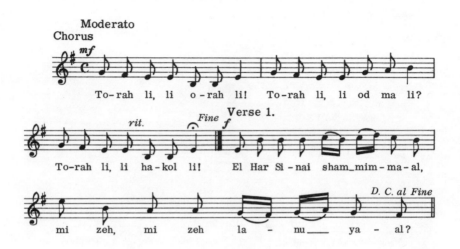

2. Ka-ra Mo-sheh, ish ha-pe-le:
   A-ni la-khem el Si-nai e-e-leh!   (Chorus)
3. Ma-ha-u khu-lam kaf ve-kar-u:
   Hish a-leh, a-leh ha-ha-rah!   (Chorus)
4. Mah sham ta-a-seh, na sa-pe-rah!
   Im El Sha-dai a-da-be-rah!   (Chorus)
5. Sha-a-lu khu-lam et ha-na-vi:
   Mah mi-Si-nai la-nu ta-vi?   (Chorus)
6. Az ha-na-vi Mo-sheh a-nah:
   To-rah a-vi ve-ma-ta-nah!   (Chorus)
7. Mi ha-To-rah ye-lam-de-nu?
   Mo-sheh ra-be-nu, Mo-sheh ra-be-nu!   (Chorus)
8. Hin-no yo-red, ha-bi-tu ho
   Ve-ha-lu-hot i-to, i-to!   (Chorus)
9. Mo-sheh ra-be-nu, Mo-sheh ra-be-nu,
   Et ha-To-rah hish lam-de-nu!   (Chorus)

Torah Tzivah Lanu

The Torah is Israel's inheritance.

Liturgy   Music: Harry Coopersmith

Barukh Elohenu

Blessed is our God, who gave us the Torah of truth.

Liturgy

Hasidic
Arrangement: Harry Coopersmith

* Yisrael ve-Oraita

The people of Israel, the Torah, and the Holy One, blessed be
He, are one.

Liturgy

Hasidic
Arrangement: Harry Coopersmith

With joy

1. Yi-yi-yi-yisra-el, yi-yisra-el ve-o-rai-ta
2. Yi-yi-yi-yisra-el, ve-o-rai-ta ve-Kud-sha berikh Hu

had____ hu. ve-o-rai-ta had__ hu.
had____ hu. ve-kud-sha berikh hu had__ hu.

To-rah o-rah To-rah o-rah Ha-le-lu-yah, To-rah o-rah

To-rah o-rah Ha-le-lu-yah, Ha-le-lu-yah. Ha-le-lu-yah.

*Yismaḥ Mosheh

Moses joyfully welcomes the gift of the Torah.

Folk Song
Arrangement: Judith K. Eisenstein and Frieda Prensky

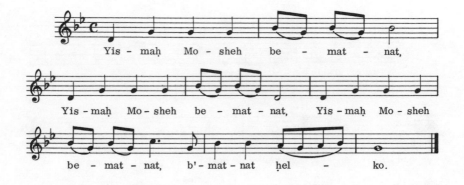

Yis - maḥ Mo - sheh be - mat - nat,
Yis - maḥ Mo - sheh be - mat - nat, Yis - maḥ Mo - sheh
be - mat - nat, b' - mat - nat ḥel - ko.

*Yismehu Adirim

Rejoice in the great gift of the Torah!

Folk Song
Arrangement: Ruth Rubin

Gay

Yis-me-ḥu a - di - rim, a - di - rim, Be - sim - ḥat ma-tan

To - rah. Be-sim-ḥat ma-tan To - rah. Be-sim-ḥat ma-tan

To - rah. Gi-lah, ri-nah, di-tzah, ve-ḥed-vah Be-sim-ḥat ma-tan

To - rah___ Gi - lah, ri - nah, di - tzah ve-ḥed-vah Be-

sim-ḥat ma-tan To - rah. To-rah ya - a, To-rah na - a,

1.
Mo-sheh ki - bel mi - Si - nai.

2.
Mo - sheh ki - bel mi - Si - nai.

*Dundai

Without the Torah, Israel is like a body without a soul.

Arrangement: Harry Coopersmith

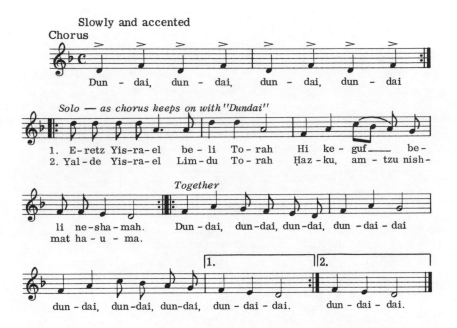

Slowly and accented

Chorus

Dun - dai, dun - dai, dun - dai, dun - dai

Solo — *as chorus keeps on with "Dundai"*

1. E - retz Yis-ra - el be - li To - rah Hi ke - guf___ be -
2. Yal - de Yis-ra - el Lim - du To - rah Ḥaz - ku, am - tzu nish -

Together

li ne - sha - mah. Dun - dai, dun - dai, dun - dai, dun - dai - dai
mat ha - u - ma.

dun - dai, dun - dai, dun - dai, dun - dai - dai.

1.

2.

dun - dai - dai.

*At Mount Sinai

This song captures the mood of the moment when Israel received the Torah at Mount Sinai.

Judith K. Eisenstein   Based on the *Akdamut* chant
                              Arrangement: Judith K. Eisenstein

Like a chant

In the wil-der-ness no wind_ blew,_ In the heav-ens
No_ bird_ flew,_ In the mea-dow no cow was_ low-ing,
In the riv-ers the wa-ter stopped_ flow-ing.
Cam-el bells were no-where_ ring-ing, E-ven the an-gels
ceased_ their_ sing-ing. O-ver the whole world si-lence was fall-ing,
On-ly the voice of the Sho-far_ call-ing. At the foot of the
moun-tain we stood, and re-ceived_ the To - rah!

Der Oibershter Iz Der Mechutten

Based on the legend depicting the Lord as the Father of the bride, the Torah as the bride, Israel as the groom, and Moses as the matchmaker.

Yiddish Folk Song   Arrangement: A. Zhitomirsky

1. Der Oi-bersht-er iz der me-chut-ten, Die Toi-reh iz die ka-leh, Moi-she Rab-be-nu iz der shad-chen ge-ven Der o-rem-er Yis-rol-ik, iz der chos-son der shehn-er oif dem hei-lig-en barg Si-nai, iz die T'noi-im ge-ven.

Refrain — Allegretto

Es fli-en Yid-e-lech, zing-en lid-e-lech ye-der-er shreit be-zund-er: Chos-son's tsad,__ Ka-leh's tsad__ "Maz-zol Tov!"

2. Dek oif dein dek-tuch, du tei-er-e ka-leh,
   Be-veiz unz dein po-nim mir vill-en dich zehn,
   Zeht nor ihr Yid-en un kukt tsu ihr al-le;
   Dos iz die e-mu-noh die ka-leh ge-ven.
   (REFRAIN)

3. A ka-leh, a rei-ne, zie iz reich un shehn,
   O-rent-lich un fein, zie iz bes-ser vi alts,
   Pe-rel bei ihr gist zich fun moil,
   A gil-de-ne keit bei ihr oif'n halz!
   (REFRAIN)

*Naaleh le-Har Tziyon
(Three Times Yearly)*

A song about the three pilgrimage festivals when the Jews traveled to Mount Zion: Sukkot, Pesah, and Shavuot.

English verse: Harry Coopersmith
and F. Minkoff

Composer unknown
Arrangement: Harry Coopersmith

Rhythmically, with marked accent

Na - a - leh le-Har Tzi - yon___ be - ri - nah.___
Three times year-ly to Mount Zi-on, we've been told,___
Three times year-ly to Mount Zi-on, did they climb, on

na - a - leh le - Har Tzi - yon___ be - ri - nah.
All of Is-rael trav-elled in the days of___ old.
Suk-kot and on Pe-sah and Sha - vu - ot___ time.

Yom___ gi - lah___ Yom___ ri - nah___
Those were hap-py days of sing-ing and of praise and

Yom ke-du - shah___ Yom me-nu - hah.
Eve-ry one did share___ of-fer-ing a prayer.

Na - a - leh le - Har Tzi - yon___ be - ri - nah___
Three times year-ly to Mount Zi - on as of yore, Our

na - a - leh le - Har Tzi - yon___ be - ri - nah.
hearts re-peat the an-cient jour-ney ev - er - more.

*Kumu ve-Naaleh

Arise, let us go up to the mountain of the Lord, our God.

Israeli Folk Song
Arrangement: Judith K. Eisenstein

*Alu, Alu
(Arise, Arise)

Arise, arise, for we go to our land with song and dance.

English verse: Samuel Dinin   Music: Yemenite
                                        Arrangement: Harry Coopersmith

Joyously

A - lu, a - lu le - e - retz a - vot. Le-ar -
A - rise, a - rise and min-gle in the throng! We—

tze - nu a - lu be - shir u - vim - ḥo - lot. To -
go to our land with danc - ing and with song. A

rat e - met ha - El na - tan___ la - nu, To -
Law of truth the Lord has grant - ed to us; a

rat ḥa - yim ha - El na - ta___ ba - nu.
Law of life the Lord has plant - ed in us,

Ya ri - bon o - lam,___ Ya ri - bon o - lam Ra -
Lord Al - might - y God,___ Lord Al - might - y God have

ḥem ra - ḥem Ra - ḥa - ma - na ra - ḥem, Ra -
mer - cy, have mer - cy Most Mer - ci - ful and kind, For-

ḥem na, ra - ḥem Ra - ḥa - ma - na ra - ḥem.
give us, and give us the land for which we pine.

NOTES

*1 Shavuot in the Bible

1. Abraham I. Sperling, *Sefer Taame ha-Minhagim u-Mekore ha-Dinim* (Lvov, 1890), 619–20; Abraham ben Nathan ha Yarhi, *Sefer ha-Manhig* (Constantinople, 5729), pp. 71b–72a.
2. Selections from the Pentateuch in this chapter are from *The Torah: The Five Books of Moses: A New Translation . . . according to the Masoretic Text,* 2d rev. ed. (Philadelphia: Jewish Publication Society of America, 1973).
3. *The Five Megilloth and Jonah: A New Translation,* introductions by H. L. Ginsberg, drawings by Ismar David, 2d rev. ed. (Philadelphia: Jewish Publication Society of America, 1974), pp. 21–27, 29.

*2 Shavuot in Postbiblical Writings

1. R. H. Charles, ed., *The Apocrypha and Pseudepigrapha of the Old Testament* (Oxford: Clarendon Press, 1913), 2: 11–12.
2. H. St. J. Thackeray, trans., *Josephus* (Cambridge, Mass.: Harvard University Press, 1930), 4:353–61.
3. F. H. Colson, trans., *Philo* (Cambridge, Mass.: Harvard University Press, 1937), 7: 7–15.
4. Ibid., pp. 21–29.
5. Charles, *Apocrypha and Pseudepigrapha,* 2: 22, 45.
6. Ibid., 1: 205–6.

7. Ralph Marcus, trans., *Josephus* (Cambridge, Mass.: Harvard University Press, 1943), 7: 353–55.
8. H. St. J. Thackeray, trans., *Josephus* (Cambridge, Mass.: Harvard University Press, 1927), 2:339.
9. Charles, *Apocrypha and Pseudepigrapha,* 1:149.

*3 Shavuot in Talmud and Midrash

1. Gerald Friedlander, trans., *Pirke de-Rabbi Eliezer* (London: Kegan Paul, 1916), pp. 314, 321.
2. William G. Braude, trans., *The Midrash on Psalms,* 2 vols. (New Haven: Yale University Press, 1959), 1:542–44.
3. Selections from *The Babylonian Talmud* are from the translation under the editorship of Isidore Epstein (London: Soncino Press, 1935–1950).
4. Selections from *Midrash Rabbah* are from the translation under the editorship of H. Freedman and Maurice Simon (London: Soncino Press, 1939–1951).
5. William G. Braude, trans., *Pesikta Rabbati: Discourses for Feasts, Fasts and Special Sabbaths,* 2 vols. (New Haven: Yale University Press, 1968), 1:398–99.
6. Jacob Z. Lauterbach, trans. and ed., *Mekilta de-Rabbi Ishmael,* 3 vols. (Philadelphia: Jewish Publication Society of America, 1933–1935), 2:229–30.
7. Ibid., 2: 234–36.
8. Ibid., 2: 198–200.
9. Nahum N. Glatzer, ed., *Hammer on the Rock: A Short Midrash Reader,* trans. by Jacob Sloan (New York: Schocken Books, 1948), p. 52.
10. Lauterbach, *Mekilta de-Rabbi Ishmael,* 2:236–37.
11. Ibid., 2: 220–21.
12. Moses Gaster, trans., *Ma'aseh Book,* 2 vols. (Philadelphia: Jewish Publication Society of America, 1934), 1:4–6. This version varies slightly from the talmudic source.
13. Ibid., 1:2–4. This version varies slightly from the original source.
14. Braude, *Pesikta Rabbati,* 1:399–400.
15. Friedlander, *Pirke de-Rabbi Eliezer,* p. 322.
16. Braude, *Pesikta Rabbati,* 1:410–11.
17. Friedlander, *Pirke de-Rabbi Eliezer,* pp. 324–25, 327.
18. Ibid., pp. 321–22.
19. Braude, *Midrash on Psalms,* 2:102.
20. Lauterbach, *Mekilta de-Rabbi Ishmael,* 2:237–38.
21. Ibid., 2:230–31.
22. Friedlander, *Pirke de-Rabbi Eliezer,* pp. 355–56.
23. Glatzer, *Hammer on the Rock,* p. 73.
24. Braude, *Midrash on Psalms,* 1:122–23

25. Friedlander, *Pirke de-Rabbi Eliezer,* pp. 361–62, 366.
26. Braude, *Pesikta Rabbati,* 1:443–46.
27. Ibid., 1:415–16.
28. Glatzer, *Hammer on the Rock,* p. 38.
29. Ibid., pp. 55–56.

4 Shavuot in Medieval Jewish Literature

1. Judah Halevi, *Kuzari: The Book of Proof and Argument,* ed. Isaak Heinemann (Oxford: East and West Library, 1947), pp. 43–44.
2. Abraham S. Halkin, ed., *Moses Maimonides' Epistle to Yemen,* trans. Boaz Cohen (New York: American Academy for Jewish Research, 1952), pp. vi–vii.
3. Moses Maimonides, *The Guide for the Perplexed,* trans. M. Friedlander (London: George Routledge & Sons, 1904), pp. 221–23.
4. Joseph Albo, *Sefer ha-Ikkarim (Book of Principles),* ed. and trans. Isaac Husik, 5 vols. (Philadelphia: Jewish Publication Society of America, 1929), 1: 169, 171.
5. Ibid., 3:246–47, 251–53.
6. The *Zohar,* 5 vols. (London: Soncino Press, 1931–1934), 3: 280–81, trans. Harry Sperling, Maurice Simon and Paul P. Levertoff.
7. Ibid., 1:296, trans. Harry Sperling and Maurice Simon.
8. Ibid., 32–33.
9. Ibid., 5:121.
10. Maimonides, *Guide for the Perplexed,* p. 352.

5   Laws and Customs of Shavuot

1. Judah D. Eisenstein, *Otzar Dinim u-Minhagim* (New York: Hebrew Publishing Co., 1938), p. 419.
2. *Kitzur Shulhan Arukh* 103.14.
3. *Shulhan Arukh, Orah Hayyim,* Rema 494.
4. *Kitzur Shulhan Arukh* 120.11.
5. *Zohar,* Emor.
6. *Magen Avraham* 494.1.
7. *Shulhan Arukh, Orah Hayyim* 494.
8. Shlomoh Yosef Zevin, *Ha-Moadim be-Halakhah* (Tel Aviv: Betan Hasefer, 5709). pp. 325–26.
9. *Shulhan Arukh, Orah Hayyim,* Rema 494.
10. *Levush* 494.5
11. Rosh Hashanah 16a.
12. *Magen Avraham* 494.5.
13. *Hayye Adam* 131.13.

14. Bikkurim 3.3.
15. *Shoshan* may also mean lily.
16. *Sefer Maharil, Hilkhot Shavuot* 21.

*6   The Liturgy of Shavuot

1. Arthur Davis and Herbert M. Adler, trans., *Service of the Synagogue: A New Edition of the Festival Prayers with an English Translation in Prose and Verse: Pentecost* (London: George Routledge & Sons, 1909), p. 152.
2. Theodor H. Gaster, *Festivals of the Jewish Year: A Modern Interpretation and Guide* (New York: William Sloane Associates, 1953), p. 64.
3. Judah Leb Fishman, *Haggim u-Moadim,* 2d. ed. (Jerusalem: Mosad Harav Kook, 1944), pp. 264–68; Eliyahu Kitov, *The Book of Our Heritage: The Jewish Year and Its Days of Significance,* trans. Nathan Bulman (New York: Feldheim Publishers, 1970), 3:65–68.
4. *Sabbath and Festival Prayer Book: With a New Translation, Supplementary Readings and Notes* (New York: The Rabbinical Assembly and United Synagogue of America, 1946), pp. 185–88.
5. Yerushalmi Berakhot 81.5; Hayyim Leshem, *Shabbat u-Moade Yisrael,* 3 vols. (Tel Aviv: Niv, 1965), 2:527–30.
6. David de Sola Pool, ed. and trans., *Prayers for the Festivals according to the Custom of the Spanish and Portuguese Jews* (New York: Union of Sephardic Congregations, 1947), pp. 328–29.
7. Davis and Adler, *Service of the Synagogue,* p. 121.
8. Ibid., p. 185.
9. There was also a liturgical poet named Jacob ben Meir Levi, who may have been confused with Rabbenu Tam. See *Jewish Encyclopedia,* 7:38.
10. David de Sola Pool, trans., *The Traditional Prayer Book for Sabbath and Festivals* (New York: Behrman House, 1960), p. 514.
11. Taanit 4.8.

*7   Shavuot in Modern Prose

1. A. Alan Steinbach, *Spiritual Cameos: Reflections and Meditations on the Holy Days and Festivals* (New York: Gertz Bros., n.d.), p. 29.
2. Abraham Joshua Heschel, *God in Search of Man: A Philosophy of Judaism* (New York: Farrar, Straus and Cudahy, 1955), pp. 167, 171, 185, 187, 189.

3. Samson Raphael Hirsch, *Judaism Eternal: Selected Essays*, trans. I. Grunfeld, 2 vols. (London: Soncino Press, 1956)1: 88–89, 101–3, 105–8.
4. David Polish, *The Higher Freedom: A New Turning Point in Jewish History* (Chicago: Quadrangle Books, 1965), pp. 62–64.
5. Ahad Ha-Am, *Selected Essays*, trans. Leon Simon (Philadelphia: Jewish Publication Society of America, 1912), pp. 320–22.
6. Ludwig Lewisohn, *What Is This Jewish Heritage?* (New York: B'nai B'rith Hillel Foundations, 1954), pp. 2–3.
7. Arthur A. Cohen, "Why I Choose to Be a Jew," *Harper's Magazine* 218, no. 1,307 (April 1959): 61–65.
8. Joseph H. Hertz, *The Authorised Daily Prayer Book: Hebrew Text, English Translation with Commentary and Notes* (New York: Bloch Publishing Co., 1948), pp. 790–91.
9. Aron Barth, *The Modern Jew Faces Eternal Problems*, trans. Haim Shachter (Jerusalem: Religious Section, Youth and Hechalutz Department, Zionist Organization, 1965), pp. 147–48.
10. Chaim Pearl, *A Guide to Shavuoth* (London: Jewish Chronicle Publications, 1959), pp. 71–72.
11. Joseph Cooper Levine, ed. and trans., *Echoes of the Jewish Soul: Gleanings from Modern Literature* (New York: Bloch Publishing Co., 1931), pp. 30–33.
12. Morris Joseph, *Judaism as Creed and Life* (London: George Routledge and Sons, 1903), pp. 226–39.
13. Uri Zvi Greenberg, "Le-Hag ha-Shavuot," *Mahanaim* 57 (1961): 17–19.
14. Grace Aguilar, *The Women of Israel*, 2 vols. (New York: D. Appleton & Co., 1854), 1:249–51.
15. Philip Birnbaum, *A Book of Jewish Concepts* (New York: Hebrew Publishing Co., 1964), pp. 442–43.
16. Louis Finkelstein, *The Pharisees: The Sociological Background of Their Faith*, 2 vols. (Philadelphia: Jewish Publication Society of America, 1938) 1:115–18. See Solomon Zeitlin, "The Takkanot of Rabban Jochanan Ben Zakkai," *Jewish Quarterly Review* 54, no. 4 (April 1964): 288–310; Leon Nemoy, trans., *Karaite Anthology: Excerpts from the Early Literature* (New Haven: Yale University Press, 1952), pp. 215–25.

*8   *Shavuot in Art*

1. Cf. Bezalel Narkiss, *Illuminated Hebrew Manuscripts* (New York, 1969), pp. 98–99, 108–9.
2. Lionel David Barnett et al., *Treasures of a London Temple . . .* (London, 1951), pp. 67–68. Cf. Joseph Gutmann, *No Graven Im-*

ages (New York, 1971), pp. xxxi ff.

3. Stephen Kayser and Guido Schoenberger, *Jewish Ceremonial Art* (Philadelphia, 1959), pp. 25ff.

4. Rachel Wischnitzer-Bernstein, *Symbole und Gestalten der jüdischen Kunst* (Berlin, 1935), pp. 43ff.

5. Ernst Róth, "Sinai und Chederunterricht im Zeichen des Wochenfestes," *Israelitisches Wochenblatt für die Schweiz,* May 15, 1964, 57–61; "Torah Instruction of Children at Shavuot," *Yeda-'Am* 11 (1965): 9–12. Cf. Bezalel Narkiss in *Mahzor Lipsiae,* ed. Elias Katz (Leipzig, 1964), pp. 96ff.

6. Cf. Joseph Gutmann in *Die Darmstädter Pessach-Haggadah* (Berlin, 1972), p. 90.

7. Johann C. G. Bodenschatz, *Kirchlicher Verfassung der heutigen Juden* 2 (Erlangen, 1748): 334–37. Cf. also Akiva Ben-Ezra, *Minhage Haggim* (Jerusalem, 1962), pp. 278–96.

8. Joseph Gutmann, *Jewish Ceremonial Art* (New York, 1964), p. 26. Barnett, *Treasures of a London Temple,* p. 66. Cf. Heinrich Frauberger, "Omerrollen," in *Mitteilungen der Gesellschaft zur Erforschung jüdischer Kunstdenkmäler* 5/6 (Frankfurt-am-Main, 1909): 17ff.

9. Giza Frankel, "Jewish Paper Cuts," *Polska Sztuka Ludowa* 19 (1965): 135–47 and "Paper Cuts: A Folk Art," *Jewish Heritage* 10 (1967): 40–41. Cf. also Otto Kurz, "Libri cum characteribus ex nulla materia compositis," *Israel Oriental Studies* 2 (1972): 244ff.

*9 Shavuot in Many Lands

1. Solomon Zeitlin, *The Rise and Fall of the Judaean State: A Political, Social and Religious History of the Second Commonwealth, 332–37 B.C.E.* 2 vols. (Philadelphia: Jewish Publication Society of America, 1964), 1:233–35.

2. Zev Vilnay, *Legends of Palestine* (Philadelphia: Jewish Publication Society of America, 1932), p. 152.

3. Hirsch Loeb Gordon, *The Maggid of Caro* (New York: Pardes Publishing House, 1949), pp. 105–8.

4. *Encyclopaedia Judaica,* 16 vols. (Jerusalem: Keter Publishing House, 1971), 14:742–43.

5. Erich Brauer, *Yehude Kurdistan: Mehker Etnologi,* ed. Raphael Patai (Jerusalem: Palestine Institute of Folklore and Ethnology, 1947), pp. 245–48.

6. J. I. Benjamin II, *Eight Years in Asia and Africa from 1846 to 1855* (Hanover, 1859), pp. 71–75.

7. Nahum Slouschz, *Travels in North Africa* (Philadelphia: Jewish Publication Society of America, 1927), pp. 331–32, 357.

8. *The Jewish Chronicle* (London), no. 3,397 (May 18, 1934), p. 15.

9. Hayyim Schauss, *The Lifetime of a Jew throughout the Ages of Jewish History* (Cincinnati: Union of American Hebrew Congregations, 1950), pp. 101–2.

10. Hayyim Schauss, *The Jewish Festivals: From Their Beginnings to Our Own Day,* trans. Samuel Jaffe (Cincinnati: Union of American Hebrew Congregations, 1938), pp. 90–93.

11. Shmarya Levin, *Forward from Exile: The Autobiography of Shmarya Levin,* trans. Maurice Samuel (Philadelphia: Jewish Publication Society of America, 1967), pp. 56–57.

12. Benjamin Schreiber, *Zechor Yemos Olam (Remember the Early Days)* trans. Paul Forchheimer (New York, 1969), pp. 150–52, 157.

13. Hana Valavkova, *A Story of the Jewish Museum in Prague,* trans. K. E. Lichtenecker (Prague: Artia, 1968), pp. 201–3.

14. Moshe Mosenson, *Letters from the Desert,* trans. Hilda Auerbach (New York: Sharon Books, 1945), pp. 66–67, 114–15.

15. S. B. Unsdorfer, *The Yellow Star* (New York: Thomas Yoseloff, 1961), pp. 199–200.

16. Joshua Rothenberg, *The Jewish Religion in the Soviet Union* (New York: Ktav Publishing House; Waltham: Philip W. Lown Graduate Center for Contemporary Jewish Studies, 1971), pp. 92–93.

17. F. B. Dexter, ed., *The Literary Diary of Ezra Stiles,* 3 vols. (New York: Charles Scribner's Sons, 1901), 1: 367–77.

18. Hyman B. Grinstein, *The Rise of the Jewish Community of New York, 1654–1860* (Philadelphia: Jewish Publication Society of America, 1945), pp. 249–50.

19. Israel Kasovich, *The Days of Our Years: Personal and General Reminiscence (1859–1929),* trans. Maximilian Hurwitz (New York: Jordan Publishing Co., 1929), pp. 288–89.

20. Yehuda Haezrahi, ed., *Shavuot Sheaves* (Jerusalem: Jewish National Fund Youth Department, 1965), pp. 26–28.

21. Ibid., pp. 31–32.

22. *Petahim,* no. 4 (June, 1968), p. 16.

23. Yaacov Luria, "A Harvest of Spring Holidays in Israel," *The American Zionist* 63, no. 9 (June 1973): 28–29.

*10 Shavuot in Poetry

1. Alice Lucas, trans., *The Jewish Year: A Collection of Devotional Poems* (London: Macmillan, 1898), p. 128.

2. Ibid., pp. 35–36.

3. Nina Davis [Salaman], trans., *Songs of Exile by Hebrew Poets* (Philadelphia: Jewish Publication Society of America, 1901), pp. 115–17.

4. Joseph Leftwich, ed., *The Golden Peacock: An Anthology of Yiddish Poetry* (Cambridge, Mass.: Sci-Art Publishers, 1939), pp. 696–97.

5. Ruth F. Brin, *Interpretations for the Weekly Torah Reading* (Minneapolis: Lerner Publications Co., 1965), p. 53.

6. *The Menorah Journal* 32, no. 1 (April-June, 1944): 1; reprinted in *The Menorah Treasury: Harvest of Half a Century,* ed. by Leo W. Schwarz (Philadelphia: Jewish Publication Society of America, 1964), p. 712.

7. Nelly Sachs, *The Seeker and Other Poems* (New York: Farrar, Straus and Giroux, 1970), p. 95.

8. Ruth Whitman, trans., *The Selected Poems of Jacob Glatstein* (New York: October House, 1972), pp. 68–70.

9. Harry H. Fein, trans., *Gems of Hebrew Verse: Poems for Young People* (Boston: Bruce Humphries, 1940), p. 18.

*11   Shavuot in the Short Story

1. Hayyim Nahman Bialik, *And It Came to Pass: Legends and Stories about King David and King Solomon,* trans. Herbert Danby (New York: Hebrew Publishing Co., 1938), pp. 14–15.

2. *The Jewish Chronicle Supplement,* no. 101 (May 31, 1929), pp. iv-v.

3. *East and West* 1, no. 1 (January 1916), pp. 307–9.

4. Sholom Asch, *Kiddush Ha-Shem: An Epic of 1648,* trans. Rufus Learsi (Philadelphia: Jewish Publication Society of America, 1926), pp. 113–28.

5. Martin Buber, *For the Sake of Heaven,* trans. Ludwig Lewisohn (Philadelphia: Jewish Publication Society of America, 1945), pp. 103–9.

6. S. Y. Agnon, *A Guest for the Night,* trans. Misha Louvish (New York: Schocken Books, 1968), pp. 278–88.

*12 A Shavuot Sheaf

1. Taanit 18a; Shabbat 87a; Abraham I. Sperling, *Sefer Taame ha-Minhagim u-Mekore ha-Dinim* (Lvov, 1890), 610–12.

2. Yom-Tov Lewinski, *Shabbatot Meyuhadot be-Luah ha-Shanah* (Tel Aviv: Tarbut Vehinukh, 1969), pp. 31–32.

3. Numbers Rabbah 13.15, 18.21.

4. Yerushalmi Betzah 61b; Yerushalmi Hagigah 78a; Yom-Tov Lewinski, *Sefer ha-Moadim . . . Shavuot* (Tel Aviv: Oneg Shabbat and Dvir, 1950), pp. 186–87.

5. Dan Ben-Amos and Jerome R. Mintz, trans. and ed., *In Praise of the Baal Shem Tov* (Bloomington: Indiana University Press, 1970), pp. 255–57; Martin Buber, *Tales of the Hasidim: The Early Masters*, trans. Olga Marx (New York: Schocken Books, 1947), pp. 83–84.
6. Solomon B. Freehof, "Hazkarath Neshamoth," *Hebrew Union College Annual* 36 (1965): 179–89.
7. Jacob R. Marcus, *Israel Jacobson: The Founder of the Reform Movement in Judaism* (Cincinnati: Hebrew Union College Press, 1972), p. 109.
8. *Jewish Encyclopedia*, 4:220.
9. Haeem Samuel Kehimkar, *The History of the Bene Israel of India* (Tel Aviv: Dayag Press, 1937), pp. 21, 169.
10. *The American Sephardi* 4, nos. 1–2 (Autumn 1970): 84.
11. Abraham Yaari, *Toldot Hag Simhat Torah: Hishtalshalut Minhagav be-Tefutzot Yisrael be-Doroteben* (Jerusalem: Mosad Harav Kook, 1964), pp. 231–36.
12. Lewinski, *Sefer ha-Moadim . . . Shavuot*, pp. 171–72; *Jewish Encyclopedia*, 10:147; Israel Cohen, *Vilna* (Philadelphia: Jewish Publication Society of America, 1943), pp. 73, 484–86.
13. Jacob S. Raisin, *Gentile Reactions to Jewish Ideals*, ed. Herman Hailperin (New York: Philosophical Library, 1953), p. 470.

13   Shavuot Wit and Humor

1. *A Thought for the Week*, adapted from the works of Rabbi Menachem M. Schneerson, vol. 3, no. 2 (October 17, 1969), p. 4.
2. Most of the stories in this chapter have been culled, with some revisions, from Philip Goodman, *Rejoice in Thy Festival: A Treasury of Wisdom, Wit and Humor for the Sabbath and Jewish Holidays* (New York: Bloch Publishing Co., 1956), pp. 227–36, 238.

14   The Culinary Art of Shavuot

1. Pesahim 68b, Rashi.
2. *Kitzur Shulhan Arukh* 103.7.
3. *Shulhan Arukh, Orah Hayyim* 494, Rema.
4. *Kitzur Shulhan Arukh* 103.7.
5. Abraham I. Sperling, *Sefer Taame ha-Minhagim u-Mekore ha-Dinim* (Lvov, 1890), 623.
6. *Kitzur Shulhan Arukh* 103.7.
7. Shabbat 88a.

8. *Yosef Ometz* 854.
9. Malkah Kohen, "Rekike Hag ha-Shavuot," *Yeda-Am* 16, nos. 39–40 (1972): 63.
10. Sperling, *Sefer Taame ha-Minhagim,* 627–28.

* *15   Children's Stories for Shavuot*

1. Charlotte Bronstein, *Tales of the Jewish Holidays as Told by the Light of the Moon,* illus. Art Seiden (New York: Behrman House, 1959), unp.
2. Sadie Rose Weilerstein, *The Adventures of K'tonton: A Little Jewish Tom Thumb,* illus. Jeannette Berkowitz (New York: National Women's League of the United Synagogue, 1935), pp. 65–70.
3. Morris Epstein, *My Holiday Story Book,* illus. Arnold Lobel (New York: Ktav Publishing House, 1958), pp. 49–54.
4. Levin Kipnis, *My Holidays: Holiday Stories for Children,* trans. Israel M. Goodelman, illus. Isa (Tel Aviv: N. Tversky, 1961), pp. 153–57.
5. Ben M. Edidin, ed., *Lag Be'Omer and Shavuot: Jewish Life and Customs: Unit Seven,* illus. Temima N. Gezari (New York: Bloch Publishing Co., 1946), pp. 16–21.
6. Jules Harlow, ed., *Lessons from Our Living Past* (New York: Behrman House, 1972), pp. 11–15.
7. Sydney Taylor, *All-of-a-Kind Family Uptown,* illus. Mary Stevens (Chicago: Wilcox and Follet, 1958), pp. 135–45.
8. *World Over* 19, no. 15 (May 16, 1958): 6–7.
9. Ezekiel Schloss and Morris Epstein, eds., *The New World Over Story Book* (New York: Bloch Publishing Co., 1968), pp. 189–93.
10. Dorothy F. Zeligs, *The Story of Modern Israel for Young People* (New York: Bloch Publishing Co., 1961), pp. 172–76.
11. Philip Goodman, *Rejoice in Thy Festival: A Treasury of Wisdom, Wit and Humor for the Sabbath and Jewish Holidays* (New York: Bloch Publishing Co., 1956), pp. 239–43.

* *16   Children's Poems for Shavuot*

1. Jessie E. Sampter, *Around the Year in Rhymes for the Jewish Child* (New York: Bloch Publishing Co., 1920), p. 60.
2. Sadie Rose Weilerstein, *The Singing Way: Poems for Jewish Children* (New York: National Women's League of United Synagogue, 1946), p. 59.

3. Louis I. Newman, *Trumpet in Adversity and Other Poems* (New York: Renascence Press, 1948), p. 130.

4. Ibid., pp. 131–32.

5. Abraham Burstein, *A Jewish Child's Garden of Verses* (New York: Bloch Publishing Co., 1940), p. 50.

6. Ilo Orleans, *The First Rainbow: A Book of Rhymes from Bible Times* (New York: Union of American Hebrew Congregations, 1954), pp. 37–38.

7. Philip M. Raskin, *Poems for Young Israel* (New York: Behrman's Jewish Book Shop, 1925), pp. 64–66.

8. Yehuda Haezrahi, ed., *Shavuot Sheaves* (Jerusalem: Jewish National Fund Youth Department, 1965), pp. 140–42.

9. Sampter, *Around the Year,* p. 63.

10. Haezrahi, *Shavuot Sheaves,* p. 139.

11. Ibid., pp. 138–39.

12. Harry H. Fein, trans., *Gems of Hebrew Verse: Poems for Young People* (Boston: Bruce Humphries, 1940), p. 19.

GLOSSARY OF SHAVUOT TERMS

AKDAMUT (introductions, prelude). An Aramaic liturgical poem recited on the first day of Shavuot at the beginning of the scriptural readings.

ASERET HA-DIBROT (the ten words). The Ten Commandments.

ATZERET (conclusion, gathering, detention: exact meaning uncertain). A name for Shavuot, which is considered the concluding feast of Passover.

AZHAROT (warnings, admonitions). Liturgical hymns dealing with the 613 commandments read on Shavuot.

BIKKURIM (firstfruits). The firstfruits of the seven species of fruits and grains enumerated in Deuteronomy 8.8, which were brought to the Temple in Jerusalem on Shavuot.

BLINTZES. Rolled pancakes filled with cheese; a favorite Shavuot dish.

CONFIRMATION. The ceremony among Reform and some Conservative Jews, usually held on Shavuot, to induct boys and girls who have completed a course of study into the Jewish community.

DAY OF THE FIRSTFRUITS. One of the biblical names for Shavuot marking it as the festival for bringing firstfruits to the Temple.

DECALOGUE. The Ten Commandments.

FEAST OF THE HARVEST. A biblical name for Shavuot alluding to the end of the wheat harvest in Israel, which occurs at the season of the festival.

FEAST OF WEEKS. A biblical name for Shavuot indicating its observance seven weeks after the second day of Passover.

FIRSTFRUITS. The firstfruits of the seven species of fruits and grains enumerated in Deuteronomy 8.8, which were brought to the Temple in Jerusalem on Shavuot.

HAGGIM U-ZEMANIM LE-SASON (festivals and seasons for gladness). The phrase used in response to the festival greeting: *moadim le-simhah* (appointed times for rejoicing).

HAG HA-BIKKURIM (Festival of the Firstfruits). A celebration in remembrance of the firstfruits offered in the Temple on Shavuot.

HAG HA-KATZIR (Feast of the Harvest). One of the biblical names for Shavuot alluding to the end of the wheat harvest in Israel, which occurs at the season of the festival.

HAG HA-SHAVUOT (Feast of Weeks). A biblical name for Shavuot indicating its observance seven weeks after the second day of Passover.

HAG SAMEAH (happy holiday). A greeting used on festivals.

HAZKARAT NESHAMOT (remembrance of the souls [of the departed]). Memorial prayer for the departed recited on the second day of Shavuot.

MAHZOR (cycle). Prayer book for the cycle of the holy days and festivals.

MATTAN TORAH (giving of the Torah). An expression referring to the revelation on Mount Sinai.

MEGILLAT RUTH (Scroll of Ruth). The biblical Scroll of Ruth read on Shavuot.

MOADIM LE-SIMHAH (appointed times for rejoicing). A greeting denoting the joyous character of the festival.

MOUNT SINAI. The mountain on which Moses received the Torah.

OMER (a dry measure, the tenth part of an *ephah*). A measure of new barley flour was brought to the Temple in Jerusalem as an offering on the second day of Passover.

PENTECOST (fiftieth). The Greek name for Shavuot since it occurs on the fiftieth day after the first day of Passover when the *omer* was given as an offering.

SEASON OF THE GIVING OF OUR LAW. The name of Shavuot found in the liturgy which denotes the relationship of the festival to the revelation on Mount Sinai.

SEFIRAH (counting). The seven-week period from the second day of Passover to Shavuot, during most of which some mourning customs prevail.

SEFIRAT HA-OMER (counting of the *omer*). For forty-nine days—starting from the second day of Passover, when the *omer* was offered in the Temple, until Shavuot—the *omer* is counted with a special benediction.

SHALOSH REGALIM (three pilgrimages). The three major festivals (Pesah, Shavuot, and Sukkot) are known as the pilgrimage festivals, when Jews traveled to Jerusalem with their offerings.

SHAVUOT (weeks). A two-day festival observed on the sixth and seventh days of Sivan (only on the sixth day by Reform Jews and in Israel), seven weeks after the second day of Passover, to commemorate the offering of the firstfruits and the revelation on Mount Sinai.

SHELOSHET YEME HAGBALAH (Three Days of Delimitation). The children of Israel were ordered to avoid going near Mount Sinai for the three days before the revelation and to prepare to receive the Torah; hence, the mourning customs during the *sefirah* period do not apply during the three days preceding Shavuot.

SIVAN. The third month of the Jewish year.

TIKKUN LEL SHAVUOT (Order of the Night of Shavuot). A compilation of selections from the Bible, the Mishnah, and cabalistic writings comprising the order of study for the first night of Shavuot.

TORAH (law, teaching). Especially the Law of Moses, the Pentateuch; also used as a term to denote the entirety of both the Written and the Oral Law.

YIZKOR (may He remember). Memorial prayer for the departed recited on the second day of Shavuot.

YOM HA-BIKKURIM (Day of the Firstfruits). A biblical name for Shavuot marking it as the festival for bringing firstfruits to the Temple.

YOM TOV (good day). A festival, holiday.

ZEMAN MATTAN TORATENU (Season of the Giving of Our Law). The name of Shavuot found in the liturgy which denotes the relationship of the festival to the revelation on Mount Sinai.

BIBLIOGRAPHY

General References

Abrahams, Israel. *Festival Studies: Being Thoughts on the Jewish Year.* Philadelphia: Julius H Greenstone, 1906, pp. 5–12, 84–90.

Agnon, Shmuel Yosef. *Atem Raitem: Sefer Rishon: Parshat Mattan Torah.* Tel Aviv: Schocken Books, 1962.

Ariel, Shlomoh Zalman. *Entziklopediah Meir Netiv.* Tel Aviv: Massada, 1960.

Ariel, Z., ed. *Sefer ha-Hag veha-Moed.* Tel Aviv: Am Oved, 1962, pp. 303–26.

Ausubel, Nathan. *The Book of Jewish Knowledge.* New York: Crown Publishers, 1964.

Ayali, Meir, ed. *Haggim u-Zemanim: Mahzore Kriah le-Moade Yisrael.* Vol. 1. Tel Aviv: Gazit, 1949, pp. 363–448.

Beker, Hayyim S., ed. *Yalkut le-Moadim: Shavuot.* Jerusalem, 1967.

Ben-Ezra, Akiba. *Hag ha-Shavuot: Kovetz le-Bet ha-Sefer ule-Bet ha-Av.* New York: Mizrachi National Education Committee, 1947.

———. *Minhage Haggim.* Tel Aviv: M. Newman, 1963, pp. 278–96.

Ben-Yehoshua, H., ed. *Shavuot: Reshimah Bibliografit,* Jerusalem: Municipality of Jerusalem, Department of Education and Culture, 1969.

Berman, Jacob. *Halakhah la-Am: Haggim u-Zemanim, Tzomot, Teshuvah ve-Yamim Noraim.* Tel Aviv: Abraham Tzioni, 1962, pp. 104–18.

Bikkurim: Moadim u-Zemanim: Hoveret 6. Jerusalem: Jewish National Fund, 1951.

Birnbaum, Philip. *A Book of Jewish Concepts.* New York: Hebrew Publishing Co., 1964.

Chomsky, Zeev, ed. *Sefirat ha-Omer ve-Hag ha-Shavuot.* New York: Jewish Education Committee of New York, 1960, pp. 26–51.

De Vaux, Roland. *Ancient Israel: Its Life and Institutions.* New York: McGraw-Hill Book Co., 1961, pp. 493–95.

Edidin, Ben M. *Jewish Holidays and Festivals.* New York: Hebrew Publishing Co., 1940, pp. 165–77.

_____, ed. *Lag Be'Omer and Shavuoth: Jewish Life and Customs: Unit Seven.* New York: Jewish Education Committee of New York, 1946.

Ehrmann, Elieser L. *Omer-Zeit und Schawuot: Ein Quellenheft.* Berlin: Schocken Verlag, 1937, pp. 30–63.

Eisenstein, Ira. *What We Mean by Religion: A Modern Interpretation of the Sabbath and Festivals.* New York: Reconstructionist Press, 1958, pp. 111–23.

Eisenstein, J. D. *Otzar Dinim u-Minhagim.* New York: Hebrew Publishing Co., 1938, pp. 26, 289, 331, 382, 392–94, 419.

Encyclopaedia Judaica. 16 vols. Jerusalem: Keter Publishing House, 1972. See vol. 1, Index.

Finkelstein, Louis. *The Pharisees: The Sociological Background of Their Faith.* Vol. 1. Philadelphia: Jewish Publication Society of America, 1940, pp. 115–18.

Fishman (Maimon), Judah Leb. *Haggim u-Moadim.* 2d ed. Jerusalem: Mosad Harav Kook, 1944, pp. 257–89.

Freehof, Lillian S., and Bandman, Lottie C. *Flowers and Festivals of the Jewish Year.* New York: Hearthside Press, 1964, pp. 123–35.

Frenkel, K. L. *Sefer Safra-Hadata: Entziklopediah le-Haggim u-Zemanim.* Tel Aviv: Agudat Hasneh, 1972, pp. 242–61.

Frishman, Y., ed. *Hag Ha-Shavuot: Homer Hadrakhah le-Morim be-Vate ha-Sefer ha-Mamlakhtiim.* Tel Aviv: Tarbut Vehinukh, 1969.

Gaster, Moses. *The Story of Shavuot.* London: M. L. Cailingold, 1930.

Gaster, Theodor H. *Festivals of the Jewish Year: A Modern Interpretation and Guide.* New York: William Sloane Associates, 1953, pp. 59–79.

Goldin, Hyman E. *A Treasury of Jewish Holidays: History, Legends, Traditions.* New York: Twayne Publishers, 1952, pp. 206–25.

_____. *The Jewish Woman and Her Home.* Brooklyn, N.Y.: Jewish Culture Publishing Co., 1941, pp. 139–46, 168–76.

Goldman, Alex J. *A Handbook for the Jewish Family: Understanding and Enjoying the Sabbath and Holidays.* New York: Bloch Publishing Co., 1958, pp. 281–310.

Goodman, Philip, ed. *Shavuot Program Material for Youth and Adults.* New York: National Jewish Welfare Board, 1946.

Goren, Shelomoh. *Torat ha-Moadim: Mehkerim u-Maamarim al Moade Yisrael le-Or ha-Halakhah.* Tel Aviv: Abraham Tzioni, 1964, pp. 359–441.

Greenbaum, M., and Vainstein, Z., eds. *Hag ha-Shavuot: Hoveret le-Vate Sefer vela-Noar.* Buenos Aires: Jewish National Fund, 1943.

Greenstein, Joseph, ed. *Shavuos: Chag ha-Bikkurim.* New York: Council for Orthodox Jewish Schools, n.d.

Greenstone, Julius H. *Jewish Feasts and Fasts.* Philadelphia, 1945, pp. 227–59.

_____. *The Jewish Religion.* Philadelphia: Jewish Chautauqua Society, 1929, pp. 50–59, 213–29.

Haezrahi, Yehudah, ed. *Shavuot Sheaves.* Jerusalem: Youth Department, Jewish National Fund, 1965.

Hag u-Moed: Divre Iyun, Mekorot. Tel Aviv: Ha-Kibbutz ha-Artzi, ha-Mahlakah le-Tarbut, n.d., pp. 29–37.

Hakohen, Shmuel, ed. *Sheloshah Ketarim: Perakim le-Hag ha-Shavuot.* Tel Aviv: Tzava Haganah le-Yisrael, Ha-Rabanut ha-Tzavait ha-Reshit, 1950.

Hamiel, Hayyim, ed. *Mayanot: Maasaf le-Inyane Hinukh ve-Horaah.* Vol. 6. Jerusalem: Department of Torah Education and Culture in the Diaspora, World Zionist Organization, 1957.

Horowitz, Israel M., and Starkman, Moshe, eds. *Shavuot.* New York: Farband Labor Zionist Order, n.d.

The Jewish Encyclopedia. 12 vols. New York: Ktav Publishing House. See *Akdamut, Azharot,* Decalogue, Festivals, Harvest, Pentecost, Revelation, Ruth, Second Day of Festivals.

Joseph, Morris. *Judaism as Creed and Life.* London: George Routledge and Sons, 1903, pp. 224–35.

Kaplan, Louis L., ed. *Material and Methods for Teaching of Customs and Ceremonies: Bulletin II: Shavuot.* Baltimore: Board of Jewish Education, 1934.

Kaplan, Mordecai M. *The Meaning of God in Modern Jewish Religion.* New York: Jewish Reconstructionist Foundation, 1947, pp. 188–201, 297–329.

Kariv, Abraham, ed. *Shabbat u-Moed be-Derush uve-Hasidut.* Tel Aviv: Dvir and Oneg Shabbat Society, 1966, pp. 141–208.

Karlebach, Azriel, ed. *Shavuot: Yalkut le-Hag ha-Torah veha-Bikkurim.* Jerusalem: Efer, n.d.

Kitov, Eliyahu. *The Book of Our Heritage: The Jewish Year and Its Days of Significance.* Vol. 3. Translated by Nathan Bulman. Jerusalem–New York: Feldheim Publishers, 1970, pp. 47–185.

_____. *Sefer ha-Todaah: La-daat Huke ha-Elokim u-Mitzvotav Hagge Yisrael u-Moadav.* Jerusalem: Alef Makhon le-Hotzaat Sefarim, 1964, pp. 263–356.

Lag ba-Omer: Hag ha-Shavuot: Homer Hadrakhah le-Morim le-Vate ha-Sefer ha-Mamlakhtiim. Jerusalem: Ministry of Education and Culture, 1966.

La-Moed: Kovetz Sifruti le-Hag ha-Shavuot. Jerusalem: Hamizrah, 1946.

Lehrman, S. M. *The Jewish Festivals.* London: Shapiro, Vallentine & Co., 1938, pp. 59–70.

Leshem, Haim. *Shabbat u-Moade Yisrael be-Halakhah, be-Aggadah, be-Historiah, uve-Folklor.* Vol. 2. Tel Aviv: Niv, 1965, pp. 499–548. Vol. 3, 1969, pp. 165–70.

Levi, Shonie B., and Kaplan, Sylvia R. *Guide for the Jewish Homemaker.* New York: Schocken Books, 1964, pp. 115–20.

Lewinski, Yom-Tov. *Eleh Moade Yisrael.* Tel Aviv: Ahiasaf, 1971, pp. 199–209.

———, ed. *Sefer ha-Moadim.* Vol. 3. *Shavuot.* Tel Aviv: Oneg Shabbat and Dvir, 1950.

Lipson, M., ed. *Moadim: Sefer Shavuot.* Tel Aviv: Jewish National Fund and Omanuth, 1947.

Malkiel, Alexander, and Avi-Tzedek, Eliyahu, eds. *Shavuot: Yalkut le-Hag ha-Torah.* Jerusalem: Tzava Haganah le-Yisrael, Ha-Rabbanut ha-Tzavait ha-Reshit, 1949.

Markowitz, S. H. *Leading a Jewish Life in the Modern World.* Rev. ed. New York: Union of American Hebrew Congregations, 1958, pp. 278–89, 312–14.

Mervis, Leonard J. *We Celebrate Shavuos.* New York: Union of American Hebrew Congregations, 1953.

Mikhael, B., ed. *Haggim u-Moadim le-Yisrael: Aggadot Shirim ve-Sippurim.* Tel Aviv: M. Biran, 1954, pp. 49–59.

Newman, Aryeh, ed. *Shavuot: Mayanot III.* Jerusalem: Department for Torah Education and Culture in the Diaspora, World Zionist Organization, 1963.

Noerdlinger, Henny S. *Moses and Egypt: The Documentation to the Motion Picture "The Ten Commandments."* Los Angeles: University of Southern California Press, 1956.

Pearl, Chaim. *A Guide to Shavuoth.* London: Jewish Chronicle Publications, 1959.

Petuchowski, Jakob J. *Ever Since Sinai: A Modern View of Torah.* New York: Scribe Publications, 1961.

Picker, Shlomoh. *Shabbat u-Moadim be-Aretz.* Tel Aviv: M. Newman, 1969, pp. 169–74.

Pougatch, I., ed. *Chavouoth.* Paris: Editions O. P. E. J., 1950.

Rabinovich, Abraham Hirsch, ed. *Yalkut ha-Moadim.* Vol. 2. *Ateret Yekutiel le-Hag Zeman Mattan Toratenu.* Buenos Aires: Sadeyah, 1943.

Rabinowitz, Esther, ed. *Haggim u-Moadim be-Hinukh: La-Mehankhim be-Gan uve-Kitot ha-Nemukhot.* Tel Aviv: Urim, 1954, pp. 308–30, 385–87.

Rosenau, William. *Jewish Ceremonial Institutions and Customs.* New York: Bloch Publishing Co., 1925, pp. 81–83, 149.

Roth, Cecil, ed. *The Standard Jewish Encyclopedia.* Garden City, N.Y.: Doubleday & Co., 1959.

Rothschild, Lothar, ed. *Schawuoth: Ein Festbüchlein.* Geneva: Editions Migdal, 1948.

Sadan, Dov. *Galgal Moadim: Shabbat ve-Shalosh Regalim: Gilgule Piyyut, Aggadah ve-Shaashua.* Tel Aviv: Massada, 1964, pp. 101–60.

Schauss, Hayyim. *The Jewish Festivals: From Their Beginnings to Our Own Days.* Cincinnati: Union of American Hebrew Congregations, 1938, pp. 86–95.

Seidman, Hillel. *The Glory of the Jewish Holidays.* Edited by Moses Zalesky. New York: Shengold Publishers, 1969, pp. 182–95.

Shavuoth Bulletin. Miami Beach: Bureau of Jewish Education of Greater Miami, n.d.

Shecter, Tzvi, ed. *Moade Yisrael: Pirke Kriah ve-Niggun.* Jerusalem: Ministry of Education and Culture, Youth Department, 1966, pp. 33–46.

Sobel, Minna B., ed. *Shevuoth Program.* New York: Young Judea, 1937.

Soltes, Mordecai. *The Jewish Holidays: A Guide to Their Origin, Significance and Observance.* Rev. ed. New York: National Jewish Welfare Board, 1968, pp. 17–19, 36–37.

Sternbuch, Moshe. *Moadim u-Zemanim ha-Shalem.* Vol. 4. Jerusalem, 1970, pp. 128–70.

Stolper, Pinchas, ed. *NCSY Shavuot Manual.* New York: National Conference of Synagogue Youth of the Union of Orthodox Jewish Congregations of America, 1961.

Thieberger, Friedrich, ed. *Jüdisches Fest: Jüdischer Brauch.* Berlin: Jüdischer Verlag, 1936, pp. 280–312.

Tselnik, Nachman Halevi. *Atzeret: Masekhet Arukhah u-Mekifah al Yeme ha-"Atzeret" be-Shanah: Shevii shel Pesah, Hag ha-Shavuot, Shemini Atzeret.* Jerusalem: Harry Fischel Institute for Research in Jewish Law, 1973, pp. 51–372.

Tverski, Shimon, ed. *Hilulim: Massekhet le-Hag ha-Shavuot.* Tel Aviv: Tzava Haganah le-Yisrael, Ha-Rabbanut ha-Tzavait ha-Reshit, 1952.

Unger, Menashe. *Chasidus un Yom-Tov.* New York: Farlag Chasidus, 1958, pp. 291–327.

The Universal Jewish Encyclopedia. 10 vols. New York: Ktav Publishing House, 1968. See *Akdamut, Azharot,* Decalogue, Firstfruits, Holidays, Revelation, Ruth, Shabuoth.

Unterman, Isaac. *The Jewish Holidays.* 2d ed. New York: Bloch Publishing Co., 1950, pp. 241–56.

Wahrmann, Nahum. *Hagge Yisrael u-Moadav: Minhagehem u-Semalehem.* Jerusalem: Ahiasaf, 1959, pp. 181–200.

———, ed. *Moadim: Pirke Halakhah, Aggadah ve-Tefillah le-Khol Moade ha-Shanah.* Jerusalem: Kiryat Sepher, 1957, pp. 129–45, 193–94, 208, 224–27, 241–43.

Werblowsky, R. J. Zwi, and Wigoder, Geoffrey, eds. *The Encyclopedia of the Jewish Religion.* New York: Holt, Rinehart and Winston, 1966.

Yedion le-Inyane Tarbut ve-Hasbarah (Tel Aviv), no. 8 (June 1965): 2–9; 2, no. 4 (May 1967): 9–19.

Zevin, Shlomoh Yosef. *Ha-Moadim be-Halakhah.* 2d ed. Tel Aviv: Betan Hasefer, 1949, pp. 305–34.

––––––. *Sippure Hasidim . . . le-Moade ha-Shanah.* Tel Aviv: Abraham Tzioni Publishing House, 1958, pp. 321–59.

Zobel, Moritz. *Das Jahr des Juden in Brauch und Liturgie.* Berlin: Schocken Verlag, 1936, pp. 189–95.

*Shavuot Liturgy

Birnbaum, Philip, ed. and trans. *Prayer Book for the Three Festivals.* New York: Hebrew Publishing Co., 1971.

Davis, Arthur, and Adler, Herbert M., trans. *Service of the Synagogue: A New Edition of the Festival Prayers with an English Translation in Prose and Verse: Pentecost.* London: George Routledge & Sons, 1909.

Idelsohn, A. Z. *Jewish Liturgy and Its Development.* New York: Henry Holt and Co., 1932, pp. 188–94, 331–44.

Levi, Eliezer. *Yesodot ha-Tefillah.* Tel Aviv: Betan Hasefer, 1952, pp. 213–16, 233–35.

Millgram, Abraham E. *Jewish Worship.* Philadelphia: Jewish Publication Society of America, 1971, pp. 199–224, 399–405.

Munk, Elie. *The World of Prayer.* Vol. 2. *Commentary and Translation of the Sabbath and Festival Prayers.* Translated by Gertrude Hirschler. New York: Philipp Feldheim, 1963, pp. 158–68.

Pool, David de Sola, ed. and trans. *Prayers for the Festivals according to the Custom of the Spanish and Portuguese Jews.* New York: Union of Sephardic Congregations, 1947.

––––––. *The Traditional Prayer Book for Sabbath and Festivals.* New York: Behrman House, 1960.

Reading and Prayers for the Pilgrimage Festivals. Vol. 1. *Pesah and Shavuot.* New York: Reconstructionist Press, 1956, pp. 61–95.

Sabbath and Festival Prayer Book: With a New Translation, Supplementary Readings and Notes. New York: The Rabbinical Assembly and United Synagogue of America, 1946.

The Union Prayerbook for Jewish Worship. Rev. ed. Part I. Cincinnati: Central Conference of American Rabbis, 1941.

*Children's Stories and Descriptions of Shavuot

Abramson, Lillian S. "Shavuot in Canaan." *Join Us for the Holidays.* Illustrated by Jessie B. Robinson. New York: National Women's League of the United Synagogue of America, 1958, pp. 53–54.

Asimov, Isaac. *The Story of Ruth.* Garden City, N. Y.: Doubleday & Co., 1972.

Bearman, Jane. *Shavuos Time.* New York: Union of American Hebrew Congregations, 1951.

Braverman, Libbie L. "The Festival of the First Fruits." *Children of the Emek.* Illustrated by Temima N. Gezari. New York: Bloch Publishing Co., 1964, pp. 102–9.

Cedarbaum, Sophia N. *Shovuos: The Birthday of the Torah.* Illustrated by Clare and John Ross. New York: Union of American Hebrew Congregations, 1961.

Certner, Simon, ed. *101 Jewish Stories for Schools, Clubs and Camps.* New York: Jewish Education Committee Press, 1961, pp. 39–45.

Cone, Molly. "The Promise." *Stories of Jewish Symbols.* Illustrated by Siegmund Forst. New York: Bloch Publishing Co., 1963, pp. 27–29.

———. "We Are the People Who Promised." *About Belonging.* Illustrated by Susan Perl. New York: Union of American Hebrew Congregations, 1972, pp. 7–9.

———. *Who Knows Ten? Children's Tales of the Ten Commandments.* Illustrated by Uri Shulevitz. New York: Union of American Hebrew Congregations, 1965.

Covich, Edith S. *The Jewish Child Every Day.* Illustrated by Mary Ida Jones. New York: Union of American Hebrew Congregations, 1955, pp. 46–48.

Daniel, David. *The Jewish Beginning: From Creation to Joshua:* Part One. Illustrated by Ben Einhorn. New York: Ktav Publishing House, 1971, pp. 137–44.

Dinah. "Shavuot and the Boy Detective." *Shavuot Sheaves.* Edited by Yehuda Haezrahi. Jerusalem: Jewish National Fund, 1965, pp. 80–89.

Edidin, Ben M. *Jewish Holidays and Festivals.* New York: Hebrew Publishing Co., 1940, pp. 165–77.

———. "One Shovuoth Day." *Jewish Child Home Library: Shovuoth.* Edited by Ben M. Edidin. Chicago: Board of Jewish Education, n.d., pp. 17–18.

Eisenstadt, Mollie. "Shovuoth Heroes." *Jewish Child Home Library: Shovuoth.* Edited by Ben M. Edidin. Chicago: Board of Jewish Education, n.d., pp. 20–24.

Epstein, Morris. *All about Jewish Holidays and Customs.* Rev. ed. Illustrated by Arnold Lobel. New York: Ktav Publishing House, 1970, pp. 68–71.

———. *A Pictorial Treasury of Jewish Holidays and Customs.* New York: Ktav Publishing House, 1959, pp. 106–13.

Farber, Walter C. *Jewish Holidays.* Detroit: Jewish Heritage Publishing House, 1967, pp. 69–75.

Fine, Helen. "One Year Old." *G'dee.* Illustrated by Hal Just. New

York: Union of American Hebrew Congregations, 1958, pp. 142–59.

Freehof, Lillian S. *Second Bible Legend Book.* Vol. 2. Illustrated by Lillian Port. New York: Union of American Hebrew Congregations, 1952, pp. 57–93.

Frischman, David. "Sinai." *Shavuot Sheaves.* Edited by Yehuda Haezrahi. Jerusalem: Jewish National Fund, 1965, pp. 62–70.

———. "Sinai." *Yisroel: The Jewish Omnibus.* Edited by Joseph Leftwich. London: James Clarke & Co., 1933, pp. 582–88.

Gaer, Yossef (Joseph). "When the Skies Open at Midnight." *The Magic Flight: Jewish Tales and Legends.* Illustrated by Robert Joyce. New York: Frank-Maurice, 1926, pp. 173–81.

Gamoran, Mamie G. *Days and Ways: The Story of Jewish Holidays and Customs.* Cincinnati: Union of American Hebrew Congregations, 1941, pp. 145–62.

———. "God's Holy Mountain," "The Best Holiday." *Hillel's Calendar.* Illustrated by Ida Libby Dengrove. New York: Union of American Hebrew Congregations, 1960, pp. 163–72.

———. "The Ten Commandments," "Be Kind to the Stranger," "Good Night, Hillel!" *Hillel's Happy Holidays.* Illustrated by Temima N. Gezari. Cincinnati: Union of American Hebrew Congregations, 1939, pp. 186–205.

Garvey, Robert. *Holidays Are Nice: Around the Year with the Jewish Child.* Illustrated by Ezekiel Schloss and Arnold Lobel. New York: Ktav Publishing House, 1960, pp. 48–52.

———. "The Powerful Goldfish." *Happy Holiday!* Illustrated by Ezekiel Schloss. New York: Ktav Publishing House, 1953, pp. 64–71.

Gersh, Harry, with Eugene B. Borowitz and Hyman Chanover. *When a Jew Celebrates.* Illustrated by Erika Weihs. New York: Behrman House, 1971, pp. 140–49.

Goldberg, David. *Holidays for American Judaism.* New York: Bookman Associates, 1954, pp. 100–19.

Goldin, Hyman E. *Holiday Tales: Jewish Holidays and Their Legends.* New York: Hebrew Publishing Co., 1929, pp. 101–13.

Goldman, Edith B. "Confirmation Day," "The Modest Mountain." *A Handbook for the Jewish Family.* By Alex J. Goldman. New York: Bloch Publishing Co., 1958, pp. 304–9.

Golub, Rose W. "Shovuos in Palestine." *Down Holiday Lane.* Illustrated by Louis Kabrin. Cincinnati: Union of American Hebrew Congregations, 1947, pp. 150–61.

Habas, Bracha. "The Roof Garden." *Shavuot Sheaves.* Edited by Yehuda Haezrahi. Jerusalem: Jewish National Fund, 1965, pp. 90–93.

Halpern, Salomon Alter. "The Girl from Moab," "Dreams and Cheesecake." *Tales of Faith.* Jerusalem: Boys Town, 1968, pp. 64–72, 190–92.

Ish Kishor, Sulamith. "The Firstfruits to God." *The Heaven on the Sea and Other Stories.* New York: Bloch Publishing Co., 1924, pp. 83–89.

―――. *Pathways through the Jewish Holidays.* Edited by Benjamin Efron. New York: Ktav Publishing House, 1967, pp. 101–8.

―――. "Shabuoth Moments." *The Stranger within Thy Gates and Other Stories.* New York: Shoulson Press, 1948, pp. 105–13.

Jaffe, Leonard. "A Holiday to Remember." *The Pitzel Holiday Book.* Illustrated by Bill Giacalone. New York: Ktav Publishing House, 1962, pp. 51–58.

Kipnis, Levin. "Moses and the Birds." *Stories round the Year.* Edited by Martha Marenof. Illustrated by Frances H. Quint. Detroit: Dot Publications, 1969, pp. 156–60.

―――. "Not a Bird Twittered." *Shavuot Sheaves.* Edited by Yehuda Haezrahi. Jerusalem: Jewish National Fund, 1965, pp. 58–61.

―――. "Not a Chirp Was Heard," "*Bikkurim,*" "Zivia and Her Little Lamb," "The Children of Jerusalem Bring *Bikkurim.*" *My Holidays: Holiday Stories for Children.* Translated by Israel M. Goodelman. Illustrated by Isa. Tel Aviv: N. Tversky, 1961, pp. 153–76.

―――. "Zeva's Gift." *Lag Be'Omer and Shavuoth: Jewish Life and Customs: Unit Seven.* Edited by Ben M. Edidin. Illustrated by Temima N. Gezari. New York: Bloch Publishing Co., 1942, pp. 28–31.

Kripke, Dorothy K. *Let's Talk about the Jewish Holidays.* New York: Jonathan David, 1970, pp. 43–46.

Learsi, Rufus. "Branches in the Desert," "The Seven Little Men." *Kasriel the Watchman and Other Stories.* Philadelphia: Jewish Publication Society of America, 1936, pp. 145–57, 276–86.

Levinger, Elma Ehrlich. "The Boy Who Could Sing," "The White Flower." *Tales Old and New.* New York: Bloch Publishing Co., 1926, pp. 180–94.

―――. "Ruth, the Girl Who Came from Moab." *Great Jewish Women.* New York: Behrman House, 1940, pp. 44–49.

―――. "Shabuoth," "A Rose for Beauty." *In Many Lands.* New York: Bloch Publishing Co., 1923, pp. 112–13, 115–23.

Levner, J. B. *The Legends of Israel.* Translated by Joel Snowman. London: James Clarke & Co., 1956, pp. 59–77.

Marenof, Martha. "A Tree of Life," "Torah Is for Man." *Stories round the Year.* Illustrated by Frances H. Quint. Detroit: Dot Publications, 1969, pp. 145–51.

Margolis, Isidor, and Markowitz, Sidney L. *Jewish Holidays and Festivals.* Illustrated by John Teppich. New York: Citadel Press, 1962, pp. 113–20.

Max, Mosheh. *The Way of God.* New York: Feldheim Publishers, 1968, pp. 147–62.

Mindel, Nissan. *Complete Story of Shavuoth.* Brooklyn, N.Y.: Merkos L'Inyonei Chinuch, 1955.

Nudelman, E. A. "A Happy Meeting." *Jewish Child Home Library:*

Shavuoth. Edited by Ben M. Edidin. Chicago: Board of Jewish Education, n.d., pp. 6–9.

Ofer, M. "Why Did Ziva Cry." *Shavuot Sheaves.* Edited by Yehuda Haezrahi. Jerusalem: Jewish National Fund, 1965, pp. 76–79.

Orenstein, Walter, and Frankel, Hertz. *Torah as Our Guide: Laws and Customs for Jewish Youth.* New York: Hebrew Publishing Co., 1960, pp. 183–94.

Pessin, Deborah. "The Story of Shavuoth," "At Sinai," "The Young Pilgrim." *Lag Be'Omer and Shavuoth: Jewish Life and Customs: Unit Seven.* Edited by Ben M. Edidin. Illustrated by Temima N. Gezari. New York: Bloch Publishing Co., 1942, pp. 10–13, 16–21, 22–27.

Petersham, Maud, and Petersham, Miska. *Ruth.* New York: Macmillan, 1958.

Posy, Arnold. "Ruth and Naomi." *Holiday Night Dreams.* New York: Bloch Publishing Co., 1953, pp. 191–213.

Rosenzweig, Marion Jordan, and Rosenzweig, Efraim Michael. *Now We Begin: A Manual of Stories and Instructions for Home and School.* Cincinnati: Union of American Hebrew Congregations, 1937, pp. 116–32.

Samuels, Ruth. *Our Ten Commandments.* Illustrated by Uri Shulevitz. New York: Ktav Publishing Co., 1961.

Shihor, S. "King Agrippa and the First Fruits." *The New World Over Story Book.* Edited by Ezekiel Schloss and Morris Epstein. New York: Bloch Publishing Co., 1968, pp. 189–93.

Sholom Aleichem. "Greens for Shavuot," "Three Little Heads." *Jewish Children.* Translated by Hannah Berman. New York: Bloch Publishing Co., 1937, pp. 79–88, 71–78.

———. "Three Little Heads." *The New World Over Story Book.* Edited by Ezekiel Schloss and Morris Epstein. New York: Bloch Publishing Co., 1968, pp. 102–7.

———. "Three Little Heads," "You Mustn't Weep—It's Yom-Tev." *Selected Stories of Sholom Aleichem.* Introduction by Alfred Kazin. New York: Modern Library, 1956, pp. 333–38, 249–62; *The Old Country.* Translated by Julius and Frances Butwin. New York: Crown Publishers, 1946, pp. 239–53, 329–35.

Silverman, Althea O. "Habibi and Yow See the Heavens Open on Shavuos Eve." *Habibi and Yow: A Little Boy and His Dog.* Illustrated by Jessie B. Robinson. New York: Bloch Publishing Co., 1946, pp. 100–6.

Smith, Harold P. *A Treasure Hunt in Judaism.* New York: Hebrew Publishing Co., 1950, pp. 120–28.

Sokolow, Helena. "Feast of the Torah," "Ruth." *Bible Rhapsodies.* Tel Aviv: Massada, 1956, pp. 25–30, 89–93.

Solis-Cohen Jr., Emily. "Amid the Alien Corn." *David the Giant Killer and Other Tales of Grandma Lopez.* Philadelphia: Jewish Publication Society of America, 1908, pp. 183–99.

Spiro, Saul S., and Spiro, Rena M. *The Joy of Jewish Living,* Cleveland: Bureau of Jewish Education, 1965, pp. 139–46, 187–89.

Stadtler, Bea. "Gleanings from the Corners." *Once upon a Jewish Holiday,* Illustrated by Bill Giacalone. New York: Ktav Publishing House, 1965, pp. 102–5.

Steinberg, Yehuda. "In the Fields of Ephrat." *Shavuot Sheaves.* Edited by Yehuda Haezrahi. Jerusalem: Jewish National Fund, 1965, pp. 55–57.

Stern, Menahem. "The Broken Tablets." *The New World Over Story Book.* Edited by Ezekiel Schloss and Morris Epstein. New York: Bloch Publishing Co., 1968, pp. 259–61.

Trager, Hannah. *Festival Stories of Child Life in a Jewish Colony in Palestine.* New York: E. P. Dutton & Co., 1920, pp. 45–65.

Weilerstein, Sadie Rose. "Where Green Things Grow." *What Danny Did: Stories for the Wee Jewish Child.* Illustrated by Jessie Berkowitz Robinson. New York: Bloch Publishing Co., 1944, pp. 98–104.

Weitz, Joseph. "The Mountain Goes Up in Flames." *The Abandoned Swing.* Translated by Shoshana Perla. Illustrated by Zvi Geyra. Ramat Gan: Massada Press, 1969, pp. 67–76.

Zeligs, Dorothy F. *The Story of Jewish Holidays and Customs for Young People.* Illustrated by Emery I. Gondor. New York: Bloch Publishing Co., 1942, pp. 173–90.

*Collections with Shavuot Music

Bar-Zimra, S., ed. *Dor Dor ve-Nigguno: Le-Lag ba-Omer vele-Hag ha-Shavuot.* Jerusalem: Ministry of Education and Culture, 1966, pp. 6–15.

Binder, A. W. *The Jewish Year in Song.* New York: G. Schirmer, 1928, pp. 22–25.

Coopersmith, Harry, ed. *More of the Songs We Sing.* New York: United Synagogue Commission on Jewish Education, 1971, pp. 124–30.

——————. *The New Jewish Song Book.* New York: Behrman House, 1965, pp. 70–76.

——————. *Songs of Zion.* New York: Behrman House, 1942, pp. 214–22.

——————. *The Songs We Sing.* New York: United Synagogue Commission on Jewish Education, 1950, pp. 206–26.

Eisenstein, Judith Kaplan. *The Gateway to Jewish Song.* New York: Behrman House, 1939, pp. 129–37.

——————, and Prensky, Frieda, eds. *Songs of Childhood.* New York: United Synagogue Commission on Jewish Education, 1955, pp. 284–88.

Ephros, Gershon, ed. *Cantorial Anthology.* Vol. 3, *Sholosh R'golim.* New York: Bloch Publishing Co., 1948.

Goldfarb, Israel, and Goldfarb, Samuel E., eds. *The Jewish Songster:*

Music for Voice and Piano. Part I. Brooklyn, N.Y., 1925, pp. 112–33.

Idelsohn, Abraham Zevi. *The Jewish Song Book for Synagogue, School and Home*. Music edited by Baruch Joseph Cohon. Cincinnati: Publications for Judaism, 1951, pp. 131–81, 406–8.

Kariv, Yosef, and Miron-Michrovsky, Issachar, eds. *Zemirot 23–24: Hag ha-Shavuot*. Jerusalem: World Zionist Organization, Department for Education and Culture in the Diaspora, 1948.

Lag B'Omer and Shavuot Songster. New York: Board of Jewish Education, 1941, pp. 3–13.

Levy, Sara C., and Deutsch, Beatrice L. *So We Sing: Holiday and Bible Songs for Young Jewish Children*. New York: Bloch Publishing Co., 1950, pp. 44–45.

Pasternak, Velvel, ed. *Songs of the Chassidim II*. New York: Bloch Publishing Co., 1971, pp. 89–114.

Rubin, Ruth, ed. *A Treasury of Jewish Folksong*. New York: Schocken Books, 1950, pp. 170–73.

Union Hymnal: Songs and Prayers for Jewish Worship. 3d ed. New York: Central Conference of American Rabbis. Part I (1940), pp. 150–65, 227–29, 488–98.

Union Songster: Songs and Prayers for Jewish Youth. New York: Central Conference of American Rabbis, 1960, pp. 226–38.

*Program and Audiovisual Materials

*FILMS

Festival of Faith. By De Witt Copp and Samuel Elkin. New York: Jewish Chautauqua Society. 16 mm, black and white, sound, 13½ minutes. Story of a rabbi who helps to restore the faith of a teen-age girl which culminates in a confirmation service on Shavuot.

Shavuoth. Produced by Yehoshua Brandstatter. New York: Israel Information Services. 16 mm, color, sound, 14½ minutes. The festival observance in Israel with emphasis on the agricultural aspect.

*FILMSTRIPS

The Book of Ruth. No. H.0120. Tel Aviv: Or and Kol, 40 Ibn-Gabirol St. 42 frames, color, Hebrew and English captions.

The Book of Ruth. Edited by Moses Singer. No. SR.0118. Tel Aviv: Or and Kol, 40 Ibn-Gabirol St. 31 frames, color, Hebrew captions.

Lag ba-Omer and Shavuot. Produced by Samuel Grand. New York: World Zionist Organization Department of Education and Culture. 55 frames, color, narration and teacher's guide. Observance of the festivals in Israel.

Saadia's Secret. Edited by Baruch Sharell. No. SR.0119. Tel Aviv: Or and Kol, 40 Ibn-Gabirol St. 33 frames, color, Hebrew captions. Suitable for Shavuot.

The Seven Varieties and the Seven Weeks. Text by Nogah Hareuveni. Photography by Yaakov Reshef and Nogah Hareuveni. Graphic art by Ran Caspi. New York: Neot Kedumim, 501 Fifth Ave. 50 frames, color, narration. The ecology of the *shivat ha-minim* and their acceptability as *bikkurim.*

Shavuot. Prepared by Irwin Soref. Los Angeles: Bureau of Jewish Education. 21 frames, color, teacher's guide. The festival story for young children; suitable for traditional groups.

Shovuos. Prepared by Irwin Soref. Los Angeles: Bureau of Jewish Education. 26 frames, color, teacher's guide. The festival story and the observance by Reform Jews.

Shovuos: Festival of Torah and Confirmation. By Nellie Reichert. Produced by Samuel Grand. New York: Union of American Hebrew Congregations. 40 frames, color, narration and teacher's guide. Observance by Reform congregations, including confirmation exercises.

The Story of Ruth. Beverly Hills, Calif: Alexander & Norsim. 34 frames, color, narration. The biblical story that is read on Shavuot.

The Story of Shavuoth. By Samuel J. Citron and Azriel Eisenberg. New York: Board of Jewish Education. 59 frames, black and white, narration and teacher's guide. The background and observance of the festival.

*RECORDINGS

Shevuot. Sung by Emanuel Rosenberg. Directed by Judith Kaplan Eisenstein. Allegro Holiday 108. For children. New York: Ktav Publishing House.

Songs for Shavuot. Directed by Harry Coopersmith. New York: Board of Jewish Education.

What Is Torah? Cantata performed by Robert H. Segal and choir. Words by Ira Eisenstein. Music by Judith Kaplan Eisenstein. New York: Jewish Reconstructionist Foundation.

*DANCES

Lapson, Dvora. *Folk Dances for Jewish Festivals.* New York: Jewish Edu-
cation Committee Press, 1961, pp. 116–23.
————. *Jewish Dances the Year Round.* New York: Jewish Education
Committee Press, 1957, pp. 76–82.

*DRAMATIZATIONS

Aronin, Ben. "Give Us Strength." *Dramatics the Year Round.* Edited by
Samuel J. Citron. New York: United Synagogue Commission on
Jewish Education, 1956, pp. 461–65. Ages 13 and up. 10 minutes.
Mass recitation for confirmation ceremony.

Ben-Gavriel, M.Y. "At the Gate of Bethlehem." *Shavuot Sheaves.* Edited by Yehuda Haezrahi. Jerusalem: Youth Department, Jewish
National Fund, 1965, pp. 94–104. 6 male, 3 female, extras, ages
11–14. 20 minutes. Based on the Book of Ruth.

Citron, Samuel J. "Induction of Beginners." *Dramatics the Year Round.*
New York: United Synagogue Commission on Jewish Education,
1956, pp. 79–82. 2 male and 2 female adults, extras (children). 15
minutes. A ceremony suitable for Shavuot.

Eisenstein, Ira and Judith K. *What Is Torah: A Cantata for Unison Chorus
and Piano.* New York: Jewish Reconstructionist Foundation,
1967. 12 or more characters. 20 minutes.

Gamoran, Mamie G. *Confirmation Service.* New York: United Synagogue Commission on Jewish Education, 1948. Adaptable for
large or small classes.

Goldin, Grace. "Come under the Wings: A Midrash on Ruth."
Adapted for radio by Virginia Mazer (Eternal Light program, no.
669, May 29, 1960), *Curtain Time for Jewish Youth.* Edited by Zara
Shakow. New York: Jonathan David, 1968, pp. 235–58. 30 minutes. 4 male, 3 female, extras.

Kaplan, Louis L. "We Pledge Allegiance." *Dramatics the Year Round.*
Edited by Samuel J. Citron. New York: United Synagogue Commission on Jewish Education, 1956, pp. 454–60. Also published
separately by Board of Jewish Education, New York, 1944. 10
male, 1 female, extras, ages 8–14. 15 minutes. A historical play
within a modern setting.

Levinger, Elma Ehrlich. "Ruth of Moab." *Jewish Festivals in Religious
Schools.* Cincinnati: Union of American Hebrew Congregations,
1923, pp. 503–15. 3 male, 6 female, extras, ages 11–14. 35 minutes. This play may be presented either in simple form or with
elaborate staging.

Mittleman, Jack. "A Shavuot Day Dream." *Dramatics the Year Round.*

Edited by Samuel J. Citron. New York: United Synagogue Commission on Jewish Education, 1956, pp. 451–54. Also published separately by Board of Jewish Education, New York, 1945. 7 male, 1 female, ages 9–13. 12 minutes. A novel presentation of appropriate legends.

Nemzoff, Samuel A., ed. *Confirmation Service Sampler.* New York: Union of American Hebrew Congregations, 1969. An anthology of cantatas, dramatic presentations, choral readings, recitative essays for confirmation classes.

Pilchik, Ely E., Greene, Barry Hewitt, and Summers, Norman. *Conflict and Concord: An Original Confirmation Cantata.* New York: Union of American Hebrew Congregations, 1967. Text and music.

————. *The Birth of the Synagogue: An Original Confirmation Cantata.* New York: Union of American Hebrew Congregations, 1968. Text and music.

Shapiro, E., ed. "The Bringing of the First Fruits." *Shavuot Sheaves.* Edited by Yehuda Haezrahi. Jerusalem: Youth Department, Jewish National Fund, 1965, pp. 109–17. Large cast, choir, ages 10–15. 40 minutes. An elaborate pageant with dance and music.

Soifer, Margaret K. *Ruth Finds a Home.* New York: Board of Jewish Education (Furrow Press, 1950). 2 male, 3 female, extras, ages 12–15. 45 minutes. This play in five scenes is written in rhyme.

Sussman, Samuel, and Segal, Abraham. "A *Bikkurim* Ceremony." *Fifty Assembly Programs for the Jewish School.* New York: United Synagogue Commission on Jewish Education, 1948, pp. 143–47. Reprinted in *Dramatics the Year Round.* Edited by Samuel J. Citron. New York: United Synagogue Commission on Jewish Education, 1956, pp. 447–51. Unlimited cast, ages 6–14. 15 minutes. A modern dramatized version of the presentation of firstfruits.

Tal, N., ed. "And Thou Shalt Observe the Feast of Shavuot." *Shavuot Sheaves.* Edited by Yehuda Haezrahi. Jerusalem: Youth Department, Jewish National Fund, 1965, pp. 118–23. 15 male or female, extras, choir, ages 10–14. A pageant with dance and music.

*ARTS AND CRAFTS

Comins, Harry L., and Leaf, Reuben. *Arts-Crafts for the Jewish Club.* Cincinnati: Union of American Hebrew Congregations, 1934, pp. 32–44, 163–76, 212–17, 286.

Gezari, Temima N. *Jewish Festival Crafts.* New York: National Jewish Welfare Board, 1968, pp. 34–36.

Kantor, Israel, ed. *Yifat: Hatzaot le-Bitui Amanuti shel Nosim Yehudiim:*

Moadim 6: Shavuot. Israel: Department of Torah Culture, Ministry of Education and Culture, n.d.

Maaseh Yadenu: Kishute Hag u-Moed: 5: Shavuot. Tel Aviv: Tarbut ve-Hinukh, Iyar, 1967.

Ness, Jack. *Arts and Crafts for Jewish Youth.* New York: Yeshiva University Community Service Division, n.d., pp. 17, 43–46.

Robinson, Jessie B. *Holidays Are Fun.* New York: Bloch Publishing Co., 1950, pp. 54–57.

Rockland, Mae Shafter. *The Work of Our Hands: Jewish Needlecraft for Today.* New York: Schocken Books, 1973, pp. 180–83.

Sharon, Ruth. *Arts and Crafts the Year Round.* Vol. 1. New York: United Synagogue Commission on Jewish Education, 1965, pp. 376–414.

*ACTIVITY AND RELATED MATERIALS

Abramson, Lillian S., and Leiderman, Lillian T. *Jewish Holiday Party Book: A Practical Guide to Parties Planned for Children Ages 5 to 12.* New York: Bloch Publishing Co., 1966, pp. 72–77.

Aunt Fanny. *Junior Jewish Cook Book.* Illustrated by Cyla London. New York: Ktav Publishing House, 1956, pp. 61–64.

Campeas, Hyman. *Workbook: All about Jewish Holidays and Customs.* New York: Ktav Publishing House, 1959, pp. 56–59.

Eisenberg, Azriel, and Robinson, Jessie B. *My Jewish Holidays.* New York: United Synagogue Commission on Jewish Education, 1958; pp. 169–81.

Engle, Fannie. *The Jewish Holidays and Their Favorite Foods: With Easy Recipes for Mother and Daughter.* Illustrated by Dorothy M. Weiss. New York: Behrman House, 1958.

Fine, Helen. *G'dee's Book of Holiday Fun.* Illustrated by Hal Just. New York: Union of American Hebrew Congregations, 1961, pp. 81–93.

Fischman, Joyce. *Holiday Work and Play.* New York: Union of American Hebrew Congregations, 1961, pp. 53–57.

Ginsburg, Marvell. *Holidays in the Jewish Nursery School and Kindergarten: A Guide for Teachers.* Chicago: Board of Jewish Education, 1970, pp. 145–57.

Goodman, Hannah Grad. *Pupils' Activity Book for Days and Ways.* New York: Union of American Hebrew Congregations, 1964, pp. 89–106.

Levinger, Elma Ehrlich. *Jewish Festivals in the Religious School: A Handbook for Entertainments.* Cincinnati: Union of American Hebrew Congregations, 1923, pp. 209–48, 503–15.

Lister, Rebecca. *Teacher's Syllabus for Grade Three.* New York: Union of American Hebrew Congregations, 1963, pp. 164–72.

————. *Workbook: Pathways through the Jewish Holidays.* New York:

Ktav Publishing House, 1967, pp. 82–87.

Pessin, Deborah, and Gezari, Temima. *The Jewish Kindergarten: A Manual for Teachers.* Cincinnati: Union of American Hebrew Congregations, 1944, pp. 291–317.

Purdy, Susan Gold. *Jewish Holidays: Facts, Activities, and Crafts.* Philadelphia: J. B. Lippincott Co., 1969, pp. 83–85.

Shakow, Zara, ed. *Curtain Time for Jewish Youth.* New York: Jonathan David, 1968, pp. 233–75.

Silverstein, Ruth. *Teacher's Syllabus for Kindergarten.* New York: Union of American Hebrew Congregations, 1960, pp. 130–36.

Stadtler, Bea, and Simon, Shirley. *Workbook: Once upon a Jewish Holiday.* Jingles by Gay Campbell. New York: Ktav Publishing House, 1966, pp. 95–98.

Sussman, Samuel, and Segal, Abraham. *Fifty Assembly Programs for the Jewish School.* New York: United Synagogue Commission on Jewish Education, 1948, pp. 142–51.